THE LIBRARY

D1426470

ESSAYS IN EUROPEAN
ECONOMIC HISTORY
1500–1800

ESSAYS IN EUROPEAN ECONOMIC HISTORY

1500—1800

EDITED

for the Economic History Society

BY

PETER EARLE

CLARENDON PRESS
OXFORD
1974

Oxford University Press, Ely House, London W. 1

GLASGOW NEW YORK TORONTO MELBOURNE WELLINGTON
CAPE TOWN IBADAN NAIROBI DAR ES SALAAM LUSAKA ADDIS ABABA
DELHI BOMBAY CALCUTTA MADRAS KARACHI LAHORE DACCA
KUALA LUMPUR SINGAPORE HONG KONG TOKYO

CASEBOUND ISBN 0 19 877054 5

© OXFORD UNIVERSITY PRESS 1974

*Printed in Great Britain by
Richard Clay (The Chaucer Press), Ltd.,
Bungay, Suffolk*

Preface

THE study of the economic and social history of Europe in the early modern period has expanded enormously since the Second World War, particularly in France, but very little of this new work has yet appeared in English. This in turn has meant that it has been virtually impossible to arrange courses in this subject for that large majority of students who read no other language but English. It is hoped that this collection of English translations of general articles and chapters from books written by some of the more distinguished students in the field will do something to improve this situation and to encourage interest in the period.

The selection of contributions for a volume of this type presents obvious problems and is bound to be somewhat arbitrary. The aim was to confine the collection to articles of a general nature dealing with problems over a long period of time in whole countries or in large regions. This proved difficult since scholars are often reluctant to generalize, but all the articles included do conform to this requirement. It was also originally intended to give as wide a geographical spread as possible. Pressure on space has, however, meant that it was impossible to cover all of Europe and with some reluctance it was decided to leave Scandinavia and most of central and eastern Europe out of the volume. Scandinavia, at least, is fairly well covered in English in the *Scandinavian Economic History Review*. In order to give some cohesion to the volume most of the articles selected are concerned with one very general theme, the dynamic changes which occurred in Europe during these three centuries as the long cycle of population and price movements had its differing effect on the economies of the various regions. Other articles are more static and descriptive in their approach and illustrate the more unchanging aspects of the European economy before the onset of industrialization.

For a volume that is meant to cover Europe over a period of three centuries this final selection incorporates both a linguistic and a temporal bias. The articles are heavily dominated by the French, in that they were either written in French or for the most part carry a heavy debt to French scholarship. There is also more on the seventeenth century than on either the sixteenth or eighteenth centuries. This is in some ways unfortunate, but all that can be said is that European economic history in this period *is* dominated by the French, and that the French are dominated by the seventeenth century.

The editor has benefited from the help of the Publications Committee of the Economic History Society and from suggestions and advice of many scholars in a number of countries. He wishes further to express his gratitude to the authors of the articles reprinted, to the editors and publishers of the journals and books in which the essays originally appeared for permission to reprint, and to the translators.

PETER EARLE

Lecturer in Economic History,
London School of Economics

Contents

1

The Mediterranean Economy in the Sixteenth Century

FERNAND BRAUDEL

*Translated by Siân Reynolds**

HAVE we here enough material to measure the Mediterranean, to construct a comprehensive, quantitative 'model' of its economy? As a unit it could then be compared to other 'world-economies' either bordering on or connected to the Mediterranean.

An attempt on this scale will provide at best some indication of orders of magnitude, the faintest of guide lines. Such a model, if we can construct it, must aim to represent not any particular year or period but the sixteenth century in its entirety looking beyond times of crisis or of plenty. What it should convey, if it is at all possible, is the mean, the water-line, so to speak, of the successive phases of the century. We shall fall far short of our aim, it is clear; but the effort will be worthwhile in spite of the difficulties ahead, not to mention the preliminary obstacles.

Can it be said for a start that the Mediterranean is an internally coherent zone? On the whole the answer is yes, in spite of the indefinite and above all changeable boundaries both on its continental and on its seaward sides: the Black Sea, the Red Sea, the Persian Gulf, the Straits of Gibraltar, and the Atlantic Ocean.

It was my original idea, in the first edition of this book, that the many dimensions of the Mediterranean in the sixteenth century could be suggested through a series of examples, by selecting certain important and indicative details:[1] a city of 700,000 inhabitants, Constantinople; a grain fleet which every year, good or bad, ferried a million quintals of wheat or other cereals; the 3,000 or so tons of wool which in 1580 lay on the quay-sides of Leghorn;[2] the estimated 100,000 combatants, both Turks and Christians, assembled in the gulf of Lepanto on 7 October 1571; the 600 vessels (totalling perhaps 45,000 tons) that participated in Charles V's expedition against Tunis in 1535; the highest recorded level of shipping at Leghorn, 150,000 tons entering

* From *La Méditerranée et le monde méditerranéen à l'époque de Philippe II* (2nd ed., Paris: Armand Colin, 1966), i., pp. 383–420. Siân Reynolds's translation of this great book has now appeared, *The Mediterranean and the Mediterranean World in the Age of Philip II* (London: Collins; New York: Harper & Row, 2 vols., 1972, 1973). The translation © 1972 is reprinted by permission of the publishers.

the port in 1592–3, probably an exaggerated figure; or two rather different annual totals at Naples: 1,300,000 ducats of business transacted in the exchanges, against 60,000 or 70,000 in insurance.[3] But this would mean leaving enormous blank spaces between the specks of colour; at best, it would only give an impressionistic notion of the distance that separates our world from that of the sixteenth century.

Today, on the other hand, I am more attracted towards the language of what economists call 'national accounting'. I should like to try to draw up a tentative balance sheet of the Mediterranean in the sixteenth century, not in order to judge its relative mediocrity or modernity but to determine the relative proportions and relationships between the different sectors of its activity, in short, to form a picture of the major structures of its material life: a difficult and hazardous project. The risks involved will be apparent to any economist who has studied the economies of underdeveloped countries which have never been fully penetrated by the monetary economy. The same was true everywhere in the sixteenth century. And the variety of moneys, real and artificial, complicate any calculations, even when precise data[4] are available, which of course they usually are not. We also have to bear in mind the casual way in which contemporary records refer to ducats or crowns in Spain, ducats, crowns, or florins in Florence. So we find in Florence itself the following: 'Ducati 1,000 d'oro di moneta di lire 7 per ciascun scudo.' The point to note here is the reference to the 7 *lire* piece.[5]

AGRICULTURE, THE MAJOR INDUSTRY

It is generally admitted that the annual consumption per head of wheat (and other cereals) was of the order of two (present-day) quintals.[6] This figure obviously conceals wide variations in actual consumption. But as an average it will do on the whole for the Mediterranean in the sixteenth century. If the population was 60 million, the total annual consumption of wheat and other bread crops must have been about 120 million quintals.* Other foodstuffs, meat, fish, olive oil, and wine were merely complementary to the staple diet. If we take the average price of the quintal in about 1600 to be 5 or 4 Venetian ducats,[7] Mediterranean consumption (assumed equal to production) must have reached 480 or 600 million ducats every year, in other words a level out of all proportion to the odd 'six millions in gold' that arrived every year at Seville.[8] Grain alone establishes the overwhelming superiority of agricultural production over all others. Agriculture was the leading industry of the Mediterranean, and of course cereals accounted for only part of agricultural revenue.

The preceding estimate is no more than a lower limit. The figures one encounters in the course of research are often higher. Venice, for instance,[9] in about 1600 was consuming, both in good years and bad, about 500,000 *staia*

---

* The modern quintal is equivalent to 100 kg (220·5 lbs).

of wheat (as well as rice, millet, and rye). The population of the city then stood at about 140,000, plus another 50,000 in adjoining territories (the *Dogado*), i.e. a total population of 200,000 inhabitants and an individual rate of consumption of 4 quintals if the figures refer only to the city and 3·1 quintals if the whole area is included. At 2 quintals per person, the supply would have fed 300,000 inhabitants. Perhaps the actual number of consumers was indeed higher than our figures suggest. Or perhaps Venice, a city with high wages, consumed more than another.

Take another example: some Venetian correspondence from Madrid[10] (February 1621) passes on the report that a tax of 2 *reales* per *fanega* of wheat ('ch'è come un mezzo staio veneziano') was to be levied before the grain was ground at the mills, 'et fanno conto di cavar da questa impositione nove millioni d'oro l'anno'. Nine million in gold, that is nine million ducats (one ducat = 350 *maravedís*, one *real* = 35) which means that there were 45,000,000 *fanegas* for a total population of 6,000,000 inhabitants, each of whom could have consumed seven and a half *fanegas*, let us say seven *fanegas*, since the size of the population is conjectural: at 55·50 litres to the *fanega*, we reach the enormous figure of 388 litres per person, which proves either that the assessment of the tax return was optimistic, or that there was a high rate of home consumption in Castile in the year 1621 when practically no grain was exported.

Another example, still in Castile: in 1576[11] ten villages in the Toledo region had a combined population of 2,975 *vecinos*, or 12,000 to 13,000 inhabitants, the very great majority of whom were peasants; declared grain production was 143,000 *fanegas* (or about 64,000 quintals). The *per capita* average is about 5 quintals, so there must have been a margin for export to the towns and even the least favoured of these villages (since its land was mainly in vineyards) could boast two quintals per person.

These estimates are borne out by the following figures, although they cannot be regarded as decisive. The first are provided by the grain-producing provinces of the kingdom of Naples on the Adriatic and the Gulf of Taranto, the Abruzzi, Bari province, Capitanata, and Basilicata in January 1580; and the second by the famous *Censo de la riqueza territorial e industrial de España en el año 1799*,[12] the findings of which can be used as a yardstick in retrospect for the sixteenth century.

The Neapolitan provinces (an important section of the kingdom), figures for which are given in a precious document in the *Sommaria*, had a total population in the winter of 1579–80 of 173,634 'hearths' or families (out of a total for the kingdom of 475,727)[13] therefore depending on the coefficient adopted (4 or 4·5) of 700,000 or 760,000 inhabitants. The harvest, according to official estimates, brought in over 100,000 *carra* of wheat. Since there were applications for *tratte* (export permits) for 8,500 *carra*, the amount available for the population's own needs must have been 92,000 *carra*, or 1,200,000

present-day quintals giving an individual quota clearly lower than 2 quintals.
And from these quantities grain required for next year's sowing had yet to be
deducted. However, the *Sommaria* which provides these figures says individual consumption is reckoned at 6 *tomoli* a year, that is about 220 kilo-
grammes. A contradiction? No, since 'per ordinario non si revela tutto il
grano che effettivamento si raccoglie', and it was on this undeclared surplus
that the Sommaria relied to make up the necessary food supply.[14]

The *Censo* of 1799 dates from much later than our period, of course, but
its percentages are very nearly identical with those of the sixteenth century.
In a Spain of 10·5 million inhabitants, wheat production totalled 14,500,000
quintals to the nearest round figure. If consumption equalled production,
the annual individual quota would be rather less than 1·4 quintals. But if
other cereals and pulses are included this would add over 13 million quintals
to the original total[15] bringing it to double the size: even if these secondary
cereals were not all used for human consumption, the projected level of 2
quintals per person would certainly be reached or exceeded. Pulses were undoubtedly very important (over 600,000 quintals[16]) even in the sixteenth century. Venetian documents constantly point out how disastrous it can be for
certain villages to lose their crop of beans or lentils in a sudden summer
storm.

These figures, while they support the general argument, cannot be taken as
proof. Since we are at any rate reasonably certain of the over-all total, let us
turn to some of its consequences:

1. Wheat shipped overseas totalled at most 1 million quintals, or 8 per cent
of consumption—which is a large volume of trade for the period (a million
people might depend on it), but insignificant as a proportion of total consumption. So Gino Luzzatto[17] is justified in minimizing it and I was justified
in giving it prominence in the early edition of this book.[18] The dramatic crisis
of 1591, of which we shall have more to say, resulted in the arrival in Spain
and Italy, even Venice, of between 100,000 and 200,000 quintals of northern
wheat, a large quantity in terms of transport, very little in relation to everyday
consumption. However it was enough to save whole towns from starvation.

But both before and after this crisis, the Mediterranean was able to live
largely off its own agricultural produce. No pattern was to emerge here comparable to that developing in the Low Countries, in the case of Amsterdam,
or which was much later to be wholeheartedly adopted by England under
free trade. Urban centres did not rely on outside sources of food. 'Wheat from
overseas' remained a last resort, to rescue the poor, rich consumers preferring
the good grain of the near-by countryside: in Lisbon the reputed wheat of the
Alemtejo;[19] in Marseilles the grain of the Provençal plains;[20] in Venice the
grain they called *nostrale*. 'We are now being given,' say the Venetian bakers
in 1601, 'grain from outside that does not produce such good results as ours,'

by which they meant *padoan*, *trivisan*, *polesene*, and *friul* grain.[21] Even those grains accounted *forestieri* were most often produced in the Mediterranean.

2. Agriculture not only assured the Mediterranean of its everyday livelihood, but also provided a range of costly goods for export, sometimes in limited quantities, such as saffron and cumin, but sometimes amounting to a large volume, such as the so-called Corinth raisins, the *uve passe*, choice wines like malmsey that continued to be highly prized until the appearance of port, Malaga, and Madeira; or the wines from the islands and ordinary table wines which a thirsty German market sent for every year, after the grape harvest, to the southern side of the Alps. Soon there were to be spirits,[22] not to mention olive oil, the fruits of the south, oranges, lemons, raw silk. This surplus combined with manufactured exports to pay for the purchases of grain, dried fish, or sugar from the Atlantic (as well as the lead, copper, and tin of the North) and as late as 1607 the balance of payments between Venice and Holland was still favourable to Venice, according to the *Cinque Savii*.[23]

3. So the Mediterranean remained a world of peasants and landlords, a world of rigid structures. Methods of farming, the balance maintained between different crops, or between crops in general and the meagre pasturelands and the vines and olives that were both making rapid progress (in Andalusia, Portugal, and Castile for instance, even more on the Venetian islands) changed very little unless there was persistent pressure from outside. It was the demand from the colonies that led to increased oil and wine production in Andalusia. And there was to be no 'internal' revolution until the introduction of maize, which arrived quite early it seems in the Basque provinces and in Morocco;[24] and took longer to reach other places. It did not appear in the Venetian countryside before 1600[25] or in the northern Tyrol before 1615.[26] The revolution of the more easily assimilated mulberry tree occurred earlier.

4. Land continued to be the most coveted of possessions. The whole countryside both inside and outside the Mediterranean region was a bewildering tangle of rents, *censos*, mortgages, tenancies, ground-rents, with numerous entailed properties, and a continual coming and going of money loans and repayments between town and countryside. Everywhere it was the same monotonous story. In the countryside around Geneva,[27] about which evidence has recently become available, it is possible to detect a very short-term circulation of money from the fifteenth century on, a decisive factor 'in a closed-circuit economy that was permanently out of breath', where the usury practised by townsfolk did not (in a Protestant country) have to be disguised under cover of rent and quit-rent. A sixteenth-century Spanish *arbitrista*, Miguel Caxa de Leruela,[28] refers to the natural tendency to invest money in land or vineyards near the town. 'As every man could see that a capital of 2,000 ducats brought in 200 a year in return, and that the capital was repaid at the end of six years, it seemed to them a good investment.'

Commerce and government loans rarely offered lenders as good returns. So land competed with them for capital, land which was such a solid and visible guarantee (if the peasant could not pay the interest or did not repay the capital the land was seized). And the investor could always see with his own eyes how his money was bearing fruit on vine or in farmhouse. Such security was worth a great deal. And since agriculture was the greatest single source of revenue in the Mediterranean, an immense amount of wealth was tied up in this sector. So there is no reason to doubt Valle de la Cerda's statement in 1618 that there were in Spain over a hundred million ducats lent in *ducados a censos*.[29]

5. The enormous cereal bill of 400 or 600 million ducats may seem either too much or too little, depending on the angle from which it is viewed. Cereals can have represented only half of the agricultural 'product' if one accepts the proportions recently established for France (in the eighteenth century it is true),[30] and for Spain in 1799.[31] So it is possible to talk in very general terms of a total agricultural production of 800,000 to 1,200 million ducats. It must be stressed that this is a very tentative estimate. The prices on the Venetian market from which we started are high and representative only of the economy of a rich city. Second, and most important, not all the grain that was consumed went on to the market. So our estimate remains extremely theoretical and could hardly be otherwise. To return to the example quoted earlier of the Castilian villages in 1576, they must have consumed 26,000 quintals of the 60,000 they produced, that is about 50 per cent; but the other half did not necessarily go on to the market, some of it went straight into the tithe barns or granaries of urban landlords. So 60 per cent or perhaps 70 per cent of the over-all production of the Mediterranean never entered the market economy to which our methods of accounting mistakenly seek to assimilate it.

6. The fact that a large percentage of the agricultural product remained outside the monetary economy with its comparative flexibility, increased the inelasticity of what was, in the Mediterranean and elsewhere, the predominant economic activity. Techniques and yields, moreover, were undistinguished. Even in the eighteenth century in Provence,[32] the seed sown was still giving a yield of only 5 to 1, and this can probably be assumed as the average yield in the sixteenth century. To obtain an annual product of 120 million quintals, at least 24 million hectares of Mediterranean land must have been under the plough: an enormous area when one remembers that 24 million hectares in any one year meant, under a two-field system, an available area of 48 million hectares (one field lying fallow for every one under crops), and when one is told that in 1600 the *total* arable surface in France was 32 million hectares.[33]

These calculations must be very tentative and the suggested figures are probably too low, for wheat (and other cereals) were not always in biennial rotation. Some land was only cultivated every three, four, or even ten years. And it is true that yields higher than 5 to 1 have been recorded.

In Cyprus, where one-twentieth of the land was cultivated, the wheat yield was 6 to 1, barley 8 to 1.[34] In Apulia, on the new lands taken over from time to time from sheep-farming, grain could give yields of 15 or 20 to 1. But these were exceptional.[35] And there were bad harvests and catastrophes. Climatic conditions continued to be the principal factor and man's unaided efforts, however determined, could not always bring him fortune. So there was inelasticity in agriculture. The figures we have for agricultural exports, which bear a certain relation to production when they compose fairly long series, generally show a constant level, whether of wool exported from Spain to Italy or wheat and silk sent to outside markets by Sicily,[36] graphically represented by a set of lines roughly parallel to the x-axis.

Progress was sometimes possible. Technically, the replacement of oxen by mules in Castile[37] meant that ploughing could be done faster and the wheat yield depended on the number of ploughings. But this replacement was by no means general. The northern plough made its appearance in the sixteenth century in Languedoc,[38] where its role remained modest, and probably in northern Italy,[39] but the swing-plough, which neither adequately turned nor aired the soil, continued in general use.

We have already discussed the improvements brought about by land reclamation schemes.[40] There is no doubt that during the fifteenth century, when the population was small, new land became available to the peasants of the Mediterranean. It was a time of expansion, or rather of recovery of a former prosperity, that of the thirteenth century. An agricultural revolution undoubtedly preceded and supported all the expansionist movements of the sixteenth century as Ruggiero Romano has rightly argued. But in the end this forward movement was brought to a halt by the very inelasticity of agriculture, under the same conditions as in the thirteenth century. The reclaimed land often gave an inferior yield. The number of mouths to feed was increasing more quickly than the resources and the logic of later Malthusian arguments was already visible.

The entire secular trend reversed direction perhaps as early as 1550, more certainly towards 1580. The foundations of a crisis were being laid, just as the improved circulation of money (let us avoid for the moment calling it the money revolution) was gathering speed. Historians of Spain are inclined to think that sooner or later agricultural investment ran into difficulties, peasants found it less easy to obtain credit, unpaid creditors seized the property,[41] and even the big landowners themselves were affected by the financial crisis of the years 1575–9,[42] when the Genoese let their own creditors bear the brunt of their losses, as we shall see. These and other explanations (in the case of Languedoc, for instance[43]) are wholly credible and valid. But the basic explanation must lie in the inelasticity of agricultural production. It had reached

its ceiling and the result of this impasse was to be the 'refeudalization' of
the seventeenth century, an agricultural revolution in reverse.

AN INDUSTRIAL BALANCE SHEET

John U. Nef,[44] writing of Europe at the beginning of the seventeenth century, reckoned that out of a total population of 70 million there must have
been two or three million artisans. A similar figure could therefore in theory
be advanced for the Mediterranean world with its 60 to 70 million inhabitants.
But if the towns represent roughly 10 per cent of the population, that is
about six or seven million people, it is unlikely that two or three million
of these, between a third and a half of the total, were actually artisans. In
one particular example, Venice, it is not difficult to reach this kind of proportion: 3,000 workers at the Arsenal,[45] 5,000 *lanaioli*,[46] 5,000 *setaioli*,[47] that
is, 13,000 artisans, with their families 50,000 people, out of the total Venetian
population of 140,000. And of course there were all the artisans in the many
private shipyards whose names and occupations we know,[48] as well as the
army of masons, the *muratori*, for the city was continually being built and
rebuilt, wood was being replaced with stone and brick, and the *rii*, which
were prone to silt up, had to be dredged. And we should include the fullers
of cloth[49] near Venice, at Mestre for example. A little further outside were
the mill-workers who ground the grain, tore up rags for paper, or sawed up
planks and beams for the great city. One should also include the coppersmiths, blacksmiths, goldsmiths, workers in the sugar refineries, the glass-
makers of Murano, stonecutters, and leather-workers,[50] the latter on the
Giudecca. And there were many more. Not to mention the printers, for
Venice in the sixteenth century produced a large proportion of European
printed books.[51]

Perhaps one should accept Nef's estimate, while making it clear that the
figure of two or three million must denote people *living off* artisan production: masters, workers, women and children, and not only the active artisan
population. It was a way of counting in Venice itself: 20,000 people were
commonly said, towards the end of the century, to be living off the many
processes of woollen manufacture.[52]

To this figure the large number of rural artisans must be added. No
village was without its artisans, however humble their work, or without its
minor manufacturing activities. But the quantitative historian will find little
joy here and, if he is guided by the habits of the past, he will tend to underestimate this obscure but vital labour in poor rural districts whose only access
it might be to the flow of precious coined money. Until recently, historians
have tended to concentrate on the impressive urban crafts, but there had
always been rural crafts in Aragon, in the Pyrenees, around Segovia,[53] in
the humble villages in Castile[54] or Léon,[55] or in the countryside around
Valencia.[56] Their presence was obvious near Genoa.[57] Villages near Aleppo[58]

worked silk and cotton. In fact there was hardly a single town that did not cause to spring up on her doorstep, or further away, the industries she needed and which could not, for lack of space, raw materials, or energy, be accommodated within her walls. This is the explanation of the foundries, mills, and paper-works in the mountains behind Genoa; of the various mines, foundries, and powder-mills throughout the kingdom of Naples and in particular near Stilo in Calabria;[59] of the sawmill at the gates of Verona,[60] on the Adige, where the boats carrying planks and timbers were all the more likely to stop because it was also an ideal place for smuggling—and of all the mill-stones grinding the grain for a neighbouring town (over eighty outside Venice), the strings of mills along the Tagus and below Talavera de la Reyna[61] or, at the other end of the Mediterranean, the thirty windmills that were visible from the city of Candia alone.[62] Languedoc had its urban industries, but in the Cévennes and the Massif Central, one finds many manufacturing villages.[63] They are also found over a wide radius round Lyons.[64] The city lived off the cheap labour of its nearby or outlying rural districts.

However, it is unlikely that these rural industries in the Mediterranean ever attained anything like the importance they had already acquired in England (the manufacture of kerseys) or in northern Europe; they never took the form of a whole group of rural centres under the control of urban merchants as was so frequently the case in France in the eighteenth century.[65] I do not even think that the cluster of rural industries around Lyons had any equivalent in the Mediterranean in the sixteenth century, at least there is so far no evidence of it. If correct this observation would prove two things: first, that the Mediterranean countryside possessed an inherently better balance of resources than so many northern regions (and possibly this is true, for vines and olives were often the equivalent of rural industries of the northern countries[66]—arboriculture balanced the peasant budget); and, second, that urban industry in the large and medium-sized towns was able to meet, virtually unaided, the requirements of an immense market. But by the end of the sixteenth century and the beginning of the seventeenth, nine times out of ten industry was moving out to small towns and villages rather than into a big city.[67] These transfers underline the actual and potential strength of rural or semi-rural regions that was still a reality at the beginning of the nineteenth century. When Murat took possession of the kingdom of Naples, in order to avoid buying expensive English red wool cloth, he clothed his army in black, peasants' wool cloth—the same as was worn by country people.[68]

If the kind of proportions one glimpses are accepted, the possibility must be envisaged that in the sixteenth century rural industry, *in terms of the number of people involved*, if not of quality or total revenue, was the equal of urban industry. This can neither be confirmed nor contradicted. The entire manufacturing community serving the Mediterranean market economy may have consisted of at most three million country people and three million poorly-off townsfolk. Of these perhaps 1,500,000 were active workers. Let us suppose that their average wages were equivalent to those received by the mine-workers in the copper mines that Venice possessed at Agordo,[69] that is, 15 *soldi* a day or 20 ducats a year (feast-days were holidays but paid). The total wage bill would be something like 30 million ducats. This is probably too low, for urban rates were much higher (and it was indeed from excessively high wages that urban industry sometimes collapsed). At Venice a worker in the *Arte della Lana* at the end of the century was earning 144 ducats a year and asking for more.[70] So our figures should or could be raised to 40 or 50 million. Finally, and this time it is practically a leap in the dark, if we reckon the value of industrial *production* as three or four times the total sum paid out in wages, we would get a maximum total of 200 million ducats.[71] Even if this figure were multiplied further, it would still remain far below the 860 or 1,200 million at which we have *hypothetically* estimated agricultural production (not altogether surprisingly, perhaps, when in discussions of the Common Market, modern experts, in countries as over-industrialized as France, have said that the commercialization of meat is one of the world's biggest industries).

As far as sixteenth-century industry was concerned the bulk of its products were more frequently absorbed into the monetary economy than cereals, oil, and wine, although here too there was a degree of self-sufficiency. But it was tending to diminish. Thomas Platter[72] notes of Uzès in 1597: 'Each family spins its own wool at home, and then takes it to be woven and dyed and prepared for various uses. They use spinning wheels as we do [in Basel; Platter was studying at Montpellier], but distaffs are never seen, for it is only the poorest people who spin hemp. The cloth may be bought from merchants and is sold at a lower price than that spun by hand.' We may seek the causes of the expansion of the textile industry and the sale of fabrics at once in the rising population, the concentration of workshops, and a probable decline in self-sufficiency.

THE PUTTING-OUT OR 'VERLAG' SYSTEM AND THE RISE OF URBAN INDUSTRY

From about 1520–40 there began a decisive period of expansion of urban industry in the Mediterranean, as capitalism gained its second wind both in the Mediterranean and Europe. The first 'industrial revolution' with which Nef credited England alone from 1540,[73] or the rise of 'big industrial capitalism' that J. Hartung[74] long ago described as taking place in Germany after 1550,[75] were in fact, given their inadequate differentiation, trends representative of Europe and the Mediterranean as a whole. Future research will perhaps show that they compensated for the brutal reverse that was sooner or later to interrupt the expansion of the sixteenth century. Commercial capitalism, its hey-day past, was being succeeded by an industrial capitalism that was to realize its full potential only with the latter, 'metallic' phase of the century. Industry compensated for recession elsewhere.

Almost everywhere (where it can be observed) this industry was of a capitalistic nature, conforming to the familiar pattern of the *Verlagssystem*[76] (the domestic or putting-out system): the merchant, the entrepreneur, or *Verleger*, puts out to the artisan the material to be worked on for a salary. This system was not new in the sixteenth century, but during the period it spread to places where it had previously been unknown (such as Castile apparently) or where it had been little practised (such as Venice). Wherever it was introduced it struck a blow against the guilds, the Italian *arti*, the Spanish *gremios*. Wherever it was introduced it benefited the merchant class which financed the slow production process and kept the profits from sales and exports. The role of these merchants 'qui faciunt laborare' was even more crucial in the relatively new process of silk manufacture than in the longer established production of woollens. Concentrations of silk looms were of course quite visible in the vast workshops, at Genoa for instance where no effort was apparently made to stop this concentration;[77] or even at Venice, where it was already provoking protests and government intervention. The law of 12 December 1497 had forbidden any silk manufacturer to employ more than six *tellari*.[78] The question was raised again in 1559, when attention was drawn to 'the greed of certain persons who since they have twenty or twenty-five looms working are causing evident inequalities'.[79]

The merchant then would advance the raw materials and money for wages, and handle sales of the finished product himself. The whole system can be reconstructed from the slightest significant detail. We are in Venice in the winter of 1530: Charles V's ambassador, Rodrigo Nino,[80] has been charged by his master to order silk fabrics; green, blue, red, and crimson damask, and crimson velvet. He will send some samples he says and negotiate about the price, but in any case once the order is placed 1,000 ducats must be advanced and the balance will be paid when the work is finished. For the weaver must buy the silk from the merchant, who has it brought from Turkey in skeins and then made up at his expense. In this case, the purchaser is taking the merchant's place, so it is he who must advance the raw material in the form of money. A minor incident at Cattaro in August 1559 is even more revealing.[81] In this lonely corner of the sea the *filatogi* had taken to working raw silk which they bought directly, contravening the law of 1547 that forbade spinners to work *per conto suo*. Order must be reintroduced, decided the Senate: the *filatogi* must from now on spin only silk belonging to the merchants so that the latter will not have to buy spun thread at prices decided by these over-independent *filatogi*—a crystal-clear example. Or again: one artisan at Genoa is giving evidence about another[82] in 1582. 'Yes, he knows what he is saying, for he has been a fellow-worker of Agostino Costa *filatore* and has seen many times in the workshop of the said Agostino, the said

Battista Montorio [the merchant] who brought him raw silk and took away finished silk.' Thirty years earlier in Spain, at Segovia, on the occasion of the arrival in 1570 of Queen Anne (Philip II's last wife) a procession of all the trades took place, first the workers of the mint, then the *tratantes en lana* (the wool merchants), then 'the clothmakers, whom the common people mistakenly call merchants [*mercaderes*]', says a seventeenth-century historian, 'when they are in fact the heads of huge families, who give a living to many people (sometimes two or three hundred) either in their own households or outside, and so by the work of many hands manufacture a great variety of fine woollen cloths ...'[83]

THE SYSTEM PROSPERED

We have to consider not only the predominant role of the merchant, the entrepreneur, but also the economic success of the system, the resistance it could offer when circumstances were no longer favourable, It led to the concentration and expansion of industry, a more rational division of labour, and increased production. Or so the evidence from places as far apart as Segovia, Córdoba, Toledo, Venice, and of course Genoa, suggests. Their vitality at the end of the century is in marked contrast to such old manufacturing centres as Florence, where the ancient arts of luxury woollen and silk cloth manufacture were to some extent suffering from old age, some said 'petty-mindedness'. Was this a structural failure? If so it would introduce an immensely interesting element to the argument—and it has been suggested by at least one well-informed historian.[84] Or possibly the more obvious reason is the correct one, that Florence was a victim of her high cost of living. Florence more than any other city (except Genoa) was affected by the arrival of precious metals and the sharp rise in prices that they brought. Banking and land competed with the *Arti* which in a Europe torn by war had difficulty finding customers, except in Spain, for their luxury goods. For whatever reason, after 1580, industrial activity at Florence was on the wane.

Other cities though, Venice in particular, continued to thrive until the following century. For this there were many reasons: plentiful labour, new techniques. Venetian woollen cloth was of medium quality, manufactured from second-grade Spanish wool and adapted to meet the tastes of the Levant which continued to be her chief customer, just as the woollen cloth of Segovia and the silks of Toledo and Córdoba were adapted both to the Spanish and American markets. A further factor was the character of the 'new men' who controlled production at the end of the century. In Venice, at least, these entrepreneurs were often foreigners who, after fifteen or twenty years of loyal service, would one day apply to the Signoria for Venetian citizenship, considering that they had amply earned it by their productions of hundreds or thousands of pieces of cloth.[85] In short, there were many new elements:

injections of new techniques and new men, both at the entrepreneur and the artisan level. For nothing was so mobile as industrial labour.

AN ITINERANT LABOUR-FORCE

The artisan community in the sixteenth century was made up of many races, rarely native to the area. Florentine crafts employed workmen from Flanders and Brabant in the fourteenth century.[86] In the sixteenth century the apprentices of the *Arte della Lana* at Florence were recruited over a large area extending well beyond the borders of Tuscany as we have already noted.[87] At Verona, which had obtained from the Signoria of Venice the right to manufacture *velluti neri*, there were twenty-five master-craftsmen in 1561:[88] not one of them was Venetian (something the Signoria would never have tolerated); fourteen came from Genoa, three from Mantua, two from Verona, two from Brescia, one from Vicenza, and one from Ferrara. As for the merchants 'che li fanno lavorare', there were only four of them: two from Verona and two from Genoa. This affords a glimpse of the mobility of both artisan and merchant classes.

The situation at Brescia was much the same: the *Arte della Ferrarezza* which manufactured armour, side-arms, and arquebuses, was continually expanding and contracting according to circumstances, losing its workers to neighbouring towns, then recovering them, and so on. At the end of the century under the impulsion of the newly appointed *Capitano* of the town, Francesco Molino,[89] it recalled one of the master-armourers from Brescia who had gone to Saluzzo taking many *lavoranti* with him; workmen were recalled from Pistoia and Milan (thirty-one at Milan's expense), and the number of *botteghe* immediately rose to twenty-three. Then there was a fresh crisis because of problems in the supply of iron and the scarcity of merchants —one or two more were needed.

For industry followed the merchants, or rather their capital: Tommaso Contarini, who was travelling in the spring of 1610[90] to England as Venetian ambassador, stopped first at Verona, then on his way to Trent passed through Rovereto. He found to his astonishment in this little place an active *negocio delle sede* with a good number of *filatogi* and over 300 'telleri che lavorano ormesini': these workers had left Verona. Four years later, in May 1614, the Signoria of Venice accepted[91] the following extraordinary proposition. In return for the services of the anonymous person who had advanced it, in reporting to the authorities any workers or master-craftsmen in important sectors of the city's industry, and in particular in the *Arte delle Seta*, 'che intendono partire', he would be granted the release of a *bandito*, an outlaw or a brigand who was, of course, in prison. Similarly, during the same period, Venice threatened reprisals on the persons or the possessions of any workers or master-craftsmen in her sugar refineries ('practico o professore di raffinare zuccari') who left the city to exercise their trade elsewhere.[92]

These journeys or flights by artisans were governed by the general situation. Over long distances and short, a mobile labour-force was constantly
responding to variations in demand. The movement from big cities to
medium-sized or small towns was typical of the end of the sixteenth century.
Over an even larger area we have the example of the spread of the silk industry throughout Europe during the fifteenth and the entire sixteenth century. In Italy the seventeenth century saw the rise of the silk industry of the
Mezzogiorno which experienced an industrial renaissance. Then quite
abruptly during the 1630s[93] this prosperity ceased and one after the other
the small towns of the north were smiled on by fortune, succeeding the
southern towns as silk manufacturers. This shift was undoubtedly accompanied by artisan emigration.

GENERAL AND LOCAL TRENDS

There is no *a priori* reason to suppose that all these rapidly developing industries followed the same general pattern. It is tempting to imagine that they
did, with some exceptions and in some places with the recovery of a former
level. But in fact the over-all picture is still a mystery to us. We may quote
in connection with the textile industries—and they were, alongside or even
after the building industry, the most important, but by no means the only
ones—some evidence of general relevance. For we know how much alum
was exported from Spain and the Papal States and therefore know the total
volume used of this mordant which was indispensable for the dyeing of
fabrics or rather in the preparation for dyeing. It is a reliable barometer and
provides an unequivocal answer. It rises and falls in time with the general
situation, reaching its highest level between 1590 and 1602.[94]

But we do not know whether other industries conformed to this pattern, as
is quite possible and indeed probable. Historians who are anxious to stress the
connection between industrial activity and the demands of the merchant
class have urged us to accept that they did; that the impetus to expansion
came from the merchants.[95] But we shall have to accept that there may have
been exceptions either in the short or the long run, for industry could also be
a form of compensation, a replacement for something else. The building
industry for instance could *sometimes* apparently move in the opposite direction to the general trend,[96] and there may have been particular local trends,
about which first-hand evidence is becoming available. We know, for example, some of the curves of textile production. The interesting thing is that
whatever the date they are all curiously alike. All industrial curves seem to
take off vertically and to decline equally dramatically. The production of
serge at Hondschoote[97] rockets up then falls sharply; textile production at
Leiden follows a similar curve. At Venice (according to Pierre Sardella[98] and
Domenico Sella[99]) it takes the classic form of a parabola. At Florence the
incomplete figures we have would fit into a similar curve.[100] The rule is con-

firmed at Mantua,[101] a minor example, and is probably true of the woollen industry of Brescia and the Val Camonica.[102] It is quite unmistakable at Segovia, Córdoba, Toledo,[103] and Cuenca. Was this a general pattern?

It seems at any rate to be true even of the most humble industries. Venice, for instance, took care to eliminate all competition from the east coast of the Adriatic, whether from shipping, manufacture, or trade. She did not always succeed. The *galere da mercato* and other ships leaving Venice were in the habit of putting in to the little port of Pola in Istria to take on crews, oarsmen, and provisions. Pola became, for the benefit of the men already aboard or about to join the ships, the best-stocked market for cloth made from the coarse wool of the islands, the *rascie* and *grigie* which we have already mentioned[104] and which came from both the Istrian and the Dalmatian hinterland. In about 1512 these cloths were reaching the fairs of the *Sottovento*, Sinigaglia, Recanati, Lanciano, where they became so popular that Pola lost what had been her usual stock-in-trade. This was to last ten or fifteen years, until about 1525 when Venice stepped in to restore order. In the interval there had been time for a steep rise followed by a fall.

Similar trends can be detected in the Ottoman Empire, where manufacture was often in the hands of immigrants. At Constantinople and elsewhere there were Christian prisoners who became master-craftsmen[105] manufacturing precious fabrics;[106] even more numerous were Jewish artisans. The latter imported the textile industry to Constantinople and Salonica.[107] In Salonica, for instance, we know that production of woollen cloth began to fall off after 1564, and that many measures were taken by the rabbis, the leaders of the Jewish community, in an attempt to stop the rot (the prohibition of free purchase of wool, the obligation to buy clothing manufactured in the town). From this evidence the peak of an impressive production curve must have occurred in 1564. This pattern is confirmed by the little town of Safed, capital of Galilee on Lake Tiberius: between 1520 and 1560–80, it was to become a prosperous wool-manufacturing town thanks to the Jewish immigrants and the crafts they imported.[108] A traveller noted in 1535, 'The manufacture of cloth prospers daily. It is said that over 15,000 kerseys have been made this year in Safed without prejudice to heavier fabrics. Some are equal in quality to those of Venice. Anyone, man or woman, who plies a trade to do with wool can make a very good living ... I have bought a few kerseys and others cloths to sell and made a good profit from them ...' Turkish tax records confirm the rise of this small town: in 1525–6 the tax paid by the dyers was 300 aspers; by 1533 it had risen to 1,000; in 1555–6 (for only four dye-works) it was 2,236 aspers. It was at about this time that the tide turned, that is the decline of Safed *roughly* coincided with the collapse of Salonica. In 1584 the Jews left Safed and its industry quickly collapsed (in 1587 a printing works, opened ten years earlier, closed down). By 1602 no cloth was manufactured there at all.

This is further evidence to add to the dossier on the probable pauperization of Jewish communities in the Near East as well as an indication of the general economic level of the Ottoman Empire in mid-century. In circumstances attributable to this decline difficulties arose in obtaining supplies of wool and in the 1580s cloth from England was being shipped direct to the Levant in English vessels. The rise of the Italian industry must also be taken into account, as well as the crucial economic and monetary crisis which was to launch the Ottoman Empire into the spiralling troubles of inflation.[109]

In any case, the peaks of industrial activity have their own particular interest.

1. It is important to note that in about 1520–40 there began a period of general expansion almost everywhere;

2. that peaks of production occurred in about 1564, 1580, 1600;

3. that although industry was not of course the paramount economic force it was on the way to being in the eighteenth century and definitely became in the nineteenth, it was already exceptionally developed. Industrial success came rapidly;

4. that its decline was equally spectacular and relatively easier to chart than its rise. In Venice, for example, the woollen industry apparently made a brilliant debut in about 1458;[110] was clearly stagnating towards 1506,[111] at least on the mainland, and made a long-lasting recovery after 1520.[112] It was not until about 1600–10 that this burst of activity began to run out of steam[113] and it was probably just then, in 1604 or so, that a period of expansion was opening in the Protestant Low Countries.[114]

There was a distinct relationship then between industrial expansion and decline in places often very far apart. Industry—or perhaps one should say pre-industry—was governed by a perpetual shifting of the balance, a continual new deal. When one hand had been played, the game began again. The loser might be lucky next time: Venice seems to prove this. But the last player to arrive was always the favourite, as the triumph of new towns in the sixteenth century in Italy and Spain was already proving. And the northern victory of the seventeenth century, although there had always been a textile industry in the Low Countries, was that of a young rival.

Present everywhere, even in the humblest towns where the historian would never have suspected their existence, even in sun-baked cities with a reputation for idleness, like Naples, industries were springing up[115] like fitful fires[116] scattered over a wide plain of dry grass. Their flames might spread afield or die down perhaps to flare up again further away. A gust of wind in one direction or another and the flames might reach grass as yet untouched. Even today the same can still be true.[117]

THE VOLUME OF COMMERCIAL TRANSACTIONS

Commerce is a many-sided activity. It will not fit easily into our calculations. 'Commerce' can mean the fruit that a peasant woman takes to market or the glass of wine which a poor man drinks at the door of the rich man's cellar (for the wealthy often indulged in this kind of retail trade) or it can mean the goods handled by the Venetian *galere da mercato* or the *Casa de la Contratación* at Seville. The range of activities it may embrace is immense. Besides, in the sixteenth century all goods were not commercially handled, far from it. The market economy covered only a fraction of economic life. More primitive forms—barter and autarky—rivalled it everywhere. If one accepts the view[118] that commerce is the final stage of the production process, in other words, that it adds surplus value to the goods it transports, one must recognize that this plus-value, and especially profits, are difficult to estimate, even in an example on which we are apparently well-informed. In the 1560s something like 20,000 quintals of pepper were annually transported to Europe from India and the East Indies. It was bought in Calicut for 5 *cruzados* per light quintal, and sold at Lisbon for 64, that is at twelve times the price. It was clearly more than a simple matter of the same individual buying and selling: the cost of transport, taxation, and risks involved were both very great and variable and we do not know how much of the 1,300,000 *cruzados* selling price went into the merchant's pocket.

Handling merchandise was moreover only one of the occupations of the sixteenth-century 'merchant', as is clear from his books, clearer still from the countless bankruptcy records. Every kind of operation and speculation appears there higgledy-piggledy: purchases of land or houses, industrial investment, banking, marine insurance, lotteries,[119] urban rents, peasants' quit-rents, stock-farming, advances from the loan banks (*Monti de Pietà*), speculation on the foreign exchanges. Actual transactions involving merchandise and artificial transactions on the money market figure side by side. The importance of purely financial transactions, with all their sophisticated ramifications, increases the further one goes up the scale of merchants and with the passing of the relatively prosperous years of the late sixteenth century. It was becoming widely known that commercial operations could be settled at the fairs almost *miraculously*. In 1550 de Rubis talks of the Lyons fairs where 'a million pounds can be paid sometimes in a morning without a single sou changing hands'.[120] Fifty years later, Giovan Battista Pereti, who kept the *giornale* of exchanges at the Banco di Rialto, explains in a report to the Signoria of Venice, that 3 or 4 million crowns' worth of business is transacted at every Piacenza fair, and that most of the time 'non vi è un quatrino de contanti'.[121] Exchange and re-exchange, the *ricorsa* bills[122] that were to extend their good and not always loyal services in the seventeenth century, had begun their career much earlier in the fifteenth century at Genoa,[123] by the end of the sixteenth century more or less everywhere,[124] and even at Lyons, where in January 1584,[125] we find a typical example: two Italian merchants agreed to advance money to the Bishop of Langres and his two brothers, the sum being taken 'ad cambium et recambium' by a third merchant, 'a gentleman called Guicciardini'.

Let us however attempt an estimate. The results are certain to be wide of the mark but the exercise will be instructive.

Our first clue comes from the fiscal records of Castile. I need hardly dwell on their shortcomings. But the *alcabalas*, or sales taxes, fluctuate according to the current economic situation and are not entirely negligible indicators. They also underline the varying degrees of activity, wealth, and income existing in the different cities and regions. At Valladolid[126] in 1576, a revenue of 22 million *maravedís* (the *alcabala* in theory representing one-tenth of all sales) must correspond to an approximate turnover of trade of 220 million *maravedís*, or 5,500 *maravedís* for each of the city's 40,000 inhabitants, that is slightly over 15 ducats per head, which does not of course mean that every citizen could have made this sum in profits from commercial transactions. This was the total volume of business that theoretically flowed through the city. As the reader will realize, commercial activity, often within a closed circuit, embraced a wide range of compensatory, speculative, and deceptive transactions. And the figure of 220 million is probably an underestimate. For the crown contracted with the cities for fixed annual payments in lieu of *alcabalas*, letting them reimburse themselves afterwards, sometimes with interest. But after the 1580s the towns no longer paid tax at a fixed rate, and the *alcabalas*, which no longer gave the old profits, reverted to central control.[127] But, in any case, the figures of 220 million and 15 ducats per head denote a fairly high turnover in 1576. An even higher figure is found at Seville in 1597,[128] for this was a far richer city than Valladolid and between 1576 and 1598 inflation had also played its part. The resulting figure is 15,900 *maravedís* per head of the Sevilian population (100,000 inhabitants and *alcabalas* of 159 million *maravedís*), that is triple the figure for Valladolid in 1576.

Let us now move on from these local figures (which provide a revealing geographical picture of the wealth of Castile[129]) to the more general problem of estimating the total turnover of trade. For the whole of Castile in 1598 the total income from the *alcabala* (unfortunately including the *tercias* as well) amounts to a thousand million *maravedís* (the *tercias* represent two-thirds of certain tithes paid to the church and must obviously be excluded from the calculation). But our hypothetical figure of ten thousand million *maravedís* gives us some idea of the scale of the total volume of internal trade. The *per capita* rate this yields is 1,500 *maravedís*, or just 4 ducats. This figure is lower than that for Valladolid in 1576 or Seville in 1598, but that need not surprise us: urban economies are always the most dynamic.

It is possible to base some calculations (though without certainty) on the customs revenue for external trade. If the relation of customs duties to total value of goods is arbitrarily assumed to be 1 to 10, it yields a figure of 3·63 milliards of *maravedís* (imports). Although the balance of payments was unfavourable to Spain, it is not totally arbitrary to assume that exports also equalled 3·63 milliards; let us add 700 million for the entry of precious metals, and without regarding it as in any way infallible, we can then, by adding together the 10 milliards (corresponding to the *alcabalas*) and the 7,960,000,000 *maravedís* of external trade, reach a total of nearly 18,000 million *maravedís*, or 9 ducats per head of the population (Castile had a population of 5 million). As the reader will have noted the relation of external trade (imports) to internal trade is something like 1 to 3.

Our second clue is provided by France between 1551 and 1556. Here we have only one certain figure, that of the total value of imports,[130] 36 million *livres tournois*, of which according to the source of the figures, 14 or 15 million represented luxury articles, superfluous *bifferies*. These 36 million (at 2 *livres* 6 *sous* to the *écu*) are the equivalent of 15·7 million crowns (*écus*). This figure can be doubled to obtain the total volume of imports and exports (31·4 millions) and can be multiplied by 3 to obtain the volume of internal trade (47·1 million). This would give an over-all total of 78·5 million crowns. If the population of France was 16 million (a figure generally accepted by historians, but by no means proved) the *per capita* rate would be nearly 5 *écus*, which expressed in Spanish ducats is about 5·6. This figure, applicable only to the years 1551–6, is of course lower than the Spanish figure for the end of the century. But Castile was richer than France, the 1598 Spanish figure is swollen by inflation, and finally the divisor (16 million as the population of France) is by no means certain. But even the sum of these uncertainties cannot entirely deprive us of the satisfaction of seeing that the two 'indicators' can at least be mentioned in the same breath.

Can the lower figure be used as an index for the Mediterranean as a whole? There are good reasons for and against. Let us solve the problem by reducing the French result to the nearest round figure. We may then conclude *without any guarantee of certainty* that the total turnover of trade for the 60 million or so inhabitants of the Mediterranean was something like 300 'million in gold'.

This figure is far from reliable. No economist would accept it. But we can say in the first place that this volume is far superior to that of profits, the income of the merchant class—which might be 10, 20, or 30 per cent of all trade; second, that the volume of goods available for commercial transactions was, if our figures are correct, only about a third, if that, of production; third, that it is important to locate in this no doubt imperfect but revealing context, the part played by the long-distance trade, *Fernhandel*, the very lifeblood of commercial capitalism. And this of course requires some comment.

THE SIGNIFICANCE AND LIMITATIONS OF LONG-DISTANCE TRADE

The *raison d'être* of long-distance trade is that it connects, sometimes with difficulty, regions where goods can be bought cheaply with others where they can be sold for high prices: buying kerseys or having them made in the Cotswolds, for example, and selling them in Aleppo or Persia; or buying linen cloth in Bohemia and selling it in Lisbon, Venice, or Lübeck. To make them worthwhile, these long journeys presupposed wide differences in economic levels, indeed enormous differences at the beginning of the sixteenth century, particularly at Lisbon, where commercial profits sprouted like tropical plants. As Porchnev[131] said of Baltic trade in the seventeenth century, what counted was not so much the volume of trade as the ultimate rate of profit. Capitalism in its agile youth (for it was now the most modern and wide-awake economic force) was attracted by these profits and their rapid rate of accumulation. In the long run of course all differences in price levels tend to be eliminated, particularly when business is good. Long-distance trade then has to chance its opinions. So there were periods when it was more or less profitable: very profitable was the first half of the sixteenth century;[132] profits levelled off in the second half; and there was renewed prosperity in the seventeenth century. It was the relative slump in trade that no doubt encouraged so many businessmen to invest their money in government loans and on foreign exchanges, culminating in a kind of financial capitalism in the second half of the sixteenth century. Let it be understood that there is no question of a drop in the volume of trade, which indeed continued to increase during this period. Our remarks apply exclusively to the *profits* obtained by the larger merchants.

The historian Jacques Heers[133] has protested against the exaggerated importance usually attributed to the spice and drug trades, which are sometimes spoken of as if they far outweighed any other traffic in the sixteenth century. 'When the history comes to be written not only of the alum trade[134] but of the trade in wine and grain, salt, cotton and even sugar and silk,' he writes, 'we shall see a very different economic history of the Mediterranean world emerge, in which pepper and drugs will only play a very minor role, particularly after the fourteenth century . . .' It all depends which way one looks at it. From the point of view of economic geography, Heers is right. From the point of view of the history of the rise of capitalism and of profits he is wrong. We should remember Porchnev's observation. In the area with which we are concerned the only thing that matters is the rate and facility of gain, the accumulation of capital. There is no doubt at all that in volume the grain trade far outweighed pepper. But Simón Ruiz was unwilling to commit himself to buying grain, because it was riskier for the merchant. Grain was not like pepper or cochineal, a 'royal merchandise' and a relatively safe risk. When dealing in grain one had to reckon with the demands of transporters, and the vigilance of states and cities. Except when large sums of money were involved, as in 1521[135] or 1583[136] or on the occasion of the massive purchases of 1590–1, large-scale capitalism did not participate in any regular way in the grain trade,[137] at least during the second half of the century; nor always in the closely supervised salt trade.

So long-distance trade depended on a very fine balance. The entire economic history of Castile under Genoese influence provides clear evidence of this now that its workings have been analysed by Felipe Ruiz Martín.[138] It was when they had difficulty in exporting American bullion from Spain that the Genoese bought alum, wool, oil, and even wines from Andalusia in order to obtain from their sale the specie they needed either in the Netherlands or in Italy. The last wool boom in Venice seems to have been the result of one of these operations.[139] I am convinced that a similar system guided from above also operated in the kingdom of Naples, for the occasional purchase of saffron, silk, oil, or even Apulian wheat. A whole army of merchants, Milanese, Florentine, Genoese, and Venetians (especially merchants from Bergamo) was stationed in the towns of the kingdom of Naples, for the most part small traders, despite the airs of importance they gave themselves and the large stocks of oil or grain they possessed; they were only there to provide their masters or correspondents with the advantages of rights and privileges acquired locally over the years. And they operated only to order: just as the Marseilles merchants who bought up large quantities of specie at Aleppo or Alexandria[140] were only executing the orders of the merchants of Lyons, who manipulated the strings according to the state of the market. The Spanish merchants too were in the service of influential foreign businessmen.[141]

So at the top commercial capitalism consisted of a series of careful choices; or one might describe it as a system of supervision and control, intervening only when large profits were assured. An entire 'strategy' can be glimpsed, sometimes even emerging into broad daylight, intervening in one place then another according to variations in the price of commodities and also in the degree of risk involved. One often stood to gain more but also to lose more by handling merchandise than by playing the money markets. Giovanni Domenico Peri, who is a reliable informant, tells us that 'there is often more profit to be made with 1,000 crowns in merchandise than with 10,000 crowns on the exchanges'.[142] But we know that on the exchanges businessmen were more likely to risk other people's money than their own and that the transfer of huge sums of money was concentrated in a few hands. No doubt greater over-all gains could be made on the 5 million ducats that the sea-borne grain trade represented in the Mediterranean at the end of the century than on the million ducats that pepper from Asia may have been worth on its arrival in Europe. But in the one case literally thousands of parties were involved, in the other a few powerful combines dominated the market. It was in their favour that the accumulation of capital operated. In 1627 the Portuguese *Marranos* who ousted the Genoese bankers were after all originally spice and pepper merchants.

And similarly the extremely powerful Genoese bankers and financiers even in their hey-day controlled only one sector, and that by no means the most important, of the economic life of imperial Spain. But they derived great profit from it since their numbers were so small. Contemporaries were often aware of this relative importance. In June 1598, the Genoese 'financiers' wanted to postpone the fairs of Medina del Campo, which would give them an opportunity to keep a little longer in their hands the money entrusted to them by investors. But the merchants of Burgos, formerly their liegemen and now their bitterest enemies, refused to co-operate. They explained that, of the total business transacted at the fair, that of the *asentistas* who advanced loans to the king represented less than the dealings of the ordinary merchants, and was in fact hardly comparable. 'Indeed,' the plaintiffs explained, 'we may assure your Majesty that the sums to be paid at the fair by those who are not included in the decree are far superior to the payments due from those merchants who are mentioned in the same decree.'[143] The decree was that of 29 November 1596, so as our text shortly puts it: 'es mucha más cantidad la que han de pagar en las ferias que no son decretados que los que lo son'. Clear evidence, but it does not affect the main issue. The essential point is that in certain sectors concentration of business had become an established pattern.

CAPITALIST CONCENTRATIONS

This concentration of firms was a fairly frequent occurrence in the sixteenth century. But its progress might be accelerated or slowed down by the general situation. During the 'first' sixteenth century, when every sector was expanding, there arose the great family concerns, the empires of the Fuggers, Welsers, Hochstätters, and Affaitati.[144] After the mid-century recession a different situation began to emerge favouring the rise of larger numbers of small firms. At this point, the spread of information and the possibilities of speculation increased, as Wilfrid Brulez[145] stressed in his study of Flanders. In order to integrate these smaller firms into the outside world, transport had to become independent, work on a commission basis had to become generalized, the role of the broker had to be accepted and extended, and credit had to become easier to obtain and therefore more risky. And indeed a series of bankruptcies marks every flurry of change after 1550.

Little is known about the higher spheres of Mediterranean capitalism. The silence of the Genoese archives reduces us to incomplete explanations. It would be extremely interesting to see how far these higher sectors of commerce, finance, and banking depended on the lower strata of small merchants and large numbers of naïve investors. Without everyday affairs, the common-

or-garden transactions of economic life, the banks at Naples or elsewhere would soon have been out of business. Without the cargoes they carried for very small clients, even the fleets of the New World would have been in difficulties. And finally, without the savings of Spain and Italy, which they were the first to mobilize, the *asentistas* of Philip II would never have been able to engineer their enormous financial operations.

In the Mediterranean the usual pattern was the family firm at both upper and lower levels, and short-term associations that were rarely renewed. Close ties, divorces, and remarriages could be effective on a certain scale. The Genoese, for instance, who lent money to the king of Spain, were in fact a permanent association, although no formal legal constitution bound them together before the *medio general* of 1597. They operated in twos and threes, or all together in times of crisis or particularly favourable conjunctures. Their small numbers and class solidarity kept them firmly together. They were commonly known as the *contratación*, proof if one is required, that they were considered as a group. For firms that were not brought together by necessity, connections could be useful as appears from the genealogical research undertaken by Hermann Kellenbenz, which has shed much light on the network of marriages, family ties, friendships, and partnerships stretching from Amsterdam to Lisbon, Venice, and the Portuguese Indies. They prepared the way for, or followed the great geographical shift, of world riches that marked the transition from the sixteenth to the seventeenth century.[146]

The availability of these networks may help to explain why the Mediterranean unlike the north never felt the need to set up large combines, the joint stock companies to whom the future was to belong.

THE TOTAL TONNAGE OF MEDITERRANEAN SHIPPING[147]

We have little in the way of reliable figures to help us estimate the total tonnage of shipping in the Mediterranean. England, France, the rebel provinces of the Netherlands, and Spain each possessed in about the 1580s 200,000 tons of shipping, the Netherlands probably more[148] (an estimated 225,000 tons in 1570), the three others certainly less, Spain something in the region of 175,000 (estimates in 1588);[149] France and England considerably less, but we do not know exactly how much. If we accept the total of 4,000 ships given by Saint-Gouard[150] (he says between 4,000 and 5,000 ships) for the whole of the French fleet, and if we accept an average tonnage per vessel of 40 or 50 tons, the minimum estimate would be 160,000 tons. If we accept that in 1588[151] the English fleet consisted of 2,000 ships, the highest possible figure would be 100,000 tons. It is true that according to the same source the figure in 1629[152] was 200,000 tons, following the expansion of English ship-building. So in the Atlantic there were perhaps 600,000 or 700,000 tons, not counting other northern navies and without subtracting the ships in Mediterranean ports in France and Spain. But we need go into no further detail since the tonnage of

Atlantic shipping is only marginal to the central issue.

If we now try to calculate the tonnage of Mediterranean shipping during the last thirty years of the century, we can first of all include a third at most of the Spanish fleet, 60,000 tons. The Venetian shipping fleet in 1605,[153] according to fairly reliable figures, consisted of 19,000 tons in big ships only, and a total of 30,000 or 40,000 tons for all classes of ship. The same figure of 40,000 tons can be accredited to Ragusa, Genoa, and Marseilles, to the fleets of Naples and Sicily and double that for the Turkish empire, i.e. a maximum of 280,000 tons which, added to Spain's 60,000, gives a total figure for the Mediterranean of rather under 350,000 tons. Even so the disproportion between the sea and the ocean is not too ludicrous: 300,000 or 350,000 on one side and 600,000 or 700,000 on the other, that is a ratio of 1 to 2. On one side the not insignificant Mediterranean, and on the other the Atlantic and the Seven Seas. And voyages within the Mediterranean were of course more frequent than those on the oceanic routes. A Ragusan vessel could easily make two or three voyages a year.

Should we include as 'Mediterranean' shipping the northern vessels that appeared there after the 1570s, possibly a hundred in number, that is at about 100 or 200 tons per ship, a total of 10,000 or 20,000 tons? It does not greatly signify: this tonnage is to the Mediterranean tonnage as 1 to 15 or 1 to 35; not much at most. Nor have we counted the hundred or so roundships of the Barbary corsairs, which may have totalled 10,000 tons at the beginning of the seventeenth century.

The figure of 300,000 or 350,000 thus reached is far from certain, but this calculation does establish: (1) that the Mediterranean was predominantly the province of Mediterranean vessels and their crews; (2) that the northerners were an anomaly, their presence did not drastically alter the structure of Mediterranean shipping, which as we have seen was solidly based; (3) that at least half of these northern ships were in any case in the service of Mediterranean cities and economies, sailing round the sea from port to port, picking up cargoes, leaving through the Straits of Gibraltar now and then, to return later the same way. So let us neither exaggerate nor minimize the role of these intruders which were in fact serving cities too rich to be self-sufficient.

May we extend to the Mediterranean as a whole the authoritative figures now available for the Ragusan shipping fleet:[154] 55,000 tons in 1570, 32,000 towards 1600; its crews: 3,000 to 5,000 men; its total value: 200,000 ducats towards 1540, 700,000 in 1570 and 650,000 in 1600; and finally its annual income, between 180,000 and 270,000 ducats—all well-documented figures? If so, the total value of shipping in the Mediterranean would be something in the region of 6 million ducats, its income about 2 million ducats and the crews would number about 30,000 men. If, as was the case at Ragusa, at least half the income from freighting went to the crews, the rest going to the 'share-holders', the average annual income of a seaman would be 30 ducats, a modest sum. Nevertheless these wages made a dent in the profits of the ship-owner, who also bore responsibility for the ship's maintenance and repair: one time it might be a rudder, another time a mast (never easy to obtain), sometimes merely a few barrels or a skiff. He had to provide food for the officers' table and for the sailors; and insurance on a ship's hull and freight might amount to 5 per cent or more of the capital investment. If the share taken by the officers and seamen increased, if the price per ton of construction (or purchase) was also rising, as it was at Lisbon[155] and Venice,[156] the capitalist merchant might have second thoughts about this expensive form of business: an income of 2 or 3 million ducats might seem a large sum, but shared among 10,000 ships it brought comparatively little to the individual ship-owner. At Venice, if the norms on which our calculation is based are correct, ships brought in 180,000 to 200,000 ducats, a mouthful of bread but no more.

This is all guesswork. But we have only a few ships' accounts to work from, one or two inadequate pages, a notebook in the *Archivio di Stato* at Venice,[157] a late document (1638) concerning the great Venetian galleon *Santa Maria Torre di Mar*.[158] Although such documents must exist, one has to be lucky to come across them. And lastly our figures are probably more indicative of long-distance shipping than of the everyday coasting trade: this in itself is a serious omission. But one thing is certain. By the end of the sixteenth century the shipping business had been abandoned (except by a very few rich ship-owners) to the small or very small businessman. If galleons are being fitted out at Naples, it will be sufficient to send a few recruiters to the ports of Apulia to find the necessary seamen.[159] When a ship comes to the end of her life, after at least twenty years of good service, her place is often taken by a poorer and smaller vessel.

OVER-LAND TRANSPORT

We have already calculated[160] that according to the Spanish figures the ratio of goods carried by land to those carried by sea was possibly 1 to 3. If 3 million ducats represents the value of the shipping traffic, over-land traffic alone in the Mediterranean would be worth about a million. I do not for a moment believe that this ratio was general. But even if we assumed an equal volume of traffic on land and sea, the total value, 6 million ducats, would still seem absurdly low. Somehow within this slight monetary framework we have to accommodate the busy flow of goods along all the Mediterranean routes, which as we have already seen is one (among many) of the major features of the inland sea.

Our calculations inevitably contain mistakes. But there can be no mistake about the poverty and meagre living of the transporters, on one hand the ordinary seamen and on the other peasants who divided their time between carrying and farming or a trade. We have, for instance, some circumstantial accounts of the *arrieros* of Maragateria near Astorga in the kingdom of León.[161] These *Maragatos* were poverty-stricken, and looked it even after they had made their fortunes later in the eighteenth and nineteenth centuries. At the end of the reign of Philip II they were occupied in loading fish, particularly sardines, in the Cantabrian ports, transporting them to Castile and bringing back wheat and wine. Their work would be done by truck drivers today. The distribution of fish throughout the towns of Castile was remarkable even in the sixteenth century.[162] The problem of how they lived becomes clearer when one examines the detailed population returns of 1561 and 1597, and sees that the transporter, *traginero*, also engaged in stock-raising, agriculture, crafts, and commerce. If he stuck to transporting he remained poor, like the young Juan Nieto who transported fish 'e mas vezes traia alquilado que por sus dineros', and 'was more often hired than paid in his own money'. The *traginero* who bought and sold the fish he carried was better off.

So the carrier, always on the verge of extreme poverty, was not only carrier but also peasant and artisan. This was so well after the sixteenth century throughout the Mediterranean and Europe. The boats carrying salt up the Rhône from the marshes of Peccais to the Swiss cantons went no further than Seyssel. From there the salt went by cart to Geneva. But here transport depended on seed time and harvest, for the peasants undertook to carry goods only during slack periods of the farming year.[163] The transport trade cannot easily be separated from the rural community that provided its labour and even from that of the little towns that often derived a great deal of their income from it. Cartagena, at the beginning of Philip II's reign, appears to have been a town specializing in transport, *acarateo*.[164]

So the circulation of goods was assured by many activities, which brought little reward either by land or by sea, and were only attractive to the seaman or muleteer for the small profits to be made from constant exchange, for each travelled on his own account too. In this way, the transporter, who was often in touch with a primitive economy, came into contact with a monetary economy; his position as middle-man had its advantages of course when he returned to do business in his own village. Nevertheless, viewed in a general context, transport in the sixteenth century was cheap and this comparative cheapness was accentuated with the years, the sums received by the transporters failing to keep pace with the rise in prices.[165] This was undoubtedly a stimulus to trade.

THE STATE: THE PRINCIPAL ENTREPRENEUR OF THE CENTURY

The state in the sixteenth century was increasingly emerging as the great collector and redistributor of revenue; it derived income from taxation, the sale of offices, government bonds, and confiscation, an enormous share of the various 'national products'. This multiple seizure of funds was effective because state budgets on the whole fluctuated with the general situation and followed the rising tide of prices.[166] So the rise of the state is in the mainstream of economic development, neither an accident, nor an untimely force, as Joseph A. Schumpeter was perhaps a little too ready to believe.[167] Whether intentionally or not the state became the principal entrepreneur of the century. It was on the state that modern warfare depended, with its constantly increasing requirements in manpower and money; as did the biggest economic enterprises: the Seville-based *Carrera de Indias*, the shipping route between Lisbon and the East Indies, for which the *Casa da India*, in other words the king of Portugal, was responsible.

The *Carrera de Indias* worked, *mutatis mutandis*, on the same principle as the Venetian *galere da mercato*, proof that this form of state capitalism was beyond its initial stages. In the Mediterranean it was indeed to remain very active: the Arsenal at Venice[168] and its copy, the double arsenal at Galata, were the greatest centres of manufacture in the known world. Also dependent on the state were all the mints[169] that were at work both in Christendom and Islam, in Christendom often under direct state control. They were farmed out but strictly supervised in the Turkish Empire or the Regency of Algiers. Dependent on the state too were the public banks whose hour of glory came at the end of the century. Here it was the city states, or at any rate states of a predominantly urban character that led the way. The territorial states had some time to wait, and the first of their banks was in fact to be the Bank of England in 1694.[170] Philip II paid no heed to the advice of the Fleming Peter van Oudegherste,[171] who tried in vain to persuade him to create a state bank.

This gap does not prevent the list of 'public' works from being very long. As a historian has pointed out, the huge installations set up by the Papal government at Tolfa and Alumiere for the extraction of alum were in fact an 'industrial complex'.[172] The Turkish government itself, outstandingly *dirigiste*, was responsible for many works; the rapid construction of the Sulaimāniye mosque[173] (and we now have an excellent recent study of work on the building site) is a good example. If we extended the label state capitalism in the west to such mixed enterprises, part public, part private, as the building of the Escorial,[174] with its remarkable constructional techniques, the list would be even longer. Through all these activities the state put back into circulation the money that arrived in its coffers, and in order to meet the demands of wars even over-spent its income. War, public works, and state enterprises were therefore more of an economic stimulus than might be supposed. What was disastrous for the economy was when money piled up in the state coffers, in the treasury that Sixtus V amassed in the Castel Sant' Angelo,[175] in the coffers of the Zecca at Venice or in those of Sully at the Arsenal.

All this having been said, it will not be too difficult to calculate the wealth of the states. We already know a good deal about their budgets and we can fairly easily find out more. If we accept the following figures for the end of the century: 9 million ducats for Castile,[176] 5 million for France under Henri

IV,[177] 3·9 million for Venice and her Empire,[178] 6 million for the Turkish Empire,[179] that is 24 million for a population of about 30 million, and if we multiply this figure by two to correspond to the 60 million inhabitants of the Mediterranean as a whole, we arrive at the no doubt artificial total of 48 million. On this showing, a man contributed rather less than a ducat a year to his ruler (and a ducat to his landlord too, no doubt).

I am sure that this figure, after the huge sums we have been conjuring with, will appear very low. Was the mighty state, striding across the stage of history, no more than this? And yet these figures are probably the most reliable of any yet mentioned. But it must be borne in mind that all the states, even the Turkish Empire, had moved beyond the primitive economy. Their yearly tribute was exacted from the 'fast-flowing blood' of the circulation of metal currencies; whereas all the other estimates we have so far given are a translation into monetary terms of transactions which for a very large part escaped the market economy. The modern state had just been born, both fully armed and unarmed, for it was not yet sufficient to its task. In order to make war, collect taxes, administer its own affairs, and conduct justice, it was dependent on businessmen and the bourgeoisie hungry for social advancement. But even this is a sign of its new energy. In Castile (which is a particularly clear example) everyone participated in state enterprise; merchants, noblemen, and *letrados*. The competition for honours and profits had begun. And a competition for hard work too. From even the humblest secretaries of the *Consejo de Hacienda y Junta de Hacienda* we have reports, letters, proof of their devotion to the king and the public good, alongside requests and denunciations dictated by self-interest.

Whether the rise of the state was beneficial remains an open question. It was in any case inevitable, just as the sharp-eyed capitalism of the merchants was inevitable. An unprecedented concentration of resources operated to the advantage of the prince. Forty or fifty million ducats (an actual figure this time, not a tentative estimate) was an extraordinary lever to have at one's command.

PRECIOUS METALS AND THE MONETARY ECONOMY

In history as in other scientific disciplines, classic explanations lose their force after a time. We no longer regard the sixteenth century as a period characterized by the uncontrolled competition of precious metals and prices, the view of François Simiand.[180] Frank Spooner and I[181] put forward a tentative estimate of the total amount of metal money in circulation in Europe and the Mediterranean *before the discovery of America*. The figure we obtained, based on simple but unverifiable equations, was an approximate total of 5,000 tons of gold and 60,000 of silver. The arrivals of bullion from America during the century and a half between 1500 and 1650 according to Hamilton[182] amount to 16,000 tons of silver and 180 of gold. Let us assume for the moment that these figures are roughly correct. They alter some problems and confirm others.

1. They paint a more optimistic picture of the situation before 1500, and therefore of the fifteenth century, which already has its advocates among historians.[183] It is in this period that we can locate the considerable advance made *in the west* by the monetary economy: by 1500 it had taken over the entire sphere of government taxation, and part of the dues payable to the landed gentry and the Church.

2. Simiand thought American minerals were the decisive factor. The stock of bullion according to him doubled between 1500 and 1520, doubled again between 1520 and 1550, and more than doubled between 1550 and 1600. 'Over the whole sixteenth century,' he wrote, 'this stock therefore increased more than five-fold. In the seventeenth century by contrast, as well as the eighteenth and the first half of the nineteenth, stocks barely doubled over any hundred year period.'[184] We can no longer accept this interpretation. The sixteenth century did not loose unprecedented riches on the world. The rising population, currency devaluations, a relative economic expansion, and certainly the accelerated circulation of coined money and the means of payment are other explanations for the high levels and revolutions (or *pseudo-revolutions*) of the sixteenth century.[185]

3. In any case, the Mediterranean, despite the expansion of credit, in the sixteenth century possessed neither the specie nor the paper equivalents sufficient to effect the annual balance of the exchanges and wages of a population of 60 million inhabitants. This shortage was endemic. At Venice, in 1603, although the city's coffers were well filled, there were not enough silver coins to pay the wages of the workers.[186] How much greater was the shortage in backward regions, where payments in kind had constantly to fill the gap. Not that payment in kind was altogether lacking in flexibility: it prepared the way for the monetary economy, but only payments in cash could make it work and prosper. On the shores of the Baltic, the small amounts of money invested by Hanseatic and western merchants helped to accelerate an economy that was still primitive. Towards the end of the century, of course, bills of exchange became more general and perhaps compensated for the slowdown (if there was one)[187] in arrivals of bullion from America during the second and third decades of the seventeenth century. In 1604[188] a Venetian tells us there was an annual turnover of 12 to 16 million crowns at the Piacenza fairs. Peri talks in terms of a turnover of 30 million towards 1630.[189] But these figures are unsupported. And such exchanges stimulated circulation only at the very pinnacle of economic life.

4. The monetary economy undoubtedly made progress. In the Turkish Empire this progress accompanied by a spate of currency depreciations virtually took on the dimensions of a revolution. Evidence of this is daily becoming available to historians. All prices were rising. All the old social patterns

were breaking up and the dramatic upheavals of the West were prolonged
there almost independently. They had the same causes and the same effects.[190]

5. But the important and unsurprising conclusion is the following. The
circulation of money (here understood to mean every type of currency, even
the lowest) only penetrated certain areas of human life. The natural flow of
rivers is drawn by gravity towards low-lying regions. The flow of money on
the other hand seems to have been restricted to the upper reaches of economic
life. It thus created a series of inequalities: inequality between the most
dynamic regions—the towns—and those where little or no money circulated
—the countryside; inequality between advanced zones and backward zones,
developed countries and underdeveloped countries (for this distinction already existed, the former constantly moving ahead, the latter even when
making progress, like Turkey for example, never catching up with the
leaders); inequality between forms of human activity, for only transport, industry, and above all commerce and government taxation had access to the
flow of money; inequality between the very few rich (perhaps 5 per cent)
and the great mass of poor and very poor, with the gap between the small
minority and this huge majority continually widening. I believe that if the
observable attempts at social revolution failed, were not even clearly formulated, it was because of the intense, relative pauperization of large numbers
of the population.

WAS ONE-FIFTH OF THE POPULATION IN GREAT POVERTY?

An estimate made with the help of parish priests in 1559 at Málaga,[191] which
we shall take as an example (a fairly well-off one), gave a total of 3,096 households (*vecinos*), that is at four persons to a household, a little over 12,000
inhabitants. Three classes were distinguished according to income: the
razonables, the *pequeños*, and finally the *pobres*. Of the last there were
over 700 widows and 300 workers (widows counted for a half-*vecino*, workers
for a whole one), that is, about 2,600 poor people, over 20 per cent of the
whole. The 'reasonably well-off' (and this does not mean rich) numbered 300
vecinos, that is about 1,200 people (10 per cent). The *pequeños* formed the
immense majority, 70 per cent, about 8,500 people. These proportions may
well be representative. Twenty per cent of the population living in extreme
poverty constitutes a large but quite credible percentage both inside and outside the Mediterranean region.[192] Contemporary observers, moreover, noted
abject poverty at the heart of the most prosperous cities: in Genoa, where
it was aggravated every winter,[193] at Ragusa, so rich and yet socially
so unbalanced, where in 1595, according to one report, 'there is also
much misery'.[194] We have no proof, of course, that the findings of Málaga
are relevant to larger or less-favoured towns or above all that the same
scale of measurement can be applied to peasant communities, whose income measured in money would be very small, but whose way of life

though less sophisticated might be better balanced. If this percentage is accepted it would mean that 12 to 14 million Mediterranean inhabitants were living near the starvation level: it is a possibility that cannot be ruled out.[195]

For we are never dealing with full-employment economies. An ever-present pressure on the labour market was the mass of underemployed workers, vagrants, or semi-vagrants that had been a constant, indeed one might say a *structural*, feature of European and Mediterranean life since at least the twelfth century.[196] As for the standard of living of the peasantry, we know next to nothing about it, so we shall be obliged to make the most of a few surveys which of course cannot be considered universally representative.

A village in the Brescia region was destroyed by fire on 8 May 1555.[197] A dependency of the Alpine commune of Collio de Valnopia, the small settlement at Tizzo nevertheless measured half a mile around, 260 houses, all burned, of which the investigator found only the walls standing. A point of detail: it paid 200 ducats annually in taxes to the Signoria of Venice. In these 260 houses, 274 families between them accounted for 2,000 people, which means if the figures are accurate (and we have every reason to think they are) that each *household* contained seven people. Not counting the price of the houses, the total damage was valued at 60,000 ducats, or 30 ducats per person. A fire in July of the same year, 1555, destroyed two peasants' houses in Trevisano, in the plains; one was valued at 250 ducats, the other at 150. In the first, furniture, hay, and grain amounted to 200 ducats, in the second, hay and grain amounted to about 90, without furniture (perhaps it had been saved). The two victims of the fire described themselves as *poveri* in their application for help, and say that they are now *nudi*, natural expressions no doubt from people asking for money, but which cannot have been in contradiction with the official estimate of their worldly goods. Now let us suppose that these individual figures can be used as a unit of measurement. Returning to Tizzo, let us complete the record of damage. Each house can be valued at 200 ducats, adding another 52,000 ducats to the bill, bringing the total damage to 112,000 and therefore the accumulated capital to 56 ducats, instead of 30, per head of the population. If we suppose that each family received a harvest similar to that of the poorer of the Trevisano fire victims, about 100 ducats, the total annual income of the village would have been about 27,400 ducats, or 13·7 ducats per head. This series of calculations brings us to the borderline of extreme poverty, perhaps it would be more correct to say of destitution. But we are never quite sure where this borderline lies.

I discovered too late to make full use of their extraordinary resources the documents of *Sommaria*, the accounts office of Naples. Through these fiscal records we are led along a multitude of paths into areas of extreme poverty and hardship. Pescara[198] on the Adriatic was a humble little town of 200 or 250 households, about 1,000 inhabitants in all, and all foreigners, *romagnuoli*, *ferraresi*, *comachiesi*, *mantovani*, *milanesi*, and *slavoni*. Of these thousand immigrants, 'fifty families [200 people] own their own houses, vines, and ply a craft; the other have absolutely nothing but their huts or rather their piles of straw; they live from day to day, working at the salt-pans or digging the ground'. If only, the text goes on, the better-off peasants could afford to buy oxen to plough with, proof that they had none. This is utter poverty, one would think. And yet the town had its port, its shops, and even its fair *della Annunziata* in March.

The *Sommaria* also gives details of the villages it sells and resells, according to the accidents of succession, to purchasers of seignorial revenues. Usually each inhabitant pays one ducat to the owner of the land, in one form or another, and this seignorial income is sold 'at five or ten per cent', that is at 10 or 20 ducats for every ducat of income. This rule of a ducat per head, a hasty calculation, is given for what it is worth. Another rule of thumb is that the *per capita* income of the peasant was approximately 10 ducats. But to take a particular case: Supertino[199] in the territory of Otranto was a village of 395 households in May 1549, a large village then, almost a small town. It had a higher population than Pescara. Its wealth lay principally in olive trees. The rule of a ducat per head rent to the landlord does not seem to work very well here. There were about 1,600 inhabitants, and the landlord received 900 ducats. But this time we have a record of tithes paid to him in kind and therefore an opportunity to calculate the village's production and income in money (3,000 kegs of wine, 11,000 *tomola* of wheat, 4,000 *tomola* of barley, 1,000 *tomola* of oats, 1,250 *tomola* of beans, 50 *tomola* of chick peas and lentils, 550 *galatri* of flax, 2,500 *staia* of olive oil—money value 8,400 ducats). The income, if the list of incomes is complete and if the tithe was indeed one-tenth, must have been a little over 5 ducats per head of the population.

But the villages of Castile, according to the *Relaciones topográficas*[200] of the 1576 and 1578 inquiries, provide higher figures. The income level calculated from a selected sample[201] is 15,522 *maravedís* or 44 ducats per family; *per capita* income, supposing a family to consist of four people, is 11 ducats.

Further calculations are undoubtedly possible. The copious guild archives have not been seriously investigated. And tax records should surely make it possible to ascertain on a larger scale the 'national product' of each of the Venetian islands of Corfu, Crete, and Cyprus. There are exceptional series of documents on Sicily both at Palermo and Simancas. I think it ought to be possible, though by no means easy, to calculate the gross product of the Venetian or Tuscan states.

I did at one time think these problems could be solved by taking as a minimum level the price of slaves or galley men, or the wages of volunteers for the galleys, or even of soldiers, or the pay of domestic servants. But I am not convinced that these prices put on men were really *marginal*. A slave in Sicily or Naples could be sold for perhaps 30 ducats[202] in the first half of the century; after 1550 the price doubled.[203] One cannot conclude anything from

this, for the slave market was very restricted; if there was a temporary influx of slaves, prices dropped sharply: in June 1587, on his return from a
pirate expedition with his galleys, Pietro di Toledo (the son of the famous
viceroy of Naples) sold the slaves he had captured for a mere 30 ducats
each.[204] We might add that it was possible to find slave-labour almost for nothing. At the end of the sixteenth century, we learn on the occasion of the
liberation of the *ponentini* galley-slaves, who had been worked continuously
for twelve years, that they had been sent to the galleys without ceremony by
the *provveditore* of Cephalonia, and then passed from one galley to another,
'strabalzati di galera in galera'.[205] Equally disappointing from our point of
view are the ransoms paid for prisoners.[206] The only ones recorded were those
for the rich and influential, whose ransom did not reflect a standard selling
price for men but what their captors thought they could afford. As for the
voluntary oarsmen who were paid and fed aboard the galleys, a remark by
the naval commander Giron[207] makes their situation plain. Also known as
'voluntary prisoners' (or not entirely voluntary) are those unfortunate men
who have served their term and remain on board the galleys; they are then
given a ducat a month, says our source, whereas in Italy they are given
twice the sum. At this high wage he adds it would be easy to find many volunteers in Spain! So soldiers must always have been over-paid, attracted by the
extra wages, for a soldier was already receiving three ducats a month in
1487.[208] In short, I have come to the conclusion that oarsmen in the galleys,
even slaves, and certainly soldiers and domestic servants (at Ragusa for
instance[209]) did not always come off worst in the division of men into those
who were looked after by their society, assured of their keep however meagre,
and the others. This dividing line runs below even these miserable classes
and if anything moves downwards.

A PROVISIONAL CLASSIFICATION

Whatever the accuracy of the preceding calculations and others yet to be
made, we shall not go far wrong in the scale of retrospective values if we fix
the following rates for the active members of the population: an income
below 20 ducats a year was a subsistence wage; between 20 and 40 ducats
'small'; and between 40 and 150 'reasonable'. This scale does not allow
either for local variations in the cost of living, or for variation over the years,
which might be considerable during periods of inflation. It will do only as a
very rough classification.[210]

So we know at once, when we learn that a professor at the University of
Padua received a salary of 600 florins a year, that he was *ipso facto* a member of the privileged class, without needing to know that he held the first
chair in civil law, 'primus locus lectionis ordinarie juris civilis' and was indeed
Corrado del Buscio, and we need not take account of the generally high
wage-level in that summer of 1506.[211] It will be of some value to place any

of the many wages mentioned in the documents against this elementary grid:
to see that at the Zecca at Venice the wage pyramid began at the bottom
with the beggarly sums paid to the boys who kept watch (20 ducats a year
in 1554)[212] and went up to 60 ducats for the salary of a *partidor*[213] (1557), the
official in charge of separating gold and silver, and only became really re-
warding for an accountant at 180 ducats[214] (in 1590, it is true, after the known
rise[215] in wages); to see that a workman in the Arsenal received only a modest
wage in 1534[216] earning 24 *soldi* a day, from 1 March to 31 August, and 20
soldi from 1 September to the last day of February; the caulker, who was a
skilled worker, was in the same year paid 40 *soldi* in summer and 30 in winter. So Venice's two great centres of power, the Arsenal and the Zecca,[217] depended on a poorly paid labour-force. Even the secretaries appointed by the
Council of Ten only drew an average of 100 ducats a year.[218] By contrast
the 'inzegner' in the service of the Signoria, Zuan Hieronimo de San Michel,
who was asking in March 1556 for his salary to be increased from 20 to 25
ducats *a month*, seems to have been very comfortably off, earning in a month
as much as a worker earned in a year.[219]

In short, large sections of the community were either poor or very poor.
They formed a huge proletariat whose existence historians are gradually
beginning to recognize from the fragmentary evidence available, a proletariat
whose presence was felt in every sector of the century's activity, increasingly
so as years went by. It bred persistent outbreaks of brigandage, an endless,
fruitless form of social revolution. The general impoverishment settled
differences, relentlessly driving poor and possessionless alike towards the very
bottom of the social ladder. In Spain the survival of ancient inherited wealth
and a marked demographic decline contributed in the seventeenth century to
produce a strange social category, a proletariat comparable to the plebeians of
ancient Rome. Genuinely poor, rascals from the towns whom the picaresque
novel has made famous, highwaymen, false or authentic beggars, all this
gente de hampa, these *hampones*, tramps, had done with work maybe, but
work and employment had done with them first. They had become en-
trenched, like the poor in Moscow under the last Tsars, in their poverty-
stricken idleness. How would they have lived without the soup that was
distributed at the doors of monasteries, these *sopistas*, eaters of *sopa boba*?
Ragged folk playing cards or dice at street corners, they also provided the
enormous numbers of domestic servants in rich houses. The young Count
Olivares, when a student at Salamanca, had a tutor, twenty-one servants, and
a mule to carry his books from his lodgings to the university.[220]

This was as typical of Spain as it was of France during the wars of religion,
of Italy under Sixtus V, or even of Turkey at the end of the century. The
growing burden of the poor was sufficient in itself to announce the impend-
ing violent economic change, from which the poor, on whatever shore of
the Mediterranean, were to gain nothing.

FOOD, A POOR GUIDE: OFFICIALLY, RATIONS WERE ALWAYS ADEQUATE

Our calculations and surveys will need revision: they can be much improved. By contrast we must not expect too much from an inquiry into sixteenth-century diets.[221] There is no shortage of documents. They are only too easily found. But they offer what seems very suspect evidence on the lower standards of living. According to them everything was for the best in the best of all possible worlds. That the Spinola family should have an abundant and varied diet is not surprising. Nor will it astonish us to find that the diet of the poor should consist very largely of cheap foodstuffs such as bread and biscuit. Cheese, meat, and fish were also eaten. The gradual decline in meat consumption throughout Europe, and no doubt in the Mediterranean too, had begun, but was not yet far advanced. The unexpected element in these past diets is that when the rations allotted to soldiers, seamen, galley-slaves, and poor-house inmates are measured for calorie content, they yield something like 4,000 calories a day.

All would indeed be for the best if we did not know that official menus were always and without exception *officially* good. Everything on the menus posted up or sent to the authorities looks satisfactory, even very satisfactory. But we hardly need the evidence of a few disputes about the distribution of food on board the galleys to sow doubt in our minds. And yet there are the figures, or the comments for example of the *veedor* of the Naples galleys, who had been in charge of supplies for years and who speaks freely before the investigators from the *Sommaria*.[222] Even on board the Turkish galleys, ordinary rations included generous distributions of biscuit.[223] So we shall have to resign ourselves to accept what we find, that is, the balanced diet that is described and confirmed by so many documents, and which may simply mean that galley-slaves and soldiers were servants precious enough to have their health cared for. And let us say at once and quite emphatically, for nothing that has gone before would suggest it: these menus were those of privileged people. Any man who had a regular diet of soup, *vaca salada*, *bizcocho*, wine, and vinegar was sure of his keep. Diego Suárez as a very young man worked on the building site of the Escorial, where he found that the rations were good: *el plato bueno*. The true poor were those who found no official provider, whether warlike or charitable. And they were legion. They form the dramatic background of the century of which we occasionally catch a violent glimpse: on 27 May 1597, at Aix-en-Provence, according to a chronicle, 'the rectors and bursars of the Church of the Holy Spirit were giving out bread to the poor, and in the crush of the said poor, six or seven persons died, children, girls and a woman, having been pushed to the ground, trampled and suffocated, for there were more than 1,200 poor people there'.[224]

CAN OUR CALCULATIONS BE CHECKED?

If we add together all the different sources of income (although they are both indeterminate and partly overlapping) the gross annual product of the Mediterranean lies between 1,200 million and 1,500 million ducats, giving a *per capita* share of 20 or 35 ducats. These figures are by no means reliable and are certainly too high. The average income could hardly have reached this level. The error arises from the misleading process of estimating everything in terms of money, and it is impossible to proceed otherwise. This *would be* the average level if everything had passed through the market economy, which is not of course the case. But that need not cause us to dismiss all our hypothetical figures as meaningless, still less as irrelevant. Our object has been to make the necessary initial survey, to situate, as it were, the huge inaccessible regions of the Mediterranean landscape in relation to each other. Let us now turn the page and leave an area where as yet quantitative history is unrewarding, where all the valid statistics are hidden from our gaze. Ten years from now, if the paths suggested here are followed and explored with success, this chapter will have to be rewritten from start to finish.

NOTES

1. F. Braudel, *La Méditerranée et le monde méditerranéen* (1st ed., Paris, 1949), pp. 342 ff.

2. F. Braudel and R. Romano, *Navires et marchandises à l'entrée du port de Livourne, 1547–1611* (Paris, 1951), p. 101.

3. Archivio di Stato [A.d.S.], Naples, *Sommaria Consultationum*, 1, f. 216, 28 Apr. 1559.

4. I hope the reader will not be shocked to find these approximate calculations expressed in 'ducats' with no further specification. There were of course many kinds of ducats, Venetian, Genoese, Florentine, Neapolitan, and Spanish. Each had its own particular and by no means fixed value. However we can still accept the ducat for the purposes of our extremely approximate calculations as a valid unit without reference either to its local value or the exchange rate. Any errors this may contain will be absorbed by the highly approximate nature of all our figures.

5. Maurice Carmona, 'Aspects du capitalisme toscan aux XVIe et XVIIe siècles', *Revue d'histoire moderne* (1964), p. 85, note 5.

6. See in particular J. Gentil da Silva, 'Villages castillans et types de production au XVIe siècle', *Annales* (1963), pp. 740–1, where an annual consumption of 2 quintals is accepted for the Castilian villages. This average is open to much debate. According to Sundborg, in 1891–3, *per capita* consumption in Italy was 1·2 quintals; 1·5 in Spain, 2·5 in France. Cf. Dr. Armand Gautier, *L'alimentation et les régimes chez l'homme sain et chez le malade* (Paris, 1908), p. 296; Andrzej Wyczanski refers to a consumption rate in 1571 of 2·2 quintals of rye in the Polish *starosti* of Korczyn, *Kwartalnik historii Kultury materialej*, viii (1960), 40–1; I. Bog, *Die bäuerliche Wirtschaft im Zeitalter des Dreissigjährigen Krieges* (Coburg, 1952), p. 48, a consumption rate of 2·5 quintals at Nuremberg, and of 1·9 at Naples in the sixteenth century, W. Naude, *Getreidepolitik der europäischen Staaten vom 13. bis 18. Jahrhundert* (Berlin, 1896), p. 156. For France, Vauban gives 3·4 quintals (3 *setiers*); the abbé Expilly (1755–64) 2·7 quintals, etc.

7. F. Braudel, *La Méditerranée* (2nd ed., Paris, 1966), i. 540 for wheat prices at Venice.

8. According to the calculations of F. Ruiz Martin.

9. Museo Correr, *Donà delle Rose*, 217, f. 131, 1 July 1604. Ibid., 218, f. 328 (1595), 468,000 *staia*.

10. A.d.S., Venice, *Dispacci Spagna*, Alvise Correr to the Doge, Madrid, 11 Feb. 1621.

11. Carmelo Viñas and Ramón Paź, *Relaciones de los pueblos de España ordeñadas por Felipe II*, ii (Toledo, 1951), 99, 132, 140, 169, 272, 309, 397–8, 342–3, 348, 408, 426, 470.

12. Re-edited in 1960.

13. G. Coniglio, *Il Viceregno di Napoli nel secolo XVII* (Rome, 1955), p. 24.

14. A.d.S., Naples, *Sommaria Consultationum*, 7, f. 204, 18 Jan. 1580.

15. *Censo*, p. xiii.

16. Ibid.

17. G. Luzzatto, 'Il Mediterraneo nella seconda metà del Cinquecento', *Nuova Rivista Storica* (1949).

18. F. Braudel, *La Méditerranée* (1949 ed.), pp. 450 ff.

19. L. Mendes de Vasconcellos, *Do sito de Lisboa* (1608), ed. Antonio Sergipe, p. 114.

20. In the eighteenth century, R. Romano, *Commerce et prix du blé à Marseille au XVIIIe siècle* (Paris, 1956), pp. 76–7.

21. Museo Correr, *Donà delle Rose*, 217.

22. On spirits from Candia, A.d.S., Venice, *Cinque Savii*, 1, f. 14, 6 Oct. 1601 and 14 Mar. 1602, aquavit and lemon juice, 'soliti condursi per Ponente'. Spirits do not appear on the customs registers of Venice until the final years of the sixteenth century.

23. A.d.S., Venice, *Cinque Savii*, Risposte 1602–6, ff. 189v, 195.

24. V. Magalhães Godinho, 'O milho maiz—Origem e difusão', *Revista de Economia*, vol. xv, No. 1.

25. According to the unpublished study by R. Romano, F. Spooner, and U. Tucci, 'Les Prix à Udine'.

26. Hans Telbis, *Zur Geographie des Getreidebaues in Nord-Tirol* (Innsbruck, 1948), p. 33.

27. J. F. Bergier, *Les Foires de Genève et l'économie internationale de la Renaissance* (Paris, 1963), pp. 82 ff.; quotation p. 83.

28. Miguel Caxa de Leruela, *Restauración de la abundancia de España* (1713), p. 50.

29. Luis Valle de la Cerda, *Desempeño del patrimonio de S.M. y de los reynos sin daño del Rey y vassalos y con descanso y alivio de todos* (1618), quoted by J. Vicens Vives, *Historia social y economica de España* (Barcelona, 1957), i. 300.

30. J. C. Toutain, 'Le Produit de l'agriculture française de 1700 à 1958', *Cahiers de l'Institut de Science Économique appliquée*, No. 115 (July 1961), esp. p. 212.

31. See above, note 12.

32. René Baehrel, *Une Croissance: la Basse-Provence rurale (fin du XVIe siècle—1789)* (Paris, 1961), p. 152. The following rapid calculations assume 1 quintal of seed-corn to the hectare.

33. J. C. Toutain, art. cit., p. 36.

34. Biblioteca Casanatense, Rome, MSS. 2084, ff. 45 ff.

35. A.d.S., Naples, *Sommaria Consultationum*, 2, f. 140, 13 Mar. 1563, yield of 20 to 1.

36. F. Braudel, *La Méditerranée* (1966 ed.), i. 541, 546 for graph and table illustrating this.

37. Idem, i. 261.

38. E. Le Roy Ladurie, *Les Paysans de Languedoc* (Paris, 1966); last chapter printed as chapter 7 below.

39. Carlo Poni's admirable book, *Gli aratri e l'economia agraria nel Bolognese dal XVII al XIX secolo* (Bologna, 1963), unfortunately only begins with the eighteenth century. The *piò* plough, which is recorded from 1664 (p. 4) must have appeared earlier, but the text is unclear.

40. F. Braudel, *La Méditerranée* (1966 ed.), i. 59 ff.

41. B. Bennassar, *Valladolid au siècle d'or* (Paris, 1967).

42. This is the explanation suggested by Felipe Ruiz Martin in his important introduction to the *Lettres marchandes échangées entre Florence et Medina del Campo* (Paris, 1965). As soon as the Genoese had the opportunity of settling with their creditors in *juros*, they shifted the burden of their losses on to other shoulders. Among their clients there were of course many landowners.

43. E. Le Roy Ladurie, op. cit.

44. John U. Nef, 'Industrial Europe at the time of the Renaissance', *Journal of Political Economy*, vol. xlix (1941).

45. R. Romano, 'Aspetti economici degli armamenti navali veneziani nel secolo XVI', *Rivista Storica Italiana* (1954).

46. Museo Correr, *Donà delle Rose*, 42, f. 77v (1607) of whom 3,300 were weavers, with a ratio of one master-weaver to two men.

47. Apparently equal in number to the *lanaioli*, which must be an exaggeration.

48. See R. Romano, 'La Marine marchande vénitienne au XVIe siècle', *Actes du IVe Colloque International d'Histoire Maritime* (Paris, 1962), p. 37.

49. A.d.S., Venice, *Senato Terra*, 53, 7 May 1569.

50. Idem, 2, 17 Sept. 1545.

51. Lucien Fébvre and Henri Jean Martin, *L'Apparition du livre* (Paris, 1958), pp. 280, 286, 287, 293.

52. A.d.S., Venice, *Cinque Savii*, 140, ff. 4–5, 11 Mar. 1598 'al numero di 20(000) et più persone computando le famiglie et figlioli loro'.

53. J. van Klavern, *Europäische Wirtschaftsgeschichte Spaniens im 16. und 17. Jahrhundert* (Stuttgart, 1960), p. 182 (1573).

54. Carmolo Viñas and Ramón Paź, op. cit., ii. 217, for example at Peña Aguilera, a poor village, there were charcoal-burners, quarrymen, 'e algunos laborantes de lana'.

55. Manufacture of peasant cloth and barrel staves in the villages of the Maragateria, cf. F. Braudel, *La Méditerranée* (1966 ed.), i. 408, note 7.

56. T. Halperin Donghi, 'Les Morisques du royaume de Valence au XVIe siècle', *Annales* (1956), p. 162: industries consisted of silk manufacture, pottery, the production of *espadrilles*, made of esparto grass for everyday use; finer ones were made of hemp.

57. Jacques Heers, *Gênes au XVe siècle* (Paris, 1961), pp. 218 ff.

58. F. Braudel, *La Méditerranée* (1966 ed.), i. 499, note 5.

59. A.d.S., Naples, *Sommaria Consultationum*, innumerable references: 13, ff. 389–90; 21, f. 51; 31, ff. 139–46, 180–4; 37, f. 41v, 42 . . .

60. A.d.S., Venice, *Senato Terra*, 30, Verona, 1 Mar. 1559.

61. Carmelo Viñas and Ramón Paź, op. cit., ii. 448.

62. S. Schweigger, *Ein neue Reissbeschreibung auss Teutschland nach Konstantinopel und Jerusalem* (4th ed., Nuremberg, 1639), p. 329 (1581).

63. E. Le Roy Ladurie, op. cit.

64. R. Gascon, *Grand Commerce et vie urbaine au XVIe siècle. Lyon et ses marchands* (Paris, 1971).

65. For a clear example see François Dornic, *L'Industrie textile dans le Maine et ses débouchés internationaux, 1650–1815* (Paris, 1955).

66. Roger Dion, *Histoire de la vigne et du vin en France des origines au XIXe siècle* (Paris, 1959), p. 26.

67. F. Braudel, *La Méditerranée* (1949 ed.), pp. 345 ff.; Giuseppe Aleati, *La popolazione di Pavia durante il dominio spagnolo* (Milan, 1957), p. 125, sees this as a crisis precipitated by the high cost of living in the cases of Pavia, Cremona, Como, and Milan.

68. A detail I owe to R. Romano.

69. Museo Correr, *Cicogna*, 2987, Aug. 1576, thirty men were employed there.

70. A.d.S., Venice, *Cinque Savii*, i. 139, 20 Apr. 1603.

71. *Censo*, table 3, the ratio of industrial to agricultural production in Spain in 1799 was 4·449 to 1.

72. *Félix et Thomas Platter à Montpellier* (Montpellier, 1892), p. 134.

73. Cf. the new departure taken by the research of Felipe Ruiz Martin for Castile, *El siglo de los Genoveses en Castilla (1528–1627)*; *capitalismo cosmopolita y capitalismos nacionales*, forthcoming; John U. Nef, 'The progress of technology and the growth of large scale industry in Great Britain, 1500–1640', *Economic History Review* (1934), and comments by Henri Hauser in *Annales d'histoire économique et sociale* (1936), pp. 71 ff.

74. J. Hartung, 'Aus dem Geheimbuche eines deutschen Handelhauses im XVI. Jahrhundert', *Z. für Sozial- und Wirtschaftsgeschichte* (1898).

75. Despite differences in technique (use of coal in England) and resources there are on the whole more points of resemblance than of divergence.

76. See M. Keul in *Annales* (1963), p. 836, note 3.

77. F. Braudel, *La Méditerranée* (1949 ed.), p. 342, following H. Sieveking, 'Die genueser Seiden-industrie im 15. und 16. Jahrhundert. Ein Beitrag zur Geschichte des Verlags-Systems' (remarkable article), *Jahrbuch für Gesetzgebung Verwaltung und Statistik im Deutschen Reiche* (1897), pp. 101–33.

78. See following note.

79. A.d.S., Venice, *Senato Terra*, 30, 11 Nov. 1559, for a reminder of the *parte* of 12 Dec. 1497.

80. Rodrigo Nino to Charles V, Venice, 1 Dec. 1530, Simancas E 1308.

81. A.d.S., *Senato Terra*, 29, 16 Aug. 1559.

82. Archivio communale, 572, Genoa, 1582.

83. Diego de Colmenares, *Historia de la insigne ciudad de Segovia* (2nd ed., Madrid, 1640), p. 547.

84. An explanation suggested by Felipe Ruiz Martin, in his introduction to the *Lettres marchandes*.

85. For example, A.d.S., Venice, *Senato Terra*, 74, 18 Apr. 1578; 106, 7 Mar. 1584; 112, 24 Nov. 1589. Negrin de Negrini, responsible for the manufacture of 1,884 woollen cloths since 1564. Innovating spirit of some entrepreneurs, ibid., *Cinque Savii*, 15, f. 21, 7 Feb. (1609).

86. Alfred Doren, *Storia economica dell'Italia nel medioevo* (Padua, 1936), p. 491.

87. F. Braudel, *La Méditerranée* (1966 ed.), i. 313. The apprentices came from Genoa, Bologna, Perugia, Ferrara, Faenza, and Mantua, according to the unpublished thesis of Maurice Carmona on Florence and Tuscany in the seventeenth century.

88. A.d.S., Venice, *Senato Terra*, 35, 15 Dec. 1561.

89. Museo Correr, *Donà delle Rose*, 160, ff. 53, 53v.

90. A.d.S., Venice, *Senato Secreta Signori Stati*, Tommaso Contarini to the Doge, Bolzano, 23 Mar. 1610.

91. A.d.S., Venice, *Cinque Savii*, 200, 27 May 1614.

92. Ibid., 16, f. 53, 15 Nov. 1611.

93. According to J. Gentil da Silva, unpublished study of Italian fairs in the seventeenth century.

94. Jean Delumeau, *L'Alun de Rome, XVe–XIXe siècles* (Paris, 1963), *passim* and esp. graph on pp. 132–3.

95. R. Gascon, op. cit., p. 89; Clemens Bauer, *Unternehmung und Unternehmungsformen im Spätmittelalter und in der beginnenden Neuzeit* (Jena, 1936), p. 9, apropos of Antwerp, following Goris and Streider.

96. Andrzej Wyrobisz, *Budownictwo Murowane w Malopolsce w XIV i XV Wieku* [*The building industry in Little Poland in the fourteenth and fifteenth centuries*] (Cracow, 1963), summary in French, pp. 166–70.

97. Emile Coornaert, *Un Centre industriel d'autrefois. La draperie-sayetterie d'Hondschoote (XIVe–XVIIIe siècles)* (Paris, 1930), pp. 493 ff. and diagram Vbis.

98. Pierre Sardella, 'L'Épanoissement industriel de Venise au XVIe siècle', *Annales*, vol. ii (1947).

99. Domenico Sella, 'Les Mouvements longs de l'industrie lainière à Venise aux XVIe et XVIIe siècles', *Annales*, vol. xii (1957).

100. Ruggiero Romano, 'A Florence au XVIIe siècle. Industries textiles et conjoncture', *Annales* (1952).

101. Aldo de Maddalena, 'L'industria tessile a Mantova nel 1500 e all' inizio del 1600', *Studi in onore di Amintore Fanfani* (Milan, 1962).

102. A. Zanelli, *Delle condizioni interne di Brescia dal 1642 al 1644* (Brescia, 1898), p. 247, situates the peak of cloth production (18,000 pieces) in about 1550; I am more inclined to place it in 1555; everything turned on the customs measures enacted at Venice, *Senato Terra*, 1, 20 May 1545. The situation after that was irremediable—the master-craftsmen who left did not return.

103. According to the forthcoming study by Felipe Ruiz Martin.

104. F. Braudel, *La Méditerranée* (1966 ed.), i. 118 and *Senato Mar*, 7, f. 26v, 18 Aug. 1461.

105. Lectures given at École des Hautes Études by Ömer Lütfi Barkan.

106. A.d.S., Florence, *Mediceo*, 4279, a Jewish merchant seeking to buy in Tripoli Christian slaves who could work velvet or damask.

107. I. S. Emmanuel, *Histoire de l'industrie des tissus des Israélites de Salonique* (Lausanne, 1935).

108. S. Schwarzfuchs, 'La Décadence de la Galilée juive du XVIe siècle et la crise du textile du Proche-Orient', *Revue des études juives* (1962).

109. F. Braudel, *La Méditerranée* (1966 ed.), i. 489 ff.

110. A.d.S., Venice, *Senato Terra*, 4, f. 71, 18 Apr. 1458: 'se ha principiado adesso el mester de la lana in questa città et lavorasse a grandissima furia de ogni sorte pani e principaliter garbi'.

111. Ibid., *Senato Terra*, 15, f. 92, 23 Jan. 1506: '... el mestier de la lana che soleva dar alimento a molte terre nostre et loci nostri hora è reducto in tanta extremità che più esser non potria'.

112. See note by P. Sardella and the much-quoted article by D. Sella, op. cit.; there were even difficulties at Venice, *Senato Terra*, 15, f. 93 ff., 9 Feb. 1506 and even clearer A.d.S., Venice, *Consoli dei Mercanti*, 128, 29 Sept. 1517.

113. Ibid.

114. Emile Coornaert, op. cit., p. 48.

115. A.d.S., Naples, *Sommaria Consultationum*, 7, ff. 33–9, 28 Feb. 1578; in 1576 there were produced 26,940 *canne* of silk cloth.

116. The cloth industry at Brescia was also precarious, hampered by customs controls on wool; it was unable to obtain further supplies at Vercelli, *Senato Terra*, 1, 20 May 1545.

117. Cf. the observations of François Simiand, *Cours d'économie politique* (Paris, 1928–9), vol. ii, *passim* and pp. 418 ff.

118. L. F. de Tollenare, *Essai sur les entraves que le commerce éprouve en Europe* (Paris, 1820), p. 3, a product 'is not complete, it does not possess its full potential exchange value until it is accessible to the purchaser. Commerce gives it its finishing touch ...'

119. Gambling held an important place not only in the life of the nobility (particularly towards the end of the century), but also in the lives of merchants. Any subject was a pretext for a wager; the number of cardinals to be promoted, the death or survival of famous men, the sex of unborn children. At Venice, when it was odds on that the French had captured Pavia, a Spaniard Calzeran insisted on wagering on the opposite. He was no doubt in touch with Lannoy or Pescara, in any case he won a fortune, A.d.S., Modena, Venezia 8.16.77. VIII, f. 66, J. Tebaldi to the Duke, Venice, 15 May 1525.

120. Quoted by R. Gascon, op. cit., p. 177, Claude de Rubys, *Histoire véritable de la ville de Lyon* (Lyon, 1604), p. 499.

121. Museo Correr, *Donà delle Rose*, 181, July 1603, f. 53.

122. Giulio Mandich, *Le Pacte de ricorsa et le marché italien des changes au XVIIe siècle* (Paris, 1953).

123. Jacques Heers, op. cit., pp. 75, 79 ff.

124. F. Braudel, 'Le Pacte de ricorsa au service du Roi d'Espagne', *Studi in onore di Armando Sapori*, vol. ii (Milan, 1957).

125. A.d.S., Florence, *Mediceo*, 4745, unnumbered, Jan. 1589.

126. Modesto Ulloa, *La hacienda real de Castilla en el reinado de Felipe II* (Rome, 1963), p. 108.

127. According to Felipe Ruiz Martin.

128. Modesto Ulloa, op. cit., p. 132.

129. Alvaro Castillo Pintado, 'El *servicio de millones* y la población del Reino de Granada in 1591', *Saitabi* (1961).

130. Albert Chamberland, 'Le Commerce d'importation en France au milieu du XVIe siècle', *Revue de géographie* (1894).

131. B. Porchnev, *Congress of historical sciences* (Stockholm, 1960), iv. 137.

132. According to G. von Below, *Über historische Periodisierungen mit besonderem Blick auf die Grenze zwischen Mittelalter und Neuzeit* (Berlin, 1925), pp. 51–2, this period was outstanding both economically and artistically. Lucien Fébvre considered it a happy age before the 'sad men' of the years after 1560; Franz Linder, 'Spanische Markt-und Börsen-wechsel', *Ibero-amerikanisches Archiv* (1929), p. 18, even claims that 1550–1600 was the age of *Ricorsa-Wechselschäft*.

133. Jacques Heers, *Revue du nord* (1964), pp. 106–7.

134. J. Finot, 'Le Commerce de l'alun dans les Pays-Bas et la bulle encyclique du Pape Jules II en 1506', *Bull. hist. et philol.* (1902); Jean Delumeau, *L'Alun de Rome, XVe–XIXe siècles* (Paris, 1963); 'The Alum Trade in the fifteenth and sixteenth centuries and the beginning of the Alum industry in England', in *The Collected Papers of Rhys Jenkins* (Cambridge, 1936); L. Liagre, 'Le Commerce de l'alun en Flandre au Moyen Âge', *Le Moyen Âge*, vol. lxi (4th series, x, 1955); Felipe Ruiz Martin, *Les Aluns espagnols, indice de la conjoncture économique de l'Europe au XVIe siècle*, forthcoming; G. Zippel, 'L'allume di Tolfa e il suo commercio', *Arch. soc. Rom. Stor. patr.*, vol. xxx (1907).

135. Cf. the many documents A.d.S., Naples, *Sommaria Partium*, 96: *1521*, ff. 131v, 133v, 150, 153, 'navis celeriter suum viagium exequi posset' (a Genoese ship), 166v (on Catalonia), 177 (Oran), 175; *1522*, ff. 186v, 199, 201, 221, 224–5, 228v and 229, 232, 244, 252v.

136. According to Felipe Ruiz Martin.

137. F. Braudel, *La Méditerranée* (1966 ed.), i. 544–5.

138. In a study to be published shortly.

139. Ibid.

140. F. Braudel, *La Méditerranée* (1966 ed.), i. 513, note 5 and Micheline Baulant, *Letres de négociants marseillais: les frères Hermite, 1570–1612* (Paris, 1953).

141. Cf. Felipe Ruiz Martin, Introduction, *Lettres de Florence*, op. cit., pp. xxxvi–xxxvii.

142. Quoted by Maurice Carmona, 'Aspects du capitalisme toscan aux XVIe et XVIIe siècles', *Revue d'histoire moderne* (1964), p. 96, note 2.

143. Archivo Ruiz, 117, quoted by F. Ruiz Martin, in *El siglo de los Genoveses*, op. cit.

144. See the admirable book by Clemens Bauer for a discussion of these questions.

145. Wilfrid Brulez, *De Firma della Faille en de internationale handel van Vlaamse firma's in de 16e eeuw* (Brussels, 1959), pp. 580 ff.

146. Notably the Hispano-Portuguese front against India and the role played by an information agency serving the interests of German and Flemish merchants: Hermann Kellenbenz, *Studia* (1963), pp. 263–90.

147. For some useful comparisons, see R. Romano, 'Per una valutazione della flotta mercantile europea alla fine del secolo XVIII', *Studi in onore di Amintore Fanfani* (Milan, 1962).

148. According to Josef Kulischer, *Allgemeine Wirtschaftsgeschichte des Mittelalters und der Neuzeit* (Munich, 1928–9), ii. 384.

149. R. Konetzke, *Geschichte des spanischen und portugiesischen Volkes* (Leipzig, 1939), p. 203.

150. Saint-Gouard to the King, Madrid, 21 May 1572, B.N., Fr. 16104, ff. 88 ff.

151. S. Lilley, *Men, Machines and History* (1948), p. 72 and J. U. Nef, *The Rise of the British Coal Industry* (1932), i. 173.

152. S. Lilley, ibid., p. 72.

153. Museo Correr, *Donà delle Rose*, 271, f. 46v, 7 Mar. 1605; see also Alberto Tenenti, *Naufrages, corsaires et assurances maritimes à Venise, 1592–1609* (Paris, 1959), pp. 563 ff.

154. Iorjo Tadić, 'Le Port de Raguse et sa flotte au XVIe siècle' in Michael Mollat, *Le Navire et l'économie maritime du Moyen Âge au XVIIIe siècle. Travaux du Deuxième Colloque Internationale d'Histoire Maritime* (Paris, 1959), pp. 15, 16.

155. B.M. Add 28478, f. 238, Apr. 1594: '... se deve ter consideração ao preço das cousas ser mayor'.

156. F. Braudel, *La Méditerranée* (1966 ed.), i. 266 ff.

157. I am indebted to Ugo Tucci for looking through it for me.

158. A.d.S., Venice, *Senato Zecca*, 39, 12 June 1638.

159. A.d.S., Naples, *Regia Camera della Sommaria*, Reg. 14, 1594, 1623–37.

160. F. Braudel, *La Méditerranée* (1966 ed.), i. 269 ff.

161. José Luis Martin Galindo, 'Arrieros maragatos en el siglo XVIII', *Estudios y Documentos*, No. 9 (1956).

162. Pedro de Medina, *Libro de grandezas y cosas memorables de España* (Alcalá de Henares, 1595), p. 209, in the case of Alcalá de Henares.

163. Brigue Archives, Stockalper Papers, Sch. 31, No. 2939, Geneva, 10 July 1650 and No. 2942, 14 July 1650; there was a break for the harvest (information supplied by M. Keul). Cf. ibid., No. 2966, 18–28 Sept. 1650 for a halt for the autumn sowing.

164. Information supplied by Felipe Ruiz Martin.

165. B. Bennassar, op. cit.

166. See the graphs in F. Braudel, *La Méditerranée* (1966 ed.), ii. 28, 31, 33.

167. Joseph Schumpeter, *Storia dell'analisi economica* (Turin, 1959), i. 174.

168. Ruggiero Romano, art. cit., *Rivista Storica Italiana* (1954).

169. Ali Sahili Oglu, unpublished study of currency minted in Turkey.

170. The Banks of Stockholm (1672) and of Amsterdam (1609) had of course preceded it, but these were predominantly city banks. It is true that the headquarters of the Bank of England were in London.

171. His first attempt was made in 1576. Felipe Ruiz Martin has drawn to my attention an important document in connection with this at Simancas E 659, f. 103.

172. Jacques Heers, *Revue du Nord* (1964).

173. Ömer Lütfi Barkan, 'L'Organisation du travail dans le chantier d'une grande mosquée à Istanbul au XVIe siècle', *Annales* (1961), pp. 1092–106.

174. For example, the stonework, the use of lead, and of machines for lifting, details of which can be seen by visiting the Escorial and the Museum commemorating its construction.

175. Cf. the remarks by Paul Herre, *Papsttum und Papstwahl im Zeitalter Philipps II* (Leipzig, 1907), p. 374.

176. Calculations and graphs by Alvaro Castillo Pintado in F. Braudel, *La Méditerranée* (1966 ed.), ii. 33.

177. A. Poirson, *Histoire du règne de Henri IV* (Paris, 1866), iv. 610–11.

178. *Bilanci generali*, seria seconda (Venice, 1912), vol. i, bk. i, p. 466 and Museo Correr, *Donà delle Rose*, 161, f. 144.

179. Ömer Lütfi Barkan, 'The Turkish budget in the year 1547–1548 and the Turkish budget in the year 1567–1568' (in Turkish), *Iktisat Fakültesi Mecmuasi* (Istanbul, 1960).

180. Op. cit., p. 128.

181. Cf. our chapter in the *Cambridge Economic History*, vol. iv.

182. Earl J. Hamilton, *American Treasure and the Price Revolution in Spain, 1501–1650* (Cambridge, Mass., 1934), p. 42.

183. J. A. Schumpeter, op. cit., vol. i, esp. p. 476, note 1; Jacques Heers, Raymond de Roover ...

184. Op. cit., p. 128.

185. Carlo M. Cipolla, 'La Prétendue Révolution des prix. Réflexions sur l'expérience italienne', *Annales* (1955), pp. 513 ff.

186. Museo Correr, *Donà delle Rose*, 181.

187. Evidence from Holland passed on to me by Morineau suggests that there may have been rather more clandestine imports during this crucial period than is usually thought.

188. Museo Correr, *Donà delle Rose*, 181, f. 62, 3 to 4 million crowns per fair.

189. Gino Luzzatto, *Storia economica dell'età moderna e contemporanea* (Padua, 1932), i. 179 ff.

190. Verbal information supplied by Ömer Lütfi Barkan.

191. Simancas, *Expedientes de Hacienda*, 122, 1559. I might equally well have taken Medina del Campo as an example and used the excellent article by B. Bennassar, 'Medina del Campo, un exemple des structures urbaines de l'Espagne au XVIe siècle', *Revue d'histoire economique et sociale* (1961). At Venice, the official documents always distinguish between *poveri, mendicanti*, and *miserabili*: there are degrees of destitution, Ernst Rodenwaldt, *Pest in Venedig, 1575–1577* (Heidelberg, 1953), p. 16.

192. For example, the estimates reproduced by Hektor Ammann, *Schaff-hauser Wirtschaft im Mittelalter* (Thayngen, 1948), table on p. 306.

193. F. Braudel, *La Méditerranée* (1966 ed.), i. 234, note 2.

194. Museo Correr, *Donà delle Rose*, 23, f. 23v.

195. Heinrich Bechtel, *Wirtschaftsgeschichte Deutschlands* (Munich, 1951–2), ii. 52, note 6, at Erfurt in 1511, 54 per cent of the population included in the census were in the lowest category of property-owners, possessing 0 to 25 florins, and 15 per cent were persons *ohne jedes Vermögen*.

196. Cf. *L'Unterschicht*, Franco-German Colloquium of 1962.

197. A.d.S., Venice, *Senato Terra*, 22, Treviso, 22 July 1555; Treviso, 30 July 1555; Brescia, 11 Aug. 1555 for the fire at Tizzo.

198. A.d.S., Naples, *Sommaria Consultationum*, 2, ff. 68v, 69, 27 July 1564.

199. Ibid., f. 59v, 22 May 1549.

200. See Noël Salomon, *La Campagne en Nouvelle Castille à la fin du XVIe siècle, d'après les 'Relaciones Topograficas'* (Paris, 1964).

201. J. Gentil da Silva, 'Villages castillans et types de production au XVIe siècle', *Annales* (1963), pp. 729–44.

202. A.d.S., Naples, *Notai Giustizia*, 51, f. 5, 17 Oct. 1520, 36 ducats to be paid in new cloth; ff. 177v, 178, 24 Aug. 1521, a black slave aged twelve, 36 ducats; ibid., 66, ff. 41v, 152, the price of a horse was 33 ducats.

203. Ibid., *Sommaria Partium*, 595, f. 18, 28 Jan. 1569, a black slave aged thirty purchased at Lecce for 60 ducats.

204. Ibid., *Sommaria Consultationum*, 9, ff. 303–5, Naples, 18 June 1587.

205. A.d.S., Venice, *Senato Mar*, 145, 24 Mar. 1600.

206. See J. Mathiex, 'Trafic et prix de l'homme en Méditerranée aux XVIIe et XVIIIe siècles', *Annales* (1954), pp. 157–64.

207. Simancas Napoles E 1046, f. 25, Com[or] Giron to H.M., Naples, 17 Sept. 1554.

208. Museo Correr, *Donà delle Rose*, 46, f. 65, 11 Mar. 1487: these were *stradioti* employed in Morea. In 1522, the janissaries were paid between 3 and 8 aspers a day, that is at 50 aspers to the ducat, between under 2 and under 5 ducats a month (Otto Zierer, *Bilder aus der Geschichte des Bauerntums und der Landwirtschaft* (Munich, 1954–6), iv. 29). At Zara in 1533, a bombardier was paid 40 ducats a year. But bombardiers were specialists.

209. The figures obtainable from the Archives at Ragusa make this quite plain. The many contracts between master and servant preserved in the registers of the *Diversa di Cancellaria* (for example, vols. 98, 122, 132, 146, 196) made it possible to conduct a brief survey. For apprentices, who came under a separate category, there was no formal payment specified at the end of their training, but according to the practice of the trade, the new artisan might receive clothing, new shoes, or his tools. The others were paid on expiry of the contract (which might be after two, five, six, seven, or ten years). This was in addition to payments in kind (board, lodging, clothing, and care during sickness). This payment which was graded according to the year of service gradually rose: from 1 to 2 gold ducats in 1505–6 to 2·5 in 1535; to 3·4 and 4·5 in 1537 and 1547; to

just above or below 3 in 1560–1; to 4 in 1607; to 8 or 10 in 1608. But since the ducat was devalued, the situation scarcely improved over the years. There was structural *ceiling*.

210. See the table in Hektor Ammann, above note 192.

211. A.d.S., Venice, *Senato Terra*, 15, f. 106.

212. Museo Correr, *Donà delle Rose*, 26, f. 46v.

213. Ibid., f. 48v.

214. Ibid., f. 100.

215. Clearly established for the period 1572–1601 from the claims of the bakers: wages had doubled in the interval, Museo Correr, *Donà delle Rose*, 218, f. 302.

216. A.d.S., Senato Mar, 23, ff. 36, 36v, 29 Sept. 1534, that is a little over 63 ducats a year.

217. Museo Correr, *Donà delle Rose*, 161, f. 80, 1606, there were 72 workers employed at the Zecca (54 for silver, 18 for gold). The total wage bill was 5,280 ducats, an average of almost 72 per worker. On average, workers in silver tended to be paid more. Sometimes one employee held two posts.

218. Museo Correr, *Donà delle Rose*, 161, f. 208v, 1586, 28 secretaries, total wage bill 2,764 ducats.

219. A.d.S., Venice, *Senato Terra*, 23, Venice, 20 Mar. 1556.

220. Juan Regla, in J. Vicens Vives, *Historia Social y Economica de España* (Barcelona, 1957), iii. 300.

221. Frank C. Spooner, 'Régimes alimentaires d'autrefois, proportions et calculs de calories', *Annales* (1961), pp. 568–74.

222. A.d.S., Naples, *Sommaria Consultationum*, 3, f. 204 ff., 28 Mar. 1571.

223. Piri Re'is, *Bahrije*, ed. Paul Kahle (1926), *Introduction*, vol. ii, p. xlii.

224. Foulquet Sobolis, *Histoire en forme de journal de ce qui s'est passé en Provence depuis l'an 1562 justqu'à l'an 1607* (1894), p. 245.

2

Rural Industries in the West
From the end of the Middle Ages to the
Eighteenth Century

HERMANN KELLENBENZ

*Translated by K. E. M. George**

BEFORE embarking upon such a vast subject, it seems to me that it was necessary first of all to point out the opinions and problems which have been raised in this field. I must therefore begin with an historical account. We will then be in a better position to tackle the heart of our subject.

1. SOME THEORETICAL APPROACHES

In his work on the *Wealth of Nations* (1776), Adam Smith dealt, among other things, with the relationships between country-folk and town-folk.[1] In an attempt to describe the true situation as accurately as possible, he contrasted the rural, farming population—squires, farmers, and servants—with the towns as centres of trade and skilled crafts. The country-folk were characterized, according to him, by the 'puerile vanity' of the nobility and by non-rational working methods, whereas the trading and craft activity of the towns was stimulated by self-interest and professional ambition.

This picture which Smith drew of town and country, of their functions and their specific economic possibilities, was to reappear time and time again, with mere shifts of emphasis, in the economic theories of subsequent years, and was to influence the majority of studies in economic history. In particular, it was Karl Bücher's formulation of the concept of urban economy (*Stadt-wirtschaft*) which helped to establish the idea of an urban–rural economic dualism. Meanwhile, a new approach had been discovered, thanks to the theory of industrial location formulated in 1826 by J. H. Thünen for agriculture, and later by Alfred Weber for modern industry.[2] But this theory too has its weaknesses; at all events, historical evolution—which is precisely what we are concerned with here—is scarcely taken into account either by this theory, or by the 'market area' theory which is derived from it, the more so since these theories were developed mainly in terms of the current situ-

* From 'Industries rurales en Occident de la fin du moyen âge au XVIII siècle', *Annales*, xviii (1963), 833–82.

ation of the national economy.[3] One should not however forget the ideas that economic theory has introduced; I am thinking particularly of the 'costs theory', and of the importance of the distribution of population and of capital and material investment, i.e. developmental factors. Bruno Kuske has shown how the historian can benefit from such approaches with regard to the history and geography of the world economy.[4] Economic geographers too have studied these problems and have advanced some interesting ideas concerning the notions of central places, market regions,[5] and market areas.[6]

The theories concerning the different stages in man's evolution, as well as the industrial location theory,[7] have given rise to a great deal of discussion. The historians joined in the debate and made valuable suggestions, thanks to which it finally became possible to distinguish between, and to correct, theories which were far too elementary. The works of Theodor Mayer (1924)[8] in particular were of great importance in this connection. Following certain ideas of Othmar Spann, notably his definition of the concept of market economy (*Verkehrswirtschaft*), Mayer defined towns, within a national economy, as the focal points in which the concentration and distribution of goods continually takes place. But in his opinion, this is not always valid for industry. Industrial production can also be distributed over rural areas (home crafts), or concentrated in a centre which is not necessarily a town (factory).[9] Mayer considers that the location of non-urban industries can be accounted for either in 'geographical' terms—the fact that certain raw materials are only found in certain places—or in 'historical' terms, a particular circumstance favouring the setting up, or the development, of a type of production in a given place. For modern industry, Mayer recognized the priority of other considerations based on 'economic rationalism', which become less significant only when an artistic as well as a technical process is involved.

Thus, historians have realized that, ever since the Middle Ages, relationships between town and country have been more complex than the theory of phased economic development, with its concept of urban economy, allows for. Their work, in the form of detailed studies, has had a bearing on all aspects of these relationships. Among the most important contributions, I would place first that made by Rudolf Häpke, who criticized the concept of the typical town,[10] a concept too far removed, in his opinion, from the diversity of historical reality; he prefers to adopt as a basis of classification a series of types 'taken from real life'. Studying in particular the main branches of activity in the northern Netherlands, he developed the concept of the 'market region': one or several towns form an economic community together with the surrounding countryside. But as he points out, the 'market region' was there before the towns appeared; thus in the rural areas, industry and trade already existed, along with agriculture and stock-farming; this was so in the time of the Frisians, and also, later on, in the fertile areas of Friesland, the *Marschen*, which remained a rural area without any towns, and yet enjoyed industry and trade.[11] Still taking Holland as his example, Häpke went on to show the process of the division of labour between a large town, small towns, and villages: 'Amsterdam became more and more the commercial centre; the *Waterland*, with its little harbour towns and its villages, became the centre of navigation; Hoorn, Enkhuizen, Medemblik, the group of towns in western Friesland and the islands along the coast also became part of the complex of activities centred on Amsterdam.'[12]

The 'market region' idea was also used by Ludwig Beutin, one of Häpke's students, to refer to the unit created by the convergence of natural resources, economic activity, and administrative action. He preferred it to the concept of the 'market area', as being more concrete.[13]

The industrial location theory, the market region concept, the studies on the *Verlagssystem**[14] as well as the recent progress made by research in the field of urban history[15]—all these things make it easier for us today to establish the centres of concentration of rural industries, and their size. The linen industry was set up in the flax-growing area which extends from Ireland to the eastern part of central Germany—passing through north-western France, Westphalia, and Lower Saxony; the metallurgical industry was established in the hilly regions rich in forests and in water, especially in areas possessing mineral resources. But these general considerations must be completed by a whole series of other factors: the demographic situation, the social and agrarian structures, communications, and economic policy.

Another approach must also be mentioned, one to which Eli F. Heckscher in particular has called attention.[16] K. Bücher's theory of development in stages, including the urban economy stage, fails to take into account the fact that the organization of towns in the Mediterranean world, which derived from the cities of antiquity, did not spread uniformly throughout Europe, notably in those areas of Germanic settlement; in the latter, and especially in the coastal regions, the Germanic conception of freedom of labour was maintained in spite of the economic power of the Hanseatic League and, later, in spite of the political economy of the absolutist principalities. And it is precisely here, in the coastal zones, from Friesland to the reefs of Finland, that one finds numerous examples of rural and peasant industry.[17] But inland too, in marginal areas, a certain freedom was apparent, for example in the hilly regions, which were relatively inaccessible to traffic, and where they still continued for a long time to reclaim the land for cultivation—work for which settlers were granted certain liberties.[18] There were also some free trades, for example mining and glass-making.

These are the problems raised by the German historians: in Switzerland, in the Netherlands, in France, and in England there has also been some research, to which we will return later. On the subject we are concerned with here there are, in fact, few systematic studies. We refer the reader par-

* i.e. the putting-out or domestic system [ed.].

ticularly to the most recent work by E. Carus-Wilson,[19] Joan Thirsk,[20] B. H. Slicher van Bath,[21] to the discussion provoked by the *Annales*, for example the historical part of the French colloquium 'Town and Country',[22] as well as to the work of Bodmer and Braun in Switzerland.[23]

2. ENGLAND AND THE BRITISH ISLES

After these general considerations, we will attempt to determine the extent to which the rural and peasant population engaged in industrial activity, from the beginning of the modern period up to the birth of industrialization in the course of the eighteenth century. The region concerned will be western Europe, in particular England, France, the Netherlands, western Germany, and Switzerland. We will concentrate on the textile industry, and also on mining and metallurgy.

In the English countryside, rural crafts seem to have enjoyed, from the Middle Ages onwards, a great freedom of action; at all events, the town guilds did not succeed in restricting this freedom.[24]

It was in cloth manufacture that the activity of the rural craftsmen reached its height. The English woollen industry began to flourish well before the time of Edward III, as E. Carus-Wilson has shown. In order to be able to appreciate this evolution in its entirety, she tells us, one must consult not only municipal records and the archives left by the guilds, but also documents which come not from the towns but from the country areas.[25]

She notes, in the twelfth century, an important technical improvement in woollen manufacture: the cloth is no longer fulled by hand or by foot, but mechanically, by means of a wooden hammer worked by a paddle-wheel.

These fulling-mills were in existence in England by the end of the twelfth century. The Templars and other religious orders seem to have been the first to use the new technique, but it was used also on episcopal estates, and in the enterprises of lay landowners, especially in those belonging to the king. In the course of the thirteenth century, the fulling-mills spread throughout England and beyond the Welsh border. Not surprisingly, the city guilds lost control of this movement, and thanks to the recent technical improvements, the woollen industry was introduced into quite new areas, far removed from eastern England, its former centre, and became established in the hilly regions of the west and north, particularly in the West Riding, the Lake District, Cornwall, Devon, Somerset, the Cotswolds, Wiltshire, and the Kennet valley. Around these mills were formed groups of workers, composed of weavers as well as fullers, who had no connection with the city guilds; for there was to be found on the spot, not only hydraulic power, but a cheap labour-force, free from urban taxes and from guild restrictions. Soon, even a part of the town labour-force left for the country. In the course of the subsequent expansion of the English cloth industry,[26] three great centres of production were formed: the west, especially the southern Cotswolds which, at the end of the fifteenth century, were to provide perhaps half of England's total cloth production: broadcloths, kerseys, and other cheap cloths; then East Anglia, which produced kerseys, especially along the banks of the Stour, where the fine churches bear witness to the wealth of the villages; and finally the West Riding of Yorkshire, which also produced kerseys, and a few minor centres such as Westmorland, known for its kendals.

E. Carus-Wilson stresses that it was above all the use of water power which gave the English cloth industry superiority over that of the Netherlands and so encouraged the emigration towards England of Flemish and Belgian weavers.[27] Building fulling-mills in the land of the windmills was hardly practicable. Other factors became important when the English cloth industry began to spread to the country. Thanks to the agrarian structure and farming methods, labour was readily available, since many small farmers could turn to weaving as a part-time occupation when work on their small-holdings did not demand all their attention or when work for the lord of the manor was slack, while the wives carded, combed, and spun the wool. Unlike the urban economy which was of an essentially corporate type, the situation in the country areas was such that it was possible to allow the workers a relatively large degree of freedom, so that people from all social classes found it quite easy to become clothiers. There were those who had begun as skilled craftsmen: weavers, fullers, dyers, and shearers; others came from outside: sheep-owners, traders in foodstuffs, butchers, country noblemen. Often, small-time clothiers would combine their activity not only with farming, but with another trade, for example as millers or butchers. In many cases, the large-scale manufacturer was at the same time a landowner, and his own sheep would provide some of the wool which he worked. In this world of villages, many of which grew within the squire's estate to become townships, there reigned also a great freedom, which favoured technical innovations. Thus, in the early years of the fifteenth century, or even before that, the teazling process was mechanized for the first time, by means of a gig-mill. In 1435, three of these mills are mentioned among the property of William Haynes of Castlecombe, a peasant who had become wealthy but who, as a villein, had to ask his lord's permission for his daughter to be married outside the estate.

Feudal ties did not, then, prevent one from working as a business contractor, nor from becoming rich. Another such contractor, Jack Winchcombe of Newbury, who died in 1519, appears to have employed 1,040 people. His example shows clearly the extent to which the *Verlagssystem* could be made to work. Often, the wool was carded, combed, spun, and woven at the clothier's house; but more frequently, the latter distributed the raw material to local craftsmen, who worked in their own homes.[28] This system also spread to certain parts of Ireland, at least as far as spinning is concerned.[29]

After the invention of spinning-machines and power-looms, that is, from the middle of the eighteenth century, the cloth industry underwent a complete change. The factories were concentrated in the towns or in large villages which were soon to become towns. Weaving in the homes fell into decline, and more and more, spinners and weavers left their homes to work in the factories. As is well known, this movement of population is closely connected with the adverse effects of enclosures which, by denying the peasant right of access to the commons, often forced him to seek a new way of life. Recent work has shown, however, that one should not attach too much importance to enclosure as a cause of migration, but rather that we should place it within the framework of a general tendency towards overpopulation.[30]

The second sector of the English textile industry based on the use of cotton and the production of the mixed cloth, known as fustian, is of more recent origin, and only began to flourish in the sixteenth century. Just like the woollen-cloth industry, cotton weaving spread in the country areas, notably in Lancashire, around Bolton and Manchester,[31] and in Dorset, Cheshire, and Derbyshire. Here too we find the *Verlagssystem*, but also independent master-craftsmen, in fairly large numbers, living in the country. It is only in the middle of the eighteenth century that the dependence on the town merchants seemed to have reached its peak. At that time, salaried weavers began to band together in support of their claims. In this sector as in the other, technical inventions, the enclosure movement and certain other factors caused grave concern with regard to industrialization, militating against rural crafts, and in favour of factory labour. Nevertheless, the number of rural fustian-weavers in the district of Manchester around 1772 was still higher than that of the town weavers: in Manchester itself there were 55 fustian manufacturers, i.e. master-craftsmen, with their journeymen and apprentices, as against 73 in the rural districts around Manchester.[32]

Finally, we must mention briefly the rural linen industry in Scotland and Ireland which up until the eighteenth century provided considerable competition for the central European industry in overseas markets.[33] In Ireland, the small farmers could not make a living without the help of their home crafts. Thanks to the low wages, Irish linen withstood foreign competition for a long time.

With regard to the iron industry, the technical improvements at the end of the Middle Ages, particularly blast-furnace smelting and the use of hydraulic power to work the tilt-hammers, resulted in the spread of the metallurgical industry in hilly areas rich in water and forests, and especially where there were iron deposits. Thus in the Sussex Weald there appeared ironmasters' works.[34] In the mountains of the north-west one found lead and tin mines, as well as copper deposits, worked partly thanks to foreign capital.[35] J. U. Nef stresses that, in many parts of Europe, small enterprises run by landowners, employing less than a dozen villagers, were common in the mining industry and in metallurgy; similarly in the coal fields set up on

Tyneside in Durham, and in the south of Nottinghamshire.[36] As the charcoal supplies became scarce, and as the iron-ore deposits dwindled, production shifted to other areas, in the north and west of the country; in the search for fuel, they even went as far as the west coast of Scotland. Recent research has shown that, in the critical stage at the beginning and middle of the eighteenth century, it was the Quakers who introduced important technical improvements, such as the use of coal, and who provided the capital necessary for production: first and foremost the Rowlinsons and the Lloyds, the Yorkshire group, and the Darbys.[37] The manufacture of iron destined for export gradually focused around Birmingham and Sheffield. In the Birmingham area this industry flourished in Dudley, Wednesbury, and Wolverhampton, villages which later became towns. Another centre was Hallamshire.[38]

In addition to this, there existed rural localities where iron was worked for the local market. Paul Mantoux points out that, in Scotland especially, and as late as the middle of the eighteenth century, almost all metallurgical activity was in the hands of rural master-smiths. The organization of this industry differed slightly from that of the textile industry. Production, particularly in the Birmingham area, was of course based on the *Verlagssystem*, but whereas, in the case of the woollen and cotton industries, the rural crafts had broken the control of the city guilds, in metallurgy on the contrary the guilds, which were tightly organized, took over the rural crafts; thus in Hallamshire, one finds a rural company of cutlers.[39]

Mention must also be made of the part played by the country areas in ship-building, fishing, and associated industries.[40]

Finally, the area around London could be given as an example to illustrate the way in which, in England, the great economic centres extended their influence over the surrounding countryside and encouraged the setting up of industrial concerns. One could quote the silk manufacture at Spitalfields, and the mills, breweries, distilleries, tanneries, and other industrial concerns at Mark Lane and Southfield.[41]

Everything that we have said so far leads to the main question: what are the reasons for which the rural industries, in their various forms, spread to the extent they did in England? Does the location theory alone offer an adequate explanation?

The favourable distribution of natural resources, of wool, of hydraulic power, and of fuel provided by the forests, did of course play an important part, as did the enterprise of rural landowners and of merchants who, from the large cities, were able to organize the rural labour-force. But all this does not provide a complete explanation. Clearly there were other factors, which were the result of the agrarian and social structure of the rural population. Joan Thirsk recently examined these problems in a most fruitful way.[42] She showed that, in the western half of England, mining occurred in areas where stock-farming was predominant, and where the demand for labour was less great than in the case of arable farming; the head of the family could therefore turn to mining, while his family looked after the fields and the cattle. Further, Joan Thirsk noted that in every region in England where mining co-exists with stock-farming, the villages are large and well-populated. She quotes in this connection a document from Derbyshire, dating from 1620, where it is stressed that 'several thousands of people derive their living from the lead-mines, coal mines, quarries and ironworks', and this would explain why the local population depended so heavily on supplies of cereals from elsewhere.

She went on to analyse in the greatest detail the areas occupied by the textile industry. She gave as her first example the manufacture of cloth in Wiltshire. At the end of the fifteenth century there were several rural cloth-producing centres: in the north-west, between Malmesbury and Westbury, and in the south, around Mere; it is significant that in the first region cheese was produced, and in the second butter. The author points out here that the peasant farms specializing in dairy produce are found in areas where scattered properties were regrouped early, contrary to the situation in cereal-producing areas and large sheep-rearing areas, where many fields and commons remained open until the end of the eighteenth century. In the former independent peasant labour persisted, in the latter on the contrary, the landlord system of organization was predominant.

Joan Thirsk again discovered this close relationship between the textile industry and dairy produce in Suffolk, particularly in the south of the region which, in the sixteenth century, provided London with butter and cheese. She also tried to show the connection between the division of estates and the overpopulation which results from it, notably in the Kent Weald, once a forest area. According to her findings, the clothiers provided, at the beginning of the seventeenth century, the significant link between the wool trade and cheese manufacture.

Joan Thirsk quotes finally the textile industry in Westmorland. This was an infertile region consisting of pasture-land and small-holdings, but with vast commons on moor-land; the villages had a high level of population and, during the period for which the author has records, the inhabitants supplemented their peasant incomes by working in ironworks, lead-mines, and stone- and slate-quarries. When the woollen industry disappeared, it was replaced by the manufacture of stockings, mentioned for the first time in documents dating from the last few years of the seventeenth century. Another example: the Lincolnshire marshes, where sheep and cattle were raised; vast commons made it possible for the villages to divide the estates, and the population grew more quickly there than in villages where primogeniture was in force. This increase in population made it necessary to look for supplementary means of existence, and these were found in the weaving of hemp, flax, and wool.[43]

3. FRANCE: THE RURAL AREAS AND INDUSTRY

Since the work of Henri Sée and Henri Hauser, much interest has been taken in the rural industries of France, and extensive research has been devoted to the subject, particularly following Marc Bloch and Lucien Fébvre. In France, as in England, the city guilds never acquired the dominant position they held in the Netherlands or in Germany. Even when guilds did exist, they were mainly restricted to the large towns, whereas in the small towns one still found free master-craftsmen, alongside whom the rural artisans held their own, having long since become firmly established, and occupying an important position. Nothing changed in the sixteenth century, nor in the so-called mercantilist period, when the government, in an attempt to control the guilds, organized craftsmen in the strictest possible manner. In the course of the eighteenth century, rural crafts became increasingly flourishing, while skilled labour organized in the form of guilds declined. Turgot, influenced by the Physiocrats, even went so far as to suppress the guilds in 1776. After his fall they were in fact re-established, but only for a short time, since the Revolution was to eliminate them once and for all.[44]

In France, just as in England, the textile industry was most widespread in the country districts. From as early as the twelfth and thirteenth centuries, linen cloth from Burgundy and Franche-Comté, and woollen cloth from Languedoc were being exported via Marseilles. Yet the home-crafts did not expand as much as in England or in the Netherlands.[45] In the sixteenth century, the *Verlagssystem* spread into the cloth-producing regions[46] of Poitou and Picardy, the Orléans area, Berry, and Languedoc; and later into Beauce, Sologne, and Gâtinais, whereas Brittany, Normandy, lower Maine, and Burgundy[47] produced linen and hemp cloth, and the Lyons region worked cotton. Still later the cotton industry expanded in Normandy, in the Vosges, and in the region of Orléans. Finally, mention must be made of the 'saieterie'[48] of Amiens and the surrounding area, which flourished in the seventeenth century.[49]

Luxury goods were also manufactured in the country areas: for example lace-making in Bourbonnais, Auvergne, Velay, Alençon, and Normandy.[50] Silk yarn was twisted and spun in Touraine, lower Languedoc, the Nîmes region, Vivarais, and in Provence.[51]

Metal was worked in Dauphiné,[52] Franche-Comté,[53] the Comté de Foix, Nivernais, Champagne, and Lorraine.[54] In Lyonnais and Beaujolais, Jacques Coeur worked lead and copper mines which were rich in silver.

Knives were manufactured around Thiers; and in the Laigle region they made needles. Under Colbert, the metallurgical industry was developed around Saint-Étienne and Forez. There was also a small naval ironworks in upper Normandy.[55] And one must not forget the salt works on the Atlantic coast[56] and in Provence, nor the glass works on noblemen's estates in the wooded areas of Champagne, Nevers, Forez, upper Poitou, Auvergne, Languedoc, and Guyenne.[57]

The ever-increasing need for fuel focused attention on coal; it began to be mined in several provinces in southern and central France, especially in Lyonnais and Forez.[58]

This rapid sketch shows the wide spread of rural industry in France up to the eighteenth century; one should also bear in mind however the changing history of the industries themselves, for example the period of decadence in the last few years of Louis XVI's reign ...

To sum up, one can say that in every part of France rural industry existed on a much larger scale than is commonly thought, although nowhere does one find either the concentration or the intensity one meets in England, in southern Holland, or in certain areas of Germany. Unfortunately, we do not yet possess detailed studies showing the way in which the peasant population took part in this activity. At all events, the majority of peasants did not own enough land to be able to live entirely from the soil; those who did not have the necessary means to become tenant-farmers were obliged to supplement their incomes by working as day-labourers or servants, or else turn to a trade, as merchants, millers, innkeepers, or craftsmen. They were known as the 'industrially employed'.[59] In general they had every chance of succeeding in those trades which processed local goods; whereas the woollen, silk, and cotton industries, and to a certain extent the mining industry, were in the hands of contractors from the towns, the nobility, or the Church. There was an obvious reason for this: silk, as a luxury industry, required heavy investment; the cotton industry depended on the wholesale merchants who imported the cotton and distributed the raw material; and in the case of the mines too, considerable sums had to be invested from time to time.[60] Under the Ancien Régime, there were in northern France a fairly large number of non-propertied rural workers, and it is precisely here that the cotton industry could be established. But even then, only some of the workers were employed in industry full-time, the others only worked there during breaks in farm-labour.[61]

4. THE NETHERLANDS

Thanks to the work of Georges Espinas, Henri Pirenne, N. W. Posthumus, Paul Harsin, and their followers, extensive information is available concerning the northern and southern Netherlands. As early as the Middle Ages the southern Netherlands was one of the most highly industrialized areas in Europe; of particular importance was the textile industry of Flanders, Hainaut, Brabant, and the Meuse valley.[62] Although production first began in the towns, the growing market, together with the conservatism of the city guilds, resulted in the industry being transferred to the country areas.[63] The unrest in both Church and State in the sixteenth century, and the resulting exodus of merchants and specialized labour, had serious adverse effects here. With the capture of Kortrijk in 1580, the linen industry's centre was ruined; the country weavers, who were robbed and held to ransom, left their districts in great numbers. When the situation had returned to normal, the linen industry was to some extent re-established in a few villages in the region of Lille.[64] Around Nieuwkerke and Ypres this industry persisted into the second half of the eighteenth century.[65] The cotton industry, of more recent date, fared rather better; it was this industry which, after the destruction of Hondschoote in 1583, supported a large number of localities in the Bruges area, for example Poperinge. The linen industry, for whose products the Spanish ports provided the best market, expanded appreciably up to the end of the seventeenth century. The importance of the old markets of central Flanders, such as Tielt, Roeselare, Itzegem, and Eeklo decreased, while the rural producers sent their thread and their linen to Bruges, Ghent, Oudenaarde, or Kortrijk. After the wars at the end of the seventeenth century, the linen industry had a new lease of life. Meanwhile, Hainaut's production had been organized too, being based particularly on Geraardsbergen and Aalst. The extent of this rural industry emerges from an estimate made in 1765 by a Ghent magistrate: the total production of Flemish cloth amounted, according to him, to 100,000 items, a figure which, in the opinion of van Houtte, is probably an underestimation. Moreover, the bulk of the linen was exported to France, England, and Germany, the producers apparently acting largely on their own account; the wholesaler, i.e. the merchant, was only involved in the purchase of the ready-made cloth. Generally, he would buy as an agent for other merchants, who bleached and finished off the cloth. But whereas in the seventeenth century they were totally dependent on Dutch bleaching, in 1700 there opened in Borgerhout, on the outskirts of Antwerp, a large bleaching factory, and several others followed later.[66]

Another industry, both urban and also rural, which flourished—thanks to fashion—was lace-making. The finest lace was of course produced in the towns; but even the less delicate work done by the peasant women found a market, not only at home but also in Spain and in Spanish America.[67]

It has been said that the misfortune of the Spanish Netherlands was the good fortune of the industry in the region of Liège. The prejudice against Flemish production and exportation gave a boost to the woollen industry of Verviers and encouraged it to seek new markets in the German hinterland. It was favoured by the fact that, at this very time, the change from tilling to stock-farming in the Herve region (between the Vesdre and the Meuse) made labour available. Thus it was that woollen manufacture prospered in the Verviers region; during the next two hundred years, it proved to be one of the foremost branches of the European textile industry.[68] Even though, in the seventeenth century, a certain number of workers left for Leiden, manufacturers continued to find advantages in the Liège and Limburg areas, because of low salaries and the protectionist policy of the bishop-princes. To a very large extent, the rural districts of the region of Herve, Limburg, and the extreme north-eastern foothills of the Ardennes, shared in this movement, as is proved by the number of employees: in the period just after the middle of the eighteenth century, the figure is put at 25,000 for the cloth industry of the Vesdre region.[69] Thanks to an administrative peculiarity, Hodimont, a town situated on the Vesdre opposite Verviers, became a serious rival to the latter, since Verviers belonged to the bishop-prince of Liège, whereas Hodimont was a dependency of Limburg and belonged to the Hapsburgs. On the whole, rural labour in these areas was dependent upon the contractors from the towns. In the country, the first cloth-mill—which however only produced shoddy-cloth—was built shortly before 1750 at Dison, near Verviers, on Limburg territory.[70]

Jean Lejeune has shown how, in the wooded region between the Sambre and the Meuse, in the Hoyaux valley and in the marquisate of Franchemont, the presence of deposits had offered the rural population the possibility of turning to metallurgy, and how later on, towards the end of the sixteenth century, 'new' industries, in the hands of contractors from Liège (alum, sulphur, copper-ore mines), had encouraged the development not only of the town of Liège but also of the Liège basin,[71] whereas the region between the Sambre and the Meuse had not followed the same pattern, because of the greater insecurity with which the low country was threatened. Unfortunately, J. Lejeune does not deal with the subject we are here concerned with in the required amount of detail.[72] At all events, in the seventeenth and eighteenth centuries, the Liège region and the area between the Sambre and the Meuse were the most important centres for iron-workers; most of the factories employed a number of people who, in addition to this work, tended their fields. Towards 1740, the number of these iron-workers is put at some 15,000 in the whole of the Liège region. In 1602, Charnoy, later to become Charleroi, had 49 peasants, all of whom were nail-smiths.[73] Production was directed by merchants who provided the iron-workers with iron and paid them on a piece-work basis, on delivery of the goods.

In the Liège region, coal-mining also played a greater role—as early as the fourteenth and fifteenth centuries—than in any other country in Europe.[74] From the middle of the sixteenth century onwards, coal was used in glass-making, an industry which was widespread in the Liège region at that time.[75] The high technical standard of coal-mining in the Liège, Meuse, and Charleroi regions is revealed by the fact that the first steam-pump, invented by Newcomen and put into service in 1705 in England, was installed as early as 1720 near Liège, in 1725 in the Charleroi district, and in 1734 near Mons.[76]

With regard to the northern Netherlands, Jappe Alberts has stressed that much of industrial activity was not restricted to the towns at the end of the Middle Ages,[77] but was carried out in the country areas. The 'Informacie' of

1514, for Holland and Friesland, gives a clear picture of this distribution.[78] In Friesland, naval transport and fishing, together with the manufacture and sale of butter and cheese and cattle-trading, formed the basis of the economy.[79] In the marshlands they collected peat, a most important fuel in a region with little forest-land. In Holland, where urban industry experienced a remarkable expansion, there was, it is true, a rural linen industry, in addition to the dairy trade; but it appears to have been of only local importance, since, as in the case of the few rural clothiers—the monopoly of the large towns was too strong in this field.[80] Two industries were prevalent on the Zealand islands: salt-works and the milling of madder-root, which was used as a dye. Following the Belgian emigration, the textile industry of Leiden flourished again towards the end of the sixteenth century, thanks to the introduction of the cloth known as Flanders serge (*saye*). But it remained an essentially urban industry, although it later transferred part of its production to Brabant; the bleaching industry of Haarlem and the silk-weaving of Amsterdam were also of a distinctly urban type.[81]

Furthermore, it was not possible to use hydraulic power as much in the lowlands as in the hilly areas. Only on the outskirts of Utrecht could the silk industry make good use of the sloping terrain, and it is here, between 1680 and 1690, that the silk factory of Jacob van Mollem was established.[82] In certain regions, such as that of the Zaan, wind-power was used to set up industrial concerns in the country, in spite of difficulties created by the towns. In the Zaan region, there were many windmills which served to saw wood, full cloth, press oil, and manufacture dyes, and paper. At the height of this activity, there were some 600 windmills, and in the period from 1630 to 1731, the number of sawmills increased from 53 to 256, while on the outskirts of Amsterdam there was only a total of 82 mills in 1691.[83] Along the Zaan, ship-building was also developed, and towards the end of the seventeenth century there were about 60 yards producing large ships. In 1707 there were no fewer than 306 boats on the stocks. But like the textile industry this activity waned in the course of the eighteenth century.[84] The inhabitants of the Zaan region still practised herring-fishing and whaling, which flourished in the second half of the seventeenth century and in which they were second only to Amsterdam; in order to process the blubber, they built installations necessary for the extraction of the whale-oil.[85] One should mention too the inshore fishing, which was quite considerable.[86]

In the duchy of Limburg—one of the main textile centres in the northern Netherlands—the woollen industry spread, towards the end of the fifteenth century to the country, for example to Weert and various other villages on the west bank of the Meuse, a development which continued in the sixteenth century. This rural industry also used locally-produced wool, which was normally forbidden. In the eastern Netherlands, where flax grew, linen was manufactured.[87] Slicher van Bath has studied the textile industry in the Twente region.[88]

5. GERMANY

Germany is one of the countries where skilled labour, organized into guilds, i.e. concentrated in the town, spread most widely. But parallel with this there existed too a highly-developed rural industry, part of which was actively engaged in export work. In the textile sector, the manufacture of linen was developed in the early Middle Ages, beginning in the region around Lake Constance; to this industry was added the manufacture of fustians, which was increased particularly in the course of the sixteenth century. In northern Germany, it was the linen industry of Westphalia which had the largest export market, as well as the linen produced in the eastern regions of central Germany, including Silesia and the southern foothills of the Erzgebirge mountains.[89]

With regard to metallurgy, a large variety of rural industries, working chiefly for export, were set up in the Mittelgebirge, rich in ore, forests, and water; this was the case notably in the Eifel, with its zinc and iron deposits, in the Hunsrück, in the regions on the right bank of the Rhine, from Siegerland as far as the Harz, the Thüringerwald, and the Erzgebirge mountains, with their plentiful supplies of iron, copper, and tin.

But many rural industries did not work for the export market, and it is these that we will examine now.

August Skalweit has analysed the relationship between rural craftsmen and urban craftsmen, especially in the Brandenburg area and in Prussia; he emphasizes just how illusory was the desire of the towns to wish to monopolize skilled labour. Nevertheless, he exaggerates the differences when he claims that town and country constituted two independent, self-sufficient regions, the first being characterized mainly by a skilled labour economy, the second by agriculture.[90] The information we have shows the towns competing with rural crafts from the fifteenth century onwards. The reasons are these: the increase in population and the rising price of farm and manufactured products; and because the former rose more than the latter, there was a drop in real income in the towns, leading to unemployment and the migration of urban craftsmen towards the country areas, which strengthened the position of rural crafts as against that of urban crafts. In electoral Saxony, in Hesse, in Bavaria, in Mecklenburg, and in Schleswig-Holstein, the princes took the side of the towns in this battle and re-established an area known as the 'mile-zone', reserved exclusively for urban craftsmen. In the country it was only the small village craftsmen, who were needed for farming, who could continue to work. After the Thirty Years War, this policy in favour of the towns became even more rigorous, mainly for reasons of taxation, for the towns paid more taxes than the country areas, and tax-collecting was easier there, thanks especially to the excise. As a result of this policy, a large number of craftsmen chose to avoid urban taxation by moving to the country, where they frequently enjoyed the protection of the big landowners, the estate farmers, or the monasteries.

In Prussia, as in many other areas, this anti-rural policy reached its height in the seventeenth century. Only linen-weavers, tailors, iron-workers, and carpenters still had the right to reside in the country or in certain rural areas, and on noblemen's estates. These *Principia regulativa*, decreed for Prussia in 1718, became stricter in the course of the eighteenth century. But, in spite of everything, rural crafts continued to be of considerable importance. According to a document of 1797, 30 per cent of the craftsmen of Kurmark were rural masters, and in eastern Friesland, the number of rural craftsmen exceeded that of urban craftsmen.

One can assume that, in the other German territories, the situation was roughly the same as we have described for Prussia. This conjecture would need to be supported, however, by detailed studies. In the case of Schleswig-Holstein we are well informed, thanks particularly to the work of Fritz Hähnsen.[91]

The pattern here was largely determined by the traditional principle of freedom of labour, and by territorial division due to the particular constitutional situation of these territories. By the beginning of the seventeenth century, in 1609, the town of Krempe for example had only 31 town craftsmen, as against 99 rural craftsmen within a radius of a mile around the little town. The development of rural crafts was encouraged by the abolition in 1615 of the guilds' monopoly in royal and ducal territories. However, in the years following, the wars and the increasing opposition between the king of Denmark and the duke halted the process of liberalization in the craft industry. When, in 1651, Duke Frederick III tried to proclaim industrial freedom, he met with the refusal of the royal chancellery of Glückstadt.

In the second half of the seventeenth century, under the influence of mercantilist ideas, efforts were made—first of all by the Crown—to restrict rural crafts in favour of those of the towns.[92] Apparently on the model of the other German territories, there was enacted in 1688, in the 'royal' part of Holstein, a 'Constitution on the suppression of urban professions and occupations in the country areas'. Thereafter, only farriers, cartwrights, coopers, boot-makers, and tailors were to be allowed, within a radius of two miles around the towns of the *Geest*, i.e. in the hilly, infertile, and thinly-populated region, and within a radius of one mile in the fertile *Marsch*; the remaining craftsmen would have to move to the towns. A little later, similar measures were adopted for the ducal territories. Finally, in 1711, a 'joint' decree, both royal and ducal, was issued suppressing urban crafts in the country; by this same decree the permitted radius was increased to three miles in the *Geest* and two in the *Marsch*.

After the Northern Wars (1700–21), developments were again determined by the hostility between the king of Denmark and Duke Charles-Frederick of Gottorf, who shared possession of Schleswig-Holstein. In 1736, the duke refused to extend the validity of the 1711 decree in his territory. The royal government did not observe the restrictions policy at all closely either, and everywhere the true situation proves that the statutes were not adhered to. In the low regions, on the Elbe, the distribution of craftsmen was as wide as it would have been if freedom of labour had in fact existed, and this was even more noticeable in the dales of the west coast, from Dithmarschen to Eiderstedt and Tondern, and in the islands. But nowhere was the number of craftsmen greater, in relation to the total population, than on the nobles' estates.

As for the textile industry, the government went so far as to renounce officially its policy of restriction, and encouraged weaving in the country districts. By the decrees of 1737 and 1751, the linen-weavers received the same statute as the woollen mills, with the right to have apprentices and journeymen. In the north and north-east of Schleswig, linen manufacture became the chief industry after agriculture in the eighteenth century. In the infertile *Geest* and on the moors, lace-making too had been a prosperous industry since the seventeenth century.[93]

The *Verlagssystem* was not as widespread in Schleswig-Holstein as in other parts of Germany, but it is known to have existed in the Hamburg region. Thus in Pinneberg, at the end of the eighteenth century, the wives of agricultural workers were employed by contractors from Hamburg and Altona. Hähnsen states—and this is an interesting point—that weaving was less widespread in those areas where agriculture was well developed, for example, in the *Marschen*, i.e. the flat country along the lower Elbe.

It would appear that the rural iron-workers did not generally cater for outside markets. Nevertheless in 1770, in the Apenrade region, the local craftsmen made scythes and scissors when they were not engaged on orders for the peasants. They found profitable markets in Fünen and Jutland.

There were metal works of some importance near the economic centres of Hamburg and Lübeck, notably at Stormarn where both hydraulic power and fuel were to be found. At the end of the Middle Ages, contractors from the towns, then the nobility, led by the Rantzau family, had installed mills for a variety of industrial purposes.[94] On a large number of noblemen's estates there were also glass-works.[95] Flourishing industries were set up in the neighbourhood of Hamburg, where there was competition between the town on the one hand, and the land authorities or the nobility on the other,[96] as well as in the town of Neumünster, which enjoyed a privileged position with regard to communications: the high rate of traffic encouraged the clothiers to settle there, and as early as 1556 it became necessary to install a fulling-mill at Wittdorf, near Neumünster.[97]

On the north-west coast of Friesland pickling-brine was produced; there was also whale-fishing, and in order to process the blubber, brought back from the high seas in barrels, it was necessary to build oil-factories.[98] Workshops produced glue, and made use of whale-bones. Moreover, the fishing boats were no longer built only in the urban ship-yards, but also locally: Kappeln, for example, on the Schlei, had a large ship-yard.[99]

In Schleswig-Holstein, as in the other regions studied here, the textile industry was mainly concentrated, as we have said, in those areas which did not favour agriculture, since those peasants who did not own enough land worked part-time at a craft to supplement their income. This was the case particularly in the *Geest*, where they became prosperous craftsmen. The farm workers also turned to a craft. But in general, those whose entire income came from their craft were few in number. As they were unable to support themselves completely, craftsmen went to live on the estates of noblemen, who provided them with board and lodging, or with a plot of land for small-scale cultivation, in return for their work. When serfdom was abolished, many former serfs sought a new livelihood in skilled crafts.

For Westphalia and the Rhineland we have a wealth of material relating to our subject. We will examine especially rural industry working for export markets.

The large textile and metallurgical industry of Westphalia and the Rhineland has been studied by Bruno Kuske and his followers. In the country we find textile manufacture: woollen and linen cloth, material made from a mixture of flax and wool,[100] hosiery,[101] and knitting, the latter mainly in the areas where linen manufacture was undeveloped, particularly in the region where moorland sheep were reared, i.e. from the Ems to the Elbe, to the Harz and the mountains of eastern Westphalia, and in Sauerland; in the flax-producing regions, on the other hand, it was linen manufacture which became established. On the whole, the textile industry coincides with the area without metallurgy. Between the sixteenth and the seventeenth centuries, the woollen manufacture of Westphalia declined, whereas the linen industry, on the contrary, continued to export its products, due partly to the way in which the *Verlagssystem* was organized. Westphalia remained, together with the eastern parts of central Germany, Silesia, and Bohemia, one of the main linen-exporting regions of Germany,[102] although the quality, which was determined by the local flax, was rather inferior to that of western Europe. Linen manufacture was concentrated in the hilly regions to the north of the province, and in neighbouring areas, i.e. Ravensberg, Minden, Lippe, the Osnabrück, Diepholz, and Hoya regions, including Münsterland and Hellweg (Lippe plain), as well as in eastern Friesland. This is, in the main, hilly terrain, lowlands alternating with humid mountain ranges. The demand for strong canvas for the purposes of shipping resulted in the creation, in the northern hills, of a hemp industry alongside the flax industry. Its centres were to be found in the Tecklenburg area.[103]

Within the flax and hemp industries, spinning held an important place, and people of all ages were engaged in it, especially children. In Westphalia, a large number of children was considered desirable. Furthermore, as a result of primogeniture, which was in force at the time, a number of non-propertied people were obliged to work at a craft. In these circumstances, one can appreciate the importance of spinning in the whole of the area circumscribed by the Elbe and the Weser, between the Harz, the forest of Thuringia, and the Lüneburg moors; the export of yarn, particularly to the Rhineland and to western Europe, was greater than the export of linen. Apart from spinning, there was bleaching; it was practised in several towns, but also in the country, for example, in the county of Mark, in Schalen, and in Wuppertal, where this industry was soon to bring urbanization.[104] The most well-known bleaching centre in Westphalia was Warendorf; from about 1720, there was another establishment of this kind at Milse, near Bielefeld.

The forest, especially in the hilly areas, provided the possibility of manufacturing objects made of wood, which because of the difficulties of transportation and disposal, were sold by the producers themselves, with the result that, in places such as Medebach and Winterberg, a long-distance trade was very soon developed. Products consisted of wooden baskets, spoons, shovels, dishes, bowls, etc., manufactured in Wittgenstein and in several villages in Siegerland and Sauerland. This woodcraft industry also existed in rural areas, on the banks of the Weser and on the fringes of the Lüneburg moors.[105] In the lower Lippe region, in Münsterland, Nordland, and in the Bentheim region, people made clogs, for which there was a demand in the marshlands; they were even exported to Holland. In the Münster area, small farmers, farm labourers, and servants made clogs.

Thanks to charcoal, the hilly and wooded areas were also well placed for metal-work and glass-making: this was the case in the Nassau, Sayn, Berg, Siegen, and Mark regions, and in the western part of the duchy of Westphalia. Frequently, miners', iron-founders', and iron-workers' guilds also formed part of a guild concerned with charcoal production. In Siegerland, for example, these guilds were called *Hauberggenossenschaften*.[106] In this area, in the duchy of Westphalia and the Dill region, oak forests were worked from the thirteenth century onwards for the production of charcoal; as a by-product, tanner's bark was obtained. Sometimes the charcoal-burners would enter into an agreement with the villages for the purchase of oak and beech-wood. In the county of Mark and in the Wittgenstein district, whole villages specialized in the supply of charcoal to the iron industry.

In the forest areas of eastern Westphalia, towards the region of the Weser, wood wastes were used in the glass industry. In this connection, the forest of Kaufung, between the Werra and the Fulda, played a particularly important part: not only was fuel to be found there, but also potash, used in glass-making. In the Kaufung region, the glass-works spread along the Weser as far as Paderborn and Lippe.[107] To the east of this zone another chain of glass-works was established in the Leine area, where the streams provided—throughout the area—favourable transport conditions.

At a very early stage, the peasants of Westphalia discovered the possibility of using the coal of the Ruhr, which in many places had broken through to the surface,[108] particularly in the Hörde region. These coal-beds formed the basis of the subsequent development of the steel-works and metal-processing works in the Berg and Mark regions. As a result of the transportation which became necessary, the number of carters and boastmen also increased considerably. In the jurisdiction of Schwelm there were between 300 and 400 coal-carters, each of whom had three or four horses.[109] In the north, which had few forests, peat was dug, especially in the subdiocese of Münster, in the region of the river Ems, and towards the lower Weser. The peat-bogs of Sauerland, and the transportation of peat by its inhabitants, were well known. It is here, in 1631, that the town of Papenburg was founded.[110]

As in Styria, the upper Palatinate, and Thuringia, there were extensive iron-ore deposits in the hilly regions of north-western Germany. In the rural areas, the peasants often worked part-time in the iron industry, just as, in northern Westphalia, their counterparts worked in the flax and hemp industry.[111] In the fifteenth century, the large-scale merchants of Cologne ran the metal industry of Siegerland and Mark, while the Dortmund and Soest merchants ran the industry in Mark and Sauerland, as well as in the towns of the Hellweg, notably in Essen.[112] In addition, there were iron-workers from the mountains who sold their products themselves. In certain localities in the north, the manufacture of scythes was a flourishing industry: at Friesoythe from the fourteenth century onwards,[113] and at Libenau, in the county of Hoya, in the seventeenth and eighteenth centuries.

With regard to the mining of iron, Siegerland played a particularly important part. Here there were peasant guilds, concerned with the mining of both iron and coal. From the end of the Middle Ages, this region supplied the metallurgical industries of Westphalia and the Rhineland with raw materials and with partly processed products.[114] There were also smelting works in the Fulda area, and at Veckerhagen on the Weser, as well as factories producing iron pans, which were sold as far afield as Bremen and Holland.[115] One of the main steel-producing centres in the sixteenth and seventeenth centuries was Breckerfeld. The town of Sayn, in Westerwald, was known for its cast-iron products.

In general terms, one can say that Siegerland and the districts of Nassau, Sayn, and the duchy of upper Berg mined iron and converted it into wrought iron and crude steel; this was the work of the smelters, the iron-workers, and the steel-workers. Mark and the duchy of Westphalia added the processed-metal industry. The real centres of this industry were, however, northern Mark, i.e. the Iserlohn region and the Ennep valley,[116] the districts of Remscheid and Solingen, and the area between Velbert and Essen, in other words those regions which had no iron deposits. Here, the industry flourished particularly in the eighteenth century; further, the rising cost of charcoal was an incentive to improve the quality of production. However, Essen and Werden began to provide coal as early as the sixteenth century, and thus it was that certain branches of the metallurgical industry in the duchy of Berg came to be set up in Mark, near the coal fields.

Specialized steel manufacture was carried out in welding shops; around 1760 there were 90 of these in Mark, 37 of which were in the parish of Lüdenscheid, and 6 in the parish of Iserlohn. As early as 1662 there was in Mark a society for the distribution of welded steel, which was renewed in 1682.[117] Wire-drawing was carried out, by means of hydraulic wheels, in the Lenne, Rahmede, and Nette valleys.[118] At the close of the sixteenth century, under the influence of Cologne, the needle industry was established in the duchy of Mark, at Menden.[119] In the early eighteenth century, the manufacture of thimbles appeared, as at Iserlohn, in the jurisdiction of Hemer, partly under the impetus of Utrecht.[120]

All these industries received, from as early as the fifteenth century, the support of the authorities. The steel-working craftsmen of Siegerland, the cutlers of the Solingen district, and the wire-makers of Mark were obliged under oath not to change their place of residence. The Grand Elector restricted the manufacture of certain thicknesses of thread to the towns of Lüdenscheid, Altena,[121] and Iserlohn. In the eighteenth century, staple companies, rather in the form of cartels, were set up for the distribution of products. The centres of the metal trade constantly tried to take over the running of production in the mountainous regions; as did the towns of Nuremberg and Frankfurt in central and southern Germany; similarly with the metal merchants of Cologne and Frankfurt in north-west Germany, and the Dutch in Mark and in Essen.[122]

Here now are a few details concerning metals other than iron: in 1736 a mining company specializing in calamine and brass was founded near Iserlohn; contractors from Iserlohn ran brass-making factories at Hemer.[123] Other rural industries were: stone-cutters, for example in Braunbergen, in the country of Bentheim, or in the parish of Wetter; slate-works, lime quarries, and clay-pits in Mark.[124] In those regions of Westphalia where linen was manufactured, the tobacco industry was established in the eighteenth century,[125] due partly to a good system of communications and to the fact that they could pay for the imported tobacco with the proceeds of their exported linen. In the hilly areas of the south, thanks to hydraulic power, the paper industry was set up, particularly near the towns which provided the rags.[126]

On the left bank of the Rhine, the iron industry was to be found in the whole of the Eifel region,[127] in the Hunsrück hills,[128] and in the Saar region.[129] In the Stolberg area, calamine deposits were mined, this being a raw material in the manufacture of brass.[130] The woollen industry, which was spread over the Aix-la-Chapelle and Monschau regions, succeeded in maintaining a certain degree of freedom of labour, while at Aix-la-Chapelle itself it was subject to the usual restrictions of the guilds.[131]

One of the most interesting regions of Germany is the Black Forest, and the questions which concern us here have been dealt with by Eberhard Gothein. In the history of skilled crafts, there are two opposing groups: the plains and the valleys on the one hand, and the mountains on the other. In the plains, the towns and the guilds exercised much greater control than in the mountains. In the latter, the peasants operated their mills not just for their personal needs, but also for customers. In the valleys known as the *Viertäler*, the peasants had their own looms which were worked by the servants during breaks in farm-labour. However, the situation was not the same in all the regions. In the principality of Fürstenberg, a greater attempt was made than elsewhere to incorporate rural craft production into the guild structure. In the mountainous area which belonged to Austria (Vorderösterreich), on the other hand, there was a certain lack of concern in this respect. The greatest determination to defend freedom of labour in the crafts was shown by the peasants and journeymen of the seigneury of Triberg. In 1741 they declared 'that since time immemorial there had never been a guild in this seigneury and that, nevertheless, people had always managed to make a living; that these guilds were usually protected by all kinds of subtle clauses, which were harmful to the peasants and contrary to their old-established rights and freedoms ... Furthermore, there are in this bleak and harsh land more than a hundred people who, through their own skill, have invented this or that work, and who are self-taught.' E. Gothein goes on: 'Thus, the pride of the peasant and the pride of the servant became one, and that proud independence, which is characteristic of the settler who cultivates his land single-handed, fused with the modern feeling of the technician who is aware of his own ability, and who sets himself a task on his own initiative.'

The main rural industry was linen manufacture, though with less emphasis on export than in other regions; we must however point out that, in the seventeenth century, cloth known as *Durlach* was exported to Norway.[132] In the southern part of the Black Forest, Swiss capital came in with the cotton industry,[133] and Vorderösterreich benefited from the capital of rich Piedmontese investors.[134] From the middle of the eighteenth century onwards, embroidery made great strides, as did weaving.[135] The Black Forest's mining output cannot compare with that of the other regions of central Europe, but its rise and decline are instructive, for they show that it is possible to combine mining and forestry with agriculture. At the height of this industry, the miners of the Tyrol, Carinthia, the upper Palatinate, and Switzerland[136] moved to the Münster valley, the Todtenau mountain, and the Wildgutach valley; with their large savings they bought land, and it was thus that they were sometimes able to acquire mining shares, crushing mills, estates, and considerable capital. And when the decline of the mining industry set in, many of them, especially the more humble of the coalmen, and the woodmen, were more than ever obliged to fall back on their properties. More and more, they took to clearing their lands, in rather a haphazard fashion; instead of producing wood for lining the mine-shafts, they made shingle-boards, plates, dishes, vine-props, etc.

The Black Forest offers in addition some interesting material for the history of glass-making. In accordance with a medieval tradition, the glass-maker, just like the miner, enjoyed freedom of movement.[137] The various working rights were conceded *in toto*, as for the mines, but they were operated individually by the various master-craftsmen together with their journeymen. Since they were free of statute labour and of landlords, the glass-makers could organize their own food supplies, keep wine in their cellars, and even sell it. But as in the case of miners, an attempt was made to bind them to the soil by offering them land on a permanent lease.[138] This tendency became even more marked after the Thirty Years War.

Among the more remarkable achievements of the Black Forest peasants were straw-braiding and clock-making. Braiding first appeared at the beginning of the eighteenth century and, like spinning and clock-making, it provided the servants with an additional income. Restricted at first to the seigneury of Triberg, this activity spread, from the middle of the century onwards, into the principality of Fürstenberg, rivalling the Italian industry. These same peasants—obviously very resourceful—introduced to their region the manufacture of metal spoons,[139] which until then had only been produced in the Erzgebirge; furthermore, they borrowed from the Swabians the technique of clog manufacture, and learned to make boxes and brushes. But their finest work was produced in clock-making.[140] This industry began around 1665, but did not really flourish before 1720. It was created by landowners who made clocks in their spare time and who improved the tools which had hitherto been used. But it was the poor, humble peasants who transformed this part-time activity into an industry designed for export. In the Furtwangen and Neustadt area there were 500 independent master-craftsmen in 1796, producing 75,000 clocks every year; in 1815 production rose to more than 187,000 clocks. In the course of the eighteenth century there appeared a motley collection of automatic mechanical devices, bells, and similar objects. As opposed to the Swiss Jura, which specialized in the mass-production of fine watch- and clock-mechanisms, with a well-planned division of labour, the Black Forest produced cheap wooden clocks for the homes of the lower middle class and the peasants, and also supplied machines for display-rooms and show-cases. This type of production can be explained both in terms of the social conditions of the peasant in this region, and in terms of his character, his individuality, and his artistic bent.

From the Black Forest, let us turn eastwards towards the vast area where Swabian linen was manufactured. As Hektor Ammann has shown, the flax industry extended, from the twelfth century onwards, over the whole of the upper Rhine region,[141] working mainly—even in those days—for export.[142] Usually, the thread was produced by family labour in the area around Lake Constance, where flax was cultivated; it was sold in the towns.[143] This industry, which was developed largely thanks to the *Verlagssystem*, had as its centres first Constance, then all the Swabian towns from Ravensburg, Isny, and Wangen, to Memmingen and Kaufbeuren, to which was added the Swiss centre of St. Gallen. In the course of the fourteenth and fifteenth centuries the manufacture of fustian was developed—a cloth made with a flax warp and a cotton weft. It was then that the towns of Ulm,[144] Biberach, Augsburg, and Nördlingen became in their turn industrial centres. In addition to maintaining a very tight control over production in the towns, the guilds were soon faced with considerable competition from the rural craftsmen,[145] who were under the exclusive control of the guilds, called 'Schau'. One of the most significant developments in this struggle was the creation and subsequent expansion of the fustian industry at Weissenhorn, under Jacob and Anton Fugger, in spite of the weavers' guild of the town of Ulm and its right of control.[146] In Weissenhorn and its outskirts, which belonged to the Fuggers, weaving began during the time of Jacob Fugger. After his death, it spread to several villages in the vicinity. Finally, it freed itself of the control which the town of Ulm had the right to exercise, by creating in Weissenhorn its own controlling authority. Subsequent developments were characterized by the expansion of the linen industry in the Swabian Alb, particularly in the region of Urach,[147] and by the activity of the famous society of contractors from Calw known as the *Zeughandlungskompagnie*.[148] The attempts that were made to introduce the silk industry into this region appear to have been less successful.[149]

6. A SPECIAL CASE: THE SWISS CANTONS

The Swiss Confederation offered conditions which were particularly favourable to the expansion of rural industries working for the export market: as a mountainous country, with a high level of rainfall, Switzerland was ideal for the cultivation of hemp and flax, and especially for stock-breeding, which allowed the inhabitants—even more than farming—to work part-time at a craft.

After the Council of Constance, the Swiss linen industry became concentrated more and more in the St. Gallen region. F. Furger believes that the surrounding country districts contributed as much as the town itself which, because it owned only a very small area of land, was unable to compel the inhabitants of the outskirts to observe the craft's statutes.[150] Nevertheless, it had an effective means of influencing rural production in the form of a right of control on the manufactured linen, a right which it succeeded in enforcing throughout the whole of Switzerland. The peasant weavers, who generally used thread which they themselves had produced, were partly employed by the contractors from the towns, while others worked on their own account. F. Furger believes that, up until the beginning of the eighteenth century, there was more weaving in the country than in the towns.[151] New centres gradually appeared, some of them in the country, like Herisau, Trogen, Rorschach,[152] Arbon,[153] and Hauptwil, setting up independent control bodies and entering into competition with St. Gallen; they could thus operate more freely and, since their labour-force was cheaper, sell their goods at a better price. The fact that rural spinners and weavers often worked on their own account is clearly shown in the Chronicle of Appenzell by Walser; this states that the 'poor' did the spinning, spooling, and weaving, while the 'rich' sold the manufactured cloth.[154] If the *Verlagssystem* played a less important role in the manufacture of linen than in the fustian and cotton industry in these parts of Switzerland, it was because the raw material was produced locally, often by the spinners and weavers themselves, so that from the very start they avoided having to rely on a supplier of raw materials.

Another centre for the manufacture of linen was set up in about 1600 in the four rural jurisdictions of Aargau and in the 'bailliage' of Willisau in the canton of Lucerne.[155] Later, the Emmental region became involved.[156] In the early part of the 1760s, this textile centre extended (according to Bodmer) from Stettlen, Vechingen, and Bollingen (near Berne) as far as the border between the 'bailliage' of Lenzburg and the Freiamt region (Aargau), and from Bucheggberg as far as the districts of Münster and Rothenburg in the canton of Lucerne.[157] However, in Lower Aargau, on the Bernese side, and in the adjacent regions in the canton of Lucerne, the flax industry was being ousted by the cotton industry, which paid higher wages.

In the Zurich area, after the middle of the sixteenth century, refugees from Locarno had introduced important technical improvements in wool weaving, in dyeing, and in fulling. After early set-backs caused by the guilds, this industry spread, thanks to the *Verlagssystem*, not only throughout the canton, but apparently as far as the regions of Zug and Lucerne, Schwyz, Glarus, and the Freiamt in Aargau,[158] and even into the Töss valley and into Thurgau. Spinning and weaving usually took place in the country areas. The government tried to confine other processes, as much as possible, to Zurich, though not always with the success it anticipated. However, the dressing of cloth was limited exclusively to the city guild.

The cotton industry, which was introduced in Zurich during the fifteenth century, later than in north-eastern Switzerland,[159] had a great future. Originally, towns and rural areas alike produced fustian or *Schürlitz*, a mixed cloth. But by the end of the century they were producing pure cotton fabrics. The new financial rewards offered by cotton manufacture were partly responsible for bringing about, after the introduction of the Reformation, a reduction in the number of enrolments for foreign service. The new industry could expand the more freely since it was not subject to the rules and regulations of the guilds.[160] The town-based *Verlagssystem* was to find that conditions here were very much in favour of its expansion. Yet there were at the same time craftsmen's workshops which gradually grew into small rural factories, run by the *Tüchler*. From 1662 onwards, the town of Zurich tried hard to curb freedom of trade by repeated prohibitions, and the fabrics (*Tüchli*) could only be sold on the urban market. Short of getting round the regulations, the weavers were thus reduced either to working *for* a contracting agent, or to working *as* a contracting agent. At first the 'supplier' (*Träger*), a mere go-between dealing both with the contracting agent and the weavers, played only a humble role; but through hard work, he often succeeded in becoming a manufacturer or a small-scale independent contractor. As for the spinners who worked for a contractor, there were even some to be found outside the canton of Zurich, and indeed as far away as the Freiamt and the catholic cantons. The rural spinners and weavers fall into two groups: those for whom a craft was only a secondary source of income, thanks to the size of their property; and those who, on the contrary, owned no property—and there were many of these—and for whom spinning and weaving were the only means of living. Whereas weaving was carried out mainly in the valleys, spinning took place on higher ground. Next to Zurich, Winterthur became a second centre of large-scale contractors (*Verleger*). Furthermore, this industry spread into Lower Aargau in the canton of Berne and into the lowlands of the canton of Lucerne. Finally, the manufacture of printed calico spread from Geneva and the principality of Neuchâtel.[161]

In eastern Switzerland the situation was very different from that which obtained in the regions around Zurich. St. Gallen, which was the largest commercial centre, occupied only a very small area. The growth in production made it necessary to draw on a labour-force which was politically dependent on authorities outside the town: people from the canton of Appenzell, from the district belonging to the abbott of St. Gallen, from the Toggenburg region, from the Rhine valley, and from Thurgau. Glarus too, together with part of the Vorarlberg, southern Swabia, and the canton of Grisons, became part of this industrial zone. The freedom of production and distribution was much greater here than in the industrial zone surrounding Zurich. Thus, a whole series of secondary centres was created, to the detriment of St. Gallen. In all, between 80,000 and 100,000 people appear to have been employed in the textile industry during the last quarter of the eighteenth century, a good third of whom were engaged in embroidery.[162]

Production in this area was organized in many different ways, but the *Verlagssystem* was predominant. There were in addition various categories of intermediary workers, known locally as *Auswäger, Feilträger, Garnkempler*, etc. Many of the poor inhabitants of this region began as intermediaries and ended up as factory-owners. A large number of weavers acted as agents for spinners, though some spinners worked on their own account. In general, weaving and spinning were secondary occupations in the peasant homes, spinning especially in the poorest areas, where it was practised by women, children, and the old folk. Then there were the spool-winders, usually children and old people, often members of a weaver's family. From the middle of the eighteenth century, the manufacture of muslin began to gain ground, it too being organized on the lines of the *Verlagssystem*. Towards the end of the century, 60 firms were distributing these products in St. Gallen alone, plus about 30 in Appenzell-Ausserroden, Herisau, Trogen, Speicher-Tensen, and Walt, as well as in Altstätten, Rheineck, Rorschach, and Arbon.

Another cotton-spinning centre was created, in the course of the eighteenth century, in the canton of Glarus and in the 'bailliages' of Werdenberg, Wartau, Uznach, and Gaster.[163] The town of Zurich tried without success to put a stop to this development by industrial regulations. Here too there gradually appeared a body of contracting agents. The cotton industry had now become the most important branch of the Swiss textile industry. According to Bodmer, it extended, in the second half of the century, from Lausanne right into the Black Forest, into Swabia and the valleys of the Grisons, from the Ajoie to the foot of the St. Gotthard.[164]

The silk industry which, after a promising start in the fifteenth century, had fairly quickly disappeared, had a new lease of life in Zurich with the arrival of the refugees from Locarno in 1555. Since it was not subject to any guild, it was able to develop as a 'free trade'; in fact, it was the monopoly of urban contractors who ran it through the *Verlagssystem*.[165] It was forbidden to spin silk outside the town; however, for spooling and other processes, rural workers were required. Apart from silk fabrics, they produced floss silk for the weft-threads, and also, by using the waste, filoselle; generally, the work was carried out in the homes, mainly by women. Towards the end of the seventeenth century, the weaving of veils became the most prosperous branch of the silk industry in Zurich. Some spinners, and a few dressers, known as *Kämbler*, rose to the position of contracting agent; then, as in the cotton industry, there were the 'suppliers', who sometimes took advantage of their role as linkmen between the contractor and the workman to become in their turn contracting agents. Like other branches of industry, silk manufacture underwent certain changes in the course of the eighteenth century, with regard to the location of its production centres. Zurich thus lost its *de facto* monopoly on the manufacture of copes, for rival spinning factories had meanwhile appeared in central Switzerland, particularly in the Lucerne region.[166]

In Basel, the silk-ribbon industry or 'passementerie' was introduced in the third quarter of the sixteenth century by refugees from Locarno and by Huguenots. It was the only industry which successfully opposed the restrictions imposed by the guilds.[167] In 1612 the controversy over guild membership was ended by a decision in its favour: 'passementerie' was declared a free trade. From that moment, a great future was opened up for the Basel silk-ribbon industry, while the manufacture of other silk fabrics declined under the stifling control of the guilds. However, from about 1600 onwards, Basel became more and more reluctant to admit foreigners into the town; and as a result of this policy, French and Italian workers, banned from the town, settled in country districts in the Basel diocese, where life was less expensive; there they worked for contracting agents based in the town. Guild members were particularly anxious to keep away from their town these 'foreign ribbon-makers', who had to surrender their work to their employers. But by 1648 the ribbon-makers and their work-system had finally won their case.

In the country, both qualified and unqualified workers were employed, and unlike the situation in the guilds, they produced in the main goods of inferior quality. In about 1660 the automatic loom was introduced, and its use became widespread just before the end of the century; there was no longer any room for craftsmen who had served their apprenticeship in the traditional way, and who could now be replaced by unskilled workers. Silk-ribbon manufacture increasingly became a home craft, a part-time occupation for the inhabitants of the area around Basel. Whole families of peasants were involved: the children, often from four years of age onwards, turned the reeling-machine, the women, and occasionally also the men, wove the cloth. In the eighteenth century there were some rural workers who owned their own loom and who worked not only for Basel merchants, but also for contractors from Aargau. Others managed to hire a loom in the home of an inhabitant of Basel who was not himself a manufacturer, and worked for a contractor, from Basel or elsewhere. Most of them worked at looms which they hired from their contracting agents in Basel, while some found their looms and their agents elsewhere. As in the Zurich area, there were also workers who specialized in silk-yarn twisting; their work was directed, very appropriately, by a ribbon-maker. There was no shortage either of middlemen acting between the workers and the contracting agents; they were called *Seidenboten*. In the course of the eighteenth century, the contracting agents of Basel became more and more powerful, and strove to secure a monopoly on the manufacture and sale of automatic looms.

Another industry which developed in the Basel area from the second half of the seventeenth century was knitting; eventually there were knitters, both qualified and unqualified, well beyond the town boundaries and those of the bishop-prince of Basel, as well as in Aargau, and later in the districts of Schaffhouse, Zurich, and Lucerne,[168] and in the canton of Soleure. In the eighteenth century, embroidery manufacture was also of great importance; goods were imported mainly from the German part of the canton of Berne.[169] Mention must also be made of lace manufacture and clock-making in the principality of Neuchâtel. This latter industry extended from Neuchâtel towards the diocese of Basel and into the canton of Vaud. Finally, I shall mention the

manufacture of slate-topped tables and the cotton industry in Glarus; whence
the creation in this region of a merchant class.[170]

7. PROVISIONAL CONCLUSION

How can this investigation be summarized? Rural industry, and more
particularly that section of rural industry producing for export, has formed
the core of our studies. We have also sought to determine the degree to
which peasants assumed the role of industrial contractors. We have seen that
the rural industries were originally, and to a large extent, determined by a
given place. The woollen-cloth industry flourished in sheep-rearing areas;
linen manufacture flourished in regions where flax and hemp were cultivated.
Mineral deposits, timber, and hydraulic energy gave rise to metallurgy, wood-
working, and glass-making. In eastern Friesland, which was rich in peat,
whole villages were engaged in cutting this fuel at the time when the shortage
of charcoal began to make itself felt, and when coal was still being used only
on a very limited scale. On the coast, the development of navigation and
fishing, especially whale-fishing, led to the setting-up of the corresponding
processing industries.

All these findings have emerged from the problem of locality alone; but
from an historical viewpoint other factors appear, which must be taken into
account. One has to consider the political and geographical framework, as
well as technical advances, and improvements in the organization of trade.
These various factors account for the many different shades in the relationships between town and country, each area having its own particular characteristics; it is they which reveal the nature and degree of interpenetration
between a social structure which is determined by the geographical setting,
and the invention and initiative of the human mind. We have seen that the
criticism levelled by the historians against the concept of medieval urban
economy had led to the discovery of another reality: the so-called market
region. For side by side with the large centres of a metropolitan type, it has
been established that other centres, both urban and semi-urban, had played
an important part, in conjunction with the former. The history of the German
Empire in particular, with its principalities, its 'seigneuries', its vast estates
belonging to monasteries, noblemen, or rich townsmen, shows clearly to what
extent the economic structure of the lowlands could vary, and how numerous
and diverse were its economic centres, all of which were capable of competing with the large towns. At the time of the absolutist states and of their mercantilist policies, the trend towards the concentration of industrial and handicraft activity in the towns became much more marked, largely for reasons of
taxation; but the examples we have given in this study show that industrial
activity in the rural areas nevertheless remained remarkably healthy, especially in the coastal regions, where the peasants were traditionally free, and in
the relatively inaccessible areas of mountain clearings. But what is more, in

these latter regions, and especially in Switzerland, rural activity very soon experienced a characteristic expansion which was to pave the way for the country's transformation into a modern industrial region.

Two other factors help to shed light on the problem we are concerned with here: technical advances and improvements in the organization of trade. When, in the course of the thirteenth and fourteenth centuries, they discovered how to increase productivity in the metallurgical industry[171] by means of the hydraulic wheel, industrial workshops were set up in the valleys, which were rich in water supplies and forest-land, some distance away from the urban centres where the metal was worked and in which the metal trade was based, for example in Siegerland, Mark, and the duchy of Berg, and in the neighbourhood of Nuremberg or Lübeck, while in the dales of England, fulling-mills were set up for the woollen industry. And again, in the seventeenth and eighteenth centuries, when the textile industry began to be mechanized, the new factories were set up not only in the town, but often on the outskirts and in the country. One has only to remember the silk factories set up around the City of London, the bleaching-houses on the outskirts of Haarlem, the part played by the silk loom, perfected in the sovereign territory of Zurich, and of the automatic loom in the ribbon industry of Basel.[172]

Yet another factor of very great importance was the birth of the *Verlagssystem*—F. Furger has shown this clearly. In the last few centuries of the Middle Ages, there appeared, in the person of the large-scale manufacturer, a type of contractor who was bound to destroy the framework of an urban economy based on the trade-guild structure. His business connections, which were often international, together with buying and selling conditions, gave him an obvious advantage over the craftsman who was bound by the rules of his guild, and he could take the liberty of producing for a wider market. Of course, production had started originally in the towns, where in many respects industrial and commercial legislation curbed the enterprise of the contractors. It is thus not surprising to see merchants looking for alternative means and finding them; they ceased to call upon guild craftsmen and directed instead the labour of country-workers.[173] It has been possible to observe this process throughout the period under study, from the emigration of the Flemish textile industry up to the industrialization of Switzerland during the expansion of the cotton industry. This rural labour-force was less experienced than the urban craftsmen, but it was cheaper, and not subject to the guilds' rules. It was capable of giving better results in the manufacture of cheap fabrics designed for mass consumption; as manual labour became simplified through ever-increasing specialization,[174] or else replaced by mechanized labour, so the value of this labour-force constantly increased.

By examining the geographical distribution of industry, political factors, and the evolution of technical and commercial organization, we are neverthe-

less still not getting to the heart of the matter. The demographic situation
and the social structure also played their part. In the arable farming areas,
rural industry produced little for export, by contrast, this type of industry
prospered in the forest-lands, in the hilly regions, and in the moors, where the
yield from the soil provided an inadequate livelihood for the inhabitants. In
the predominantly stock-farming areas, similarly, more time could be devoted
to working at a craft. The right of inheritance also played its part. The law of
primogeniture, by which the farm fell to one of the sons, forced the other
children to find a livelihood elsewhere, particularly in those areas where there
was no remaining arable land. But in its way, the custom of dividing the inheritance had an even more important effect, since the peasant who inherited
a plot of land which was too small—short of taking up intensive gardening
or vine-growing—needed a supplementary income. Thus it was the small
farmers and the farm labourers who turned to an industrial occupation, much
more than the farmers proper, who at the most made things as a hobby in
their spare time, for example watches. In the most favourable cases, the
farmers employed their servants at weaving, but in view of the shortage of
farm labourers, they rather disapproved of unpropertied villagers working
at a craft.[175]

We are now in a better position to consider the relationship between the
demographic evolution, the agricultural situation, and the expansion of industry in the rural areas.[176]

To begin with, let us examine the first phase, that of the decrease in population after the middle of the fourteenth century, due to the great epidemic
diseases. Slicher van Bath has drawn attention to the fact that during the
period before 1450, a rural industry (working for export) 'appeared in certain
regions'. The difficulties in agriculture made its introduction easier, as did
the technical advances already mentioned, and the spread of the *Verlagssystem*, thanks to the opening of new long-distance markets. If we consult the
findings of E. Carus-Wilson with regard to England, we can see to what
extent events influenced one another; rural export industries began much
earlier than the agrarian history of England led us to believe.

For the subsequent development, the datings proposed by Slicher van
Bath and W. Abel[177] differ. Slicher van Bath, who is concerned with the
evolution in the whole of western Europe, lays stress on the increase in
population between 1450 and 1550, and for the 1550 to 1650 period, on the
considerable rise in prices, resulting from this increase in population, from
the massive influx of American gold and silver, and from the high level of
revenue from agriculture, wages having risen less than prices. W. Abel finds,
with reference to Germany, that there was a rise in prices from the beginning
of the sixteenth century up to the Thirty Years War, followed by a decrease
up until the end of the seventeenth century. What was the state of rural
industry at that time? Thanks to the excellent situation which obtained in

agriculture, cultivation increased to a certain extent, and as a result there appeared in north-west Germany a new category of small-holders (the *Kätner*);[178] but this expansion in crop-farming was not practicable either in the coastal areas with a dairy economy, which would have required heavy investment (short of building dykes), or in the hilly regions. The increasing density of population in these areas found an outlet in the armies of the *landsknechts*, in military service abroad; but the development of the rural industries curbed the numbers of mercenaries, thus providing small farmers, who were becoming more and more numerous (the *Tauner*) with new means of existence.[179] Another outlet was to be found in mining, which since the fifteenth century had become a flourishing industry, thanks particularly to the technical progress made at that time.

One has only to look, however, at the Netherlands, the areas of Germany devastated by the Thirty Years War, and the Swiss Confederation to see the extent to which local conditions were of prime importance. In the southern Netherlands, the 'Eighty Years War' resulted in the transfer of industry under Spanish rule to the neutral regions of the diocese of Liège. In Germany, rural industrial production suffered a serious blow during the Thirty Years War, but recovered at least partially as the result of being transferred in a similar way. In his work on the social and economic situation of western Germany during that war, Kuske notes this removal of the large urban industrial centres to the country, and points out that production, which until then had been of a medieval guild type, generally increased. This was so particularly in the Berg and Mark districts, both in metallurgy and in the textile industry; then in the region of Aix-la-Chapelle, and later in the lower Rhine area.[180] Finally, in the Swiss Confederation, which since the Middle Ages had remained apart from military operations, the Thirty Years War had a few indirect repercussions. Thus, for example, the number of cloths bleached at St. Gallen in 1610 was not reached again until 1714.[181] But from the second half of the seventeenth century, the manufacture of copes, directed by contractors from Zurich, reached peak production.[182]

We now come to the last phase which remains to be examined, the period extending from the end of the Thirty Years War to the middle of the eighteenth century. Slicher van Bath describes it as a period of recession, with a population which increased only slightly, and which even—occasionally—remained static; a period of long-drawn-out depression in agriculture, during which, however, live-stock prices held better than those of cereals. This accounts for the fact that there was some increase in the amount of pasture-land at the expense of cereal crops, for example in Schleswig-Holstein.[183] But the same situation can be observed in the Herve district,[184] in Southern Germany and in Switzerland, as well as in the Thiérache region in Northern France.[185] These areas experienced intensive industrial development, as did Maine, Twente, Westphalia, Switzerland, Silesia, Scotland, and Ireland.[186] With regard to Twente, Slicher van Bath has shown how, between 1675 and 1723, the textile industry was set up in the peasants' homes, whereas after 1723 it became concentrated more and more in the towns and villages, the link between 'industry and agriculture' becoming more slender.[187] As for Switzerland, the work that Bodmer carried out has revealed the considerable part played by the cotton industry, during the first half of the eighteenth century, in absorbing the surplus population, in becoming the first textile industry working for export in the country. Dairying, with its limited marketing possibilities, was obviously of less importance in this respect than the textile industry, which could employ a very large labour-force, working at home, even including children from four years of age upwards. When Slicher van Bath stated that the stock-farming areas did not favour population growth,[188] he was thinking of the fertile regions along the coasts, where the farmers invested capital for their equipment, encouraged by the conditions which were favourable to the transportation of their products. But he did not think of the mountainous regions of the Confederation. Whereas the surplus population in the coastal areas found employment in fishing and navigation, in Switzerland, leaving aside emigration, it was the cottage industry which offered the best solution. Moreover, this is how the people of the time saw it too. For reasons of political economy, J. H. Schinz praised this growth in population which could be noted in the course of the eighteenth century.[189] It is true that Switzerland was also engaged in selling live-stock to northern Italy[190] and in exporting its cheeses to Italy, Germany, and France.

Having thus cleared up certain important facts relating to the social history, we can now extend our investigation in two directions. First we will raise the problem of the lower classes of the rural population.[191] If, as Erich Maschke suggests,[192] we understand, by lower classes, groups 'whose livelihood depended on their labour', then the work offered by rural industry held a strong attraction for such people, since it enabled them to overcome the hardships caused by seasonal work, or by poor crops; this was the case especially for unpropertied day-labourers, and also for various categories of small-holders, who enjoyed only limited rights on the common lands. The social stratification of the rural population and the resulting frictions became even more apparent with the spread of the *Verlagssystem*: opposition, in the country areas, between specialized textile workers and unskilled labourers; a different degree of respect shown towards the spinners and the weavers; a distinction between rich weavers and poor weavers; hostility on the part of some of the land-owning peasants—because of the shortage of farm-hands—towards any expansion of rural industry.[193]

Another interesting fact can be noted, namely the growing appreciation of the labour-force provided by the lower classes. It can be seen to appear in the first phase of industrialization in the Middle Ages, at the time when manufacturers began recruiting their workers from the rural population. This reveals nothing more than a cold-blooded economic rationalism, which cannot be identified either with the work ethic of the medieval Church, or with the Protestant ethic, although the latter was no doubt partly responsible for the growing esteem in which this labour-force was held.[194] An important stage in this development was reached in the seventeenth century, when linen-weaving was declared an 'honourable' trade.[195]

Another question concerns the flexibility of social conditions. The upper strata of the peasantry were relatively closed. The lower strata thus had to strive even harder to make a living in a cottage industry or in an associated occupation. This brings us to the question of the contractors.

Can one speak of truly peasant contractors within the framework of rural industry? Other types of contractor are more important. First and foremost the large-scale merchant from the town who, through the *Verlagssystem* and through his purchasing, directed the available rural labour-force, seeking above all to compete with the guild craftsmen of the towns. Then there were the contractors from the nobility and from the Church, who enjoyed the advantage of securing from within their own estates raw materials and, if necessary, labour. Examples of this could be quoted from every part of the former German Empire. Wherever heavy investment was necessary, particularly for mining and for building factories, the advantage was with the princes and with the State. Finally there were the town craftsmen who became contractors: at various periods, as Skalweit and Kuske have shown,[196] craftsmen could be seen to leave the towns for the country, as soon as the latter offered more favourable working conditions; in settling there, they became contractors for various industries, as did a large number of rural craftsmen.

Attention should also be drawn to the most remarkable intermediary case, namely a section of the mining workers, a very mobile group which emigrated from the copper- and silver-producing centres of the Tyrol and central Germany, claiming special rights wherever they went. It was thus that Tyrolese miners settled in the Black Forest at the time when mining flourished there, and put their large savings into property-buying, sometimes making a considerable fortune in capital, landed property, mining shares, and stamping-mills. When mining declined in that area, many of them—chiefly the poor charcoal-burners and woodcutters—were forced to fall back on their farming property.[197] The social consequences of this were fairly serious since, by acquiring land, the landlords could bring about a lowering in the social standing of the miners, and also of the charcoal-burners and woodcutters.[198] The glass-makers were in a similar position.

We have just gone some way towards answering the following question: what conditions enabled the rural and peasant contractors to succeed? First of all, knowing a craft. This was already true—to quote a very early example —of the Fuggers, whose ancestor, a weaver by trade, came from his village to Augsburg. Then, in the regions far removed from the main highways, there

were many opportunities for making one's living as a pedlar,[199] as an agent
or representative of a contractor from the town, or else as an independent
tradesman; the most characteristic example of the latter case is that of the
trading companies of the Black Forest. Other opportunities were to be found
in transport, chiefly in transit areas:[200] for example for well-to-do peasants
who owned horses. It was thus that whole villages specialized in haulage; let
us not forget that it was thanks to the carters that the clothiers were able to
settle in Neumünster.[201]

We have already stressed the important part played by urban capital in
stimulating the industrial activity of the rural population, whether it be due
to the *Verlagssystem*, or to a system combining a buying contract with an
agreement on a salary based on output awarded to the producer. But these
are not the only forms taken by the organization of rural industry. The
peasants' traditional spirit of co-operation gave rise to a large variety of
societies, among which we could mention the Hallamshire cutlers, the
Hauberggenossenschaften of Siegerland for forestry work, and the trading
companies of the Black Forest.[202] The closely-knit family structure and religious conviction also played a certain part; one could quote the glass-makers
of the Black Forest and the English ironmasters, for example the Quaker
groups formed by the Darbys of Coalbrookdale.

This is only a brief outline of the most important features in the development of rural industry and peasant activity. There is no doubt that systematic
research in this field will produce further important results for the history of
industry and of industrialization in western Europe. But here a point must
be made concerning methodology. Research, which so far has chosen to concentrate on narrowly defined areas, must systematically encompass vast
areas, leading as far as possible towards a comparative history. It is by
transcending boundaries that we will discover the really important links, and
arrive at a clearer view of things. How fruitful, to take the case of Kuske for
example, the study of the whole of the Netherlands, the Rhineland, and
Westphalia proved to be, and how instructive was the widening of Hektor
Ammann's research into the textile industry in the Middle Ages.[203]

This improved knowledge of the birth of rural industries and of their
importance will provide—and this will be one of the most interesting results
—a clearer, more accurate picture of European economic growth. We shall
come to realize that the constant shifting of the industrial centres bears witness to a tremendous vitality and energy; and that the whole period under
consideration here was in no way as static as those whose judgement is
based on the period commonly known as the 'industrial revolution' are so
ready to claim.

NOTES

1. Adam Smith, *Natur und Ursachen des Volkswohlstandes* (Ger. trans., Berlin, 1879), i. 428 ff.
2. Alfred Weber, *Ueber den Standort der Industrien* (Tübingen, 1909).
3. See in particular August Lösch, *Die räumliche Ordnung der Wirtschaft* (2nd ed., Jena, 1944); Walter Isard, *Location and Space Economy* (New York, 1956).
4. Bruno Kuske, *Entstehung und Gestaltung des Wirtschaftsraumes, Beiträge zur Geschichte und Geographie der Weltwirtschaft* (Bonn, 1930).
5. N. Creutzburg, *Das Lokalisationsphänomen der Industrien* (Stuttgart, 1925); W. Credner, *Landschaft und Wirtschaft in Schweden* (Breslau, 1926); E. Fels, 'Der Einfluss der Wirtschaft auf Naturlandschaft und Lebewelt', *Beiträge zur Wirtschaftsgeographie, Ernst Tiessen zum 60. Gerburstage* (Berlin, 1931), pp. 53 ff. Walter Christaller, *Die Zentralen Orte in Süddeutschland* (Jena, 1933).
6. Theodor Kraus, *Der Wirtschaftsraum. Gedanken zu seiner geographischen Erforschung* (Cologne, 1933); id., 'Wirtschaftsgeographie als Geographie und als Wirtschaftswissenschaft', *Erde*, lxxxviii (1957), 112.
7. Theodor Mayer refers to A. Schaffle, *Das gesellschaftliche System* (3rd ed., Tübingen, 1873) who distinguishes between luxury industries and ordinary goods, the former being found in the market-towns and the estates, and the latter in the small towns and villages; but Mayer does not share this opinion.
8. Theodor Mayer, 'Wirtschaftsstufen und Wirtschaftsentwicklung', *Zeitschrift für Volkswirtschaft und Sozialpolitik*, N.S. ii (1922), 676–92; see also Werner Sombart, *Der modern Kapitalismus* (3rd ed. Munich–Leipzig, 1919), i. 247 ff.; 683, 901 ff.
9. T. Mayer, op. cit., pp. 648 ff.
10. Rudolf Haepke, *Die Entstehung der holländischen Wirtschaft. Ein Beitrag zur Lehre von der ökonomischen Landschaft* (vol. i of Studien zur Geschichte der Wirtschaft und Geisteskultur, edited by R. Häpke, Berlin, 1928), pp. 13 ff.
11. See for example J. A. Faber, 'Handel und Schiffahrt Frieslands im Lauf der Jahrhunderte', *It Beaken*, xxiv (1962), 1–11.
12. See also T. S. Jansma, 'De economiske opbloei van het Norden', *Algemene Geschiedenis der Nederlanden*, v (Utrecht, 1952), 214.
13. Ludwig Beutin, *Geschichte der südwestfälischen Industrie- und Handelskammer zu Hagen und ihrer Wirtschaftslandschaft* (Hagen, 1956), p. 11. Also Heinrich Kramm, 'Landschaft und Raum als ökonomische Hilfsbegriffe', *Vierteljahrsschrift für Sozial- und Wirtschaftsgeschichte*, xxxiv (1941), 1–14.
14. See the work of Fridolin Furger, *Zum Verlagssystem als Organisationsform des Frühkapitalismus im Textilgewerbe* (Stuttgart, 1927). [This was a system whereby a contractor (the *Verleger*) supplied a craftsman, or a group of craftsmen, with capital or raw materials; the finished articles were then returned to him, and he sold them on his own account, i.e. the German equivalent of the putting-out system. Translator's note.]
15. Karl Bosl, 'Staat, Gesellschaft, Wirtschaft', in Gebhardt, *Handbuch der Deutschen Geschichte* (8th ed. Stuttgart, 1954), i. 665 ff. (with bibliography); Carl Haase, *Die Entstehung der westfälischen Stadte* in the collection Veröffentlichungen des Provinzialinstituts für westfälische Landes-und Volkskunde, ser i, cahier i (Munster-Westfalen, 1960).
16. Eli F. Heckscher, 'Den ekonomiska innebörden av 1500-och 1600-talens svenska stadsgrundningar', *Hist. Tidskrift*, xliii (1923), 309 ff. (in Swedish).
17. Hermann Kellenbenz, 'Bäuerliche Unternehmertätigkeit im Bereich der Nord- und Ostsee vom Hochmittelalter bis zum Beginn der Neuzeit', *Vierteljahrsschrift fur Sozial- und Wirtschaftsgeschichte*, xlix (1962), 1 ff.
18. See the recent study by Friedrich Luetge, 'Das Problem der Freiheit in der frühen deutschen Agrarverfassung', *Studi in onore di Amintore Fanfani* (Milan, 1962), i. 496 ff.
19. E. M. Carus-Wilson, 'An Industrial Revolution of the Thirteenth Century', *Economic History Review* (1941), republished in id., *Medieval Merchant Adventurers* (1954), pp. 183 ff.

20. Joan Thirsk, 'Industries in the Countryside', in *Essays in Economic and Social History of Tudor and Stuart England*, ed. F. J. Fisher (Cambridge, 1961), pp. 70 ff.

21. B. H. Slicher van Bath, 'Historische ontwikkeling van de textiel-nijverheid in Twente', *Textielhistorische Bijdragen*, ii (1960), 21–39; id., *De agrarische Geschiedenis van West-Europa, 500–1850* (Utrecht–Antwerp, 1960), pp. 137 ff., 240 ff., 340 ff.

22. *Villes et campagnes. Civilisation urbaine et civilisation rurale en France*. Collection published under the direction of and with an introduction by Georges Friedmann (Paris, n.d.), pp. 3 ff. See also Georges Livet, 'La Route royale et la civilisation française de la fin du XVe au milieu du XVIIIe siècle', in *Les Routes de France depuis les origines jusqu'à nos jours* (Paris, 1958), pp. 58 ff.

23. Walter Bodmer, *Die Entwicklung der schweizerischen Textilwirtschaft im Rahmen der übrigen Industrie und Wirtschaftzweige* (Zurich, 1960); Rudolf Braun, *Industrialisierung und Volksleben. Die Veranderungen der Lebensformen in einem ländlichen Industriegebiet vor 1800* (Zurcher Oberland) (Erlenbach–Zurich–Stuttgart, 1960).

24. Georg Brodnitz, *Englische Wirtschaftsgeschichte* (Jena, 1918), i. 450 ff. does not examine the problem we are concerned with here, although he deals with the spread of the woollen-cloth industry in the country areas.

25. Carus-Wilson, art. cit.

26. For what follows see id., 'The Woollen Industry', in *The Cambridge Economic History of Europe*, ed. M. M. Postan and E. E. Rich (Cambridge, 1952), ii. 409 ff.

27. Henri-E. de Sagher, 'L'Immigration de tisserands flamands et brabançons en Angleterre sous Edouard III', in *Mélanges d'histoire offerts à Henri Pirenne* (Brussels, 1926), pp. 109 ff.

28. Carus-Wilson, 'The Woollen Industry', op. cit., p. 425.

29. Hans Hausherr, *Wirtschaftsgeschichte der Neuzeit* (2nd ed., Cologne–Graz, 1960), p. 162.

30. We cannot quote here all the works which deal with this very controversial question; we shall therefore quote only the following: J. D. Chambers, 'Enclosure and Labour Supply in the Industrial Revolution', *Economic History Review*, 2nd ser. v (1953), 319–43; id., 'Industrialization as a Factor in Economic Growth in England, 1700–1900', in *Première Conférence Internationale d'Histoire Économique. Contributions, Communications, Stockholm, 1960* (Paris–The Hague, 1960), pp. 211 ff.

31. C. W. Daniels, *The Early English Cotton Industry*, publns. of the University of Manchester, Historical Series, xxxvi (Manchester, 1920).

32. See also Louis W. Moffitt, *England on the Eve of the Industrial Revolution* (1925), pp. 128 ff.

33. C. Gill, *The Rise of the Irish Linen Industry* (1925); E. R. R. Green, *The Lagan Valley* (1949); Constantia Maxwell, *Country and town in Ireland under the Georges* (Dundalk, 1949); Hausherr, op. cit., pp. 153 ff., 295.

34. Charles Foulkes, *The Gun-Founders of England* (Cambridge, 1937); Rhys Jenkins, 'The Rise and Fall of the Sussex Iron Industry', *Trans. of the Newcomen Society*, 5th ser., i (1920), 21; id., 'Ironmaking in the Forest of Dean', *Trans. of the Newcomen Soc.*, 5th ser., vol. vi (1927); Ernest Straker, *Wealden Iron* (1931); John U. Nef, 'Mining and Metallurgy in Medieval Civilization', *The New Cambridge Economic History*, ii. 461 ff.

35. J. W. Gough, *The Mines of Mendip* (Oxford, 1930), pp. 112 ff., 206, 233; George Randall Lewis, *The Stannaries* (Cambridge, Mass., 1924), pp. 34 ff.; A. K. Hamilton Jenkin, *The Cornish Miner* (2nd ed., 1928), pp. 48 ff., 83 ff.; Herbert Heaton, *Economic History of Europe* (rev. ed., New York, 1948), p. 316.

36. Robert L. Galloway, *A History of Coal Mining in Great Britain* (1882), John U. Nef, *The Rise of the British Coal Industry* (1932); ibid., 'Mining and Metallurgy', p. 474.

37. Arthur Raistrick, *Quaker Contribution to Science and Industry* (1950), pp. 11 ff., 89 ff.; id., *Dynasty of Iron Founders. The Darbys and Coalbrookdale* (1953), pp. 1 ff.

38. Paul Mantoux, *The Industrial Revolution in the Eighteenth Century* (11th ed., 1952), pp. 280 ff.

39. Mantoux, op. cit., pp. 184 ff.; Sir John Clapham, *A Concise Economic History of Britain* (Cambridge, 1950), pp. 189 ff.

40. Clapham, op. cit., pp. 190, 236.

41. T. S. Ashton, *An Economic History of England, The 18th Century* (1952), p. 91.

42. John Thirsk, op. cit., pp. 70–88.

43. Thirsk quotes a final example: the handknitting industry in west Yorkshire, where the inhabitants made their living from stock-farming and the dairy trade; they practised the system of division of land by succession, and experienced the high rate of population growth that goes with it. From Tudor times onwards, they practised knitting as a secondary occupation, up until the twentieth century, when the centres of this industry were Dentdale and Garsdale.

44. R. Eberstadt, 'Das französische Gewerberecht und die Schaffung staatlicher Gesetzgebung und Verwaltung in Frankreich vom 13. Jahrhundert bis 1581', *Staats- und sozialwissenschaftliche Forschungen*, 17 (Leipzig, 1899); Henri Sée, 'Remarques sur le caractère de l'industrie rurale en France et les causes de son extension au XVIIIe siècle', *Revue Historique* (1923); id., *L'Évolution commerciale et industrielle de la France sous l'ancien régime* (Paris, 1925), pp. 26 ff., 38 ff., 188 ff., 191 ff.; id., *Französische Wirtschaftsgeschichte* (Jena, 1930), i. 91 ff.; Henri Hauser, *Les Débuts du capitalisme* (Paris, 1927), pp. 80 ff.; Gaston Roupnel, *La Ville et la campagne au XVIIIe siècle. Étude sur les populations du pays Dijonnais* (Paris, 1955), pp. 70 ff.

45. H. Sée, *Französische Wirtschaftsgeschichte*, i. 49, 91 ff., 226 ff., 313 ff.

46. Ibid., pp. 97 ff., 244 ff.; Ph. Sagnac, 'L'Industrie et le commerce de la draperie à la fin du XVIIe siècle', *Revue d'histoire moderne*, ix (1907).

47. F. Bourdais and R. Durand, 'L'Industrie et le commerce de la toile en Bretagne au XVIIIe siècle', *Comité des travaux historiques*, section d'histoire moderne et contemporaine (1922), pt. vii, pp. 1–48.

48. [The manufacture of light woollen cloth, known as Flanders serge. Translator's note.]

49. Ed. Maugis, 'La Saieterie d' Amiens', *Vierteljahrsschrift für Sozial- und Wirtschaftsgeschichte* (1957), pp. 1 ff.

50. H. Sée, *Französische Wirtschaftsgeschichte*, i. 245.

51. Natalis Rondot, *L'Industrie de la soie en France* (Lyons, 1894), pp. 89 ff.; Élie Reynier, *La Soie en Largentière* (Vivarais, 1921).

52. Simeon Luce, *L'Exploitation des mines et la condition des ouvriers mineurs* (Paris, 1928), pp. 192 ff.; Thérèse Sclafert, *Les Minces de fer d'Allevard au Moyen Âge* (Paris, 1925), pp. 10 ff; Pierre Leon, 'Deux siècles d'activité minière et métallurgique: l'usines d'Allevard, 1675–1870', *Revue de géographie alpine,* vol. xxxvi (1948); id., *La Naissance de la grande industrie en Dauphiné (fin du XVIIIe siècle–1869)* (Paris, 1953), pp. 52 ff.

53. Lucien Fébvre, *Philippe II et la Franche-Comté* (Paris, 1911), pp. 101 ff.

54. Marcel Bulard, 'L'Industrie du fer dans la Haute Marne', *Annales de géographie,* xiii (1904), 229 ff.; E. Greau, *Le Fer en Lorraine* (Paris–Nancy, 1908), pp. 1 ff.; Henri Rouzard, *La Mine de Rancié (comté de Foix) depuis le Moyen Âge jusqu' à la Révolution* (Toulouse, 1908), 23 ff.; J. Levainville, *L'Industrie du fer* (Paris, 1922), pp. 3 ff., 39 ff.; B. Gilley, *Les Origines de la grande industrie métallurgique en France* (Paris, 1947); John U. Nef, 'Mining and Metallurgy', op cit., pp. 468, 471 ff.

55. L. G. Gras, *Histoire du commerce local et des industries qui s'y rattachent dans la région stéfanoise et forezienne* (Saint-Étienne, 1910); id., *Histoire économique générale des mines de la Loire* (Saint-Étienne, 1922); Jean Vidalenc, *La Petite Métallurgie rurale en Haute-Normandie sous l'ancien régime* (Paris, 1946), pp. 7 ff., 27 ff.

56. See Michel Mollat, 'Une Enquête sur le sel dans l'histoire', given at the colloquium organized in Dec. 1961, in Paris, on the importance of salt in history. It contains a complete bibliography of the subject. See also the other papers given.

57. P. Boissonnade, *Le Socialisme d'état, l'industrie et les classes industrielles en France pendant les deux premiers siècles de l'ère moderne, 1453–1651* (Paris, 1927), pp. 62 ff.; E. Levasseur, *Histoire des classes ouvrières*, ii. 138 ff.

58. See Marcel Rouff, *Les Mines de charbon en France* (Paris, 1922).
59. H. Sée, *Französische Wirtschaftsgeschichte*, i. 4, 153 ff., 257 ff.
60. Ibid., pp. 98 ff., 102.
61. Ibid., p. 245; Georges Lefebvre, *Les Paysans du Nord pendant la Révolution française* (Lille, 1924).
62. Georges Espinas, *La Draperie dans la Flandre française au Moyen Âge* (Paris, 1923), ii. 103 ff., 832 ff.; id., 'Une Draperie rurale dans la Flandre française au XVe siècle. La Draperie rurale d'Estaires (1428–1434)', *Revue d'histoire économique et sociale*, xi (1923), 429 ff.; id., *Documents relatifs à la draperie de Valenciennes au Moyen Âge* (Paris–Lille, 1931); L. Verriest, *La Draperie d'Ath, des origines au XVIIIe siècle* (Brussels, 1942); Emile Coornaert, *Un Centre industriel d'autrefois. La Draperie-sayetterie d'Hondschoote, XIVe-XVIIIe siècles* (Paris, 1930); Étienne Sabbe, *De belgische vlasnijverheid, i, De zuidnederlandsche vlasnijverheid tot hed verdrag van Utrecht (1713)* (Bruges, 1943), 44 ff., 88 ff.; Renée Doehard, *L'Expansion économique belge au Moyen Âge* (Brussels, 1946), pp. 47 ff.; H. van Werveke, 'De opbloei van handel en nijverheid', *Algemene Geschiedenis der Nederlanden*, ii. (Utrecht, 1950), 447 ff.
63. H.-E. de Sagher, 'Une Enquête sur la situation de l'industrie drapière en Flandre à la fin du XVIe siècle', *Études d'histoire dédiées à la mémoire de Henri Pirenne* (Brussels, 1937), pp. 481–94; cf. Henri Pirenne, *Histoire de la Belgique*, iii. 277 ff.; id., 'Une Crise industrielle au XVIe siècle. La Draperie urbaine et la nouvelle draperie en Flandre', *Bull. de l'Acad. Royale de Belgique, Classe des Lettres* (1905); Henri-E. de Sagher, *Recueil de documents relatifs à l'histoire de l'industrie drapière en Flandre*, ed. Johan-H. de Sagher *et al.* (2 vols., Brussels, 1951 and 1961).
64. J. A. van Houtte, 'Het economisch verval van het Zuiden', *Algemene Geschiedenis der Nederlanden*, v (Utrecht, 1952), 181 ff., 200 ff.
65. E. Coornaert, op. cit., p. 64; J. R. van Houtte, *Economische en sociale ontwikkeling van het Zuiden*, p. 391.
66. van Houtte, *Economische*, pp. 398 ff.
67. Sabbe, op. cit., p. 373; P. Verhaegen, 'La Dentelle et la broderie sur tulle', in *Les Industries à domicile en Belgique*, iv (1902), 30 ff.; id., *La Dentelle belge* (1912), pp. 5 ff.; G. van Bever, *La Dentelle* (Brussels, 1945), p. 9.
68. Cf. Joseph Ruwet, *L'Agriculture et les classes rurales au pays de Herve sous l'ancien régime* (Liège–Paris, 1954), pp. 270 ff.; van Houtte, 'Het economische verval . . .', p. 201; id., *Economische*, p. 393; N. W. Posthumus, 'De industrielle concurrentie tussen Noord- en Zuid-Nederlandsche nijverheidscentra in de XVIIe en XVIIIe eeuw', *Mélanges H. Pirenne*, ii. (1926), 370; id., *De Geschiedenis van de leidsche lakenindustrie*, iii, 960 ff.
69. P. Lebrun, *L'Industrie de la laine à Verviers pendant le XVIIIe et le début du XIXe siècle* (Liege, 1949), p. 271; van Houtte, *Economische*, p. 394.
70. Lebrun, op. cit., p. 221; L. Dechesne, *L'Industrie de la Vesdre avant 1800* (Paris–Liège, 1926); J. Mathieu, *Histoire sociale de l'industrie textile de Verviers* (Dijon, 1946); van Houtte, *Economische*, p. 395.
71. Jean Lejeune, *La Formation du capitalisme moderne dans la principauté de Liège au XVIe siècle* (Liège–Paris, 1939), pp. 157 ff., 587.
72. Cf. P. Harsin, *Études sur l'histoire économique de la principauté de Liège, particulièrement au XVIIe siècle* in Bureau de l'Inst. archéol. liégeois, vol. lii (1928); Jean Yernaux, *La Métallurgie liégeoise et son expansion au XVIIe siècle* (Liège, 1939), pp. 33 ff.
73. V. Tahon, 'L'Industrie cloutière au pays de Charleroi', *Doc. et rapports de la Soc. royale de paléontol. et archéol. de Charleroi*, xxxvi. 11 ff.
74. J. U. Nef, 'Mining and Metallurgy', pp. 472 ff.
75. F. Torent Pholien, *La Verrerie et ses artistes au Pays de Liège* (Liège, n.d., about 1900); A. Baer, 'Evolution de la fabrication due verre en Belgique . . . du XVIe au XVIIIe siècle', *Federation archéol. et hist. de la Belgique*, XXIXe Congrès (Liège, 1932), pp. 261 ff.; V. Lefebvre, *La Verrerie à vitres et les verriers de Belgique depuis le XVe siècle* (Charleroi, 1938), pp. 16 ff.

76. G. Hansotte, 'L'Introduction de la machine à vapeur au Pays de Liège', *La Vie wallonne*, xxiv (1950), 47 ff.

77. Cf. the manuscript 'De Nijverheid in de latere Middeleeuwen', which Professor Jappe Alberts of the University of Utrecht very kindly made available to me.

78. R. Fruin (ed.), *Informacie up den staet . . . van Holland ende Friesland in den jaare 1514* (Leiden, 1866).

79. See also O. Postma, 'De fryske Boerkery en it Boerelibben yn de XVIe en XVIIe ieu' and Faber, 'Handel und Schiffahrt . . .'

80. Cf. J. F. Niermeyer, *Delft en Delftland* (1944), p. 92.

81. Ernst Baasch, *Holländische Wirtschaftsgeschichte* (Jena, 1927), p. 49; T. S. Jansma, 'De economische opbloei van het Noorden', *Algemene Geschiedenis der Nederlanden*, v (Utrecht, 1952), 222 ff.

82. J. G. van Dillen, 'Honderd jaar economische ontwikkeling van het Noorden', id. vii (Utrecht, 1954), 297 ff.

83. Baasch, op. cit., p. 90; van Braam, *Bloei en verval van het economisch en sociaal leven aan de Zaan* (Wormeveer, 1944); S. Hart, 'De Zaanstreek in 1731', *De Zaende*, ii (1947), 102 ff.; id., 'Bijdrage tot de Geschiedenis van den houthandel', *De Zaende*, iii (1948), 4; id., 'De personele quotisatie te Oost-Zaandem, zoals ze in 1742 is vastgesteld', *De Zaende*, iii (1948); id., 'De personele quotisatie te Zaandijk, zoals die in 1742 is vastgesteld', *De Zaende*, iv (1949), 257 ff.; id., 'De personele quotisatie te Krommenie en Krommeniedijk, zoals die in 1742 is vastgesteld', *De Zaende*, v (1950), 257 ff., 289 ff., C. A. Schillemans, *De houtveilingen van Zaandam in de jaaren 1655–1811* in *Econ. hist. Jaerboek*, xxiii (1944–5), 171 ff.; P. Boorsma *Duizend Zaanse molens* (Wormerveer, 1950); G. J. Honig, 'Duizend Zaanse molens', *De Zaende*, vi (1951), 97 ff.; Joop Goudsblom, 'De molens van Krommenie', *De Zaende*, vi (1951), 294 ff.; L. A. Ankumi, 'Een bijdrage tot de geschiedenis van de Zaanse olieslagerji', *Tijdschrift voor Geschiedenis*, lxxiii (1960), 39 ff.

84. J. G. van Dillen, *Honderd jaar*, p. 299.

85. Baasch, op. cit., pp. 59, 67 ff.; S. Lootsma, *Bijdragen tot de Geschiedenis der Nederlandische Walvisvaart, meer speciaal de Zaansche* (1937); J. G. van Dillen, op. cit., p. 303.

86. Cf. J. J. M. Heeren, 'Uit de geschiedenis der Helmondische textielnijverheid', *Ekon. Hist. Jaarboek*, vol. xii (1926); Baasch, op. cit., pp. 65 ff.

87. Z. W. Sneller, 'De opkomst van de plattelandsni verheid in Nederland in de XVIIe en XVIIIe eeuw', *De Economist*, lxxvii (1928), 690–702.

88. B. H. Slicher van Bath, 'Historische ontwikkeling . . .', pp. 21–39, and also Z. W. Sneller, 'De Twentsche weefnijverheid omstreeks het jaar 1800', *Tijdschrift voor Geschiedenis* (1926); J. H. Gietelink, 'Handel en verkeer in het oude Twente, 1795–1820', ibid. lxix (1956), 196 ff.

89. Our study will not deal with these regions of East Germany; we refer the reader to Gustav Aubin and Arno Kunze, *Leinenerzeugung und Leinenabsatz im östlichen Mitteldeutschland zur Zeit der Zunftkäufe* (Stuttgart, 1940); Gerhard Heitz, *Ländliche Leinenproduktion in Sachsen 1470–1555* (Berlin, 1961).

90. Cf. August Skalweit, *Das Dorfhandwerk vor Aufhebung des Städrezwanges* (Frankfurt–Main, 1942), pp. 9 ff.; id., 'Vom Werdegang des Dorfhandwerks', *Zeitschrift für Agrargeschichte und Agrarsoziologie*, ii (1954), 11.

91. Fritz Haehnsen, *Die Entwicklung des ländlichen Handwerks in Schleswig-Holstein* (in the collection Quellen und Forschungen zur Geschichte Schleswig-Holsteins, vol. ix, Leipzig, 1923), *passim;* Sven Henningsen, *Studier over den ökonomiske Liberalismeus Gennembroud i Danmark. Landhaandverket* (Göteborg, 1944), pp. 36 ff.

92. See also Aksel E. Christensen, 'Tiden indtil c. 1730', *Industriens historie i Danmark* (Copenhagen, 1943), p. 103 ff.; Holger Hjelholt, 'Tidsrummet c. 1660–1805', *Sönderjyllands Historie*, iii (Copenhagen, n.d.), 278 ff.; Hermann Kellenbenz, 'Die Herzogtümer vom Kopenhagener Frieden bis zur Wiedervereinigung Schleswig-Holsteins', in *Geschichte Schleswig-Holsteins*, v (Neumünster, 1960), 360 ff.; Olaf Klose, 'Die Jahrzehnte der Wiedervereinigung', ibid. vi (Neumünster, 1959), 104 ff.

93. A. E. Christensen, op. cit., p. 175; *Danmark för og nu. Red. af Johannes Brönsted,*

under medvirken af Sv. Aakjaer og T. Sölvsten. Vest- og Sydjylland (Copenhagen, 1954), pp. 181 ff.; Hermann Kellenbenz, 'Bäuerliche Unternehmertätigkeit im Bereich der Nord- und Ostsee', *Vierteljahrsschrift für Sozial- und Wirtschaftsgeschichte*, xlix (1962), 32.

94. I shall not give any further details on this subject here, since I have dealt with it elsewhere on several occasions. See H. Kellenbenz, 'German Aristocratic Entrepreneurship. The Economic Activity of the Holstein Nobility in the Sixteenth and Seventeenth Centuries', *Explorations in Entrepreneurial History*, vi (1953–4), 103 ff.; id., *Unternehmerkräfte im Hamburger Portugal- und Spanienhandel, 1590–1625* (Hamburg, 1954), pp. 278 ff.; id., 'Die unternehmerische Betätigung der verschiedenen Stände während des Uebergangs zur Neuzeit', *Vierteljahrsschrift für Sozial- und Wirtschaftsgeschichte*, xliv (1957), 15 ff.; id., 'Die Harzogtümer vom Kopenhagener . . .', pp. 336 ff.; id., 'Die Betätigung der Grossgrundbesitzer im Bereich der deutschen Nord- und Ostseeküste in Handel, Gewerbe und Finanz (16.–18. Jahrhundert)', in *Première Conférence Internationale d'Histoire Économique. Contributions, Communications, Stockholm, 1960* (Paris–The Hague, 1960), pp. 501 ff.

95. Kellenbenz, 'Die Herzogtümer', p. 343.

96. Ibid., p. 354.

97. Kellenbenz, 'Bäuerliche', p. 24.

98. Kellenbenz, 'Die unternehmerische', p. 10; id., 'Bäuerliche', p. 22; id., 'Die Herzogtümer', p. 362; Wanda Oesau, *Schleswig-Holsteins Grönlandfahrt auf Walfischfang und Robbenschlag vom 17. bis 19. Jahrhundert* (Gluckstadt–Hamburg–New York, 1937), pp. 255 ff.

99. Oesau, op. cit., p. 267.

100. For the early period see Hans Joachim Seeger, *Westfälens Handel und Gewerbe vom 9. bis zum Beginn des 14. Jahrhunderts* (vol. i of the collection Studien z. Geschichte der Wirtschaft und Geisteskultur, ed. Rudolf Häpke, Berlin, 1926), pp. 8 ff.; for the following period see Bruno Kuske, *Wirtschaftsgeschichte Westfälens in Leistung und Verflechtung mit den Nachbarländern* (Munster, 1949), p. 72.

101. Kuske, op. cit., p. 75.

102. Ibid., pp. 82 ff.

103. Ibid., pp. 97 ff.

104. Ibid., pp. 92 ff.; *Zeitschrift des Bergischen Geschichtsvereins*, xviii. 11 ff.; *Dortmunder Beiträge*, xi. 90–1.

105. Kuske, op. cit., pp. 103–4.

106. With ref. to these see H. Achenbach, *Die Haubergs-Genossenschaften des Siegerlandes. Ein Beitrag zur Darstellung der deutschen Flur- und Agrarverfassung* (Bonn, 1863), pp. 3 ff.; Theodor Kraus, *Das Siegerland, ein Industriegebiet im rheinischen Schiefergebirge* (Stuttgart, 1931), pp. 47 ff.

107. Kuske, op. cit., pp. 11, 146–7.

108. Ibid., pp. 112 ff.

109. Ibid., pp. 112 ff. In the hilly regions of the north, coal was mined in the Burke mountains near Obernkirchen. Coal-mining centres of lesser importance were established in the Osnabrück region, near Osede and Borgloh, on the Piesberg, and on the Schafberg near Ibbenbühren in the county of Lingen; it was from here that the town of Osnabrück and the salt-works of Rothenfelds and Rheine obtained their fuel supplies. Cf. Walter Heidorn, 'Der niedersächsische Steinkohlenbergbau', *Jahrbuch der Geographischen Gesellschaft zu Hannover für das Jahr 1927* (Hanover, 1927), pp. 18 ff.

110. Kuske, op. cit., p. 117.

111. Cf. Franz Sondermann, *Geschichte der Eisenindustrie im Kreise Olpe. Ein Beitrag zur Wirtschaftsgeschichte des Sauerlandes* (vol. x of the collection Münstersche Beiträge zur Geschichtsforschung, Munster, 1907), pp. 6 ff.; E. Voye, *Geschichte der Industrie im märkischen Sauerland* (1910) especially ii. 13 ff.; W. Luesebrink, *Die Osemund-Industrie* (Ludenschei, 1920); Wilhelm Quast, *Die Entwicklung der Eisenindustrie im Sauerland* (Cologne thesis, 1928); Wilhelm von Kurten, *Die Industrielandschaft von Schwelm, Gevelsberg und Milspe-Vörde* (Cologne thesis, Emsdetten, 1939),

pp. 33 ff.; Klaus Rockenbach, 'Der Bergbau der Mark', *Heimatblätter für Hohen-limburg und Umgebung*, xxiii (1962), 67–72, 83–92.

112. Kuske, op. cit., pp. 118 ff.

113. Cf. I. Göken in *Oldenburger Jahrbuch*, xxxvi. 42–3.

114. Cf. also Richard Utsch, *Die Entwicklung und volkwirtschäftliche Bedeutung des Eisenerzbergbaues und der Eisenindustrie im Siegerland* (Gorlitz, 1913); E. Broecker, *Eisenindustrie des vorderen Westerwäldes* (Cologne thesis, 1921); Th. Kraus, *Das Siegerland*, pp. 30–1, 73 ff.; K. W. Klein, *Entwicklungsgrundzüge und wirtschaftliche Bedingungen der Siegerländer Eisenhütten* (Cologne thesis, 1948), pp. 22 ff.; Fritz Schulte, *Die Entwicklung der gewerblichen Wirtschaft in Rheinland-Westfalen im 18. Jahrhundert* (Cologne, 1959), pp. 21, 25–6.

115. Kuske, op. cit., p. 121.

116. See in particular Margarete Asbeck Haspe, *Die Sensenindustrie an der Enneper Strasse* (MS. thesis, Hamburg, 1922); W. Wernekinck, *Die Kleineisenindustrie an der Enneper Strasse vom Beginn bis zur Gegenwart* (Berlin thesis, 1937); Schulte, op. cit., pp. 28 ff.

117. Kuske, op. cit., p. 129; Luesebrink, op. cit., p. 33; F. Schmid, *Das Osemundgewerbe im Süderland* (Altena, 1949), pp. 3 ff.

118. See also O. Döhner, *Geschichte der Eisendrahtindustrie* (Berlin, 1925); K. Knapmann, *Das Eisen- und Stahldrahtgewerbe in Altena* (Münster, 1907); W. K. Rieck, *Die deutsche Drahtindustrie, ihre Entwicklung und ihr heutiger Aufbau* (Wurzburg thesis, 1928).

119. Röttgermann, *Die Entwicklung der Industrie im Wirtschaftsraum Menden (Sauerland) und ihre Probleme seit Beginn des 19. Jahrhunderts* (Cologne thesis, 1938).

120. Eversmann, p. 280.

121. For Altena see also Karl Rüsse, *Die Entwicklung der Industrie im Altenaer Wirtschaftsraum seit Beginn des 19. Jahrhunderts* (Cologne thesis, Emsdetten, 1934).

122. Kuske, op. cit., pp. 131, 133–4.

123. Ibid., p. 136.

124. Ibid., p. 143.

125. Ibid., pp. 151–2.

126. Ibid., pp. 152–3.

127. Cf. E. Virmond, *Geschichte der Eifeler Eisenindustrie* (Schleiden, 1896); Justus Hashagen, 'Zur Geschichte der Eisenindustrie vornehmlich in der nord-westlichen Eifel', *Eifel-Festschrift* (Bonn, 1913); Schulte, op. cit., pp. 34 ff.

128. Robert Schmitt, *Geschichte der Rheinböllerhütte* (vol. i of the series Schriften zur rheinisch-westfälischen Wirtschaftsgeschichte, Cologne, 1961), pp. 9 ff.

129. Cf. Anton Hasslacher, *Der Steinkohlenbergbau des Preussischen Staats in der Umgebung von Saarbrücken*, vol. i, *Geschichtliche Entwicklung des Steinkohlenbergbaues im Saargebiet* (Berlin, 1904); id., *Das Industriegebiet an der Saar und seine hauptsächlichesten Industriezweige* (Saarbrucken, 1912); Walter Lauer, *Die Glasindustrie im Saargebiet* (Braunschweig thesis, 1922); Carl Schnur, 'Die Entwicklung der Kulturlandschaft im Saargebiet', *Jahresbericht des Frankfurter Vereins für Geographie und Statistik*, lxxxvii–lxxxix (Frankfort/Main, 1922–5), 5–127; Jacques Gayot and Robert Herly, *La Métallurgie des pays de la Sarre moyenne jusqu'en 1815* (Nancy–Paris–Strasbourg, 1928); Josef Collet, *Das Wirtschaftsleben in der Grafschaft Saarbrücken im Zeitalter des Merkantilismus, 1697–1793* (Frankfort on Main thesis, 1930); Hermann Overbeck and Georg Wilhelm Sante, *Saar-Atlas* (Gotha, 1934).

130. R. A. Peltzer, *Geschichte der Messingindustrie und der künstlerischen Arbeiten in Messing in Aachen und den Ländern zwischen Maas und Rhein* (Aix-la-Chapelle, 1909); A. Becker, *Die Stolberger Messingindustrie und ihre Entwicklung* (Bonn thesis, 1913); K. Schleicher, *Geschichte der Stolberger Messingindustrie unter besonderer Berücksichtigung ihrer technischen Entwicklung* (Cologne thesis, 1952); A. Voigt, 'Bergbau und Hüttenwesen in der Geschichte des Dürener Landes', *Dürener Geschichtsblätter*, xxv (1961), 490 ff.

131. Cf. Alphons Thun, *Die Industrie am Niederrhein und ihre Arbeiter* (Leipzig,

1879), 18–19; E. Barkhausen, *Die Tuchindustrie in Montjoie, ihr Aufstieg und Niedergang* (Aix-la-Chapelle, 1925).

132. Eberhard Gothein, *Wirtschaftsgeschichte des Schwarzwaldes* (Strasbourg, 1892), p. 663; Henri Berg, *Trondhjems Sjöfart under Eneveldet*, vol. i (Tronhjems Sjöfartsmuseums Tidskrift, 1938), p. 4.

133. Walter Bodmer, *Die Entwicklung der schweizerischen Textilwirtschaft im Rahmen der übrigen Industrien und Wirtschaftszweige* (Zurich, 1960); Gothein, op. cit., pp. 723 ff.

134. Gothein, op. cit., pp. 736 ff.

135. Ibid., p. 762 ff.

136. E. Gothein, 'Beiträge zur Geschichte des Bergbaus im Scharzwald', *Zeitschrift für Geschichte des Oberrheins*, N.S. ii (1887), 435–6.

137. Gothein, *Wirtschaftsgeschichte*, pp. 806 ff.

138. Ibid., p. 812.

139. Ibid., pp. 824–5.

140. Ibid., pp. 831 ff.

141. Cf. Hector Ammann, 'Die Anfänge der Leinenindustrie des Bodenseegebietes', *Alemannisches Jahrbuch* (1953), pp. 251 ff.

142. See in particular Hektor Ammann, *Die Diesbach-Watt-Gesellschaft. Ein Beitrag zur Handelsgeschichte des 15. Jahrhunderts* (St. Gallen, 1928); Aloys Schulte, *Geschichte der Grossen Ravensburger Handelsgesellschaft* (3 vols., Stuttgart, 1923).

143. Fridolin Furger, *Zum Verlagssystem als Organisationsform des Frühkapitalismus in Textilgewerbe* (Stuttgart, 1927), p. 58.

144. Cf. E. Nubling, *Ulms Handel und Gewerbe im Mittelalter* (Leipzig, 1890); id., *Ulms Baumwollweberei im Mittelalter* (Ulm, 1891).

145. Furger, op. cit., p. 71.

146. Cf. Gotz Freiherr von Pölnitz, *Anton Fugger*, ii (Tübingen, 1962), 4 ff., and note 38.

147. Cf. Grete Karr, *Die Uracher Leinenweberei und die Leinwandhandlungskompagnie* (Stuttgart, 1930), pp. 20 ff.

148. Walter Troeltsche, *Die Calwer Zeughandlungskompagnie und ihre Arbeiter. Studien zur Gewerbe- und Sozialgeschichte Altwürttembergs* (Jena, 1897), pp. 19 ff., 24 ff., 49 ff.

149. Kummerlen, 'Die Leinenweberei Leutkirchs', *Württembergische Jahrbuch für Statistik und Landeskunde* (1903), p. 147.

150. In addition to the works of Hektor Ammann which we have quoted see for what follows: Furger, op. cit.; Bodmer, op. cit.; Hans Conrad Peyer, *Leinwandgewerbe und Fernhandel der Stadt St. Gallen von den Anfängen bis 1520* (2 vols., St. Gallen, 1959–60), ii. 12 ff.

151. Furger, op. cit., p. 80.

152. Bodmer, op. cit., p. 139.

153. A. Oberhölzer, *Geschichte der Stadt Arbon* (Arbon, 1902), pp. 39 ff.

154. Gabriel Walser, *Neue Appenzeller Chronik oder Beschreibung des Kantons Appenzell* (St. Gallen, 1740), p. 41; cf. Furger, op. cit., pp. 82–3.

155. Bodmer, op. cit., pp. 125–6, 157, 204 ff.

156. Wolf Buerkli-Meyer, *Zürcherische Fabrikgesetzgebung vom Beginn des 14. Jahrhunderts bis zur schweizerischen Staatsumwälzung von 1798* (Zurich, 1884), pp. 8 ff., and *Dreihundert Jahre Entwicklung einer Emmentaler Firma, 1630–1936. Geschichte der Leinenweberei Worb & Scheitlin AG Burgdorf* (Burgdorf, 1936).

157. Bodmer, op. cit., pp. 205–6.

158. Furger, op. cit., pp. 84 ff.; Bodmer, op. cit., pp. 118, 145.

159. Bodmer, op. cit., pp. 43, 98 ff., 181 ff.; E. Kunzle, *Die zürcherische Baumwollindustrie von ihren Anfängen bis zur Einführung des Fabrikbetriebes* (Zurich, 1906), pp. 7 ff.

160. Kunzle, op. cit., pp. 5 ff.; Bodmer, op. cit., pp. 151–2.

161. Bodmer, op. cit., pp. 186–7; A. Dreyer, *Les Toiles peintes en Pays Neuchâtelois* (Neuchâtel, 1928), pp. 19 ff., 24 ff.

162. A. Jenny-Trumpy, 'Handel und Industrie des Kantons Glarus', *Jahrbuch des Hist. Vereins des Kantons Glarus* (1899); Furger, op. cit., p. 104.

163. Furger, op. cit., pp. 114 ff.

164. Bodmer, op. cit., p. 233.

165. Adolf Buerkli-Mayer, *Geschichte der zurcherischen Seidenindustrie vom Schlusse des 13. Jahrhunderts bis in die neuere Zeit* (Zurich, 1884); ibid., *Zurcherische Fabrikgesetzgebung*, op. cit., *passim*; Bodmer, op. cit., pp. 147–8, 189 ff.; William E. Rappart, *La Révolution industrielle et les origines de la protection légale du travail en Suisse* (Berne, 1904), pp. 88–9; Furger, op. cit., pp. 120 ff.

166. Bodmer, op. cit., pp. 208 ff.

167. Cf. Traugott Geering, *Handel und Industrie der Stadt Basel* (Basle, 1886), pp. 433–4, 470 ff.; Emil Thurkauf, *Verlag und Heimarbeit in der Basler Seid–industrie* (1909), pp. 11 ff.; Furger, op. cit., pp. 129 ff.; Bodmer, op. cit., pp. 121–2, 154 ff., 193 ff.

168. Bodmer, op. cit., pp. 156, 217; A. Ass, *Das wirtschaftliche Verhältnis zwischen Stadt und Land im Kanton Basel, vornehmlich im 18. Jahrhundert* (Breslau thesis, 1930).

169. Bodmer, op. cit., p. 216.

170. Ibid., pp. 237 ff.

171. Cf. Abbot Payson Usher, *A History of Mechanical Inventions* (rev. ed., Cambridge Mass., 1954), pp. 179 ff.

172. Bodmer, op. cit., pp. 149, 155.

173. Furger, op. cit., p. 73.

174. See, for example, for the clock-making industry of Geneva, Bodmer, op. cit., p. 126.

175. Gothein, *Wirtschaftsgeschichte des Schwarzwaldes*, p. 821.

176. B. H. Slicher van Bath, *Historische ontwikkeling*, pp. 21–2, analyses these relationships during the first period of the history of the textile industry and of agriculture; see also ibid., *De agrarische geschiedenis*, pp. 137–8, 145–6, 240, 340 ff.

177. Cf. Wilhelm Abel, *Agrarkrisen und Agrarkonjunktur in Mitteleuropa vom 13. bis 19. Jahrhundert* (Berlin, 1935), p. 8.

178. Cf. Slicher van Bath, *De agrarische geschiedenis*, p. 143; Wilhelm Abel, *Geschichte der deutschen Landwirtschaft* (Stuttgart, 1962), p. 198.

179. Bodmer, op. cit., p. 124, with reference to Berne.

180. Bruno Kuske, 'Das soziale und wirtschaftliche Leben Westdeutschland im Dreissigjährigen Kriege,' *Jahrbuch der Arbeitsgemeinschaft rheinischer Geschichtsvereine*, iii (1937), 81–7, reprinted in id., *Köln, der Rhein und das Reich, Beiträge aus fünf Jahrhunderten wirtschaftsgeschichtlicher Forschung* (Cologne–Graz, 1956), pp. 177–99.

181. Bodmer, op. cit., p. 118.

182. Ibid., p. 147.

183. See the most recent study on the subject by Volkmar von Armin, *Krisen und Konjunkturen der Landwirtschaft in Schleswig-Holstein vom 16. bis 18. Jahrhundert* (vol. xxxv of the series Quellen und Forschungen zur Geschichte Schleswig-Holsteins, Neumünster, 1957), p. 59.

184. Mentioned by Slicher van Bath, *De agrarische Geschiedenis*, op. cit., p. 146.

185. A. Lequeux, *L'Accourtillage en Thiérache au XVIIe et XVIIIe siècles*, Mem. de la Soc. d'Hist. du droit des pays flamands, picards et wallons, ii (1939), 21 ff.

186. Cf. E. J. Hobsbawm, 'The General Crisis of the European Economy in the 17th Century', *Past and Present*, vi (1954), 51–2.

187. Slicher van Bath, *De agrarische Geschiedenis*, p. 24.

188. Ibid., p. 45.

189. Hauser, *Schweizerische Wirtschafts- und Sozialgeschichte*, pp. 176–7.

190. Ibid., pp. 85–6, 139 ff.

191. With regard to these classes see Werner Conze, 'Vom "Pöbel" zum "Proletariat" ', *Vierteljahrsschrift für Sozial- und Wirtschaftsgeschichte*, xli (1954), 333; id., 'Staat und Gesellschaft in der frührevolutionären Gesellschaft', *Historische Zeitschrift*, vol. clxxxvi (1958).

192. Cf. Erich Maschke, *Die städtischen Unterschichten im späten Mittelalter*, paper given at a colloquium held at Saint-Cloud, 1 Nov. 1962.

193. Bodmer, op. cit.

194. See for Switzerland, Braun, *Industrialisierung*, pp. 181 ff.

195. Cf. Kuske, 'Das soziale', p. 197.

196. Ibid., p. 190.

197. Gothein, *Wirtschaftsgeschichte des Schwarzwaldes*, p. 603.

198. Ibid., p. 667.

199. In the Sauerland for example; see Hedwig Kleinsorge, *Die Hausierer des oberen Sauerlandes* (Münster thesis, 1919), especially pp. 30 ff.; see also R. B. Westerfield, *Middlemen in English Business particularly between 1660 and 1760* (New Haven, Conn., 1915), pp. 218 ff., 255 ff.

200. Cf. Bruno Kuske, 'Die wirtschaftliche und soziale Verflechtung zwischen Deutschland und den Niederlanden bis zum 18. Jahrhundert', *Deutsches Archiv für Landes- und Volksforschung*, vol. i (1937), reprinted in Kuske, *Köln*, pp. 206 ff.

201. Cf. Kellenbenz, *Bäuerliche*, p. 24; id., 'Unternehmertum im süddeutschen Raum zu Beginn der Neuzeit', in *Gemeinsames Erbe. Perspektiven europäischer Geschichte* (Munich, 1959), p. 121.

202. See also Bruno Kuske, *Die kulturhistorische Bedeutung des Genossenschaftsgedankens* (Halberstadt, 1928), pp. 12 ff., 21 ff.

203. Cf. also Paul Leuilliot, 'Houille et coton en Belgique: Pour une histoire industrielle comparée', *Annales*, vii (1952), 199 ff.

3

Monetary Circulation and the Use of Coinage in Sixteenth- and Seventeenth-Century France

JEAN MEUVRET

*Translated by Patrick Doran**

I

'FRANCE ... produces in abundance foodstuffs and merchandise which are useful and even indispensable to her neighbours, so that commerce always draws money to the kingdom ... Moreover has it not nearly always been estimated that in the return of the fleets from the Indies up to a third has accrued to the French and that much of the remaining two-thirds found its way into the kingdom through the need of other nations for French merchandise?'[1] It is not at all certain that France's trade balance was positive when these lines were written in 1686. It is even more doubtful if the stock of specie was on the increase. These assumptions, which seem to beg the question, were popular because they were the faithful echo of a long tradition, the old legacy of the sixteenth-century *monétaristes* to their successors. The real reason why Nicolas Desmerets seemed to make this debatable thesis his own was his wish to spotlight through contrast another aspect of the financial problem of which he, in common with all the administrators of the time of Louis XIV, had first-hand knowledge: the scarcity of money. If it is accepted that France was becoming increasingly prosperous then this statement has a paradoxical character. Logically it should have followed that 'money was in greater supply' and it should have been truly astonishing that 'the exhaustion of the provinces' was as bad as was proclaimed. The reduction of 'consumption' was, however, an indisputable fact as was, 'by a natural consequence', the decrease in 'commerce from within the provinces'.

If the contrast thus presented appears to be somewhat strained, it retains all its force if one side of it is placed in the past. It must be admitted that in a previous period France had received considerable quantities of specie from abroad, either in coin or bullion; for the amount of precious metals mined in France was always insignificant. Whether this supply had slowed down

---

* From 'Circulation monétaire et utilisation économique de la monnaie dans la France du XVIe et du XVIIe siècle', *Études d'histoire moderne et contemporaine*, i (1947), 15–28.

or even ceased—contrary to what Desmerets seemed to believe—is a major question for present-day historians.

On the other hand the above text invites another reflection in stressing the particular aspect which this monetary scarcity assumed. It was not Paris or the great centres which suffered most, but 'the interior of the kingdom', 'the provinces'. It was there that a profound crisis occurred, of consequence to the mass of the people. Whether the question to be considered is that of the scarcity of money or its manifestations, some light on the conditions which they brought about can be generated by going back to the sixteenth century, to the period when the major part of France's monetary stock was formed.

The difficulties involved in an investigation of this kind cannot be under-estimated. To treat monetary circulation in a realistic manner all economic activities must be examined from this angle. It is hardly necessary to say that for the sixteenth and seventeenth centuries many of these activities are still obscure. The existing bibliography, particularly on the mechanism of monetary phenomena, is extremely meagre. At the most, there are some valuable suggestions scattered here and there. The substantial studies of M. Doucet constitute a happy exception, but Lyons is not, perhaps, the best example for the activity of the country as a whole. In this situation it would be presumptuous to advance a premature synthesis. Nevertheless it would be useful, at this stage, to formulate several working hypotheses, these, of course, being open to revision.

II

The influx of precious metals from Spanish America and the rise in prices brought about by this are among the principal themes of sixteenth-century European history. Yet the global views to which comprehensive studies lead still leave unanswered many questions concerning the degree and mode of absorption of the new stock of monetary material by different countries, taking into account the particular structure of each country. Before going any further, it will therefore be necessary to examine from this point of view the actual conditions operating in the French economy.

Firstly, foreign trade must be looked at.[2] Through this, it is clear, a large amount of precious metals entered the kingdom. In default of precise quantitative data contemporary records are reasonably agreed at least on the origin, nature, and relative importance of imports and exports. Moreover from the routes taken by them the direction of monetary flow can be conjectured. And no less significant is the quality of the goods sold. The surest starting-point for all research on the various uses to which specie, acquired by trade, was put is the information to be gleaned about manufacturers and distributors.

What goods were exported? The most important were corn, wines and spirits, salt, and linens. Secondly came various fabrics of medium quality:

sheeting, butter-muslins, serges, or camlets. Lastly came various small items of ironmongery and hardware and divers agricultural products such as hemp, saffron, fats, wool, fruit, or honey and, in a class apart, wood. This group of goods has two predominant characteristics.

The first of these was its rustic character. This is true not only because of the strong representation of vegetable products, but also because of the rural origin of most of the products, even those which might, with some justice, be categorized as industrial.

Domestic industry existed throughout the French provinces. Hemp-dressers, tow-dressers, linen-weavers, rope-makers, wool-carders, pit-sawyers, *'tireurs de mines'*, were active, barely distinguishable from the mass of manual workers, day labourers, or *'brassiers'*. They often worked in the fields and almost always took part in seasonal work, particularly at harvest-time. The same was true, to a certain extent, of various artisans who were a little more specialized, such as potters, edge-tool makers, and curriers. Even if they themselves did not guide the plough or tend the vine a large proportion of them had small parcels of land from which they drew some of their food. Yvonne Bezard's observations on the southern part of the Paris region are valid for the whole of France: 'artisans for the most part ... do not form ... a separate class from the peasants, generally they combine both activities'.[3] Rural products were low-grade products. Because they were too crude to acquire much commercial value, their selling price was low. This low return was itself made possible by the fact that they were only a source of supplementary income for the manual worker or artisan whose subsistence was otherwise assured.

Today the export of French wines comes under the heading of luxury goods. Certainly on the basis of volume wine has always been a far more valuable product than other fruits of the earth. Consequently it has, from an early period, enjoyed a wider commercial value. But when Dutch merchants signed a charter-party for a shipment of wine 'of the new vintage' they did not attribute to different growths the particular values of the present day. And this was even more the case for cereals. Next to wheat, which held the place of honour, rye and chestnuts were the chief exports.

On the marshes of the Atlantic coast French salt was produced by simple processes requiring neither capital nor expertise. No costly installations were necessary, just the sun to evaporate the sea-water. Harvesting the salt was the main operation.

Why did linen hold the principal place in textile exports if not because it was, *par excellence*, the popular rural product? One should not be led astray by the names associated with certain varieties: great city- or big town-names are those of the markets in which these varieties were mainly concentrated, but it was in the thatched cottages that manufacture took place.[4] These 'canvases' which brought wealth to part of Brittany were nothing more than pack-cloths, and sailcloth, though more exalted in its use, was more robust than elegant. Many of them, like those of Vitré, were only rough unbleached linen.

A second fundamental characteristic which is no less important proceeds immediately from the first. Because it was an export of little value in proportion to its weight and volume this product could be distributed only through very favourable channels. In this respect trade-routes obeyed a geographical imperative. Only the rivers could provide profitable transport for such common goods. And the destination of all this traffic was the sea which offered numerous opportunities for the transport of such modest goods even if only to complement a cargo or as return freight. Hence the activity, alongside the great stars of maritime trade such as Rouen or Bordeaux, of a number of small ports on the Channel and Atlantic coasts. It is very difficult to estimate the past importance of some of these, such as Morlaix or Brouage.

Thus at the bottom was a crowd of 'pin-money earners' and at the top the merchants. Without doubt a good many traders and ship-owners were of small means, forwarding cargoes prudently spread over a number of small ships. Everything seems to point to this conclusion, but much more detailed studies are needed to prove it.[5] Between the peasant producer and the retailer at the port of embarkation the principal go-between was the rural trader. On this last point there is a little more information available, at least for upper Poitou, thanks to the celebrated monograph of Raveau.[6] But it must be said, however, that up to the present it has not encouraged any imitators.

There were also other ways, more modest still, by which quantities of Spanish gold and silver were brought into France. From the provinces in the neighbourhood of the Pyrenees but also from Limousin and Auvergne Frenchmen went to Spain each year to do seasonal work in agriculture and even to take up all kinds of itinerant jobs such as grinders and pedlars.[7] Here too other French industries played a part, many of which were as rural in character as those previously mentioned: portable cutlery, small wares, small objects of wood, bone, or pasteboard, the most important of which were rosary beads. Each of these men, returning to France, brought back *reals*, perhaps even some *pistoles*.

III

Sixteenth-century France encompassed but a small part of the territory in which a relatively advanced agriculture was, in time, to develop parallel with heavy industry. Lorraine, Alsace, Artois, and Flanders were not yet French, and elsewhere, exluding the Paris region, almost all the peasantry lived under a régime of domestic quasi-autarky. The 'silent communities' of the west or centre or the southern 'brotherhoods' represented the most advanced types, but the daily lives of the artisans, even of the petite bourgeoisie, obviously obeyed the same principle of living primarily from the fruits of the earth which they owned or exploited. Among them buying and selling was negligible.

The use of gold or silver was unnecessary for the satisfaction of ordinary needs, nor were coins indispensable for the few purchases usually made. Notarial acts specifying prices, in the same way as accounts calculated in *livres* and *deniers*, did not always accurately reflect the movements of coinage. In a very great number of cases a credit adjustment could be made. Sometimes the balance was paid in legal currency but there could also be agreements specifying payment in produce, in useful rights, or even in property.

Undoubtedly cash payment was customary in retail trade, in the local market, and in settlements for various services. But the amount of money involved in such transactions was extremely low, so low that gold was never used. Even silver coinage was sometimes too strong a currency. The *teston* of the first half of the sixteenth century was worth ten or eleven *sous tournois*. That was considerably more than the value of those quantities in which cereals were sold: the bushel, quart, *émine*, or *bichet*.

It was, therefore, the low-value coinage which the people used in their normal transactions.[8] And that was often of mediocre quality, more often the detested 'black money' than 'white money'. The ordinary people were accustomed by tradition to give a conventional value to the *piècettes*, the low-value coins which represented divisional tokens, and were not too particular as to their weight and quality. Because of this the traders became prone to the temptation of changing their silver against an intrinsic equivalent value in weak money which was circulated at a nominal value higher than its intrinsic worth.[9] Among the quantities of metal circulating in France in the sixteenth century was a little gold, a fairly large amount of 'white money', and much bad *billon* which kept increasing throughout the century.[10]

It can be shown that the traders, on their side, could carry on business almost entirely without a floating capital of money. Those inventories taken after death which have come down to us rarely involve large sums of ready cash.[11] On the other hand all the sources indicate a very extensive use of credit. Numerous references can be found to 'schedules' or 'obligations' forming an interconnecting web of debts. Bills of exchange were already in frequent use as a method of settling accounts, as well as a means of transfer. Above all the role of barter must be emphasized. Merchants in the big ports engaged in it.[12] All the more reason for the local traders, who sometimes used ordinary foodstuffs as a negotiable currency to do so. This was still the case in Quercy in the mid-seventeenth century where salt was used.[13] These practices were encouraged by the absence of specialization, for almost all the traders were engaged in several different lines of business. This was true at all levels of the business hierarchy. That banking remained tied to business for so long[14] was due to the fact that merchandise served as an instrument of credit, and that coinage was regarded merely as a particular kind of merchandise, less fungible perhaps than some others.

Among the precious metals imported into France were coins from various countries, ingots, and gems.[15] There was not always any hurry to convert all of them into French money. People were often deterred by the taxes; for in addition to the exchange tax there was the seigniorage which was relatively high, as well as the foreign trade duty.

Besides, the mint masters were sometimes no more than moderately wealthy and did not have much credit.[16] Often they lacked materials as the frequent and prolonged closures of many mints showed. Hence the maintenance in circulation of many foreign coins,[17] a number of which were tolerated to the extent of receiving an official rate. Of these the most famous was the *pistole*, which became the usual term for the gold coin in the classical language.

On the other hand a sizeable amount of these precious metals went to supply the goldsmiths' industry. There was the manufacture of plate, 'for there is no councillor, treasurer, bishop, or abbot who does not have some in his cupboard ... and even the small tradesman wants to have a basin, an ewer and a bowl, or at least a salt cellar with half a dozen of spoons'. There were, too, all the ornaments: 'so many gold chains, so many half-girdles, belts, rings, buttons, necklaces, and other such items'. To these must be added silver and gold which were used 'in enormous quantities in churches, and in the making of sacred vessels or chalices, in candlesticks, crosses, crucifixes, lamps, and above all in shrines and reliquaries'.[18] These precious objects were not always lost to the commercial world. Plate and sacred vessels were sometimes melted down, as much from government decree as from the initiative of some Huguenot leader. Melting and mintage, however, required both money and time. If metal reserves were more often mobilized than the treasures of the Middle Ages these were not disposable assets and could not be used as a cash reserve.[19]

IV

The question still remains as to what became of the genuine coinage which entered commercial circulation. Taking into account the foregoing inquiry it can be stated that despite the diversity of operations carried out by the coinage, the reliance on a coinage of weight and soundness almost certainly implies the existence of a need which could not be satisfied in a provincial framework. At the end of the chain of exchanges there must have been a vendor who was not satisfied with the usual methods of payment. The sound and strong currency was an export currency, from the province towards the great city or towards foreign parts. Whether the utilization of this currency was for profit or for the payment of consumer goods its common features can be recognized.

Was it a question of lending money to an individual? An inhabitant of the country needed only food and basic materials for his daily sustenance. If supplies ran out they were readily obtainable by the means already described. The loan of seeds, combustibles, or raw materials were all transactions which involved no break with time-honoured habits. But matters were very different when the tax-collector harried the parish collectors and put pressure on them to carry out their orders. In that case the leading citizen who had advanced money could claim the most varied objects or services as reimbursement and the *testons* and *écus* paid by him were taken out of the village or even out of the province.

The same was true in the exploitation of property: if an owner lived in the vicinity it was in his interest to make use of his land, in default of direct development by share-cropping or renting. It is clear from ledgers of the sixteenth and seventeenth centuries that it was possible to live in relative comfort under these conditions. But not only the squires lived like this. Many townsmen ate their own corn and drank their own wine. The case was different, however, for someone who travelled around, who went to court or became a soldier.

Even without travelling, circumstances changed once extravagance was introduced. For luxury goods were bought from outside. From the Field of the Cloth of Gold to the be-ribboned and laced marquesses of Molière, masculine as well as feminine fashions were costly to the nation. Dress was a field which exercised the ingenuity of the inventor.[20] Extravagance in furnishing was no less great, while that of the table was also redoubtable because of the profuse use of spices. The nobility wasted its possessions in this sort of excess[21] and neither the bourgeois[22] nor even the simple labourer[23] was slow in following their example.

Despite all this it was not yet possible to speak of encouragement being given to French industry. According to Doucet,[24] Lyons was almost exclusively an import centre. Silks, brocades, glassware, and *objets d'art* flowed in from Italy. Account must be taken of this fact to appreciate Barthélémy Laffemas's virulent attacks on the commerce of Lyons. Good-quality cloth, fine linens, and tapestries were brought in from Flanders and England. The Levant trade was also distinguished by the export of money. From Germany more useful but still costly products were introduced. These were, mainly, metals and metal objects, also horses, for French breeding was insufficient to ensure remounts for cavalry.

Besides, importation was easy to arrange. It supported, because of its worth, long-distance freightage, even over-land. It offered a substantial income in a trade which had preserved its caravaning character. Merchants rode in groups to the fairs of Paris, Lyons, and Beaucaire.[25] In remote cities haberdashers continued to sell exotic products.[26] This is not the place to distinguish between state and private expenditure. Both attracted sound money

to several privileged centres and, to a considerable extent, from these to
foreign countries.

To a large extent this second monetary circuit was unique. The great
cities, the court, the king, all bought less from the provinces than the amount
of silver which they took out of them. Occasionally some middle-men were
enriched by undertaking provisioning operations. There is no doubt that
rural manufacturers and craftsmen succeeded in selling some of their products to urban customers, but the balance remained weighted against the
open country and the small towns.

V

Despite our limited knowledge of the sixteenth-century rise in prices and its
mechanism it is possible to make a comparison between it and what has been
said above. The rise was, on the whole, the result of monetary inflation, an
inflation that had two distinct aspects. From the point of view of the nation
at large, particularly the rural population, it was in the main an inflation of
bad money, the depreciation of which expressed itself in an increase in the
value of sound specie and a corresponding devaluation of the money of
account, and by that fact alone by a rise in prices.[27] Still there is no doubt
that because of exportation certain foodstuffs, especially cereals, became
scarce leading to the same kind of real inflation of gold and silver which in
Andalusia brought about a rise in all prices, even wages, to a point reached
nowhere else.[28]

Taking this twofold influence into account it is perhaps possible to find
the real reasons for the differences between prices, according to their nature
and place. The degree of fluctuation between the ceilings reached through
violent and irregular oscillations in the price of cereals and those of other
categories was slowly to become less marked as were differences, too, of a
geographical nature between the prices of the same product not only in
different countries but in the markets of the same state.[29]

Anyway the changes which the seventeenth century brought about in the
general movement of prices modified neither the basis nor the orientation of
the economic life of each people; for these maintained their long-established
structure. But the deflation[30] was particularly difficult to support for the
French economy. French exports did not enjoy high profit-margins.[31] Their
exportation was based primarily on the differences between Spanish and
French prices. From the day on which the inflow of precious metals slowed
down this difference shrank.

From another point of view this period of deflation was marked by a remarkable effort of economic rationalization among those nations most reso-
lutely engaged in capitalistic production,[32] the United Provinces and England.
Capitalistic production, that is to say the effort to use the accumulation of
money so as to produce maximum profit from production, supposes, of

course, the existence among the public of buyers of sufficient means.

By comparison, it is easy to understand why French manufacturing effort was never—from Henri IV to Louis XIV—more than a series of more or less happy attempts to develop luxury industries while limiting imports. Despite everything, the whole country remained in the state of monetary poverty described by Desmerets and recognized by Colbert in 1670,[33] when he confessed to the king that 'the general difficulty' facing tax-farmers and collectors was 'to get money from the provinces'.[34] And he ended by saying that there was much less of it 'in the public commerce'.[35]

NOTES

1. 'Mémoire de M. Desmeretz sur l'état présent des affaires', printed in A. M. de Boislisle, *Correspondence des contrôleurs généraux* (1874), i. 543.

2. Information on this subject can be extracted from French and foreign writers of the sixteenth and seventeenth centuries. Unfortunately, these writers tend to repeat each other with monotonous regularity. A more realistic analysis of imports for the period 1551–6 can be found in the well-known MS. from the Bibliothèque Nationale, fds. fr. 2085, printed by Chamberland in the *Revue de géographie*, vols. xxxi, xxxii, and xxxiii. The whole trade of the countries of the North Sea and the Baltic has been the subject of important documentary publications, both Dutch and Scandinavian. Nina Bang's work on the customs of the Sound should be particularly noticed. On Franco-Dutch trade in the sixteenth century see especially Zw. Sneller and W. S. Unger, *Bronnen tot de geschiedenis van den handel met Frankrijk*, vol. i (The Hague, 1930). For highly interesting critical comments on the value of these sources, as well as some comprehensive views and an extended bibliography see A. E. Christensen, *Dutch trade to the Baltic about 1600* (Copenhagen–The Hague, 1941). On Franco-Spanish trade see Albert Girard, *Le Commerce français à Séville et Cadix au temps des Habsbourg* (Paris, 1932).

3. Yvonne Bezard, *La Vie rurale dans le sud de la région parisienne de 1450 à 1560* (Paris, 1929), p. 182.

4. This characteristic has been pointed out in a recent monograph: 'Like most industries of this period, the linen industry was essentially rural . . . Many peasants were weavers; to dispose of their products these isolated manufacturers were naturally dependent on merchants who served as their middle-men . . .', Yvonne Labbé, *Vitré au XVe et au XVIe siècle* (Rennes, 1944).

5. In addition to the works previously cited see the short document in Spanish printed by Schäfer, *Hansische Geschichtsblätter*, lix (1935), 143–76.

6. *L'Agriculture et les classes paysannes dans le Haut-Poitou au XVIe siècle* (Paris, 1926).

7. According to Bodin, *Réponse à M. de Malestroit*, ed. Le Branchu, p. 94, workmen in Spain could earn 'triple' that to be earned in France. Cf. the satirical picture of Frenchmen, *en route* to the peninsula, given by the author of 'Heure de tous', René Bouvier, *Quevedo* (Paris, 1929), p. 305.

8. Even in Paris low-value coins came to invade the circulation: '. . . the ordinary people are only paid in such coins', the mint declared in 1638 à propos of the double *denier*, Bibl. Nat. MS. fr. 18504, f. 35.

9. It was the poor quality of the small denominations which caused the rise in rates of the hard currency. This seems to have escaped Raveau in his article 'La Crise des prix au XVIe siècle en Poitou', *Revue historique*, clxii (1929).

10. In the last years of the sixteenth century there was practically no specie other than *douzains* in the royal returns. Henry Poullain, *Traité des monnaies*, cited by Raveau, 'La Crise des prix', p. 62.

11. Raveau provides a significant exception which perhaps proves the point: a 'very wealthy tradesman of Poitou' left, in 1542, 1,500 livres in gold coin. But of these 1,000 livres had been set aside 'to provide a dowry for one of his children', family treasure and not commercial coin; Raveau, 'La Crise des prix', p. 32. On the whole everything seems to confirm the general opinion of M. Doucet, based above all on the record office in Lyons, i.e. on a great centre of banking as well as trade. 'The inventories throw into relief the almost complete absence of specie in hand', 'La richesse en France au XVIe siècle', *Revue d'histoire moderne*, xiv (1939), 296–7. *A fortiori* this was true of the small centres.

12. Here are a few examples among many. On 6 Nov. 1505, Pierre Depretz, steward of a merchant at Middelbourg, leaves 1,345 bushels of wheat to pay a debt of 491 *francs bordelois* owed for 41 barrels of wine, Archives de la Gironde, 3E 2489, f. 94, Sneller and Unger, op. cit., p. 254, item No. 467. On 13 Mar. 1580 Sabatery of Bordeaux wrote to Simon Lecomte of Toulouse that he had done his best to 'swop' his cloth for wines 'du haut pays', Fagniez, *L'Économie sociale de la France sous Henri IV* (Paris, 1897), p. 382. In 1639 the Vitréen Hévin announced that he had loaded at San Lucar 2,071 pounds of tobacco to be exchanged for some 'Morlaix', Frain, *Le Commerce des Vitréens en Espagne* (Vitré, 1898), p. 9.

13. 'Livre de comptes et de raison' of Hugues Mario, merchant of Montaigut, summarized by Granat, *Revue de l'Agenais* (1901), pp. 425–40.

14. Hauser, 'Réflections sur l'histoire des banques', in *Les Origines historiques des problèmes économiques actuels* (Paris, 1930), p. 83. At Lyons the Capponi bank was also an importer of various products: camlets and felts from Ancona, silk and linen from Florence, feathers from Avignon, etc. Doucet, *La Banque Capponi à Lyon en 1556* (1939), pp. 6 and 7.

15. Boissonnade, 'Le Mouvement commercial entre la France et les Îles Britanniques au XVIe siècle', *Revue historique*, cxxxv. 17. Cf. Yvonne Labbé, op. cit., p. 128.

16. For example it was reported that the mint master of Saint-Lô could not afford to buy 50 marks of silver and it was more than twenty years since he had minted a single quarter écu, Bibl. Nat. MS. fr. 18504, f. 6. The mint master of Paris had 'neither belongings nor credit', so that merchants were compelled to sell their ingots and bars of gold and silver to the goldsmiths and refiners and also to foreigners who transported them out of France; ibid., f. 10. These complaints, addressed to Richelieu, came from some traders of Saint-Malo.

17. For Normandy see the 'Journal du sire de Gouberville', *Mém. de la Soc. des Antiquaires de Normandie*, vol. xxxi, *passim*; for Poitou, see Raveau, 'La Crise des prix', tables of payments with details of the coins.

18. Scipion de Grammont, *Le Denier Royal* (Paris, 1620), pp. 152–4.

19. They could be used, of course, as security on a loan. Jean de Gennes, a merchant of Vitré, gave his brother a loan against some silver cups; *Revue de Bretagne* (1914), li. 215.

20. Bernard Palissy cites an instance of enamel buttons so vulgar in their design that their price fell: *Oeuvres*, ed. A. France, p. 373.

21. La Noue, *Discours politiques et militaires, 8e discour*.

22. See the description of the attire of the bourgeoisie in E. Clouard, *La Vie à Riom aux XVe et XVIe siècles* (Paris, 1910), p. 958.

23. 'Pepper, saffron, ginger, cinnamon ... nutmeg, cloves, and other similar fripperies, brought from the towns into our villages', Noel du Fail, *Propos rustiques*, ed. Lefevre, p. 19.

24. 'La Richesse de la France au XVIe siècle', résumé in *8e Congrès intern. des Science hist. Paris* (1939), pp. 536–40.

25. Clouard, op. cit., p. 892.

26. Ibid., description of Amable Moreau's shop.

27. A fact well brought out by Hauser, 'La Question des prix et des monnaies en Bourgogne dans la seconde moitié du XVIe siècle', *Annales de Bourgogne* (1932), iv. 7–12. For the Velay see *Mémoires de Jean Burel*, published by Chassaing (Le Puy, 1875), pp. 319 and 320.

28. Cf. Hamilton, *American Treasure and the Price Revolution in Spain: 1501–1650* (Cambridge, Mass., 1934).

29. Compare the several series given by Hauser, *Recherches et documents sur l'histoire des prix* (Paris, 1936).

30. One of the clearest signs of this deflation is the general fall in interest rates, noted in the heart of the French provinces as well as in Holland and England: Latouche, *La Vie en Bas Quercy du XIVe au XVIIIe siècle* (Paris, 1923), p. 289. For Holland see more particularly the interest rates charged by the Amsterdam Bank to the East India company in J. G. van Dillen, *Bronnen tot de geschiedenis der wisselbank* (The Hague, 1925), p. 949.

31. In a Mémoire of 1636 is this reflection: 'France supplies foreigners with hardly any goods but those whose production is always accompanied by more trouble and risk than profit', Bibl. Nat. MS. fr. 18503, f. 85v.

32. They had been engaged on it from the sixteenth century. For England see J. U. Nef in *The Economic History Review*, vol. v (1934), vol. vii (1937), also in *The Journal of Political Economy*, vol. xliv (1936). On the distinction in France between 'active' and 'passive' capital see Doucet, 'La richesse en France', article in *Revue d'histoire moderne*, p. 299.

33. 'Mémoire au Roi sur les finances', Arch. Nat. K 899, item No. 4, in P. Clément, *Lettres, instructions et mémoires de Colbert*, vii. 233 ff.

34. Ibid., p. 234.

35. Ibid., p. 236.

4

The Age of Don Quixote

PIERRE VILAR

Translated by Richard Morris*

CENTENARIES have some value; they remind us that masterpieces have dates. Too often today intellectual history is treated as a discontinuous series of isolated wholes. The reality of history is thus rejected. But each masterpiece distils for us a rich potion of real history which can be enjoyed by those not frightened of the prospect. The truth is that *Don Quixote*, that 'universal' and 'eternal' work, remains first and foremost a Spanish book published in 1605; it is only in its historical context that it assumes its full meaning.

1. THE CRISIS OF POWER AND CONSCIENCE IN SPAIN, 1598–1620

It has often been said that it would be fruitless to look to Cervantes for an interpretation of the 'decadence' of his country, 'because he could not have foreseen it'.[1] This is to misunderstand completely the chronology of events. For if the word 'crisis' really means the passage from rise to collapse, then it is certainly between 1598 and 1620, between its greatness and decadence, that we must locate the decisive crisis of Spanish power, and, with even greater certainty, the first great crisis of doubt of the Spanish people. Now the two parts of *Don Quixote* were published in 1605 and 1615.

It is true there is room for discussion. The Castilian currency did not collapse until 1625; Iberian unity lasted until 1640 and the famous Infantry until 1643. Furthermore, it was almost a century before, as early as 1558 that, following a well-known state bankruptcy, Luiz Ortiz's 'Memorial' had expressed the first (but not the least vigorous) of the gloomy predictions of the future health of Spain.

The reign of Philip II had seen so many swings from hope to despair that the threatened people were encouraged to believe in miracles. St. Quentin had erased the memory of bankruptcy, as had Lepanto the revolt of the *moriscos* and of the Sea Beggars. At the time of the Armada's dispersal, the union of Spain and Portugal—the kingdom of the three Oceans—had not been in existence ten years. Spain gave the impression of being if not at the beginning of its adventure then at least at its height. Silver was arriving from the Indies in greater abundance than ever. To aristocratic ears, the com-

* From 'Le Temps du "Quichotte" ', *Europe*, xxxiv (1956), 3–16.

plaints of the Cortes no doubt sounded like the trivial whinings of the petit bourgeois.

Such signs, however, always have some significance. Scarcely had the old king died in the Escorial in the autumn of 1598 than far-seeing Spaniards dared already to confess; decline was starting. Others thought it was the edge of the abyss. In the prologue to a memorandum presented to Philip III in 1600 one can read that since the virtues of the new prince were equal to those of the deceased king, the commonwealth could rest assured of its resurgence 'however low it might have fallen'. Was this a piece of insolence? The context would indicate not, but this manner of demolishing the entire rhetorical effect in six words was to become the favourite device (now quite calculated) upon which *Don Quixote* was to be built. The moment was to come when Spain would set reality and myth face to face, for better or for worse.

The year 1600 brought harsh realities. At the height of the great price rise of the sixteenth century in which Spain had led the way, the climb suddenly steepened. Andalusian corn rose from 430 *maravedís* the *fanega* in 1595 to 1,041 in 1598; Castilian corn from 408 in 1595 to 908 in 1599. And even then, the true rise cannot be measured accurately. In spite of regular evasion, taxation was imposed here and there.[2] But then it was the producer who suffered: during the last five years of the century pamphlets abounded for or against the *tasa del pan*, for or against public granaries or *montipos*. A Doctor Cristobel Pérez de Herrera, who practised his medicine on the galleys, wanted to organize some kind of poor relief. Repressive measures against the vagabonds were all that finally came out of it. From 1599 to 1601, 'the hunger coming up from Andalusia' met 'the plague descending from Castile':[3] this was the bubonic plague, the most terrible of all, but this time not imported from the Mediterranean, for it originated quite simply, as Herrera tells us, 'among the poor divested of all means of support'. 'Almost all Spain' —especially the interior—was ravaged by it.[4]

Now such losses of human life—a familiar feature of old economies—are usually soon made good, but in this case the scourge was attacking an already worn-out population living in overpopulated towns and barren countrysides. This deficit in human life was to last. After 1600, the 'depopulation' of Spain, the hackneyed textbook theme, can be seen in the wages and the census figures. A Castilian gardener, paid 3,470 *maravedís* in 1599, received 9,000 in 1603. The real wage of the Spanish worker made a jump unique in its history between 1601 and 1610.[5] But this cannot be interpreted as a worker's golden age because there were scarcely any *paid* workers to be found. The Castilian tenant or the *morisco* demi-serf still scratched a bare living from the difficult soil. The price of grain continued to fluctuate wildly: the price of one *fanega* of Andalusian corn rose from 204 to 1,301 *maravedís* between 1602 and 1605. Once more there was famine. The dearness (or rather the absence) of a labour-force spelt death for the economy of Castile. In 1620 the subject of the profusion of pamphlets was no longer the 'bread tax', but instead the alarming invasion of foreign goods.

All the more so because the general level of prices began to decline after 1601. It was the same turning-point, but the outcome was different. The stream of silver from the Indies began to slow up; that is, it arrived costing more. Over in Mexico and Peru too, exploitation of man had found its limits. An immense fall in population[6] forced the owners of mines to turn their efforts to the semi-feudal agricultural sphere.[7] The rise of world silver prices was to stop—and in Spain first of all. One of the mechanisms of colonial parasitism, which had been supporting the country artificially far above its means, had just come to a halt.

Could Spain afford to be resigned? The sumptuous way of life of the nobles, the enormous State expenditure, and the general indebtedness together made resignation impossible. Receiving less good money and lavishing it externally, Spain took to minting an inferior quality for internal use. The century saw the beginning of the striking on a large scale of pure copper coin—the contemporary equivalent of printing bank-notes. Between 1600 and 1610, the Cortes and the financial theorists unceasingly criticized this policy and predicted catastrophe.[8]

The economic drug of inflation was joined in 1609 by a social drug, when public alarm was distracted by the expulsion of the *moriscos*. These people, the remainder of the vanquished Moors, had been forcibly converted, but never completely assimilated. Some were carters, some shopkeepers, but mostly peasants living in a closed community, serving the great Lords of the *Reconquista*: Spain had a colonial problem on its own soil which was to drag on for two centuries without solution.[9] After so many rebellions, repressions, expulsions, and massive population transfers, the threat of a general uprising in 1600 was probably unfounded. But because of the mistrust felt for the false Christian, the *mala casta*, the spy, the plunderer, the smuggler enriching himself with ducats, the *morisco* became the providential scape-goat for a time of crisis. He was said to be 'too prolific' and 'living on nothing':[10] these were the real grievances. The Castilian middle classes, on the verge of financial ruin, were envious of the colonial labour-force available to the great Lords. After the expulsion, the latter obtained cancellation of their debts to counter-balance the loss.[11] Instead of striking at the feudal economy, the measure therefore struck at its creditors: the rich farmers and the middle classes. Thus we should acknowledge the once-disputed importance of the expulsion, particularly since we must accept the figure of 500,000 departures.[12] The kingdom of Valencia lost a good third of its inhabitants. Once the operation was over, the public which had demanded it, and which had proclaimed it a holy work, remained unsatisfied.[13]

Needless to say, this turmoil was echoed by a similar crisis within the State machine. Don Quixote woke up one morning beneath a mass of hanged bandits and surrounded by forty living bandits, 'which makes me realize that I am not far from Barcelona'.[14] Mere fiction? No, the plain reality. It is, yet again, between 1605 and 1615 that one must date the worst period of Catalan brigandage. The Viceroy Almazán, not wanting to be taken for a nonentity ('por un palo'), burned and hanged; but the bandits who were put in prison negotiated with his wife and daughter.[15] His successor, Albuquerque, threatened the whole 'principality with the galleys'; but he had to reach Barcelona by sea. On land 'the brigands are more masters than the king' wrote the Bishop of Vic.[16] The situation was so bad it almost constituted revolt. Like Don Quixote, the people had sympathy for the bandit chiefs, and attempts to suppress them met with no success.[17] Thus, a prelude to the coming separatism, Madrid mistrusted Barcelona and Barcelona criticized Madrid. One of the city's envoys to the court complained 'that our country is infested by bandits, who have their centre at our city gates. All this is wrongfully imputed to us and we are treated like black slaves ... our affairs are in the hands of people who dislike us and who do not understand anything of our problems ... they enjoy themselves feasting, hunting, and gambling, while the world and its problems go up in smoke ...' This was Brother Franch in 1614. In the following year, a lawyer Rosell wrote:

The King and his ministers work so slowly in everything that it is the greatest pity in the world. They importune ambassadors from the Pope, from the King of France, from Venice, from the Emperor, and from others all in order to quiet the troubles in Italy. They can never make up their minds but, if this continues, they will be forced in the end to a less honourable decision ... It is now two years since our enemies began to stir up trouble in the Philippines. No resolution was taken and now we learn that they have taken control of all the islands, destroying a large garrison. In short, our good King may be a saint, but he is never finished with his scruples. His ministers prefer to gamble all night and to get up at noon, rather than to see to the war. All the talk is about the Duke of Lerma's festivities. Those who are in trouble complain in vain.

To have an audience with 'those gentlemen' one had to spend three days in the antechambers of confidants and confessors, but this did not bring a halt to bureaucracy. 'The amount of work done here on reports and memoranda is quite beyond belief, and not one out of ten people consulted knows what is going on.'[18]

We here touch upon a well-known evil—the mania on the part of the *arbitristas* for reports and memoranda. It is however advisable to distinguish between the street-corner tip sold for 1 *real* (this did happen), the technician's suggestions or the guild's complaints, and the ideas of the *república* which were in the jurist's study or in the monk's cell. But this plethora makes one fact quite clear, namely that the crisis was as acute in men's minds as it was in reality. In reproaching the historian for ascribing modern feelings to a people of an earlier period, one is subscribing to the view that the *Konjunkturforschung* first revealed the feeling of bankruptcy to shopkeepers or that the trade-union newspapers first made hunger known to the unemployed. As much ink was spilled in giving advice in the Spain of 1600 as in the United States of 1930. Most of it was nonsense, with the exception of a few brilliant pages (for the short-sighted *arbitristas* could see only the short-term crisis). But in the last analysis, the real interpreter was in the one case Cervantes and in the other Charlie Chaplin, since the wreck of a world and its values has about it something of a tragi-comic flavour.

For the drama of 1600 went beyond Spain. It heralded the difficult times of the seventeenth century which were experienced all over Europe, and which are now recognized as the 'general crisis' of an entire society.[19] Cervantes pronounced an ironic, cruel, yet tender farewell to that way of life and to those very feudal values whose disappearance in the world the Spanish conquerors had unwittingly promoted; and, paradoxically, whose survival in their own country they had fostered at the cost of ruin. The secret of Don Quixote is to be sought within this original dialectic of Spanish imperialism.

2. SPANISH IMPERIALISM—THE SUPREME STAGE OF FEUDALISM

The developmental rhythm of productive forces in western Europe began to make manifest the first demands of profound social change during the last third of the fifteenth century.[20] The growth of population, the extension of cultures and new techniques combined together in different ways in different countries—but with one major and global consequence: the devaluation of ordinary goods in the face of rare produce and precious metal. A twofold race resulted: a race after treasure and a race after territory. Portugal seemed to win the first, but it was Spain that finally won both at the same time.

The conquest of Granada, raids on Africa, and the Discoveries had already offered to the Castile of the Catholic Kings treasure, land, and a servile labour-force. Machiavelli's Prince, Ferdinand, founded the modern mercantile state. The empire 'where the sun never sets' finished by adding to its already rich Italo-Flemish heritage the mines of America and the spices of the east. The poor and backward Spain of today too readily conceals from us the domineering Spain of old, head of one of the most powerful empires ever to have existed.

But why was the fall even more rapid than the rise? Have we not, from Montesquieu through to modern scholarship,[21] written much more on the subject than the *arbitristas* of 1600? Arid land, deforestation, agricultural decline, emigration, expulsion, excessive mortmain, alms-giving and religious vocation, vagabondage, scorn for work, the craze for nobility, entails, high prices, high wages, taxes, wars, weaknesses of favourites and kings: these 'causes' of decadence are too numerous for one to ignore the overlapping of cause and effects, the 'general crisis' in which political impotence, productive inefficiency, and social decay were integrally bound together.

Cantillon, in a schematic analysis, saw the situation in greater depth:

When the over-abundance of silver from the mines has diminished the population of a State, when it has accustomed those remaining to too much spending;
when it has raised to excessive heights the cost of labour and of the produce of
the earth, has ruined State manufactures because landowners and mineworkers
use foreign goods, the money produced by those mines will of necessity be used
for purchasing abroad and little by little this will impoverish the State ... The
wide circulation of silver, which was general at the beginning, now stops. Poverty
and misery follow ... This is roughly what has happened to Spain since the discovery of the Indies ...[22]

A remarkable analysis, but one which is limited to purely economic
mechanisms; in order to examine the social ones, it will be necessary to have
recourse to Marxist terminology.

In so far as it instituted the *world market* and in so far as it permitted the
primitive accumulation of capital, by pouring cheap silver into Europe, the
Spanish Conquest founded a new society. Such a society, however, could only
develop with increased productive forces and with new social relationships.
This is what was to come about in northern Europe. In Spain, on the other
hand, or rather in Castile, the ruling classes managed the Conquest as they
had the *Reconquista*, namely, *in the feudal manner*. To occupy land, sub-
jugate the inhabitants, and carry off their riches was no way to prepare for
investment in the capitalist sense of the word. A nascent bourgeoisie could
have invested, and between 1480 and 1550 roughly, it did not fail to do so;
but because of its position on the monetary circuit, its first contact was with
the unstable kind of capitalism typical of ports and fairs. Furthermore, the
'productive forces' at Castile's disposal—land, men, and technical innovation
—came up particularly quickly against the law of diminishing returns. This
was the reason for the largely sterile effect of the money that was being
injected into the country. People spent freely, imported, and lent money for
interest; but little was produced. Prices and salaries soared. Parasitism prevailed and enterprise died; only poverty was left for the morrow.

There is however another cause of ruin not mentioned by Cantillon which
should not be overlooked. Imperialism also has its political aspect. If the
silver which came privately from the Indies was finally to serve only to
balance foreign imports, that which arrived for the king was committed in
advance into the hands of the bankers, in Augsburg and later in Genoa. High
politics diverted away from Spanish soil the wealth which footed the bill for
nascent capitalist production in Europe. From 1570 onwards, the king had
to fight his own subjects; by initiating the costly war in the Netherlands, the
'Gueux', who represented the most advanced bourgeois nation, challenged
the Catholic and feudal empire of Philip II. Thus it was that Spanish
imperialism indeed represented the 'supreme stage' of the society it had
helped to destroy. But on home soil in Castile in 1600 or thereabouts, feudal-

ism went into its death-agony without there being anything to replace it. The drama was to last; it exists to the present day. This is why Don Quixote has remained a symbol.

3. PARADOXES OF A CONDEMNED SOCIETY

One should not be too hasty to accuse the author of dealing in abstract dialectics lest one be bound also to accuse writers of the period of the same thing. 'So then,' wrote the *licenciado* Martín González de Cellorigo, 'if there is no gold and silver coin in Spain, it is precisely because she possesses both; and it is her richness that constitutes her poverty: despite the logical impossibility of reconciling these two contradictory statements, they must both be regarded as true in our Spain.'[23] The *arbitrista* theologian who in 1600 wrote this stab at scholasticism did not do so purely for the sake of form. He penetrated to the heart of the matter better than did Cantillon. He noted the opposition between the productive and the parasitical masses. Although he no doubt exaggerated the relative importance of the latter, he at least revealed clearly the role played by public indebtedness (the *juros*) and by private indebtedness (the *censos*); because of this, the guarantee offered by the silver coming from the Indies caused inflation of paper titles. Anticipating Lenin, he described for us what happens to people when they try to 'squeeze out maximum dividends'.

And the whole trouble stems from the fact that they have scorned society's natural foundations, and that they have adopted the destructive attitude of all commonwealths: the belief that richness lies only in money and in the interest from that money. The securities which yield this interest have plunged the country into the depths of poverty, as a widespread plague might have done; for all Spaniards, or the majority at least, have been eager to live off their securities and revenues without stopping to think from where the means to support such a way of life could possibly come.

Deceived by the certainty of profit from these securities, the shopkeeper gives up his business, the artisan his trade, the farmer abandons his fields, the shepherd leaves his sheep, and the nobleman sells his lands, exchanging the hundred which they are worth for five hundred in securities. But the fact remains that they do not realize that if everyone does the same, the real revenue from such holdings will become exhausted and money will go up in smoke. Let us take the example of a ploughman who, in addition to meeting his own needs, has to pay the local Lord, the bondholder, the tithe-collector, the tax-farmer, and others who have some claim on the land. One may guess that throughout the entire hierarchy the proportion of workers to non-workers is one to thirty. This is the reason for the frequent legal recourse against creditors, for the accumulation of letters relating to payments falling due, and for the large number of people cornered into borrowing who would otherwise be forced to dishonour their own obligations. This system of unearned income is supporting an army of distrainment officers, many of whom have doubtful consciences, who serve only to destroy the nobility and the whole body of the State ...

Wealth has not sent its roots deep because it has never come down to earth, remaining in the form of papers, bills of exchange, and gold and silver coin—and not in the form of goods capable of yield or of attracting foreign wealth through interior strength.[24]

Finally, Cellorigo wrote:
'It really seems as if we have been trying to make of this commonwealth a commonwealth of enchanted men who live outside the natural order of things.'

That was written in 1600—'the enchanted man who lives outside the natural order of things'. Upon this man Cervantes was in 1605 to bestow immortality. The remarkable thing about Cellorigo was that he detected the divorce between his country's way of life and its economic situation, forcefully contrasting the illusory, mythical, mystical superstructure with the parasitical character of the society of his day.

Now this example is not fortuitous. When, at the turn of the century, the harsh reality of the crisis began to destroy the illusions born of inflation and the Indies, the device of 'contradictory statements' invaded the works of many writers. Spain is rich—she is poor. She has the Indies—she is the 'Indies' of the foreigner. She is having a feast—while her people die of starvation. She runs an empire—but she has no more men. In a context of scholastic and Latin-based rhetoric, one may guess that such antitheses were in danger of passing unheeded. But, for the moment at least, the *arbitristas* were saved from banality by their touching love for their commonwealth and by their naïve hope of a return to a more realistic attitude.

Indeed, their greyest pages are suddenly illuminated by a tender anxiety, as when Cellorigo wrote: '*our* Spain'. It is really with him (and not sooner despite some over-early diagnoses) that the passion for analysis and the feeling of vital insecurity experienced by Spaniards for their country triumphed, a feeling which has been well defined, though incorrectly dated, by Américo Castro.[25] Here, as elsewhere, the historian's job is to 'date accurately' rather than to make hasty generalizations. Round about 1600, the *textes en séries*, the only valid collective evidence, never ceased to emphasize the three creative realities: *population*, *production*, and *labour*. But after 1620, and particularly after 1626, thinkers tended more and more to take refuge in mysticism, rationalism, 'laudatio temporis acti', and at times in defiance or even absurdity. At the high point where these two currents separate stood the smiling face of Cervantes.

4. THE SOCIAL FOUNDATIONS OF SPANISH IRRATIONALITY

It would of course be well worthwhile to analyse in greater depth the social foundations of this Spanish irrationality—but there would not be the space.

The polarization of wealth at different levels produced nothing of long-standing value. The huge revenues of feudal or colonial origin permitted lives of gay intrigue; but if these revenues fell (which they in fact did) the

lord went into debt; as for example did the *moriscos*' overlords and the duke
who played the high-living host to Don Quixote and Sancho.

Among the bourgeois of 1600 there remained from the previous century
virtually nothing of the wealth of bankers and rich merchants, of whom Mercado said: 'although they embraced a world and an ocean, they retained so
little that everything collapsed about them'.[26] Already the son of the bank-
rupt, Guzmán de Alfarache, had become a *pícaro* and was to finish on the
galleys.

There was, to be sure, the village potentate. Several of Cervantes's villagers
bore the epithet 'rich', which defined a typical exception: the peasant who
was capable of amassing money. Usually he was a usurer, a tax-farmer, a
hoarder in time of famine. But the universal *kulak*, who was elsewhere
potentially bourgeois, was in Spain condemned by inflation to assume the role
of a permanent *nouveau riche* whose money was no sooner earned than devalued, so quickly indeed that it seemed best to spend it all on Gargantuan
weddings. He might have lent it at a high interest, but to poor repayers, be
they poverty-stricken (the poor peasant had to get into debt to live) or powerful (including the king). 'Enterprise' did not pay. So, after the old style, the
wealthy man ate, hired servants, entertained, gave (alms, etc.), stole, and in
turn was robbed. Because of its peculiar position and circumstances (and not
because of religion or temperament) Spanish society in 1600, the antithesis
of puritan society, turned its back on savings and investment.

The wealthy *ate*—so much so that doctors were worried. Dr. Herrera, who
styled himself 'doctor of the galleys, of the king, and of the kingdom' only
dared to suggest a limitation of four to six courses a meal, so many entrées,
so many desserts.[27] A happy mean! Unfortunately, the guests invited to these
feasts were few. The starving masses dreamt only of gleaning the scraps, or
of gaining access by pure chance, as Sancho did when he became governor.
(One understands only too well why he gave such a poor welcome to the
doctor instructed to supervise at the dinner-table!) Hunger and feasting:
these were the *pícaro*'s two obsessive dreams.

Even in less well-off circumstances the Spaniard hired servants. The blind
beggar had always had his servant.[28] The humanist confined by the In-
quisition kept four servants with him.[29] The *arbitristas* regarded the wearing
of a ruff as a scourge since the upkeep of this garment required specialized
and highly paid valets; and it cost as much as it was worth to have it
smoothed out and ironed a few times.[30] To be 'in service' brought in as much
as 'practising a trade', and many trades were in fact pure 'service'. One
would be glad of the opportunity, with regard to Spain in the sixteenth century, to work out the figures for the massive transfer of the active population
to the non-productive sector, that 'tertiary' sector which today is held up as
an example and consequence of progress, but which of course for Spain of
the period represented only social parasitism and the ensuing decline.

The Spaniard gave. The accumulated wealth of the Church maintained a growing number of non-producers. Now for capitalism to emerge, beggars must become paid workers, and this never happened in Spain, despite favour from certain quarters.[31] It was not 'temperament' that prevented it happening, but rather an economic climate in which the rich man could afford to be generous, and in which the poor man was better off living from hand to mouth than accepting wages which, in the face of rising prices, held less promise than a life of adventure.

Finally, the Spaniard stole and allowed himself to be robbed. The servant's 'levy' on his master's finances, petty thievery (the *sisa*), was in evidence at all social levels:[32] the family, the community, and the administration. Cervantes, once a professional soldier, who had held a charge as a collector, would seem to have practised it clumsily, since he was found out and sent to prison. As he himself put it later: 'necessity' on the one hand and 'opportunity' on the other could lead so easily to the galleys. This is why Don Quixote frees the galley-slaves.[33] In Catalonia, a frontier country, more dynamic and less charitable, social unrest produced more bandits than beggars and *picaros*. In cahoots with aristocratic groups, gangs of bandits had their agents in offices and banks[34] whose job it was to earmark convoys of good coin (counterfeit —*boscatera*—was produced in the woods).

All in all, it was a picturesque society, more likeable in many ways than puritan society. In other ways, however, it was rotten and in any case doomed. The law of production, which in other countries was more quickly appreciated, brought about its inexorable results. Detached from reality, Spain in 1600 preferred to dream.

Cellorigo, Deça, and even Cervantes tell us that, in the hope of a better life, people put their faith not only in the expulsion of the *moriscos* but also in plague![35] Both would enable them to appropriate their neighbour's inheritance! This no doubt because 'rich uncle in America' was less generous to them; for of course all derives ultimately from the huge mirage of the Indies. Spain, said Deça, was truly flourishing only when her inhabitants, from the Pyrenees to the sea, 'had no reason to wander off, and when her aspirations for the future were not based upon fresh embarkations but rather upon the exploitation of their land, their flocks, their fish, their trades, and their *own* affairs'.[36]

Don Quixote's housekeeper shouted at Sancho: 'Go till your plot of land and govern your house, and cease to think of the Islands and their inhabitants.'[37]

Cervantes issued his warning as much for the benefit of Sancho and the Spanish people who felt they were gaining something by imitating their masters, as for the benefit of Don Quixote who derived from books his idealistic interpretation of his forefathers' exploits.

From books: this is the last point under consideration. The growth of the

non-productive sector in Spanish society was not limited to the material services; the same trend can also be seen in the intellectual field, in the writers
who captivated and put their public under a spell—in the good and bad
senses of the term. There were the jurists[38] and the *arbitristas* (the bad were
heeded more than the good); there were also the hawkers of legends. A flood
of literature swept through the Madrid of Phillip III: Góngora, the most
perfect of pure poets, was of the period under review. Mateo Alemán, who
best described the 'sick' life of the *picaro*, published the two parts of the
Guzmán in 1599 and 1604. Lope de Vega—the theatre was the only national
product to continue merrily supplying its demand. Now the masses in the
provinces were as greedy as the élite at Court; but both, through lack of anything better, fell under the spell of peddled picaresque novels, rose-coloured
pastorals, and adventurous chivalresque romances. The Spanish villagers
were fooled by the exploits of these puppets as much as we today fall for the
most outworn and dated westerns. Any escape is better than none. And those
with the most leisure are invariably the easiest fooled, such as Don Quixote.

Thus in the twilight of a society spent by the course of history, in the
country which had carried her contradictions to extremes, there came the
moment when a severe crisis began to disclose her defects. Her streets were
overrun with idle men-about-town, ruined rentiers, and impressive gangsters,
while the unemployed were reduced to begging in them. Clerks existed on
pure art and the average man on twopenny-halfpenny literature. This was the
background from which emerged a masterpiece which fixed for ever in image
form the tragi-comic clash between the mythical superstructure and the
reality of human relations. If it was a light-hearted work with the old anec-
dotes and classic grimaces, it was also a parody, one which far surpassed its
worthy models, of every aspect of the art of escapism. It did not portray the
world but, better than any learned treatise, it revealed its inner workings
with strokes of genius. 'The soul of this soulless world' was the puppet (Don
Quixote) overwhelmed with misfortune and pursued by fantasies who, in the
tattered garb of an outdated respectability, lived twenty lives (with a single
love-affair): he rose to the defence of honour, weakness, friendship, and the
homeland; he captured princes and addressed long speeches to the world.
His life was an anachronism and therefore of little practical use, but it
affirmed the value of human kindness and was a reserve of sympathy: a
comforting sign for the future, therefore. From the refined amateur of pure
poetry to the hunger-threatened pauper, the bygone age was evoked and
admired in the character of the hero. The crisis had thrown up an interpreter
to match.

I have written of 1605–15, of Cervantes, of Don Quixote with his helmet
and armour. I might well have written of 1929–39, of Charlie Chaplin, of
'Charlot', with his black jacket, bowler, and cane. Never were two masterpieces more nearly akin. The two great stages of modern history have been

treated in precisely the same way. We would admire Cervantes less if we were not part of the age of Charlie Chaplin.

But let us not insist too much on this; let us not persuade some minister that Chaplin and Cervantes, these 'entertainers', these 'character actors', are also 'social novelists'. Their work would be promptly banned.

NOTES

1. A. P. V. Morel-Fatio, *Études sur l'Espagne* (Paris, 1888–1904), pp. 1, 330. A. Castro, *El pensamiento de Cervantes* (Madrid, 1925), p. 219.

2. E. J. Hamilton, *American Treasure and the Price Revolution in Spain* (Cambridge, Mass., 1934), appendix V. In Old Castile, the quoted prices are tax prices and not market prices.

3. So says Mateo Alemán in *Guzmán de Alfarache* (1599).

4. 'Dubitationes ad maligni popularisque morbi qui nunc in tota fere Hispania grassatur exactam medellam ... a Doctore Ch. Perez a Herrera' (Madrid, 1599), f. 3. Martín González de Cellorigo, *Memorial de la política necessaria y útil restauración de la república de España* (Valladolid, 1600), First part.

5. Hamilton, op. cit., Ch.: 'Wages; money and real', and appendix VII.

6. Woodrow Borah, *New Spain's century of depression* (Los Angeles, 1951), gives: Mexico, 1519: 11,000,000 inhabitants; 1597: 2,500,000; 1607: 2,000,000.

7. F. Chevalier, *La Formation des grands domaines au Mexique* (Paris, 1952), p. 234.

8. Actas de la Cortes (Castilla): xviii. 157, 568, 596, xix. 443, etc. and P. J. de Mariana, *Tratado de la moneda de vellón que al presente se labra en Castilla* (1609) (among others).

9. F. Braudel, *La Méditerranée et le monde méditerranéen à l'époque de Philippe II* (Paris, 1949), pp. 576–82.

10. Cervantes, *Coloquio de los perros* (*Obras*, ed. Aguilar, 1825). He takes up (ironically?) these two arguments which were very common in the twenty or so works justifying expulsion.

11. Regla Campistol, 'La expulsión de los moriscos y sus consecuencias', *Hispania* vols. li, lii (1953), shows the importance of this hitherto neglected fact.

12. Ibid., against Hamilton who reduced the number to 100,000 and contested the economic consequences of the expulsion on the grounds that wages did not rise. (But could they rise yet again?)

13. This dissatisfaction was felt earlier by some people: 'May the Lord take me before I see such evils without being able to help' (The patriarch of Valencia to Phillip III, 19 Dec. 1608).

14. *Don Quijote*, ii. 60.

15. Municipal Archives of Barcelona. Private papers 1612. f. 196.

16. F. Soldevila, *Historia de Catalunya* (Barcelona, 1934–5), ii. 258, n. 4, text of 1615.

17. Gilabert, *Discursos sobre la calidad del Principado de Cataluña*. Disc. I, f. 9v.

18. Municipal archives Barcelona. 'Cartas comunes originales', 1614, p. 15.

19. E. J. Hobsbawm, 'The general crisis of the European economy in the seventeenth century', *Past and Present*, Nos. 5 and 6 (1954).

20. Everything in this matter confirms Engels's opinion (cf. letter to Lafargue, *Économie et politique* (Mar. 1955), p. 14).

21. Cf., in the way of recent work, the special numbers of *De Económica* (Madrid, Sept. and Dec. 1953). ('Sobre la decadencia económica de España') and Hamilton, 'The decline of Spain', *Econ Hist. Rev.*, viii. 168–79.

22. Cantillon, 'Essai sur la nature du commerce en général', uned., 91–2.

23. Cellorigo, op. cit., f. 29r.

24. Ibid.

25. A. Castro, *La realidad histórica de España* (Mexico, 1954) ch. i.

26. Fray Tomás de Mercado, *Suma de tratos y contratos* (ed. Seville, 1571), iv. 67.

27. Herrera, *Remedios para el bien de la salud del cuerpo de la República* (1610), f. 15r.

28. The 'moço de ciego', hero of *Lazarillo*, the first picaresque novel.

29. M. Bataillon, *Érasme et l'Espagne* (Mexico), ii. p. 51. [Translator's note: the much revised Mexico ed. bore the Spanish title *Erasmo y España*.]

30. Lison y Viedma, *Discursos y apuntamientos* (1622), vol. i.

31. Among those in favour in the controversy of 1545 was the very modern Juan de Medina and in 1599 (although for different reasons) Dr. Herrera, *Amparo de los pobres*.

32. Herrera, *Remedios*, 'not a course arrives at table but that half its content has been deducted'.

33. *Don Quijote*, i. 22.

34. Soler y Terol, *Perot Roca Guinarda* (Manresa, 1909), and J. Carrera Pujal, *Historia económica y política de Cataluña* (Barcelona, 1946–7), ii. 4 and Regla Campistol, *Est. Hist. Moderna*, iv (1954), 197, 199.

35. Cellorigo, op. cit., First part. Cervantes, *Coloquio*, not quoted.

36. Lope de Deça, *Govierno de Agricultura* (1618), f. 22r.

37. *Don Quijote*, ii. 2.

38. Deça, op. cit., f. 26v. The law faculties left agriculture bereft of manpower.

5

The Atlantic Economy and the World Economy[1]

PIERRE AND HUGUETTE CHAUNU

Translated by Elizabeth Mortimer[*]

I

THE Spanish Atlantic is the oldest of all the Atlantics known to historians. It came into being during the two decades following the fateful year 1492. The beginnings of this ocean, which, in the middle of the twentieth century, carries more than 400 million tons of merchandise (70 per cent of the world's sea trade), were modest indeed by the standards of today: by those of that period, none the less, the volume of trade was already a presage of future greatness. It is of course impossible to know exactly what proportion of all the Atlantic trades of the period fell specifically to the Spanish Atlantic. Studies corresponding to the present work have yet to be made for Portugal, France, England, and Holland. It seems, however, that until about 1600 the Spanish Atlantic remained the most important; until the end of the sixteenth century the trade between Spain and America appears to have been the dominant part, indeed virtually the whole, of the trade between Europe and America. Under pressure from 1600 to 1650, it must none the less have accounted for more than half the total until about 1630–40.

A detailed account of the Spanish–American trade, from 1504 to 1650, was therefore eminently desirable. Our contribution to the world of learning will be the large-scale work on this subject which we have compiled in the way described below, and which will shortly be completed and published.[2] It comprises, in some 2,500 pages, a full reconstruction of outward and homeward voyages of ships throughout this long period, and a partial one of the goods transported in them. In the meantime, we thought it worthwhile to give the following brief outline.

The state of economic archives being what it is, it may appear surprising that a study of this kind has proved possible.[3] We owe it to two pieces of good luck: the extreme concentration within Spain of the trade with

* From 'Économie atlantique. Économie mondiale', *Cahiers d'histoire mondiale*, i (1953), 91–104.

America, and the solicitude of the Spanish state for a trade which, while not run by the state, was not a free trade either.

Much has been written on the Seville monopoly;[4] its existence is less paradoxical than it may seem: Castile does not possess many good ports on the Atlantic coast which are linked to a vast hinterland of plains. The only possible hesitation would have been between Andalusia and Cantabria; Andalusia took the lead right from the start, sharing its monopoly with the ship-building north; the south offered its ports, and the wealth of its agricultural hinterland. It is therefore possible (with a few notable exceptions) to study Spanish–American trade by studying Seville alone, provided that by 'Seville' is understood a vast port-complex, including notably Seville itself, San Lúcar, and on its rock, south of the Guadalquivir, the old Phoenician site of Cadiz; and beyond, the various harbours of the Canaries, a kind of extreme outpost thrown far out into the Atlantic by the Guadalquivir. The Spanish state, which in its Atlantic policy was barely distinguishable from the group of men in Andalusia who conducted the business, kept a strict check on the observance of the monopoly, which had the advantage (among others) of facilitating effective state supervision. And it is the efficiency of this supervision which makes possible the efficiency of the modern historian.

The second piece of good luck hinges on the first. Not only was this trade virtually under state control (or the state under Seville control): from 1503 onwards it was kept under close bureaucratic supervision by the *Casa de la Contratación* (beginning in fact before 1503, but formalized from then on). Very soon offices were proliferating in Seville; their growth kept pace with that of the trade itself, and the documents emanating from the services of the *Casa de la Contratación* form the main body of our documentation: the papers of the *Contratación* itself (more than 5,000 files in the *Archivo de Indias*), and parts of the *Contaduria* papers and of the *Indiferente general de la Seccion Quinta*. The activity of the Spanish Atlantic—of its ships, its men, and its merchandise—is all there: you only need to go and look for it.

This is not such an easy task, however, for it has frightened off such historians[5] as have given some thought to the problem. The difficulty is twofold: it lies both in the sheer volume of the documents (some 10,000 files) and, perhaps even more, in their incompleteness. It is true that the greater part of these archives has the rare good fortune to have travelled very little (the *Casa Lonja* housed the *Casa de la Contratación* and its offices before the *Archivo General de Indias*); but time has done its work—and men theirs. A mere glance at the catalogues, then at the files, gives a rough idea of the inroads made by haphazard destruction.

Only an Ariadne's thread could lead us through this mass of archives, and give the measure of its gaps; but such a thread exists: it is the *Libro de Registros*.

We do not claim to have discovered this unique document;[6] at most we have found a methodical way of using it. It comes in the form of several thick, bound ledgers, in which are entered, from 1504 to 1786, the ships entering and leaving the port of Seville and its annexes, with the name of the ship, the ship's master, and, from 1548 onwards, its destination and place of origin. Occasionally other facts are noted: events taking place on the voyage; ships plundered or sunk; a few dates; a great number of things, in short, but hard to interpret. The *Libro de Registros* is full of afterthoughts and second thoughts. A full understanding of it requires a precise knowledge of the way in which it was compiled. These and other difficulties no doubt explain why some excellent historians have passed by this precious document without according it the attention it deserves.

There is a further and more serious difficulty: is the *Libro de Registros* complete? Most of the historians who have tackled this problem have refused to solve it. In fact, a careful study of the administration of the *Casa de la Contratación* and of the services which compiled this *Libro de Registros* enables us to answer: 'Yes, the *Libro* is complete.' But in order to reach this conclusion, we first had to go through the whole mass of archives concerning trade between Spain and America. We found that not a single document, whatever its source, contained a reference to a ship which ought to have been entered in the *Libro de Registros* but was missing from it. 'Ought to have been entered?' *There* is the third and most serious difficulty.

For the only ships recorded are merchantmen or warships officially engaged in trade i.e. carrying a register. There were therefore, besides the merchantmen, a whole series of ships which escaped supervision. A list of these had to be drawn up from other documents: warships, the king's ships, etc. It is precisely the absence, or at least the deceptively haphazard presence, of these *armada* ships in the *Libro de Registros* that has raised doubts, wrongly, about the reliability of this document, and which has put researchers off. This aspect of the problem could not, however, be set aside, for in the sixteenth century there were no warships which did not transport merchandise, and the dividing line between merchant ships and *armada* ships is extremely vague. A study of ships' movements which confined itself, as does the *Libro de Registros*, to merchant ships in the strict sense of the term, would in certain cases involve an error of as much as a 100 per cent; moreover, it would systematically underestimate the seventeenth century in favour of the sixteenth.

Using the *Libro de Registros* and the archives it illumines as a starting-point, we have tried to reconstruct a record of the Spanish–American Atlantic, of the kind a modern administration would compile for its own purposes. To this end we have consulted a considerable number of documents, which form the basis for tables showing every ship which left Spain for America and vice versa between 1504 and 1650 (including those sailing via Portugal or from any port other than the Seville port-complex as defined above). These tables give the name of the ship, the name of the captain, the destination, and place of origin. The first two items are always given by the *Libro de Regis-tros*, as is the third after 1548. The *Libro* also sometimes gives an indication of a ship's class (galleon, caravel, *nave*, etc.). To these basic data for each ship we have added, where possible, the following:[7] name of owner or owners (principal members of a shipping company); details as exact as possible on the nature of the ship and its origin (Biscayan, Andalusian, Portuguese, French, English, Flemish, Dutch, Hanseatic, from the Indies, or the Mediterranean); number and composition of crew, indicated by a four-figure code; and—the keystone of the system—for each of the 25,000 ships which figure in our tables: the tonnage.

Tonnage (in the sixteenth century ships very rarely sailed in ballast, least of all in the *Carrera de Indias*) is an element of great importance in the understanding of trade, and therefore in modern economic history as a whole. Establishing these 25,000 tonnages was feasible in so far as the ships of the *Carrera de Indias* constitute a stable volume which renews itself more or less rapidly according to periods and class of vessel, but on the whole at a rather slow pace, so that it can be studied on the basis of averages.

In this way we have been able to trace the career of each ship, and so to use the information on tonnage provided for a single voyage as a guide to the tonnage carried on all other voyages made by the same ship. As for the ships whose precise tonnage is not given in the documents (some 50 per cent), we have nearly always managed to collect enough details to make the margin of error very narrow, in guessing the tonnage: this is because in the sixteenth and seventeenth centuries only a limited number of types of ships were used for any given purpose; thus it is possible to get to know them and work out a scale which makes reckoning almost infallible. It need hardly be said that for such a method to bear fruit a great deal of patience was required.

Finally, we have written for each year one or more historical notes, of varying length,[8] giving without commentary the chief events of the maritime year: departure- and arrival-dates of ships; losses, with their cause and location; state of the market in the broad sense on departure and arrival; shortages, high prices, facility of distribution; competition from foreign contraband; saturation; indications pointing to the existence of a cycle; difficulties in provisioning, varying availability of crews, epidemics—and the infinite range of conflcting interests within a *Carrera* which is vaster and more varied than one could have imagined.

We have always done our best—by indicating the source of all data supplied on the tables with conventional signs—to make our work easy to assess, and, if necessary, to improve, especially with the help of materials which might have escaped us by being preserved only in transatlantic archives. In

short, we intended our study to be flexible enough for one or more of its component parts to be altered at any later stage, without affecting the balance of
the whole. For this reason it is impossible to publish the graphs, diagrams,
and calculations derived from these tables without first giving a full defence
of the bases of such calculations. Besides, the historian of any one Spanish–
American state may find in the tables points whose interest has escaped us,
and which the curves, mere generalizations as they are, have smoothed away.
Accidents, too, can be the raw material of industry.

Our study therefore allows us to measure in volume, and, to some extent,
in weight, the Spanish–American trade: one might say, for the sixteenth
century, the European–American trade. So much is certain, and the achievement is perhaps, by its very modesty, as indisputable as any we could have
hoped for. We have none the less aimed at reaching other aspects which are
nobler, but for that very reason easier to dispute. The sole advantage we have
over our predecessors in this field is our ability to judge these aspects in the
light of the 'tonnage standard' which our research has established. Starting
from the different *ad valorem* taxes levied on the Indies trade—the *avería* and
almojarifázgo of the various American ports—and interpreting these data,
with the help of the indispensable commentary on them provided by the
correspondence of the *Casa de la Contratación* in its effort to apply legislation
about whose effectiveness it had no illusions, we have tried to plot the value
curve of a trade already measured in weight. As it turns out this curve differs
from the weight curve, when all allowances have been made, much more than
could have been expected *a priori*. But even in more stable times than our
own, it would be surprising if one and a half centuries of history did not bring
with them structural changes.[9]

II

For the above reasons and others which are obvious, there can be no question of setting out here and now, in ten pages, the conclusions of a study
which fills 2,500. The most we can attempt is to sketch two or three of the
main themes which a careful study of the work would reveal.

First, a question of method: the economic history of the sixteenth and
seventeenth centuries has so far hardly got beyond the qualitative stage[10]
—with one exception, that of prices. For the sixteenth and seventeenth
centuries, prices are the only subject to have been studied simultaneously
and systematically in all the European countries where this was possible.[11]
This has certainly brought a leap forward in economic history. Such a
study, however, does not come to grips with the volume of an economy,
and therefore does not really enable one to take the measure of a century. Marxist historians have sharply criticized 'bourgeois' historiography
for deliberately and systematically leaving aside this volumetric aspect, and
more especially that of production. They would no doubt have done better

to utter fewer strictures and set more of an example. In fact, a study of production in the sixteenth and seventeenth centuries is virtually impossible. History cannot be manufactured from philosophical systems: the notion of production is a recent one and the archives, by definition, will hardly yield evidence about something which never preoccupied the men whose memories they embody.

But even if the attempt to measure production has to be abandoned for lack of documents, it may be possible to assess the volume of modern economies by measuring their exchanges. For our part we supply the measure of one exchange—to be precise the measure of the exchanges between Spain and America from 1504 to 1650. As exchanges constitute the vulnerable side of an economy, by which we mean the side most susceptible to fiscal or state control, it may be hoped that by one approach or another, and on condition that they know the right standpoint, historians will be able to detect and measure a considerable number of exchanges.[12]

What limit, what conditions, can be set for such a plan of study? Of course, compared to the mass of goods which hardly left the sphere in which they were produced, and which, since they remained confined to a limited economy, elude our scrutiny, the volume of the exchange economy was doubtless smaller, even in the sixteenth and seventeenth centuries, than it is nowadays. Yet may not this small negotiable area of the economy constitute a marginal value whose very position as marginal multiplies its effect on history? The dynamic history of negotiated 'volumes' in modern economies must surely constitute a decisive chapter in macro-history.

It is therefore important to identify the great exchange-axes of the modern economy and measure them. This and the history of prices will provide a solid hold on the economy of modern times which will be quite as valuable as any that could be procured by a quantitative knowledge of production—a notion which in any case is very probably an anachronism.

Over-land trading seems unfortunately very refractory. There is nothing to foreshadow the statistics of the railway companies for the second half of the nineteenth century. Road traffic is dust on the hands of illiterates, of which scarcely a trace remains. In such conditions, a toll is a stroke of luck, and a 'dry harbour' an extremely rare piece of good fortune. We must therefore direct our efforts towards maritime trade. Luckily for the historian, the advantage of sea over land was much clearer in the sixteenth and seventeenth centuries even than in our own times, and it may be asserted that the great trade of those days, the commercial ventures that led the world, were those that went by sea. There are certainly many ports in the Old World where one may hope to count ships, for there were very few where the authorities were unable to keep an effective check on incoming and outgoing vessels. So that with a certain amount of ingenuity and patience it should be possible to classify these vessels according to the main types of ships in use during the sixteenth and seventeenth centuries, and thus make a fair estimate of the volume of incoming and outgoing goods.

It is in fact the volume, i.e. the tonnage, which is the most desirable quantitative datum. It should always be preferred to estimates of value deduced from *ad valorem* taxes. The returns relating to the collection of these taxes are always much more capricious and fluctuating than one might think, ready as one is to take the easy path. In order to make use of them, a perfect knowledge of the legislation is called for (which is far from easy), and (which is infinitely more difficult) a knowledge of the tax-collectors' practice, the margins of tolerance, the various and changeable ways in which different commodities react to the tax; throughout this labyrinth there is always the risk of losing one's way, unless there is a fixed model by which to correct mistakes and false biases.

There is undoubtedly not much chance that the exceptionally favourable conditions which made possible Nina Ellinger Bang's study of the Sound and ours of Seville and its dependent port-complex will obtain in many European archives. One may nevertheless wonder to what extent our empiricism might not guide us to a method of adding together the separate empiricisms of a series of port studies; and hence wonder whether the time has not come to open, in the quantitative economic history of modern times, a second chapter: after the study of prices, parallel to it and indeed supported by it, the study of tonnages.

The graphs based both on the volume of merchandise (tonnage) and on its value (*ad valorem* taxes interpreted with the aid of tonnages and with such knowledge of the application of these *ad valorem* taxes as could be obtained from the various correspondences of the *Casa de la Contratación*) and also on the nature and direction of the various trades, are so complex, and their interpretation requires such long commentaries that it is out of the question to print them here: the most we can provide is a general impression, a simplified 'trend'.

From 1500 to 1580, the Indies trade is, so to speak, borne up on a rising swell, the rising swell of the sixteenth century which brings an increase in the global volume of outgoing goods from between 3,000 and 4,000 tons in its first years to 30,000 in the record years of the second-last decade of the century. This is not a uniform rise, but includes many setbacks, advancing through a succession of plateaux: the first in about 1530–5; then a sheer ascent leading to a second plateau around 1560; after this an almost steady climb, bringing total tonnage from the 15,000 or so tons achieved in 1565–70 to the 25,000 or 30,000 tons of the years preceding the catastrophe of the Invincible Armada (1588). 'Catastrophe' is perhaps an excessive word: the big ships lost are soon made up; at most one may glimpse a severe tonnage crisis between 1589 and 1598 which pushes up the price of freight and increases the speed of rotation of tonnage to its limits. After which a very slight decline from 1598 to 1605 leads on to the two apogees of Spanish–American trade, one situated, according to our calculations, between 1605 and 1610; the other, between 1615 and 1620. The record year, 1608, reaches the impressive figure of 45,078 tons. After 1620 the curve turns downwards; but this is not regular either. As in the rising curve, a cycle of ten to eleven years may be observed. Above all, this descent is much less rapid and much less deep than one might be tempted to think *a priori*, because one may readily overlook three fundamental facts: the prodigious increase in tonnage capacity of individual ships, which over a long period more than compensates for reduced numbers; the proliferation of *armada* ships (warships commissioned for defence either by the king or by the port authorities, the *avería*), huge vessels well-provided with cannon, whose holds (see the correspondence of the *Casa de la Contratación*) were just as crammed with merchandise as those of merchant ships proper; and finally, the change in the nature of cargoes.

For the decline of the trade, from 1620 to 1650, was less important in value than in volume. The nature of the cargoes which went from Spain to America changed radically during the first two or three decades of the seventeenth century. In the sixteenth century, and as late as about 1580–90, they consisted chiefly of grain, biscuits, wine, and oil. The huge convoys of the second half of the sixteenth century (huge by the standards of the period) brought to the Spanish settlers the three basic elements of the Mediterranean diet, the wheat, wine, and olive oil which enabled these Mediterraneans exiled in the land of maize to keep up long-established eating habits at the price of a veritable economic lunacy. By contrast, from the first decades of the seventeenth century, cargoes consisted chiefly of manufactured goods, mainly cloths, which moreover were not Spanish, but were brought through Spain from Italy and northern Europe. To be convinced of this reversal of the trend one need only consult the records of the *Casa de la Contratación*, and read the simplistic remedies suggested by those who were its worst victims, the great Andalusian landowners, who, in that aristocratic century,[13] were closely allied to the Spanish government. As a result of this noticeable change in the nature of exports, their value increases as their volume diminishes.

How can this important change be explained? By the fact that as the Spanish colonies developed, so they increased their mastery over their natural surroundings. (An example: the triumphant implantation of the vine beside the Pacific, in the oases of the dry Peruvian coast, despite the ineffectual prohibitions obtained by the Andalusian aristocracy from a docile Spanish government.) And equally by this other fact, that the new generations of Spaniards, born in the Indies and among the Indians, did not share the prejudices about the local cuisine that their fathers had brought with them, transplanted as they were from one universe to another.

Finally, and above all, the economic madness of transporting at enormous cost products of little value, and highly unsuitable for long-distance transport, between Spain and America, was only possible because of the very high profitability of the silver mines in the New World. When profits fell for a complex set of reasons (exhaustion of surface deposits, scarcity of labour around the mines, higher price of mercury needed for the amalgam—above all, the reduced purchasing-power of silver resulting from the sixteenth-century price revolution) the silver was exported less to Europe, and used more in America to create a more stable and more self-sufficient economy.

On this point our studies fully support those of Earl J. Hamilton. At the beginning of the seventeenth century, the mines could only maintain their profitability if they continually improved their techniques; that they did improve techniques of amalgamation is certain, but this was not enough to compensate for the fall in the value of silver. One may speak of a drive towards 'industrialization' on the Mexican plateaux in the early seventeenth century. The same phenomenon appears as for wine : the cheap *panos* from the Anahuac Plateaux and the equally cheap silks brought in galleons from Manila barred the way to European cloths of mediocre quality, only letting through luxury goods, the products of highly-developed techniques, which were indispensable to the Creole aristocracies intent on enjoying the fabulous incomes of which a world in full internal expansion assured them. An amazingly outward-looking Atlantic economy in the sixteenth century (we would readily term it a 'Manchester School' century) is succeeded by an inward-looking 'autarkic' seventeenth century—without any accompanying economic regression, in fact quite the opposite. Such a change of atmosphere we in the French school of history have, following François Simiand, been accustomed to call the passage from the 'A' phase to a 'B' phase.

This too-hasty outline calls for a few comments. The sixteenth-century price rise, which Earl J. Hamilton has so fully demonstrated for Spain, is reflected in the great sea-going trade by a prodigious increase in volume—a paradox for anyone not versed in dynamic economics.[14] The general volume-curve of the Atlantic trade thus 'sticks' in a certain sense to the general economic-curve of the sixteenth and seventeenth centuries. It sticks to it more closely than the curve of the arrivals of precious metals in Spain[15] plotted for the same period (1500–1650) by Earl J. Hamilton, perhaps because (as we think after an exhaustive perusal of the *Casa de la Contratación* correspondence) Earl J. Hamilton, admirable as is his contribution—without which, as we cannot repeat often enough, our own work would have been unthinkable—has not taken sufficient account for the seventeenth century of the factor of contraband, which plays an exceptionally active part in the domain of precious metals. It is therefore all the more satisfying to observe how the volume-curve of Atlantic trade 'sticks' to the curve of the price revolution so perfectly worked out by the great American economist.

Since the economic cycle of the Spanish Atlantic is a faithful reproduction of what may be considered as the European economic cycle, we deduce from this and from the size of the trade that the economic cycle of the Spanish Atlantic must be one of the major components of the European economic cycle from 1500 to 1650. We use the word 'European' in order to avoid delving into that great problem, not yet elucidated, which is posed for this period by the economic cycle of the Far East, linked as it undoubtedly is to the European economic cycle, but by a correlation which is not direct but probably inverse.

The economy of the Spanish–American Atlantic such as it is perceived in its great East–West axis is thus an economy of long phases, those long phases so dear to the hearts of French historians. It is, however, possible to discern within the great movements—first the rise, then the levelling-off or decline —a series of short fluctuations. This study may help to clarify the problem, which remains intact, of short-term cyclical fluctuations in sixteenth- and seventeenth-century economies: fluctuations which in the absence of statistics can be guessed at rather than perceived.

Cyclical fluctuations ripple through the massive movement of merchandise between Spain and America from 1504 to 1650. From 1590 to 1650, a cycle of about 10 to 11 years may be clearly distinguished, lagging slightly behind the decade—the declining phase corresponding roughly to the first half of the decade, and the rising phase to the second half.[16] It remains to be seen what these short fluctuations imply; whether, on closer analysis, they may not be reduced to simpler and shorter fluctuations, and finally what they reflect in the economy as a whole. But such an analysis is beyond the scope of this study.

Nor is it impossible that between the 10–11 year fluctuations and the centennial ones (rising phase 1508–1620; declining phase 1620–80) we may be able to discover intermediate fluctuations of 15 or 20 years, or longer, according to the period; fluctuations known to historians of the French school as 'interdecennial fluctuations'. Most likely they could be deduced from the figures provided. For maritime trade we have in fact a quite convenient means of feeling the economy's pulse: by studying the relation between supply and demand for freight. For one can quite easily discern in this century of the history of the Spanish Atlantic certain periods when, under pressure from an expanding trade, the supply of shipping fails to satisfy the demands of trade. These are the periods when the price of freight increases faster than the general price-curve, when the rhythm of rotation of ships is particularly rapid, when the *cargadores* (traders) complain of the impossibility of loading their merchandise.

But there are also even more easily recognizable periods when the available shipping greatly exceeds the available trade. At such times the rhythm of rotation of ships slows down, and long queues of ships stretch down the estuary, as it were, waiting for a cargo which the traders dole out in driblets. At such times as these the ship-owners, in order to avoid a disastrous drop in freight, turn to the state, which allots a number to each ship in the queue waiting for provender.

The first periods naturally correspond to long phases of expansion; the second to long phases of recession. It may easily be imagined that ship-building is stimulated in the first phases, and, on the contrary, discouraged in the second. The phase of freight crisis normally ends in the sixteenth century when there is a strong upsurge of trade; in the seventeenth century it normally ends, or at least its effects are attenuated, when the stock of existing vessels runs out (the less they are used, the faster they deteriorate). Then again, but one stage lower, the available shipping falls short of the available trade. Ship-building regains its prosperity, but not for long, since it is power-less to reverse the decline of trade.

The periods of the first type (not enough ships), which may be called '*a*', are longer in the sixteenth century, when young ships predominate. The periods of the second type, which may be called '*b*' periods, are longer in the seventeenth century: these are the periods of old ships.

This very rapid sketch naturally deals with only part of the facts; it leaves out the effects of technical change which nearly always and in every period, with very rare exceptions, worked in favour of big ships. It also leaves aside state intervention through legislation, a far from negligible factor. To sum up, there is no golden rule for determining short- and medium-term fluctuations in the Spanish-Atlantic economy from 1504 to 1650; the most one can do is to sketch a probable outline on the strength of a careful analysis which brings to bear the maximum number of statistics, without neglecting the qualitative judgements of contemporaries.

Nor is there, and on this point we wish to conclude, a *single* economic cycle for the Spanish Atlantic, which was a world much vaster to the men of the sixteenth century than is the entire planet to our own technology today. There are *several* economic cycles, of which that of the Spanish Atlantic is at most a resultant. The economic space of the sixteenth century, and even more that of the seventeenth, was certainly much more partitioned than that of the twentieth, and *a fortiori* the nineteenth.

Two examples among a thousand: the 1600–20 ceiling, the period when trade between Spain and America reaches its highest averages, is marked by a curious collapse of trade between Spain and Tierra Firma i.e. between Spain and South America. It is to New Spain (Central America and Mexico) that this apogee of the first two decades of the seventeenth century is due. Thus, in the Spanish Atlantic between 1600 and 1620 the general economic situation is diametrically opposed to that of Tierra Firma, but coincides with that of New Spain: for twenty years—an unparalleled occurrence in the Spanish Atlantic—New Spain becomes the driving force of the economic cycle. After 1620 there is a gradual return to the state of affairs before 1600: Tierra Firma once more takes precedence. This vital episode in the economic history of the New World stems from causes which must be sought in Tierra Firma and in New Spain. In Tierra Firma, the period 1600–20 marks a brief capture of trade by the Dutch, who settled in the salt-pans of the Araya Peninsula, and who, in collaboration with a sizeable colony of Portuguese (Portuguese Jews perhaps) driven out of Brazil and lately installed in this part of America, syphoned off, to their own advantage, a commerce which up to then had gone through Seville. It seems that after 1620 the Spaniards managed to stabilize the situation. On the other hand, 1600–20 seems to mark a high point in all spheres of activity in New Spain: the size of the Vera Cruz fleet, greater than ever before or after; activity on the Anahuac Plateau; trade with China at its apogee (cf. our studies on the Pacific); activity also, no doubt, in the mines, the profits from which, partly invested on the spot, might perhaps be largely responsible for this prosperity?

There is no doubt an economic cycle particular to each province of the Castilian Indies: consider for instance the amazing stability of trade in the islands throughout the period, which seems more or less the reverse of the continental trade cycle: decline of the islands in the sixteenth century when New Spain and Tierra Firma emerge, because these new, more alluring countries draw away the settlers; then a timid recovery at the end of the period, when these 'poor relations' of the Castilian Indies seem to become more attractive, once the *el Dorado* of the mainland shows signs of fatigue.

The Spanish-Atlantic economic cycle, a major component of the world economic cycle, is itself therefore no more than the result of an infinity of lesser cycles which only patient research can bring to light.

NOTES

1. This article was commissioned by the editor of the *Cahiers d'histoire mondiale*, Professor Lucien Fébvre.

2. [This great work has now been published. *Seville et l'Atlantique* (11 vols., Paris, 1955–9).]

3. There was, it is true, the precedent set by Nina Ellinger Bang, but that was concerned with the traffic through a 'narrow sea', which is easier to pin down. (Nina Ellinger Bang, *Tabeller over stribsfart eg varetransport gennem Oresund, 1497–1660*. Publication of this work, begun in Copenhagen in 1906, extended over 25 years; after the death of Nina Ellinger Bang it was taken over by Knud Korst.)

4. A complete bibliography may be found in the classic *Trade and Navigation between Spain and Indies*, by Clarence Haring (Cambridge, Mass., 1918). Many articles followed: cf. especially the interesting views of Ramón Carande, in the first volume of his *Carlos V y sus banqueros*, Madrid, *Revista de Occidente* (1943).

5. R. Carande, op. cit., especially ch. IX, pp. 184–90; C. Haring, op. cit.

6. First mentioned by Haring, op. cit.

7. Drawn from existing ships' registers, the *papeles de armada*, etc.; the correspondence received by the *Casa de la Contratación* from its various services and from in-

dividuals; series contained in the *Contratación* papers; fragmentary series in the *Indiferente General* Collection; and also the various series of accounting documents in the *Contratación* and *Contaduria* papers, the accounts of the *Receptores d'avería*, of the Fator of the *Casa de la Contratación*, and notably the accounts of the counting-houses at the various ports of the Viceroyalties of the Indies.

8. From half a page to 15 or 20 pages in the most eventful years.

9. Regarding the nature of the cargoes, the results are more fragmentary, being copious for homeward voyages (America–Spain) but very sporadic for outward ones— quite adequate, however, as an indication of changes over the period under consideration.

10. Earl J. Hamilton, in his book, *American Treasure and Price Revolution in Spain* (Cambridge, Mass., 1934), has supplied another very interesting quantitative element, that of the arrival of precious metals (gold, and especially silver) in Spain. The global volume of trade in the form of tonnage is a less spectacular datum, but should it not also be a less suspect one?

11. Of all the branches of economic history, the history of prices is the one which has made the greatest progress in modern times. For the sixteenth and seventeenth centuries in Europe the first classic works were already written in the nineteenth century; the Vicomte G. d'Avenel for France, *Histoire économique de la propriété, des denrées et de tous les prix en général depuis l'an 1200 jusqu'en l'an 1800* (7 vols., 1894–1926); Georg Wiebe for Germany, *Zur Geschichte der Preisrevolution des XVI. und XVII. Jahrhunderts* (Leipzig, 1895), and for England, Thorold Rogers, *A History of agriculture and prices in England from the year after the Oxford Parliament to the commencement of Continental War* (7 vols., Oxford, 1866–1902). And later, Magoldi e Fabri, Bartolini, for Italy; Johann Falke, Bahlmann, G. von Below, Dittmann, Friederesberg, Helferich, Hildebrand, Keller, Kins, Unger, etc., for Germany; P. Raveau, for France; van Houtte, for Belgium.

Closer to the present-day, but more in line with the requirements of contemporary economic history, we would remind the reader of François Simiand's indispensable guide, *Recherches anciennes et nouvelles sur le mouvement général des prix du XVIe au XIXe siècle* (Paris, 1932). For France, the fundamental works of C. E. Labrousse are unfortunately limited to the eighteenth century : *Esquisse du mouvement des prix et des revenus en France au XVIIIe siècle* (Paris, 1933), and *La Crise de l'économie française à la fin de l'ancien régime et au début de la Révolution*, vol. i (Paris, 1944); for England, Sir William H. Beveridge, *Prices and wages in England from the XIIth to the XIXth century* (1939); for Holland, N. W. Posthumus, *Inquiry into the history of prices in Holland*, vol. i, *Wholesale prices at the exchange of Amsterdam, 1585–1914, Rates of Exchange at Amsterdam, 1609–1914* (Leiden, 1946), and for Spain, Earl J. Hamilton's classic (op. cit., cf. note 10).

12. It is for precisely this purpose that the series *Ports. routes. trafics* has been initiated by the VIth *Section* of the *École Pratique des Hautes Études*.

13. The Count-Duke of Olivarès is the best known of these great landowners who exported the produce of their estates to America.

14. This study fully corroborates the hypotheses put forward by Fernand Braudel in his lectures at the Collège de France.

15. Arrivals of precious metals would seem to decline from 1595 onwards, but price increases continue until 1650. Even taking inflation into account, it is difficult to explain this phenomenon if one accepts a sudden collapse of silver shipments, and therefore of European–American trade, from the end of the sixteenth century. After a sudden bulge between 1595 and 1605 the Spanish price-curve plotted by E. J. Hamilton resumes its climb after 1610 as the exact prolongation of the line from 1550 to 1595. Now before 1625 inflation by itself does not seem a sufficient explanation of this phenomenon. In this sense our curve (tonnage) 'sticks' even better to the price-curve than does the curve of 'official' arrivals of precious metals.

In Holland, according to Posthumus (op. cit., note 11), the reversal of the main price trend appears not to be earlier than 1636–7. The Spanish Atlantic thus 'sticks' to the European economic cycle.

16. Between 1600 and 1620 (at least) an analogous fluctuation is clearly readable in Hamilton's precious-metals curve. The rhythm of silver arrivals and that of the trade as a whole are identical, but the 'trend' of our curve differs from that of Hamilton's, because, we think, Hamilton underestimated the sudden increase in the share of contraband in precious metals during this period.

6

Economic Decline in Poland
from the Sixteenth to the Eighteenth Centuries

JERZY TOPOLSKI

Translated by Richard Morris*

I

THE subject of economic decline in Poland from the sixteenth to eighteenth centuries is not a new one, although it has attracted a large body of fresh research since the Second World War. From the beginning of the seventeenth century onwards many Polish economic writers drew attention to the rapidly deteriorating economic state of the country and tried to work out the causes of this situation. The main factors which were emphasized included the progressive decline of the towns and, even more, the worsening conditions in which the peasants lived, as well as the poor state of agriculture in general. The luxurious way of life enjoyed by the nobility and the oppression suffered by the peasants were both condemned.

Eighteenth- and nineteenth-century writers continued to emphasize the country's economic decline. Two main factors were brought forward to explain the situation. Much emphasis was placed on the terrible devastation caused by war, particularly in the seventeenth century, but nearly all writers were convinced that no real progress could be made so long as the social system of the country remained the same. The system of serfdom and the strict subordination of the towns, many of which were the property of nobles or lords, made it virtually impossible for the bourgeois and peasant classes ever to achieve an adequately active economy.

Twentieth-century historians have not sought to challenge these two basic explanations of Poland's economic decline, but have brought a far more scientific method to bear on the analysis of these and other problems in Polish economic history. Since the Second World War economic history has been integrated into other themes of Polish history and a large number of detailed monographs have appeared dealing with both the rural and urban history of the country. They have amply confirmed the judgements of contemporaries about the decline of the country during the period in question, and have provided a body of well-documented statistical and descriptive material, thus

* From 'La Regression économique en Pologne du XVIe au XVIIIe siècle', *Acta Poloniae Historica*, vii (1962), 28–49.

preparing the way for much more complete studies dealing with the problems as a whole.[1]

II

In order to study the problem of economic decline in Poland properly, several preliminary questions must be taken into consideration. First of all the actual term must be defined as precisely as possible. Only then can one look at the research methods applicable to such a complex phenomenon. It is necessary to establish on the one hand the causes, and on the other the dimensions, of this economic decline. And, in order to explain its causes, we must have recourse to statistics and to some comparative data concerning other countries.

Decline, when considered on the scale of the economy as a whole, means a decrease in the global volume of production in the country in question. Moreover, it is not a matter of a mere passing phase of collapse, but rather of a prolonged phenomenon involving a decisive downward trend in production. So far as Poland is concerned, the period to be discussed will be from the last years of the sixteenth century right up to the end of the eighteenth century, in spite of certain signs of economic recovery noticed by historians in the second half of the eighteenth century. In general, however, the index of the volume of production does not rise during this period, and indeed shows a downward tendency. The usefulness of the criterion 'volume of production' is emphasized because certain authors consider the mere fact of farming based on labour by peasant-serfs to be a regressive step. The phenomenon of decline could also be defined as an economic crisis but, in view of the manifold meanings this word takes on in certain studies, this definition is not a desirable one.

It is also necessary to determine whether it is in fact a matter of decline, or merely of a state of economic stagnation, though this is usually a forecast of decline itself. This problem can be solved if suitable sources are available and if one is in a position to compare the volume of production at given periods. The same problem can arise indirectly when facts are lacking and one is obliged to analyse symptoms which bring to light the variations in the volume of production. These symptoms can, obviously, be of greater or of lesser significance. Thus, so far as agriculture is concerned, symptoms which are important indicators of a change in the volume of production include information about the area of arable land, the number of farms, the quantity of seed used, and the size of the harvest. Facts of this kind, when one lacks direct information on the volume of agricultural production, can illustrate the trends in economic development and, at the very least, can show whether it is a matter of growth or decline. So far as industrial or artisan production is concerned, this can be judged from information on the number of houses in the towns, the number of workshops, the number of inhabitants, and even from the amount of taxes paid by the middle-class citizens. It is evident however that in the period under discussion, and especially where Poland is concerned, economic development depended primarily on the volume of agricultural production which served in turn as the basis for industrial activity. For that reason this branch of the economy will figure predominantly in the subsequent discussion.

Most important among the symptoms indicating variations in the different parts of the economy are the facts concerning the volume of trade, both internal trade which can be studied through the income derived from the levy of stallage taxes at fairs, and certain branches of foreign trade, such as the export of corn. It is a common procedure to include among the most important symptoms of economic change details of price fluctuations, and then to point out that a prolonged downward trend means a weakening of the pace of the country's economic life. In Poland, however, the rise and fall of prices is a misleading symptom of the country's economic trends. In the first place, monetary exchanges did no more than brush the surface of economic life, leaving aside its main structure and, notably, most of the peasant-farms. Secondly, the prices paid for cereals to the nobility at Danzig (Gdańsk), which might have had considerable importance for our analysis, were under the influence of the West European economy. Fluctuations in these prices are more or less identical with those in the price of corn in the countries of western Europe. Finally, it cannot be maintained, in the period under discussion, that a downward trend in prices is proof of a weakening of economic activity, and therefore of a decrease in output.

In Poland, as elsewhere in western and central Europe, there was a check to rising prices in the first half of the seventeenth century.[2] But from the end of the wars of the middle of the century onwards there can be seen a rise in prices lasting for a long time (exact figures are available for the town of Warsaw) which is linked to the lack of a sufficient quantity of various goods on the market. There was therefore an upward trend at the very moment of total economic stagnation. On the other hand, if Amsterdam during the second half of the seventeenth century is taken as an example, the research of N. Posthumus shows prices falling and reaching their lowest level between 1680 and 1684.[3] And yet Holland, like England, was a leader among those countries enjoying economic growth in the seventeenth century.

Other difficulties concerning method arise in the course of study of the causes of decline. First of all, it is extremely difficult to trace the influence exerted by the system of forced labour upon agricultural production. Sources give no direct information on this point and, moreover, from the middle of the century onwards, one must add to the considerations already mentioned the extensive devastations resulting from the wars, since these seriously harmed rural production for a long time. It is sufficient to say that out of 68 years (1648–1716), 55 were war years. From then on, the effects of these

devastating wars in addition to a whole series of other factors joined and
acted together. It is for this reason that the research carried out on the Polish
economy before the middle of the seventeenth century is of such importance,
since in that period devastations resulting from hostilities did not have such
a widespread significance.

Research into the variations in agricultural production must be concerned
as much with the lands of the nobility as with the farms of the peasants. It
is possible at a given time for production from the lands of the nobility to
increase, while that from the peasant-farms decreases; while the total agricultural production of the country may be either stable or declining.

III

It has been possible to determine the extent of economic decline from the
end of the sixteenth to the eighteenth centuries from research into the landed
property of the archbishopric of Gniezno. These vast estates, which towards
the end of the eighteenth century included 426 villages and 13 towns, did
not constitute a well-defined territorial region, but were scattered about in
Masovia, in the region of Sieradz and Lęczyca, in Greater Poland and also,
though to a lesser extent, in Pomerania and Lesser Poland. Conclusions
drawn from an analysis of the situation as seen in these various areas will
thus have the merit of being more or less representative of the whole of
Poland, though the emphasis will naturally be principally on western and
central Poland. The extant documents and sources, after numerous statistical
calculations, illustrate the variations in the volume of agricultural production and in stock-farming for the whole of the period under discussion. Until
now, no other comparable data have been made available. There has only
been more or less incomplete material which confirms in one way or another
the facts supplied by analysis of the economic history of the Gniezno estates.

Research into the property of this archbishopric tells us both directly and
indirectly about changes in the volume of production. Data concerning the
surface area of cultivated land supply indirect information. In the sixteenth
century there was a slight increase in the areas of cultivated land. Taking
the index 100 to express the state of affairs at the beginning of the century,
the index rises to 110 by its close. But by the beginning of the following
century the arable land had shrunk and the index falls to 98. The devastations
caused by the wars of the middle of the seventeenth century brought about
a considerable further decrease in the area of cultivated land, and around
1685, a quarter of a century after the end of hostilities, the index was only 65.
Wars at the beginning of the eighteenth century brought about a further
decrease, and right up to the end of the century the area of arable land never
equalled that of the late sixteenth century. The figure climbed to 89 or, if one
includes new areas, to 94. Variations in the area of uncultivated land have
also been examined; by the end of the eighteenth century one-quarter of the

land was uncultivated, double the proportion at the beginning of the sixteenth century.

These changes in the areas of arable land would directly reflect the volume of agricultural production if both cultivation techniques and yield had remained the same. In fact the yield might well have increased with the result that the decreases of cultivated area might well point to the disuse of marginal land rather than to a parallel decrease in production. On the other hand, if the yield had decreased, the real fall in production would be much greater than would appear from the mere fact of reduction in area. Now this is just what did happen in Poland during the period under discussion. On the basis of the numerous pieces of research so far undertaken, it can be stated generally that the average harvest-yield in the second half of the sixteenth century was of the order of 5 to 1, whereas it was no more than 3 or 4 to 1 during the second half of the eighteenth century. This decrease in yield had begun as early as the beginning of the seventeenth century. This can be shown from data concerning the Gniezno estates, as well as from other estates in different regions. Mrs. Wawrzyńczyk has collected enough material to demonstrate the decrease in harvest crop in the region of Sandomierz. As far as crown property was concerned, she showed that the average harvest from ninety farms in 1564 was 4·99 to 1, whereas in 1615 it was no more than 4·08.[4] In the archbishopric estates the average for the first half of the seventeenth century was roughly 4 to 1 against 5 to 1 for the second half of the preceding century. A similar decrease has also been noted in connection with farms belonging to the town of Poznań.[5]

Calculations concerning the volume of production also testify to a decrease in yield. The decline in cereal production (largely grain which accounted for 95 per cent of the fields) was faster than the reduction in arable acreage. Cultivated land decreased by 14 per cent between the end of the sixteenth and the beginning of the eighteenth centuries, whereas the decrease in production of cereals on large farms and on peasant holdings in the same region of the archbishopric lands was 39 per cent for a similar period. Assuming that the decrease in harvest was in the order of 25 to 30 per cent, it could be stated that one-third to one-quarter of the over-all decrease of cereal production in the seventeenth and eighteenth centuries can be accounted for by the reduction in arable acreage and two-thirds to three-quarters by the decrease in yield.

Production from peasant-farms diminished much more than that from the large farms. The decrease in production from the latter for the period from the end of the sixteenth to the end of the eighteenth centuries is only 6 per cent, while that of the peasant-farms reached approximately 37 per cent. The conclusion is clear; given the considerable over-all decrease in cereal production in the whole country, one is bound to acknowledge that it was due mainly to failing production from the peasant-farms.

The over-all production of cereals had increased only slightly in the second half of the sixteenth century. The first half of the following century brought with it a decrease which was as yet barely perceptible. The wars of the middle of the century brought with them serious slackening of agricultural production which was felt more among the peasants than among the great landowners. In 1685 production from the archbishopric estates represented only 35 per cent of what it had been a hundred years before, and only 40 per cent of the years 1620–40. After the devastation caused by the third war against Sweden in the early eighteenth century can be seen a period of reconstruction. Production from the large properties almost reached the level of the end of the sixteenth and beginning of the seventeenth centuries, although production from small peasant-holdings was still far inferior to what it had been a century before. Over-all cereal production in the last quarter of the eighteenth century reached no more than 60 to 65 per cent of the volume produced during the closing years of the sixteenth century.

A decrease in stock-breeding ran concurrent with the decrease in cereal production, although to a lesser degree. Taking the end of the sixteenth century as a base, the cattle population had declined one-third as much as had the area of arable land by the end of the eighteenth century. This decrease is considerable, and nearly all of it is accounted for by the small peasant-farms. Once again it is clear that research into economic decline in Poland must be primarily directed at an analysis of peasant productivity. In addition it should be stressed that in the archbishopric estates it was the small peasant-farms which provided more than 80 per cent of the total volume of cereal production and which reared between 85 and 90 per cent of the total number of domestic animals.

As is apparent from the above figures, the decrease in production of cereals and of stock-breeding was considerable, roughly one-third between the end of the sixteenth and eighteenth centuries. The potential productivity of Polish farms was thus much lower at the time of the partitions than it had been two centuries earlier. There can be no doubt that these facts are of importance for research and speculation on the causes of the loss of Polish independence at the close of the eighteenth century.

IV

Research on data supplied by the Gniezno estates has rendered possible a concise statement of the dimensions and chronological background of the economic regression. This provides a starting-point for analytical studies in the course of which various facts can be pointed out, though these are only contributory details by comparison with the decline as a whole. First will be mentioned regional differences in the symptoms of decline so far established.

In Masovia it was relatively early that regressive tendencies became apparent, as much in the urban as in the rural economy. Masovia was favourably situated for the transport of corn by water to the Baltic; hence this province's rapid emergence as part of the export route. The 1616 inventory of royal property indicated a decrease of roughly one-quarter in the number of farms, by comparison with that of 1569, and noted the appearance of uncultivated land in the villages. The number of industrial workshops in the countryside grew less too. Thus, for example, there was a 20 per cent reduction in the number of village mills during the same period.[6] The decline of the region continued to make itself felt. In the *starosti* of Sochaczew there were 180 arpents of uncultivated land in 1602, whereas in 1630 the figure had more than trebled. In the same year in the *starosti* of Gostynin 27 per cent of its land was uncultivated. A very distinct decrease in stock-breeding can also be observed. For example, in those of the Gniezno estates which were situated in Masovia, the average number of domestic animals per peasant-farm during the first half of the seventeenth century was 4·2 as against 13 or 14 in the middle of the preceding century.

Regressive tendencies are clearly to be seen in the Masovian towns, and they can best be examined by comparing the 1569, 1616, and 1630 inventories. The number of houses and artisan-workers gradually diminished. Public and industrial installations fell into ruins. The town markets lost influence. According to the research of Irena Gieysztor on the economic history of eighteen Masovian towns, in 1616 there was 37 per cent less landed property than there had been in 1569.[7] For the purpose of comparison with 1630, the author chose five towns and was able to discover that the decrease in the number of houses in these towns for the period 1569–1630 was roughly 41 per cent.[8] The decrease in the number of houses is an indirect pointer to the decrease in the number of artisans. The same author was able to show that these towns had lost proportions of their artisan population ranging from 15 to 37 per cent between 1564 and 1630.[9] Economic activity at the fairs and markets slowed down; their numbers fell and the exchange of money grew rarer.

In summary, it can be said that in Masovia economic decline began during the last years of the sixteenth century, while in the first two decades of the seventeenth century it can be seen more easily as its manifestations became more pronounced.

In southern Poland too, that is in Lesser Poland, are to be found early signs of growing stagnation and economic depression, although these symptoms are not as clear as in Masovia. But in numerous villages uncultivated land is to be found more and more frequently. Thus, for example, in the *starosti* of Luków more than 10 per cent of the countryside was idle.[10] Production from large properties had not yet decreased, but it was already stationary. In 1554, on 45 farms of the royal estate of the *voivodi* of Sandomierz, almost 66,500 bushels of breadcrops had been harvested. A similar harvest was reaped in 1615.[11] In metallurgy, decline had already set in. B. Zientara, who has specialized in this branch of Polish industry, noticed its sharp decline in the seventeenth century, worsened further by growing imports and the decrease in artisanship in the towns. At this period, the only branch of the industry which was still expanding was the manufacture of weapons.[12]

As for eastern Greater Poland, there are many signs of decline from the end of the sixteenth century onwards. The state of the small peasant properties worsened considerably and their equipment grew more limited and of poorer quality. Horses, which were frequently used by the peasants in the sixteenth century, were henceforth replaced by oxen which tended to be slow, undersized, and generally weak. As in other regions, the peasants' houses, sheds, and haylofts fell into decay and sometimes into total ruin.[13] Industrial activity in the towns declined appreciably.

During the first half of the seventeenth century, symptoms of economic regression are also to be observed in western Greater Poland. Here, methods of farming based on serfdom developed later, hence the negative results of these methods was not immediately apparent. However, from 1620 onwards, the area of uncultivated land grew larger. Between 1591 and 1593 there had been scarcely a hundred idle acres in the estates of the archbishopric, but this number had increased tenfold by the middle of the following century. According to W. Rusiński, it was the years 1630 to 1635 that saw the beginnings of the abandonment of very extensive areas of arable land.[14] Concurrent with the increase in the area of idle land is growing evidence of the poor state of peasant-farms, low-quality tools, and insufficient cattle. This led to fields being poorly sown and attacked by weeds, a hazard often mentioned in the sources. The towns of western Greater Poland also supply evidence of some decline, although to a lesser degree than those in Masovia. The results of research undertaken on this topic are still imperfectly known.

Pomerania, and in particular the province of Danzig, had followed a different course of development. Since its union with Poland, this region had undergone a period of economic prosperity. The corn business had its centre in this province, and the towns offered attractive opportunities for merchants coming from western Europe, and thus managed to resist the crisis better and longer than other areas. The nobles used mainly day-labourers on their farms, and only to a very small extent was serf-labour employed. The peasant-farms had managed to retain their economic position. For these reasons, until the devastating war of 1626–9, Pomerania showed no symptoms of decline. However, destruction caused by the hostilities was considerable. Three-quarters of the peasant-farms were destroyed on certain royal estates, while in the royal estate of Malbork almost all the farms were ruined and did not recover before 1636. By the time of the Swedish invasion of 1655, the province still had been unable to recuperate from the destruction caused by the 1626–9 war.[15] Western Pomerania was also to suffer badly from the Thirty Years War. Farms owned by nobles developed continually while the small peasant-farms grew correspondingly poorer.

Up to the Thirty Years War no signs of decay are to be seen in the economy of Silesia. But the war implacably destroyed nearly 1,100 villages, either completely or partly. Decades were required before they could be rebuilt.

V

Economic decline in town and country, already perceptible in the first half of the seventeenth century, was violently hastened by the terrible destruction of the wars which extended over the entire country in the middle of the century. Fighting, and in particular the ensuing epidemics, reduced the population by half. Masovia lost 64 per cent of its inhabitants, Pomerania nearly 60 per cent, Podlachia nearly 50, Greater Poland roughly 42, and southern (or Lesser) Poland nearly 27 per cent.[16]

Almost 10 per cent of Masovian villages were annihilated, and 85 per cent of the land was left uncultivated. An inventory of 1660 reveals that out of 101 farms, 13 had been completely ruined and abandoned, 27 no longer had any buildings standing and had been burnt. The remainder were in poor condition: 20 per cent of them no longer had either cattle or work-horses, and the others suffered similar serious losses. By comparison with the 1616 figures, head of cattle had been reduced by roughly one-third, and sheep-raising had almost entirely ceased. In 1660 only 15 per cent of land cultivated by peasants was sown. The corresponding percentage for Church property varied between 20 and 45, and it is probable that noble-owned properties had suffered in like proportion. The latest research shows that in the years immediately following hostilities, only 40 per cent of peasant-owned land was sown. In the royal estates of Masovia, the average amount of seed sown for any given farm fell by roughly 57 per cent. Harvests were very poor, since the amount of crop reaped was reduced in proportion to the decrease in seed sown. Agricultural production on the royal estates of Masovia was 76 per cent lower than in 1616, and harvest-yields had fallen from 5·6 to 3·1 for each unit sown.[17]

Such precise figures are not available for Lesser Poland, but there are numerous indications of the reduction in the arable area of peasant-farms, the decrease in stock-breeding, and the destruction of kitchen gardens, bee-hives, ponds, and other equipment. In 30 villages belonging to the crown in the *voivodi* of Cracovia, peasants tilled nearly 170 measures of land, but after the war more than half of this was left untilled. In the village of the Uszwia, owned by the Bishop of Cracovia, the figures were approximately the same, while, in the 61 villages in the *voivodi* of Sandomierz whose history has been studied, scarcely 30 per cent of the peasant land was being tilled after the war. In the villages belonging to rich landowners the figures were less striking.[18] An even bigger decline in the land tilled by peasants has been found in the *voivodi* of Lublin. Thus, for example, in the *starosti* of Luków more than 80 per cent of the land tilled by peasants had been abandoned by 1660.[19]

In Greater Poland 72 per cent of the fields in the Gniezno district were abandoned and 50 in Kościan.[20] In the hundreds of villages belonging to the Gniezno archbishopric, 70 per cent of the land was uncultivated after the war. Altogether the reduction in agricultural production in the peasant-farms of Greater Poland after the war can be estimated at some 50 to 70 per cent. In the farms of the district of Kalisz the 1661 harvests were hardly a quarter of what they had been in 1616.[21] Eastern Greater Poland suffered the worst devastation. The village of Blonie, belonging to the *starosti* of Leczyca, had in 1661 a mere 3 measures of peasant-tilled land as against 50 before the war. Entire villages had been destroyed to the extent that not a single peasant-farm or -house had been spared.[22]

The same happened in eastern Pomerania. Here the hostilities lasted for nearly five years. Despite continual devastation, the province was expected to feed whole armies and even to equip them with weapons and various supplies. In 1664, a few years after the end of the war, nearly 30 per cent of the villages were still completely destroyed. More than half the property in another third had been destroyed, and only one-third had been able to keep half its possessions and buildings intact ... As for crown estates in eastern Pomerania, it is estimated that hardly one-third of the villagers' means of production had escaped destruction.[23] Out of the 163 farms mentioned in the 1664 inventory, 77 had been completely devastated. The others, too, had been laid waste.[24] In 1664 cereal production in these farms failed to reach a third of the pre-war figure.

Podlachia had also suffered a great deal from the war. The decrease in cultivated land reached 85 per cent, and on noble-owned land 50 per cent. These small noble farms had resisted the war better. Almost 11 per cent of royal villages were totally destroyed, and cereal production on the royal estates scarcely reached 20 per cent of the volume produced in 1616.[25]

The devastation in the countryside was not without a parallel in the towns. It has been estimated that 60 per cent of the houses in Greater Poland were destroyed.[26] In Masovia almost 35 per cent of the towns were razed to the ground. From the 1660 inventory it can be seen that barely 14 per cent of the houses mentioned in the 1564 list were still standing.[27] The urban population of Podlachia had fallen to 36 per cent of its pre-war figure.[28] In the light of this, it is easy to understand why craftsmanship and business had declined so much. A study has been made of six towns in Lesser Poland in which could be seen a decrease of roughly 53 per cent in the number of craftsmen.[29] In Podlachia it has been estimated that there was a fall of approximately 80 per cent in the number of craftsmen in towns belonging to the crown.[30]

As can be seen, the devastation caused by the wars of the middle of the century was truly catastrophic. Agriculture was ruined. A start was made towards reconstruction, but it was a long and difficult task. An analysis of this reconstruction has provided completely new data which are generally unknown, but here is not the place to deal with this matter. The slow process of reconstruction was brutally interrupted by the third war against Sweden at the beginning of the eighteenth century. The economic effects and the devastation caused by this war have not yet been properly studied. Nevertheless, the destruction was on a vast scale. Reconstruction during the eighteenth century received a certain amount of support from new agricultural techniques (for example, the development of colonization by the farmers of Greater Poland), but although this reconstruction was more rapid than the equivalent period of regrowth following upon the 1655–60 war, it was nevertheless impossible, even by the end of the eighteenth century, to reach the level of productivity enjoyed at the end of the sixteenth century.

VI

The following question may now be asked: what were the causes of the economic decline of Poland during the seventeenth century? Why was productivity in the second half of the eighteenth century inferior to that of the end of the sixteenth?

It is not to be doubted that frequent and prolonged wars caused serious damage to the country's economy and heavy losses in population both of which contributed to economic decline. However, these wars, for all the devastation they caused, cannot be regarded as the only cause of the prolonged economic decline in Poland for several reasons.

In the first place, the regressive tendencies had already become apparent, as was shown in section IV of this outline, before the worst of the wars of the middle of the century. War-time destruction therefore preyed upon an already weakened organism. It is clear that some other factor must have intervened earlier, and then exerted its influence concurrently with the ravages of war, thereby reinforcing its economic consequences.

Secondly, available sources dealing with the reconstruction period which followed the seventeenth-century wars reveal that its rhythm was independent of the extent of destruction. In other words, certain of the worst-hit regions embarked upon recovery much more quickly than provinces which suffered less. Among the first to recover was Pomerania, and in particular the region of Danzig. This region had been the battleground of the first (1626–9) and second wars against Sweden (1655–60); and yet it rapidly repaired the damages and losses wreaked by those bloody campaigns. It should be emphasized that agricultural recovery did not occur as a result of widespread use of serf-labour, as was the case in other regions, but by the use of three other methods: firstly tenant-farming; secondly a system in which rent constituted the main charge on the peasants; and thirdly with the help of day-labourers, the principal labour-force used on the larger farms.

Source-material in other countries, and in particular those dealing with the economic consequences of the Thirty Years War, testify to the fact that this war did not entail long-lasting economic decline in the countries in which it was waged. Recovery was relatively rapid, and was generally based upon more modern methods. Thus, for example, in Bohemia one can see an appreciable development in the food industry, an increase in the number of workshops, and the formation and growth of a large internal market including Bohemia and Moravia. A. Klima defined the period 1648–1781 (the latter date marking the abolition of serfdom) as one of preparation for the victory of capitalism.[31] Similar conclusions emerge from a remarkable work by O. Placht.[32] In Germany, too, industry recovered quite rapidly. R. Ludloff, in his study of industrial development in Germany in the sixteenth and seventeenth centuries, estimated that the seventeenth century did not bring with it industrial decline, but rather that industry modified its organization by returning to more primitive forms, to become later the object of capitalist development.[33] It is clear that agriculture must have felt for a long time the effects of losses and destruction caused by war, but it never sank into economic depression or stagnation.

As can be seen, there are good reasons for looking for factors other than the wars of the middle of the seventeenth century to account for Poland's economic decline. This does not mean that the present author would wish to minimize the importance of the consequences of the wars on the Polish economy. It is rather a matter of defining this main cause whose influence on the economy was as multi-faceted as it was disastrous.

It is generally thought today that economic decline in Poland during the seventeenth and eighteenth centuries was caused mainly by the particular kind of farming system which spread rapidly over the whole country. This system, which operated on large and medium-sized properties belonging to nobles, was the use of a labour-force which consisted almost solely of peasant-serfs. The development of this kind of rural system was largely due to the attraction of the corn markets of western Europe and the opportunities thus made available to property-owners in Poland. Exports of cereals towards the Baltic ports had quickly taken on such proportions as to dominate the entire economic structure of the country. The use of forced labour for the farming of the properties of the nobles was a serious threat to the potential of the small peasant-farms. Furthermore, the growth of the towns was gravely prejudiced by the nobility's monopoly in foreign trade, and by the limitations of the home market—a direct consequence of the impoverishment of the countryside. The reasons for the worsening of the lot of the small peasant-farmers were many, but they generally arose from the same major causes. Among these reasons was the decrease in area of the arable land which the peasants had the right to cultivate for their own profit. In addition, in the seventeenth century, they had less time to spend on their own land because of an increase in the number of dayworks and dues owed to the lord. More and more of the rural population found themselves gradually forced into serfdom and feudal labour. Opportunities for the peasants to sell freely either their own labour or the produce of their land were seriously decreased, partly because of heavy charges in kind and money, and partly because of the limitations imposed by the nobility on the peasants' contracts with local markets. The development of noble landed property at the expense of the peasants had begun to have harmful effects from the first half of the seventeenth century. Here and there, production in the noble properties increased, though this increase was not the result of agricultural progress, but in most cases arose from an increase in arable area, achieved by appropriating land hitherto cultivated by the peasants.

The present author is in a position to present certain arguments which, in addition to the direct detailed data in the source material, will lend support to the thesis of the harmful influence on the economic development of the country of landed property using the labour of peasant-serfs, and directed solely towards the export of cereals.

First is the fact that the beginnings of the economic decline correspond chronologically with the more or less rapid establishment of the predominance of noble farms employing serf-labour. For example, in Greater Poland where this system of farming developed a little later than in Masovia and was more closely connected with the home market, regressive tendencies became apparent correspondingly later. This delay can be estimated to have been roughly a quarter of a century. Further research would probably shed more light on this point.

Secondly, there were no symptoms of economic decline in Silesia before the Thirty Years War. Now, in this region, landed properties developed in close contact with the home market. Towns were able to grow and to provide markets for agricultural produce. Even the spread of large-scale farming was unable to paralyse their development, as was the case in those areas where the essential factor contributing to the predominance of noble farms was the export of cereals to the Baltic ports, organized by the nobles themselves, without the help of the towns. Noble-owned properties in Silesia used as their labour-force mainly those members of the rural population who owned only the tiniest portions of land, or even none at all. Until the end of the sixteenth century, and even up to the beginning of the seventeenth, the Silesia peasants worked on their lords' land for a mere 50–70 days a year.[34]

Thirdly, let us look at the economic development of Pomerania (or rather of the region of Gdańsk) where, as has been seen, there was no economic decline before the first Swedish invasion of 1626–9. Large noble properties had not yet begun at this period to restrict the growth of the small peasant-farms. The towns, principally Gdańsk, made sizeable profits from the very favourable situation created by cereal export to western Europe.

It is possible to derive a further argument from analogies in Europe. Let it be said straight away that the present author does not subscribe to the view that there was in Europe in the seventeenth century a general economic crisis in the sense of a stagnation, lull, or recession caused by a weakening of economic activity. Such a phenomenon certainly did not take place. On the other hand, an increasing disequilibrium can be seen in economic development in various European countries. Such development came about faster in some countries than in others, and some were unable to maintain the rhythm to which their economy had been accustomed during the preceding years. A slightly deeper analysis reveals that those countries whose economy was most dynamic—that is England and the Low Countries—were precisely those where feudalism played almost no part in the rural economy and where industry and the towns were thriving. The countries, whose rhythm of development was slower, still possessed a fairly traditional social and economic structure in rural areas, although the situation regarding peasant properties and towns was never as difficult as in Poland. The countries of the Iberian peninsula, Spain and Portugal, bear some resemblance to Poland. Indeed, in these countries can be observed in the seventeenth century phenomena of economic stagnation and even of decline (as in Italy to a certain extent). Now, in these countries, as in Poland, social relations in rural areas were backward. The Portuguese and Spanish nobility busied itself with colonial exploitation, without a care for the internal development of their countries. Their economic activity—like that of the Polish nobility who developed a system of farming based on forced labour and the export of cereals—hindered both the economic initiative and the potential productivity of the peasant and, to a large extent, also that of the bourgeoisie. For these reasons, it is difficult to agree with F. Mauro's thesis which sees in the development of sugar production in Brazil clear signs of a so-called economic revival of Portugal in the seventeenth century.[35] This is tantamount to arguing that the fact that noble landed properties based on serf-labour developed rapidly in Poland is evidence that the country was enjoying a period of flourishing economic growth before the wars of the middle of the seventeenth century.

There have also been attempts to explain this crisis of the seventeenth century by unfavourable changes in the climate of Europe at this time. Such, for example, is G. Utterström's view.[36] Le Roy Ladurie observed rather more wisely that the changes in climate had various effects which could equally well have favoured harvests as harmed them.[37] This factor can therefore be left out of account in studies of economic decline in Poland.

In conclusion, two essential elements may be isolated from among the causes of economic decline in Poland: the destruction due to the wars, and the system of farming in the larger properties based on serf-labour and on the export of cereals.

NOTES

1. The first section of this translation is a paraphrase of the author's first section in which he gives a much fuller account of the historiography of the economic decline of Poland, together with detailed bibliographical notes. The rest of the translation follows the text of the original article.

2. S. Hoszowski, 'L'Europe centrale devant la révolution des prix aux XVIe et XVIIe siècles', *Annales* (1961), pp. 445 ff.

3. N. W. Posthumus, *Inquiry into the History of Prices in Holland* (Leiden, 1946), vol. i. p. cii.

4. A. Wawrzyńczyk, *Próba ustalenia wysokości plonów w królewszcznach województwa sandomierskiego w drugiej połowie XVIi początkach XVII wieku* (An attempt to estimate the yield from the lands in the crown estates of the *voivodi* of Sandomierz in the second half of the sixteenth and the beginning of the seventeenth centuries), in *Studia z dziejów gospodarstwa wiejskiego* (Studies in the history of rural civilization), vol. i (Wroclaw, 1957).

5. J. Majewski, *Gospodarstwo folwarczne we wsiach miasta Poznania w latach 1582–1644* (The cultivation of the rural properties of the town of Poznan during the years 1582–1644) (Poznan, 1957).

6. I. Gieysztor, *Zniszczenia i straty wojenne oraz ich skutk na Mazowszu* (Destruction and losses caused by the wars, and their consequences in Masovia), in *Polska w okresie drugiej wojny północnej 1655–1660*, ii (Warsaw, 1957), 55 and 56.

7. Ibid., p. 57.

8. Ibid., p. 60.

9. Ibid.

10. J. R. Szaflik, *Stosunki gospodarczo-społeczne we wsiach starostwa łukowskiego w XVII wieku. Z przeszłosci ziemi łukowskiej* (Social and economic relations in the villages of the *starosti* of Lukow in the seventeenth century. Outline of the past of the region of Lukow) (Lublin, 1957), p. 60.

11. Warwrzyńczyk, op. cit.

12. Cf. B. Zientara, *Dzieje małopolskiego hutnictwa żelaznego XIV-XVII wieku* (The history of metallurgy in Lesser Poland from the fourteenth to the seventeenth centuries) (Warsaw, 1954).

13. Cf. B. Baranowski, *Gospodarstwo chłopskie i folwarczne we wschodniej Wielkopolsce, w XVIII wieku* (Peasant-farms and large landed properties in eastern Greater Poland in the eighteenth century) (Warsaw, 1958).

14. W. Rusiński, *Straty i zniszczenia w czasie wojny szwedzkiep (1655–1660) oraz jej skutki na obszarze Wielkopolski* (Losses and destruction during the war against Sweden (1655–1660) and their consequences in the province of Greater Poland) in *Polska w okresie drugiej wojny północnej*, ii (Warsaw, 1957), 6.

15. It was S. Hoszowski who made a special study of the destruction caused by the wars in Danzig in Pomerania: *Zniszczenia w czasie wojny szwedzkiej na terenie Prus Królewskich* (The damage caused by the war against Sweden in Royal Prussia), in *Polska w okresie drugiej wojny północnej*, ii (Warsaw, 1957), 383–427.

16. J. Topolski, *Wpływ wojen połowy XVII wieku na sytuację ekonomiczną Podlasia* (Consequences of the wars of the middle of the seventeenth century on the economic situation in Podlachia), in *Studia Historica à l'occasion de la 35e année de travaux historiques de Henryk Łowmiański* (Warsaw, 1959).

17. Gieysztor, op. cit., pp. 75 ff.

18. A. Kamiński, *Zniszczenia wojenne w Małopolsce i ich skutki w okresie najazdu szwedzkiego 1655–1660* (Destruction due to hostilities during the Swedish invasion of 1655–1660 and their consequences), in *Polska w okresie drugiej wojny północnej*, ii (Warsaw, 1957), 112.

19. Szaflik, op. cit., p. 61.

20. Rusiński, op. cit., p. 35.
21. Ibid., p. 34.
22. Baranowski, op. cit., p. 39.
23. Hoszowski, op. cit., pp. 141 ff.
24. Ibid.
25. Topolski, op. cit., p. 337.
26. Rusiński, op. cit., p. 21.
27. Gieysztor, op. cit., p. 72.
28. Topolski, op. cit., p. 341.
29. Kamiński, op. cit., p. 105.
30. Topolski, op. cit., pp. 340 ff.
31. A. Klima, 'Industrial development in Bohemia, 1648–1781', *Past and Present*, xi (1957), 87–99.
32. O. Placht, *Lidnatost a společenska skladba Českeho Štatu w XVI–XVIII stuleti* (The population and social structure in the state of Bohemia from the sixteenth to the eighteenth centuries) (Prague, 1957).
33. R. Ludloff, 'Industrial development in 16th and 17th century Germany', *Past and Present*, xii (1957), 58–75.
34. R. Heck, *Studia nad położaniem ekonomicznym ludności wiejskiej no Śląsku w XVI wieku* (Studies on the economic situation of the rural population in Silesia in the sixteenth century) (Wroclaw, 1959).
35. F. Mauro, *Le Portugal et l'Atlantique au XVIIe siècle, 1570–1670* (Paris, 1960).
36. G. Utterström, 'Climatic Fluctuations and Population Problems in Early Modern History', *Scandinavian Economic History Review*, iii (1955).
37. E. Le Roy Ladurie, 'Histoire et climat', *Annales*, vol. i (1959); id., 'Climat et récoltes aux XVIIe et XVIIIe siècles', *Annales*, vol. iii (1960); id., 'Aspects historiques de la nouvelle climatologie', *Revue historique*, vol. ccxxv (1961).

7

A Long Agrarian Cycle: Languedoc, 1500–1700

EMMANUEL LE ROY LADURIE

Translated by John Day*

WITCHES' black magic at the end of the sixteenth century; prophets' white magic at the beginning of the eighteenth century—the radical antithesis in mythical content must not be allowed to obscure the affinities of certain mental structures, nor the long persistence, in the early modern period, of a capacity for anxiety and for wonder; of a faith in miracles which today is lost. Is this one sign, among scores of others, of a certain cultural continuum between 1500 and 1700—itself resting on the social continuum and the specific unity of a long agrarian cycle?

PERIODIZATION

I have endeavoured in the present book[1] to observe, at various levels, the long-term movements of an economy and of a society: base and superstructure; material life and cultural life; sociological evolution and collective psychology—the whole within the framework of a rural world which remained very largely traditional in nature. More particularly, I have attempted to analyse, in their multiple aspects, successive phases of growth and decline. These phases taken together in chronological sequence (lift-off, rise, maturity, and decline) imply a unity and serve to describe a major, organized, multi-secular rural fluctuation spanning eight generations.

To put it more simply, my book's protagonist is a long agrarian cycle, lasting from the end of the fifteenth to the beginning of the eighteenth century, studied in its entirety. I have been able to delineate and to characterize it thanks, naturally, to the price-curves; but more particularly thanks to demographic studies (of tax-paying and of total population) to indices of production and business activity, to the series of diagrams reflecting land, wealth, and income distribution.

The early modern cycle thus defined is not merely a figment of the imagination, one of those abstractions raised to a fetish which have been so justly criticized by Pierre Jeannin for their inability to explain what they pretend

* From the last chapter of the abridged edition of *Les Paysans de Languedoc* (Paris: Flammarion, 1969). The English translation of this book was published in 1974 by the University of Illinois Press and the present chapter is reproduced with their permission. The notes to this chapter were translated by the Editor.

to explain. Happily a solid documentation, rich in diverse, continuous, indicative series of data, has made it possible to dissociate in a fruitful manner 'the elements and components' of the long-term movement. These sources have divulged its internal connections; 'its significance, modalities, and chronology'.[2]

The complete cycle can be broken down into several distinct phases.

Phase one: the low-water mark (pre-conditions of growth). People were scarce (because the demographic structure had collapsed at the end of the previous—medieval—long-term cycle, which was also multi-secular, spanning the period from the eleventh to the fifteenth century). Arable land and even forests were once again abundant, constituting reserves of unemployed resources available for a resumption of expansion. Landed property was consolidated into large holdings; families into powerful clans. Low land-rent tended little by little to stimulate the activities of assarters, farm-operators, and peasants. Food was more plentiful and people were better nourished, healthier, and, in other respects, less vulnerable to the plague microbe after a good hundred years of selective slaughter. All of these things helped set the stage for a new period of advance.

Second phase: the advance. It came about, as has been seen, essentially of its own accord, fuelled by the simple accumulation of endogenous factors. The combustible material had been piling up for a long time and the slightest spark (a series of good harvests, a supplementary injection of precious metals into the monetary circulation; the influence of new circuits of trade or of new poles of urban growth; or simply a period of peace and prosperity) was sufficient to ignite the fires of expansion.

The expansion—a rapid mutation at the end of a period of silent gestation —thus made its local début quite abruptly in about 1490–1500. It was population that got off to a fast start; the economy itself made little headway at first. For this reason, by 1530 a serious contradiction developed: on the one hand, there was the dynamic elasticity of population; on the other, the stubborn inelasticity of agricultural production. Was the latter, which has been widely noted elsewhere in western Europe—in the north[3] as well as in the south—the 'fruit' of technical conservatism,[4] lack of capital, and the absence of a spirit of initiative and innovation? In all events, it brought in its wake signs of austerity—forms of 'rationing': wage-rationing through the reduction of real wages and the pauperization of hired hands and day-labourers; land rationing through the accelerated subdivision of tenures. Impoverishment proceeded at the same time from a sort of 'iron law' of wages and from the break-up of land-holdings without any increase in yields per hectare. Malthus and Ricardo had joined forces.

A disparate, discordant development of this sort is incapable, notwithstanding a rise in entrepreneurial profits, of bringing about agrarian capitalism on a large scale. True growth, which would have raised the average gross product *per capita*, remained, under these conditions, an impossible goal, situated far over the horizon.

Contemporaries—the notables no less than the people—were only confusedly aware of the real situation. Should one be surprised at their relative insensibility? No, there is nothing at all shocking about it if one reflects carefully on the mentality of the period. The people of that age had other things on their minds besides the gross product. The most representative among them—and this was one of the strongest and most typical traits of traditional society—were preoccupied to the point of self-immolation with religious questions. The civil-war combatants, whether Huguenot or Papist, were possessed by a bloody obsession with heavenly salvation. After 1560, they threw themselves body and soul into the religious struggle.

It is true that in Protestant circles, the sacred combat obscured certain social projects which raised the question of Church land, of the tithe, and taxes; and even of the three orders of society. Such projects tended, in an obscure and piecemeal fashion, to mitigate the deficiencies of social development.

But the results were mediocre. The social agitation of the end of the century degenerated into an anti-tax movement, if not into the madness of the witches' sabbaths that turned the world upside down but did nothing to transform it.

Third phase: post-1600, maturity. The Malthusian and Ricardian checks tended to become veritable social stumbling-blocks. Thus, from the point of view of population—for reasons connected with the deterioration of living standards—the death rate drew dangerously close to the birth rate. To be sure, in Languedoc (as in Provence, the Loire valley, the Beauvais region, Holland, and England) population continued to grow after 1600; and the French Midi—like many regions of continental Europe to the north—had thus far escaped the long, premature retreat of population that affected Castile and certain parts of Italy beginning in 1600.[5]

Nevertheless, as far as Languedoc is concerned, a demographic deceleration is clearly perceptible after 1600. The general curve of population had been climbing steeply under Francis I and Henry II. Between 1570 and 1650 it gradually levelled off.

New parasitic phenomena were superimposed on the cases of 'rationing' and austerity, observed in the second phase (which continued into the third): *rente* in all its forms 'took off'—interest on loans, rent from land, tithes to the Church, and taxes to the State. The rentier mentality prevailed over the spirit of enterprise. Gentleman farmers were transformed into parasitic landlords. In certain respects society tended to sink into a state of social conservatism, the paralysing consequences of which aggravated the Malthusian effects of an immemorial technical conservatism.[6]

During this third phase an enormous increase in taxation reflected in its way the temptations of prestige and of state power embodied in the policies of Richelieu. The state, which had consolidated its forces at the end of the previous phase of expansion, embarked on far-ranging wars, the costs of which were too heavy for society to bear.

This third phase of so-called *maturity* in agrarian development, which preceded a certain decline, was therefore quite different from the phase of the same name, as described by theoreticians of modern economic growth. It was not the 'healthy' maturity of industrial societies, or at least of the most favoured among them. On the contrary, it was a period beset with growing difficulties and accumulated obstacles; a period in which the gross product, in the long run, made no progress: in which the demographic advance, for this reason, was held in check: in which capital was diverted towards *rente*.

Granting this, is it correct, in connection with such a period, to employ catch-all phrases like 'the crisis of the seventeenth century', or to speak of the 'reversal of the conjuncture' beginning in the early decades of the century?

Such expressions are perfectly valid in regard to the Spanish-colonial conjuncture, to Iberian America, prematurely stricken by the silver famine, and above all by the débâcle of the indigenous population. They are equally valid in regard to Castile and Italy; and a few decades later could be applied to Germany and neighbouring Burgundy devastated by the Thirty Years War. But outside these geographical limits, vast as they are, simple extrapolation is impossible. One cannot even assert that the 'Mediterranean conjuncture', as a whole, supports the thesis of a change of direction around 1620: some violent short-lived crises, yes; a demographic slow-down (beginning in the last third of the sixteenth century), without a doubt; a universal secular depression, no—at least not yet; because Provence, Languedoc, and Catalonia[7]—all of the considerable Mediterranean littoral of the Gulf of Lion, from Tarragona to Toulon—escaped that radical reversal of the economic conjuncture which assumed henceforth a southern, peninsular, and, from a European point of view, almost marginal character.

On the northernmost shores of the Mediterranean, the conjuncture subsided; it changed pace; it grew *sluggish*;[8] it did not yet *reverse itself*. The 'chronological disparity' and the 'permanent opposition' that Pierre Jeannin called attention to in 1964 established itself along a frontier passing far to the south; a frontier that served to isolate the Spanish-colonial and 'Italo-Castilian' conjuncture condemned to a long decline beginning in 1620. North of this line, in numerous regions of continental Europe and the New World, in the huge area extending from Mediterranean France and Catalonia to the North Sea and to the Puritan countries of the Atlantic seaboard, the populations knew nothing yet, nor for some time to come, of that malady of long-term decline that afflicted Italians, Castilians, and Spain's American subjects.

In Languedoc, in any event, agricultural production, although sluggish, did not collapse. Quite the contrary, after 1620 certain sectors, like viticulture, were even fairly lively. The demographic advance continued, if at a much slower pace; and numerous categories of rentiers prospered, redoubling their outlays on prestige, piety, power, and conspicuous consumption; multiplying their chateaux and churches.

The 'carefree prosperity' of the sixteenth century was evidently at an end. Signs of sclerosis and social and demographic maturity multiplied, and it is here that one discovers an analogy with the infinitely more serious sclerosis affecting Castile and Italy; but it is here alone, for, local exceptions aside, the gross product and population for the most part held firm.

The tragedy of Languedoc, in phase III, was not the collapse but only the inelasticity and rigidity of agricultural production; not its decline, but its failure to grow significantly. Let us accept, for the sake of argument, the most favourable (counterfactual) hypothesis—that the gross product had increased substantially under Richelieu and Mazarin. In that case, it would have sustained the continuing demographic advance, the resulting sub-division of tenures, and the increased exactions of the rentier classes without difficulty and without sacrificing the standard of living. It would have financed the wars and ambitions of the cardinal ministers with Napoleonic good cheer.

Nothing of the sort occurred. The gross agricultural product from Francis I to the Fronde remained, in the long run, practically stationary, with only a slight tendency to rise. This was the reason for so much misfortune, even if the conjuncture did not 'turn around'; even if its complete reversal—marking the tragic moment of a difficult time—did not in fact occur until later, in the final phase of the great agrarian cycle that I have termed 'the recession'.

Under Colbert, the obduracy of production seemed for a moment exorcised. The gross product increased, and for a period of ten or fifteen years broke through the secular ceiling. Unfortunately, the production of wine, which was the most profitable crop of the region in normal times, did not rise; indeed it declined during this brief period of prosperity. The contradiction is not without significance, for society in the age of Colbert was not equipped, materially or psychologically, to receive and continue this partial and precarious rise of the gross product. The increase in supply, resulting automatically from the rise in production, occurred in the midst of falling prices which it served only to accentuate.

Farm profits were wiped out by 1665 to 1670. Production itself finally collapsed in the disastrous decade of the 1680s, affecting the peasant small-hold no less than the great ecclesiastical estate.

We are now well into *phase IV, the long period of recession.* Aggregate agricultural production declined, without, however, falling excessively low. The movement was limited essentially to wiping out the temporary increase registered in the days of Fouquet and Colbert. Production simply retreated more or less to the permanent, basic, depressed level it had been unable to rise above in the sixteenth and first half of the seventeenth centuries.

This return to Louis XIII, to Henry II, indeed to Francis I, at the very end of the reign of Louis XIV, had depressing consequences for peasant society. For a long time—up to 1650—the low level of production had been compatible with the continuation—increasingly slow and difficult—of the demographic advance and the process of landed subdivision. It was even compatible with the institution of increasingly heavy rents and charges. People exerted themselves a bit more, tightened their belts, and society managed somehow to make ends meet. After 1650, the momentary upsurge of production (between 1655 and 1675) had granted peasant society a new lease on life. The demographic advance, landed subdivision, and onerous exactions could continue for a while longer.

But the return to a depressed level of production after 1675–80 necessitated, in the last analysis, a readjustment, a social reassessment, a sort of cheerless process of rationalization. In which domain? There was no question, for reasons of high politics, of the government curtailing its demands in the face of a declining gross product. Quite the opposite, taxation would increase at the end of the reign contrary to all economic logic but in harmony with the grandiose designs of the Sun King, served by a ruthless bureaucracy.

The readjustment and re-ordering, therefore, would have to be in other directions. First, since nothing could be done about public exactions, certain private exactions contracted a bit. Land-rent showed unmistakable signs of decline in real terms at the close of the century. But the chief victim of social readjustment was population. Society's solution to the contraction of the gross product and its return to the secular *status quo ante* was of the cruellest sort. It reduced the number of mouths to feed, the size of the potential workforce, by brutally amputating a fraction of its human complement. It handed over a pound of its own flesh. After 1680, in fact, all demographic growth, no matter how modest, was arrested. Here we come to the capital fact, the truly unprecedented event: population, for the first time in two centuries, entered upon a long-term decline; a decline provoked not so much by the repeated famines—which were perhaps less serious than in the centre and in the north of France—as by joblessness and poverty; by chronic undernourishment; by the low standard of living which favoured the spread of epidemics; by the primitive sanitary conditions of the poor; and—very accessorily—by emigration, late marriages, and even a little birth control. A natural corollary to the decline in numbers of the poorer classes was the downfall of the small-hold tenant. Landed subdivision, which had been raging since the Renaissance, was finally arrested, and a phase of consolidation, to the advantage of the land engrossers, set in.

It was no longer a question, as it had been in the first half of the seventeenth century, of the simple abatement of a particularly lively conjuncture, but rather—from 1675 to 1680—of its complete turn-about, a turn-about reflected as clearly as one could hope to see in population statistics and in the cadasters. The movement, almost two centuries old, of rising population and landed subdivision had lasted since 1500. Extremely animated during the better part of the sixteenth century, in the seventeenth century it showed obvious signs of maturity, sclerosis, and fatigue. Finally, in 1680, it disappeared, giving way to a movement in the opposite direction. This was a perfect illustration (at least in the regional case of the French Midi, elsewhere the timing might be different) of the reversal of the conjuncture. It was the critical juncture that historians just about everywhere are rightly struggling to date, in the exhausted Europe of the seventeenth century.

TECHNICAL IMPASSES AND CULTURAL STUMBLING-BLOCKS

Throughout the present book, and in particular in the last part devoted to the 'recession'—the interrupted development and contraction of an ancient rural society—I have tried to situate the determinants, to assign the actual responsibilities, by establishing an accurate chronology. From this point of view, at least one connection seems solidly established. It was the technological weakness of this society; its inability to raise productivity; its incapacity to increase production lastingly and definitively, which created the barrier that interrupted the almost bisecular advance in population and peasant small-holding at the end of our period.

One is truly in the presence of that 'preindustrial society characterized by slow technical change' where the 'processes of growth and decline' were still dominated 'by the play between demographic expansion and limited resources'.[9] From beginning to end of the great agrarian cycle of 1500–1700, the gross product determined the outcome of this duel through sheer weight of inertia. It was the gross product that progressively bent the population-curve inward (its ballistic-like trajectory evokes this braking action on society to perfection).[10] It was the gross product that induced phenomena of pauperization in phases II and III; through its incapacity to grow, it rendered the increased exactions of phase III intolerable (exactions that a dynamic production, on the contrary, would have sustained without difficulty). Finally, in phase IV, the retrogression—or to be exact, the return to a state of inertia following a momentary upswing of the gross product—provoked the final decline of population, of small-holding, and of land development.

This denouement was logical and inevitable. The Malthusian scissors between production and population could not stay open for ever.

Under these circumstances, is one forced to reject the classic explanation which imputes the difficulties of the seventeenth century and its terminal crisis to the 'monetary famine'? By no means. Even if somewhat outmoded, the quantity theory of money does not deserve such a summary execution. But it can no longer conserve the absolutely centrol role it once enjoyed. It must be integrated into a unified system of explanation, at once more sweeping and more flexible.

If, following the lively advance of the previous period, certain European economies, populations, and societies, like those of Languedoc, levelled off and finally declined during the course of the seventeenth century, it was not only because the Spanish–American colonizers had worked out the best gold and silver mines and depleted the ranks of the mining proletariat of the Andes. A monetary impasse really existed, but it was not the only obstacle to expansion. It formed part of a whole structure of interrelated impasses: the landed impasse—the lack of unlimited reserves of fertile, easy to work, profitable land; and more important—concealed, so to speak, behind the phenomenon of land hunger—the technological impasse, which constituted the essential impediment.

The most striking evidence in the latter domain is the average wheat yield in Languedoc[11] which, according to first-hand sources, remained stabilized at a low figure (from 3 to 4·5 for 1) from the sixteenth century (our earliest data) to 1730–40. The only improvement, and it was not lasting, was registered in the age of Colbert. Yields did not really begin to rise until 1750 and even then they rose only slowly.

In other words, if society contracted and the economy lost momentum and finally fell back to its base level at the end of the seventeenth century, it was because the latter was incapable either of increasing or renewing its stocks; its stock of previous metals, to be sure; but also its stock of good land, which was limited by definition; and failing this, its 'stock' of technical progress which was so ridiculously modest in the sixteenth and seventeenth centuries. Let us pursue one of our earlier hypotheses: if grain-yields had risen a few points between 1500 and 1700 (as would occur later); if one had succeeded in planting vines on a massive scale and a continuing basis (as would be the case almost uninterruptedly between 1760 and 1870); or else in introducing widespread irrigation (like the Catalans beginning in 1720), in that case Languedocian society, through the simple increase in income per land unit, could have coped with the rise in population and the headlong subdivision of land-holdings, as well as with the growing burden of charges of all sorts. The fragmentation of peasant tenures proved excessive and the increased charges intolerable because production and productivity remained stabilized at centuries-old levels.

In fact, this technological immobility was the result of a whole series of cultural stumbling-blocks. Some have spoken of a *natural* ceiling on productive resources. But 'nature' in this instance is actually culture; it is the customs, the way of life, the mentality of the people; it is a whole formed by technical knowledge and a system of values; by the means employed and the ends pursued. The forces that first deflected the expansion, then checked it, and ultimately broke it, were not only economic in a narrow sense, but also cultural in a broad sense, and even in a certain measure spiritual. In this last category, above all, their actual impact is impossible to measure, but their power of constraint is obvious.

Despite a certain evolution, of which we shall speak in a moment, Languedocian society, as far as its ruling élites were concerned, remained—at least to the same degree as French society as a whole—theological and military; and under Louis XIV, the sons of the petit bourgeoisie, just like the sons of the nobility, were whenever possible still intended for the army or the church.

For the most gifted minds of that age, the salvation of souls was more important than the improvement of techniques. The pragmatic, 'disenchanted',[12] and profoundly non-religious universe in which we live was scarcely conceivable, at least for the masses of the people, before 1700.

In the sixteenth century, for example, in a society which was nevertheless very dynamic, the capital of human energy accumulated since the Renaissance was not invested in the economy, or consecrated to the safeguard of a minimum level of well-being. It was dissipated wholesale in the fire and flame of the religious struggle. It was only as a second thought and on the rebound, so to speak, that the Protestants of the civil wars advanced certain modest social demands—the redistribution of land and the reform of the tithe.

After 1600, the victory of Catholicism became more and more inseparable from a certain revival of 'feudal' society ('feudal' not in the narrow, institutional sense of the medievalists, but in the broad sense in which the philosophers of the eighteenth century used the term).

The comparative failure of the agronomists and Protestant leaders is a reflection of this revival. Serres, Laffemas, and Sully, who were concerned, each in his own fashion and sometimes in contradiction to one another, with questions of economic expansion—in agriculture or manufacturing—had no significant following after 1620. The nation, with Richelieu, would prefer war; and with Louis XIV, despite the Colbertian interlude, it would prefer glory. The aristocratic ideal of prowess and the Catholic ideal of salvation would determine the conduct of the ruling classes.

During what I have termed the phase of maturity (phase III), rent exacted its heavy tribute from a sluggish production; and this golden age of rent was inseparable from a certain number of styles or ways of life which aimed, as the case might be, at ostentation or security; styles of life reflected in the bourgeoisie's passion for offices or land; the clergy's investments in monasteries or baroque architecture; the libertine or military pursuits of the nobility, or of those who aspired to the nobility. These modes of life signified relative wealth; they did little to stimulate expansion.

In phase IV ('recession'), the policies pursued by the state, with the assent of a large portion of the élites, were aimed at assuring, at whatever cost, the resplendent glory of one man and his lineage; the war-making and territorial power of the realm and the absolute monopoly of a Church. Such policies are the perfectly logical consequence of a certain system of values (aberrant values in our eyes), but they ran directly counter to the recovery of a contracted economy. Versailles and the army—the military and sumptuary budgets—increased the pressure of taxation, and thus reduced further a gross product already in decline.

As for the Revocation of the Edict of Nantes—another striking aspect of these global policies—it revealed, in the person of Basville, its principal promoter in Languedoc, an exacerbated concern for a combined religious and political monism. For the Intendant of Languedoc, the unity of the faith was an absolute good, which had the added merit of guaranteeing the unanimity of the French people in their obedience to the Very Christian King.[13]

Such an attitude was not absurd, if we only place ourselves in the specious perspective of its promoters. But it was costly; and it furnishes the remarkable example of a culture that was destructive of its own economic foundations. Doubtless the Revocation was neither the first nor the principal cause of French economic decadence at the close of the reign.[14] In 1685, nevertheless, it came at a very bad moment for a Midi swarming with Huguenots and in the early stages of an economic decline (underway since 1675–80). In Languedoc, at least in the Protestant cantons, the Revocation accentuated the existing stagnation. It consummated for a time the ruin of the silk industry of the Cévennes and subjacent regions. It provoked the flight of capital from Nîmes.[15]

Catholic contemporaries were conscious of these misfortunes. 'Misery is very widespread since the change of religion,' the notary Borrely wrote at the conclusion of some notations on the subject. Nevertheless, the same Borrely had accepted in advance and would justify *a posteriori* the decree of 1685, for he saw in it a supreme sign of grace, a divine miracle, the work of God. Besides, Borrely was convinced that the Protestants, those 'ill-intentioned devils', those monsters, those fanatics, fully deserved their bitter fate. No matter if they dragged their Catholic contemporaries down to ruin in an epidemic of bankruptcies. That was the price that had to be paid.

From a certain point of view, therefore, responsible men of that age acted out their own history and consummated their own misfortunes without illusions. It was a question of the stakes; religious unity, for many of them, represented a higher value in itself than the rescue, at any price, of profits or material well-being.

By the same token, the rebels who rose up against different kinds of oppression did not always adopt a line of conduct that was—according to our own criteria—perfectly rational and capable of putting an end to their suffering. For a very long time, they confined themselves to fighting the tax-collector, whereas the real source of their difficulties lay in the social organization itself and was much more general. A single revolt in seventeenth-century France sought explicitly (at the direct instigation of English exiles influenced by their own revolution) to raise the issue of equal rights and representative government.[16] The daring programme drawn up by the *Ormée* at Bordeaux intrigued, for a time, the princes of the Fronde, but it did not awaken a lasting echo among the population; and this attempted graft of Anglo-Saxon political thought on the French rebel consciousness was destined to wither on the limb. The eighteenth century of the *philosophes*, whose activities would eventually prepare the way for the reception of political programmes from across the Channel, still lay ahead. In the seventeenth century the French and English cultural areas were at variance. To speak to a French rebel of those days, whether pre-Fronde or post-Fronde, of the actual abolition of privilege and of a national, elected assembly, would be a little, *mutatis mutandis*, like preaching socialism to an African native in 1850 or 1900. But if you had talked to that Frenchman of 1640 or 1670 about the *taille* or the salt-tax he would have seen red, even if taxes were only one of the many sources of his difficulties.

In another domain, that of religious oppression, the natives of the Cévennes during the course of the Camisard insurrection departed from what—according to our possibly subjective criteria—should have represented the rationale of such a revolt. They did not confine themselves to advocating freedom of conscience, or even to simple Protestant proselytizing, but adopted, as a line of conduct, the hysterical trance, inspired by the convulsions of the visionaries and the imminence of the Second Coming. Such behaviour was highly appreciated and where possible imitated by the Camisards' Protestant contemporaries; but in our culture of today, and even at the time among devout Catholic rationalists like Fléchier and Basville, it was considered aberrant and neurotic.[17]

In this perspective, the study of cultural impediments ought to be pursued beyond the limits of 'culture', in the narrow sense of the term, to the farthest reaches of the unconscious psyche; the *aiguillette* rites, so widespread and so terrifying; the forms of behaviour encountered during the popular revolts and 'emotions'[18] have disclosed, on several occasions, the existence of extremely well-characterized anxieties, impulses, and fantasies which were expressed in a symbolic 'language' of frightening obviousness the likes of which are no longer to be found in our contemporary culture.

A long monograph on the Camisard peasants has permitted us to elucidate in a different connection—starting with the convulsive seizures—the symptoms of hysterical 'conversion';[19] that deep-seated ethnological neurosis of traditional societies[20] which today is in the process of disappearing in the more advanced countries. Thanks to these symptoms, there emerged the underlying role of a severe sexual repression, inculcated from earliest childhood in the Cévennes by the Huguenot ethic; inculcated elsewhere—in

Languedoc or at Paris—by the Jansenist ethic which steadily gained ascendancy under Louis XIV and the young Louis XV.[21]

Jansenist or Huguenot, profound psychological motivations conformed, in this instance, to the imperatives of the social structure, and more precisely to the basic demographic facts of that age which implied, for the majority of young people, a long period of sexual inhibition prior to marriage,[22] and justified a severe repression of the biological instincts.

Materially impoverished and sexually repressed, traditional society at the end of our period seems, as far as the popular classes are concerned, to have been characterized by a double series of frustrations and deficiencies which mutually reinforced and conditioned one another.

The material aspects of the great agrarian cycle were, in a word, inseparable from its cultural aspects properly speaking. One sustained and fortified the other. The economy stagnated, society remained intractable, and population—following its early triumphs—retreated; because society, population, and the economy lacked the progressive technology of true growth. But they also lacked—at least as yet and at least to a sufficient degree, broadly diffused among the ruling classes and among the people—the conscience, the culture, the morals, the politics, the education, the reformist spirit, the unfettered longing for success, which would have stimulated technological initiative and the spirit of enterprise, and permitted an economic 'take-off'.

SEEDS OF TRUE GROWTH

The picture, however, must not be blackened excessively. I have been speaking of a multi-secular rural fluctuation, or more simply of a long agrarian cycle. Let no one be misled by my use of this convenient expression. It was not at all a question of a sort of eternal return, of a bisecular or trisecular swing of the pendulum which, following a phase of expansion, brought society back to its point of departure, to the 'zero degree' from which it started.

Such a conception would be absurd and, for that matter, inadequate in the light of the known facts. In reality, even if the contagion of true growth had not yet broken out at the close of the seventeenth century—far from it —there existed by this time, within Languedocian society, some isolated factors of real growth, shining like incandescent particles in the darkest hours of Louis XIV's reign. They portend, but as yet no more than that, a modern type of development based on an increase of individual wealth which was slow but unlimited.

First in the case of agriculture: vine cultivation (for wine and spirits) and silk culture, despite their difficulties at the end of the period, were much more widespread in 1700–10 than in the sixteenth century, as the figures cited by Basville and the *compoix* clearly show.[23] Progress in this domain, despite partial setbacks, was irreversible. Viticulture took two steps forward from Henry IV to Mazarin, and one step back under Louis XIV. It was still one step ahead.[24]

And then, it is also indisputable that, at the end of the seventeenth century, the agricultural sector lost its near-exclusive preponderance. A manufacturing sector was developing, not without difficulty. For a long time, Colbert had been preaching to deaf ears. That effective but unpopular minister (for him, as for Jules Ferry, *les roses poussent en dedans*) was largely unsuccessful in seducing the Estates of Languedoc, and when the members of that august assembly did at last agree to the minister's projects—Riquet's canal and the new manufactures—it was in their eyes a sort of bargaining counter conceded to the court in the hope of obtaining new anti-Protestant measures from the king: 'We'll give you the Canal, if you'll hand over the Huguenots.'

But little by little, beginning in 1670–2, the first seeds of an industrial mentality began to spread among the local population. The provincial Estates now accorded the 'pistole per piece' premium on woollen cloth exports readily and without being coaxed. Languedocian cloth manufacturing became a subsidized industry. By 1685–1700, it was competing successfully in the Levant with the Dutch, and trade figures for Marseilles, the obligatory port of exit, begin to swell from the moment statistical series become available, in 1700. This progress would continue, despite temporary setbacks, in the decades that followed.[25]

The Languedocian cloth industry, then, first began to prosper in about 1680–1715, at the very time that agricultural production was collapsing. The two curves—agriculture and woollen manufactures—crossed paths. The retreat of agriculture was very partially compensated for by the advance of textiles, where growth factors were undeniably present.

This is a book of rural history. It is not our purpose here to study the details of manufacturing in Languedoc, a subject that merits a book of its own. We should only point out that the present example of an antithetic development—where the decay of agriculture did not prevent certain seeds of 'maritime', industrial, and commercial progress from taking root—was not unique in late seventeenth- and early eighteenth-century Europe. One encounters other examples in Provence,[26] in Catalonia,[27] and much further afield, on the shores of the Baltic and the North Sea. In fact, the northern plains of the European continent, in the years 1680–1720, witnessed the consummation of an impressive slump of the rural economy. The production and trade in cereals, flax, and hemp regressed,[28] just like those of wheat, wine, and olive oil in Languedoc in the same period. This contraction of supply induced in the north of Europe, as it did in the French Midi, the upward movement of agricultural prices, and a general series of unhealthy, speculative, cyclical upswings; black-market phenomena which caused the *mercuriales* to spiral upward in the second half of Louis XIV's reign.

Nevertheless, the wholesale decline of a vast agricultural sector did not drag all the other segments of the north European economy down in its wake. The English export industries were spared to a degree; and they actually picked up quite briskly in the 1710s,[29] a decade fatal, in many instances, to agriculture. The case resembles that of the Languedocian woollen textile industry on a much larger scale.

Thus, despite the agrarian tragedy, the economy possessed stabilizing forces, industrial and commercial counterweights, which acted to check the decline. They represented limited growth sectors; they constituted elements of feedback and they helped forestall a total collapse, an uncontrollable chain reaction like the one which afflicted various regions in the late Middle Ages. They enhanced the approaching changes of recovery.

THE QUESTION OF ILLITERACY

In the intellectual domain too, despite some cultural stumbling-blocks and despite the economic and social regression of the late seventeenth century, an irreversible process was underway, and certain advances, if still extremely modest, did nevertheless reach 'a point of no return'.

The determining factor was the slow diffusion of some kind of elementary instruction. Let us try to take its measure from a single typical example. At Aniane, an important rural parish in the valley of the Hérault, the registers of the political council (the equivalent, more or less, of a municipal council) have been carefully conserved for the period 1571–1715. On important occasions, all the councillors (who were merchants, artisans, peasants, sometimes farm-labourers) signed the register. Among these individuals, representative for the most part of the more fortunate fraction of rural society, some were illiterate and some were literate; the percentage varied.

How did this percentage evolve along the length of a diachronic series covering a century and a half?[30] In the beginning, around 1570–1625, the series testifies to a fearsome rate of rural illiteracy. In this circle of village councillors, which was not one of grinding poverty, one individual in three, and sometimes one in two, was a complete illiterate who signed with a mark (in the form of a cross, a trowel, a hammer, etc.), thereby demonstrating his inability not only to write, but even to use his simple initials.

The generation of councillors who took their seats around 1620–30 (a generation that probably grew up under the worst conditions, during the difficult years of the war and the League, *c.* 1580–1600) broke all records for basic ignorance. Montmorency, who in his senseless revolt of 1632 often relied on the support of the municipalities, would not find it difficult to lead these illiterates around by the nose.

Beginning in 1630, on the contrary, progress was rapid and almost continuous, although it is still possible to distinguish two stages. Around 1660–70, the council counted no more than 10–20 per cent of complete illiterates who signed with a mark. In the following period, 1670–1710, the proportion declined still further, falling practically to zero. This does not mean that the entire village, especially the majority which consisted of women, manual labourers, and poor peasants, now knew how to read, write, and count. Very far from it. But the minority of petit bourgeois, the plebeian élite of artisans and peasants represented on the council, henceforth included a high proportion of individuals with some schooling who disposed of the rudiments of reading, writing, and perhaps arithmetic.

Maggiolo's literacy maps of about 1685–90 do not in reality contradict the present point of view.[31] It is true that with the 'two sexes united', they reveal a state of crass ignorance compared to north-eastern France. But if male literacy alone is taken into account, it can be seen that the Gard (a *département* that was in part Protestant and better-schooled), and even the Hérault, counted a creditable percentage of adult males able to sign their own names.

These respectable results were due to the efforts of the Protestant schools (Gard), but also, in Catholic country (the greater part of the Hérault), to the perseverance of the Roman clergy. The diffusion of a certain amount of learning was, in fact, inseparable from instruction in the rudiments of Christian doctrine; and the naming of a schoolmaster to teach the ABCs and the catechism was the Church's business.

The bishops, during the course of their pastoral visits, never forgot to inspect the village schools. They worried about the schoolmaster. (Was he meeting his classes? Did he, unmindful of his duty, collect fees from the poor? Did he sing in the choir?) They were aggrieved over the absenteeism of students who had to mind the stock or tend to the cherry-trees. The episcopate, if one substitutes the principle of secular instruction for mitre and crook, was acting as a body of elementary-school inspectors.

At the end of the century, this activity of the prelates began to bear fruit. In the diocese of Montpellier it was conducted by the bishop Colbert, meticulous like his uncle, a Jansenist, and fervent partisan of the elementary schools (*les petites écoles*) in the manner of Port-Royal. Thanks to him, all the villages that still lacked schoolmasters in 1677 were provided with them by 1704. In the latter year, in 37 villages (comprising 4,082 families), 1,887 children including 1,247 boys were attending class. The lesson of these very old educational statistics is that every second household without exception had a child in school. The proportion was low by present-day standards, above all when one considers the poor quality of instruction; it was not, however, negligible. An enormous reservoir of ignorance still subsisted in the rural areas, but the Church, in the manner of the Huguenots, had assumed, by the reign of Louis XIV, the task of cultural improvement in the south of France. The clergy had its own reasons, but the results were important and progress was steady if slow.[32]

This effort was all the more remarkable in that it was carried out at the height of the economic débâcle between 1680 and 1720. Here again the two curves cross, the descending curve of the gross product and the mounting curve of popular instruction.

In this instance, it was not economics that determined culture, for in that case one would have seen a decline in popular instruction. It was, on the contrary, culture which, in the midst of a slump in production, anticipated the future development of the economy and the resumption of economic growth, beginning in 1720.

Culture anticipated, and one might even add that it determined, developments. Beginning in the very first decade of the century of the Enlightenment, it was one of the factors that helped lay the foundations and prepare the conditions of the coming economic recovery. The diffusion, limited though it might be, of elementary instruction, in fact improved the comportment of economic man even in the most isolated villages. Thus, the large-scale tenant farmers, who as a class were still illiterate at the end of the sixteenth century, were often able to read and write at the end of the seventeenth and beginning of the eighteenth centuries, as a comparison between the number of marks and signatures affixed to the bottom of the lease contracts clearly indicates.

The farmers now knew a little reading, writing, and arithmetic and could thus market their produce in the most favourable circumstances. Now, as is well known, a good farmer is not just someone who knows how to farm. He must also, when the proper time comes, know how to sell.

Similarly, when the great noble and ecclesiastical landowners, prodded by the crisis, made up their minds, between 1690 and 1720, to take over the management of their properties and to invest their own capital in the enterprise or risk insolvency—they did not confine themselves to repeating—unknowingly—the 'anti-crisis' responses of their predecessors and ancestors of the fifteenth century who had been forced to assume the role of gentlemen farmers in somewhat analogous circumstances.

For these landowners of 1700 were no longer dealing only with clumsy, unlettered rustics, as had been the case with their forefathers. Thanks to limited but real progress in primary instruction, they could recruit their bailiffs, their foremen, and their farm managers from a stratum of already literate peasants, some of whom were capable of writing French and of adding up columns of figures. These competent individuals made effective and productive collaborators.

CHANGES IN PATTERNS OF BEHAVIOUR

Finally, the progress of elementary instruction was inseparable, even among the people, from a certain psychological transfiguration, and a general improvement in behaviour. Doctor Puech, at the end of the nineteenth century, worked through the judicial archives of the *Présidial* of Nîmes for the years

1620–1720.[33] As he approached the end of this period, the good doctor—just like Boutelet and Chaunu in an analogous study for Normandy[34]—observed some significant changes in comportment. The following are the anthropological conclusions of Puech's crime statistics: 'Man did not remain immutable. His behaviour improved. He mastered his anger better and was less prone to violence.' The virtue of self-control, so highly esteemed by the modern world, made considerable progress. Duels, sword-fights, and knife-fights grew rare in this region of the Gard in the early eighteenth century. Fencing masters were forsaken for dancing masters and musicians, the latter already in vogue by 1650–60. The *papegay*, a sort of folkloristic target-range, formerly a school for fire-arms, became a simple pretext for uproar and debauchery, to such a point that it was suppressed. Violent sports, *paume* and *ballon*, were abandoned in favour of the taverns and the bawdy-houses. Duels and brawls gave way to gambling, debauchery, and swindles. In general, aggressiveness began to take on various disguises: one passed 'from foul play to stealing'. The lions were transformed into foxes, at least in the vicinity of the towns and in the more civilized lowlands; for in the mountain districts, and especially in the Vivarais of du Roure and his rebels, fatal stabbings were still common occurrences and aggressiveness continued to express itself in physical violence.

One encounters the same phenomena of selective attenuation in the domain of religious fanaticism, or simply in religious feeling. In the Cévennes, as we have seen, this *phanatisme* survived intact, still capable of degenerating into bloody forms of exaltation. But near the towns, the hold of religion was clearly weakening by the end of the seventeenth century. John Locke and Basville noted this development for Montpellier and for Nîmes respectively apropos of both religions.[35] In 1704–11, the bishop Colbert despaired of Celleneuve and Juvignac, two villages close to Montpellier; whereas elsewhere, in the distant countryside far from the towns, he was satisfied by the perfect assiduity at mass, by the unanimity of the Easter communicants, and by the popular faith in miracles performed in the local sanctuaries to the Virgin. Now, in those two suburban villages, free of Huguenots but infected by the near-by town, most of the men had forsaken the mass; there was dancing at the very doors of the church and the taverns were packed during the holy services. A certain urban indifference, in other words, had begun to rub off little by little on the rustics of the surrounding neighbourhood.[36]

The picture, then, is full of contrasts. A great mass of people, especially mountain-dwellers, remained mostly illiterate (for example, in the region of Saint-Pons, despite some progress); prey to primitive violence (Vivarais), or to religious fanaticism with neurotic symptoms (Cévennes). But the towns and with them the neighbouring lowlands were slowly becoming literate and beginning to repudiate, in part, individual violence. If the people did not abandon religion, it no longer occupied the pre-eminent position of former times.

Do these different traits, still nebulous and embryonic, represent the germs of a new psychology—more intellectual than emotional, more cunning than aggressive, and more practical than mystical? Such changes, in any case, are not irrelevant to economic history. Formed in greater numbers, it was the educated and competent, the practical-minded, composed individuals who would one day be responsible for solid instances of economic growth.

MALTHUS WOULD BE TOO LATE

That day was no longer very far away. In Languedoc, in the five-year period 1715–20 (as in neighbouring Catalonia), the long slump of the gross agricultural product, which had lasted—on the French side of the Pyrenees—since 1675–80, was finally surmounted.[37] The recessionary wave that marked the conclusion of a multi-secular fluctuation slackened. Some original symptoms appeared. They were characteristic, not simply of a normal, ordinary advance, a *recovery*, but of a new age of growth to the measure of the incoming century—and one not entirely unworthy of our own. The forces of transformation—wine-growing and manufacturing, competent farm management, and new mental attitudes—were now sufficiently powerful to tilt the old balance. They lent the inevitable upturn a character which was more than one of simple economic, monetary, and demographic recovery, conferring upon it certain innovating aspects that were a far cry from the pauperizing processes of the sixteenth century.

Between 1720 and the end of the century, the rural landscape grew more diversified and certain sectors of production 'took-off'. Wine-growing extended its hegemony and multiplied its returns per hectare. Maize, alfalfa, and beans were planted on the fallow. Wheat yields, which had remained stationary since the time of Francis I, improved slightly beginning in 1750. There was only one serious shortcoming: irrigation was little practised in Languedoc at the very time that the Catalans were resorting to it more and more widely.

Progress also affected roads, canals, ports, and manufacturing (woollen, silk, and cotton textiles; hosiery, mining, and metallurgy) from Law to Necker. The curve that has been published for the woollen-cloth industry suggests that one is in the presence of an almost continuous rise, which shattered all the mediocre records of Colbertism. Nîmes, with 50,000 inhabitants, had become one of the great manufacturing towns of France by the end of the century. The Protestants, above all in the Cévennes—still subject to harassment but less and less to outright persecution at the hands of the authorities—were cured of their fanaticism thanks to the reasonable preachings of Antoine Court. They could devote themselves wholeheartedly to business in conformity with their ancient and profitable vocation of secular asceticism.

The indices of economic activity, tithes in kind and in money, confirm the fact that the gross product had become the determining factor. It was agricultural production that first showed signs of life. It had begun to advance by 1715–20, before prices and before population. For the space of a generation (1715–45), the rise in the gross product and in real income (nominal income increasing faster than prices) bestowed its still-modest benefits on a declining or stationary rural population. As a result, gross *per capita* income rose.

Beginning in 1740–50, it was the turn of the demographic sector, which was shaken from its lethargy by economic animation; by the growth in wealth of society as a whole; by the modest, if by no means negligible, rise in people's living standards—that is to say, in the final analysis by the decline in the death rate that resulted;[38] and which can be perceived in the civil registers and in the statistics of the provincial administration.

Population began to advance, and once again the race was on between population on the one hand, and food supplies and the gross product on the other.

It is impossible to describe the vicissitudes of that contest within the compass of the present book. Suffice it to say, that, according to our diagrams, the outcome was never in doubt. In the sixteenth century, agricultural production was completely out of the race. After 1750, on the contrary, the rise of the gross farm product matched and sometimes perhaps outdistanced the rise in rural population.[39] The average living standard was still quite low, but the threat of a general Malthusian kind of impoverishment had disappeared.

All the elements are in agreement; for it seems, in fact, that wages during the course of the eighteenth century, as was also the case in Catalonia, paralleled or very slowly overtook grain and bread prices. Here again, the evolution was radically divergent from the one encountered during the sixteenth-century price revolution.

The wage-workers were still poor, and perhaps even more acutely conscious of their poverty; but the process of pauperization had been banished, and this was in itself a fact of capital importance.

Landed pauperization was checked in the same way as the deterioration of wages. It is true that the subdivision of holdings grew rife again beginning in 1750 or 1770, a bit earlier or a bit later, depending on the village. The advance in rural population, once underway, imposed its own laws; and, as in the sixteenth century, it forced the multiplying peasants to dismember and divide up their tenements among their more and more numerous heirs. The process recommenced at the end of the reign of Louis XV when the long phase of landed consolidation which had lasted, approximately, from 1680 to 1750, came to a close. It continued under Louis XVI; traversed the Revolution without faltering and persisted under all the subsequent régimes up to the time of the phylloxera epidemic. The *compoix* and books of the *taille*; the cadasters and the land-tax rolls all attest, one after another, to the progress of landed subdivision from 1770 to 1870.

The movement appears to be of the same nature as the analogous process of the sixteenth century. Yet its significance is different; for it was a far less serious matter to carve up the family holding when income per hectare was rising and when the vine was invading every village, as it did from Louis XV to Napoleon III. The rise in earnings per unit compensated for the reduced size of the allotted holdings. The new generations of wine-growers, even if they were more cramped for space, were not necessarily poorer—far from it—than their fathers and grandfathers who ploughed and sowed.

The over-all impression is that society after 1715–20—after Louis XIV— was no longer held in check, blocked, and ultimately bowed by the perfect rigidity of the gross product. It was, on the contrary, the gross product itself which, during the entire course of a growth cycle lasting more than a century (up to 1873) and affecting principally viticulture, determined the progress of society, population, and the standard of living.

The Malthusian curse had fallen on Languedoc in the sixteenth and seventeenth centuries, just as it has fallen in very different circumstances on certain peoples of today's Third World. In the modern period (and no doubt also in the preceding medieval period) it had invested a great agrarian cycle, after a vigorous starting phase, with the character of an inexorable fluctuation. But the curse was slowly lifted in the eighteenth century, even before it had been formulated in 1798 by the man whose name it bears. Malthus was a clear-headed theoretician of traditional societies. But he was a prophet of the past; and he was born too late in a world too new.

NOTES

1. *Les Paysans de Languedoc* (Paris, 1966); abridged version (Paris, 1969).
2. Pierre Jeannin, 'Les Comptes du Sund comme source pour la construction d'indices généraux de l'activité économique en Europe', *Revue historique* (1964), p. 320 and *passim*.
3. Jeannin, op. cit., p. 335.
4. Cf. Pierre Vilar, Communication to the *Première conférence internationale d'histoire économique, Stockholm 1960* (Paris, 1960).
5. On these problems of comparative European demography see, for instance, Jeannin, op. cit., p. 325, and B. Bennassar, *Valladolid au siècle d'or* (Paris, 1967).
6. Cf. Vilar, op. cit.
7. R. Baehrel, *Une Croissance: la Basse-Provence rurale* (Paris, 1961); P. Vilar, *La Catalogne dans l'Espagne moderne* (Paris, 1962).
8. R. Romano, 'Encore la crise de 1619–1622', *Annales* (1964).
9. Vilar, Communication.
10. Ladurie (Paris, 1966), p. 937, Graph 6.
11. Ladurie, op. cit., pp. 849–52, Annexe 30.
12. M. Weber, *Le Savant et le politique* (Paris, 1963), p. 70 and *passim*.
13. Ladurie, op. cit., p. 612, fn. 1.
14. W. C. Scoville, *The Persecution of the Huguenots and French Economic Development* (Berkeley, Calif., 1960).
15. See the account book of Borrely in A. Puech, *Nîmes à la fin du XVIe siècle*

(Nîmes, 1884); C. Duthil, 'L'industrie de la soie à Nîmes jusqu'en 1789', *Revue d'histoire moderne et contemporaine*, vol. x (1908).

16. The text of the rebels' programme is in V. Cousin, *Madame de Longueville pendant la Fronde* (Paris, 1887), p. 466.

17. For the attempt of the Faculty of Medicine at Montpellier to cure the Camisards see A. Ducasse, *La guerre des Camisards* (Paris, 1962), p. 59.

18. The revolts of the Old Régime, and the 'lower classes' involved in them, have inspired, as is known, a whole series of important studies. Some seek to relate the uprisings to a finality which transcends the immediate and even the conscious interests of the rebels themselves: the 'objective' struggle against manorialism or absolutism [B. Porchnev, *Les Soulèvements populaires en France de 1623 à 1648* (Paris, 1963)]; the intrigues of aristocrats or bourgeois who openly or 'underhandedly' incited to riot [R. Mousnier, *Les XVIe et XVIIe siècles* (Paris, 1954), p. 460 and id., 'Recherches sur les soulèvements populaires en France avant la Fronde', *Revue d'histoire moderne et contemporaine* (1958)]; apocalyptic objectives [N. Cohn, *Les Fanatiques de l'Apocalypse* (Paris, 1962)]. Other authors emphasize among the motivations of these 'primitive rebels' the instinct of self-preservation and the hunger drive—the basic tendencies of the human ego in other words [F. Furet, 'Pour une définition des classes inférieures à l'époque moderne', *Annales* (1963) and G. Rudé, 'La taxation populaire de mai 1775 (la guerre des farines)', *Annales historiques de la Révolution française* (1956)]. These different analyses, all of which have proved fruitful, are by no means mutually exclusive. Our own studies of popular uprisings serve to confirm and complete them at many points. But ours also evoke, for the interpretation of the most deviant and aberrant phenomena which are inexplicable in rational terms, certain impulses underlying not only supra-individual motivations, but the conscious ego itself. Such impulses could only originate in the oldest and deepest recesses of the human psyche: the *id*. In a general way, only this appeal to the unconscious, to the intervention of deep-seated impulses, is in measure to explain the ferocious, desperate, irrational energies that were released in the old-style popular revolt. It was not just a violent means to a justifiable end; it was also the savage expression of a long-repressed resentment. In its most stupefying forms of aggression it represents a *passage à l'acte*.

19. See Ladurie, op. cit., p. 627, fn. 1 for a definition of the phenomenon.

20. R. Linton, *Culture and Mental Disorders* (Springfield, Mass., 1956); G. Devereux, 'Normal and Abnormal, the key problem of psychiatric anthropology' in *Some Uses of Anthropology: theoretical and applied, publication of the Anthropological Society of Washington* (Washington, D.C., 1956), pp. 9–10 and *passim*; R. Bénédict, *Patterns of Culture* (New York, 1960), pp. 229–33.

21. E. Lavisse, *Histoire de France* (Paris, 1911), vol. vii, pt. 2, pp. 6 ff.; E. Appolis, *Le Diocèse civil de Lodève* (Albi, 1952); id., *Le Jansénisme dans le diocèse de Lodève au XVIIIe siècle* (Albi, 1952); P. Richer, *Études cliniques sur la grande hystérie* (Paris, 1885), pp. 866–88.

22. The existence of such a period of sexual inhibition, much more rigorous and lasting much longer than in the case of our contemporary culture, can be gathered from a certain series of facts brought to light by the studies of Pierre Goubert, *Beauvais et le Beauvaisis au XVIIe siècle* (Paris, 1960), and for Languedoc by J. Godechot and S. Moncassin, 'Démographie et subsistances en Languedoc du XVIIIe au début du XIXe siècle', *Bull. d'hist. écon. et soc. de la Révolution française* (1964). These facts are namely:

(a) The absence or the minor importance of contraception prior to 1730, in Languedoc as well as in the Beauvaisis.

(b) The extremely low percentage of pre-marital conceptions and illegitimate births (0·5 per cent in Languedoc throughout the eighteenth century). If pre-marital sexual relations had been really important, they would have resulted—because of the ignorance of contraception—in a great many births of this sort. This was not the case.

(c) The constant practice of late marriage (25 years for women, 29 years for men in

Languedoc between 1700 and 1789). The period of sexual inhibition, determined by the above two factors, was thereby automatically extended.

23. Basville, *Mémoires pour servir à l'histoire de Languedoc* (Amsterdam, 1734).
24. Ladurie, op. cit., pp. 1004–5, Graph 31.
25. Gaston Rambert (ed.), *Histoire du commerce de Marseille*, vol. v (Paris, 1957), p. 545; P. Leon, Communication to *Première Conférence d'histoire économique, Stockholm 1960* (Paris, 1960), p. 197.
26. Gaston Rambert (ed.), op. cit., vols. iv and v.
27. Vilar, *La Catalogne*, op. cit., pp. 646 ff.
28. Jeannin, op. cit., pp. 328–39, diagrams 5 and 7.
29. Ibid., diagrams 1 and 4.
30. Ladurie, op. cit., pp. 883–5, Annexe 41, and pp. 1028–9, Graph 43.
31. See M. Fleury and P. Valmary, 'Les Progrès de l'instruction élémentaire de Louis XIV à Napoléon III', *Population* (1957).
32. On all these problems of elementary education in Languedoc in the time of Louis XIV see the statistical data and references in Ladurie, op. cit., pp. 882–6, Annexe 41.
33. A. Puech, *Nîmes à la fin du XVIe siècle* (Nîmes, 1884), pp. 131–2, 387–8 and note xv.
34. B. Boutelet, 'La criminalité dans le baillage de Pont-de-l'Arche', *Annales de Normandie* (1962).
35. John Locke, *Travels in France, 1675–1679* (Cambridge, 1953), p. 28; Basville, op. cit.
36. References and texts on these symptoms of 'dechristianization' can be found in Ladurie, op. cit., p. 890, Annexe 45; see also the article by M. Vovelle, 'Déchristianisation spontanée et déchristianisation provoquée dans le Sud-Est sous la Révolution française', *Bulletin de la Société d'histoire moderne* (1964).
37. Ladurie, op. cit., pp. 978–9, Graph 23.
38. Essentially, as Godechot has shown, the mortality of adults. J. Godechot and S. Moncassin, 'Démographie et subsistances en Languedoc du XVIIIe au début du XIXe siècle', *Bull. d'hist. écon. et soc. de la Révolution française* (1964).
39. Ladurie, op. cit.; compare Graph 5 on pp. 936–7 with Graph 23 on pp. 978–9.

8

French Agriculture in the Seventeenth Century

JEAN JACQUART

*Translated by Judy Falkus**

I

ANY study of the French economy in the seventeenth century must naturally begin with agriculture, which employed the vast majority of the population. Tapié goes so far as to claim that the history of the kingdom under Louis XIII and Louis XIV was truly that of its rural community.[1]

As recently as the eve of the Second World War, R. Schnerb, editor of Henri Sée's *Histoire économique de la France*, could point to virtual ignorance of the subject.[2] Although our understanding is still far from complete, such a statement could not be repeated today. Thirty years of research have shed some light on certain regional diversities. Yet much remains to be done before we can hope to comprehend fully the extremely varied pattern of development of rural communities which constituted the lifeblood of the kingdom.

All that can be done here, therefore, is to present a brief outline of the present state of knowledge. As requested, I will restrict myself to a narrow economist's approach which leaves aside all social and legal considerations.

But first I must say a few words about the general framework of rural activity. And by this I mean neither the geographical conditions, which vary so greatly from one part of the country to another, nor even the institutional structure (parishes, manorial estates, etc.), but the basic unit of production. The study of the farm itself is fundamental for it determines production potential. But it is also complex, touching as it must on questions of land distribution, technology, and availability of capital; and it is not made any easier by the availability of abundant yet disappointing documentation. A few general facts can however be established.

The overwhelming majority of farms were very small. More than 75 per cent of French peasants in the seventeenth century were cultivating insufficient land to provide what today would be considered the bare essentials of life. The two reasons for this were the low level of peasant ownership and the lack of capital and of mechanical aids. Although the average size of

* From 'La Production agricole dans la France du XVIIe siècle', *XVIIe siècle* (1966), 21–46.

small-holdings varied between regions in relation to population density and soil fertility, an over-all pattern does emerge. The nucleus of the property was a small piece of land, leased from the *seigneur*, in addition to which there might be a few plots rented from a town-dweller or from another farmer living too far away to cultivate them himself. The tools for tending these small and often widely scattered holdings were primitive and included neither plough nor draught animals.* Although the returns could be quite respectable, this was a marginal agriculture where human labour was substituted for anything that might be wanting. Historical and geographical studies reveal that these small farms were common throughout the country and therefore of greatest social significance. The *borderie*† of the western provinces was fairly typical: 5 or 6 hectares‡ of scattered plots, tilled with the spade (occasionally with the help of a neighbouring farmer), one or two cows, a few sheep, a small quantity of grain, a little hemp, some fruit gathered in the hedgerows. The pattern was universal, under different names maybe and with one characteristic feature or other.

Specialization, however, enabled some to escape from the general mediocrity. Production, even on a small scale, of marketable goods of high value could help to raise the farmer's standard of living. Such was the case for wine-growers in those regions favoured by climate, exposure, or the proximity of a consumer market or export outlet. Whereas some 10 hectares of arable land might barely support a family, 2 or 3 hectares of vineyard could suffice. No wine-grower actually owned his land, but he could always find small patches to rent from or cultivate for city-dwellers, village craftsmen, or rural landlords. Another instance of specialization was to be found among market-gardeners on the outskirts of towns. Pierre Goubert described a small group of them in the eastern suburbs of Beauvais who, on the banks of the Thérain, grew vegetables for the town and artichokes and asparagus for the Parisian market. And around the capital, in a ring gradually pushed further from the medieval centre of the city by buildings and allotments, market-gardens spread throughout the suburbs, from Popincourt to Montmartre, from Grenelle to Saint-Marcel.[3] These enclosures, hand-tilled and carefully manured, employed a whole host of highly specialized workers. It was here, according to La Bruyère, that the land and the seasons were dragooned into producing the delicacies of life.

The difference between small- and medium-sized holdings was marked. A distinctive feature of the latter was the use of draught animals. This enabled the farmer to cultivate much larger areas, by renting additional land, and thus gave promise of improved standards of living. Personal property and

---

* It must be remembered that in all but the largest undertakings livestock was usually leased from the landowner.

† This is the name given, in the west, to the *métairie*, a farm leased on the principle of sharecropping.

‡ A hectare is 2·471 acres.

leaseholds of varying tenures were combined as in small-scale undertakings, but the total size was considerably greater, averaging some 30 hectares: slightly less in Provence, where farms rarely exceeded 15 hectares, somewhat more in the upland Poitou where the majority extended to between 30 to 60 hectares. On the land around Paris, the average farm of some 100–150 arpents* was characteristic of properties owned by town-dwellers.⁴ This type of farm could be found among the bean-growers of the Beauvaisis, in eastern Normandy, and many other places throughout the country. Its equipment was still simple: a plough, one or two horses, or a couple of oxen, a cart, and little else. In many cases this would seem inadequate to us, even with the hiring of beasts of burden, so typical of those agricultural undertakings financed by urban capital.

However, medium-sized farms were generally self-sufficient. Their land was predominantly arable, though usually with some pasture, either small meadows or stretches of waste land. An orchard and a garden, even a bit of vineyard where conditions were favourable, completed a holding which could be tended by a family alone, other than at harvest time when it was necessary to hire additional labour.

Farming on this scale no doubt became more widespread as the century progressed, largely as a result of the policies of landowners. It required only limited investment, could be managed by one tenant-farmer or sharecropper with relatively little capital equipment, and yet it yielded products sufficiently varied and plentiful to afford a profit: it was thus a most attractive proposition for members of the professional and mercantile classes. Around Paris, court officials and merchants, taking advantage of the difficulties faced by small peasants, bought and exchanged plots of land, gradually establishing farms of a reasonable size. Just south of the city the same process was taking place near Dourdan, Chevreuse, and Étampes. In addition, some peasants who had managed to accumulate a little wealth abandoned their former condition and did the same. Dr. Merle points out that at the same time, in upland Poitou, local landlords (whatever their social background) worked painstakingly to create such new units of production outside the feudal system, though often resorting in their land purchases to the feudal right of preemption. These holdings, closely grouped around the farm buildings, were let on the principle of sharecropping and were geared to combine quite substantial stock-breeding with the normal agriculture of a poor region.

Throughout most of the kingdom agriculture had not, at this time, developed beyond the stage of medium-sized units, though more for social than for technical reasons. Even on this scale there were problems. Certainly there were farmers with the necessary capital and equipment; but they were mainly in the fertile Parisian basin where the stimulus of a market economy had been felt for some time. In most provinces the landowner needed to

* 1 arpent is approx. 1·5 acres.

advance seed and implements and to hire out livestock to the peasant who in turn contributed little more than his own and his family's labour. In the west as in the south, the practice of *métayage** was intimately bound up with this necessity.[5]

These problems were all the more acute in the case of large undertakings. No farmer possessed the means to build up an extensive holding, and even outside the rural community few commanded such resources. The cultivation of wide expanses required a prosperous class of husbandmen with the necessary equipment, livestock, and entrepreneurial qualities. As *métayage* involved fairly close supervision by the landlord of the conduct of affairs, it was not practical on this scale.

Thus properties of some magnitude were only to be found on the fertile plateaux of northern France. These areas, which had long been the chosen domains of the great landowners and religious communities, benefited from having been cultivated from a very early date and from being among the first to feel the effects of the awakening of urban activity. Here new methods had made a precocious appearance. From the thirteenth century at least, large farms had been characteristic of the region, covering some hundred hectares and usually situated well away from the big compact villages.[6]

The farm buildings stood in a block around a square yard, with wide gates opening on to the fields. The barns alone constituted a good proportion of the whole, testifying to the essential nature of these undertakings—the large-scale production of grain. The size of the fields and their close grouping around the farmhouse clearly distinguished this type of farm from all others. Not infrequently, and especially in the case of ecclesiastical properties, all the land was farmed by a single tenant. Thus as Corbreuse, between Paris and Orléans, the 200 hectares belonging to the Chapter of Notre-Dame were all in one piece. Such vast domains required more elaborate equipment than was to be found on medium-sized farms. Corbreuse, in 1660, had 5 ploughs, a dozen harrows, and some 10 horses. Thirty years earlier, a 125-hectare farm in Brie used 4 ploughs, 3 carts, 9 horses, and 3 donkeys. For the times this was quite considerable, although nowadays it barely seems adequate. And the paucity of livestock was even more marked: on the same Brie farm there were only 13 head of cattle and 150 sheep;[7] and on the outskirts of Paris, farms of 50–70 hectares kept only 4–6 cows. Such underequipment could not but tell on the productivity of these large enterprises.

Problems of scale thus imposed a ceiling on the size of properties. Quite a few stood at between 110 and 130 hectares, but this figure was rarely exceeded in the seventeenth century. Yet in the same areas today, farms commonly stretch to 300 and not infrequently to 500 hectares.

Different methods of cultivation corresponded to these marked variations in area and agricultural equipment, although the broad classification made

* Sharecropping.

here obscures considerable diversity. However, the major distinction between small- and large-scale agriculture dear to students of the eighteenth century applies already to the previous period. The big undertakings, found only in the north of France and particularly in the Parisian basin, were devoted to the production of grain, while the smaller ones inclined to some form of mixed farming in which the predominance of cereals did not exclude a variety of other crops.

Whatever the object of one's study, whether agricultural technology or peasant income, when one looks for the reality behind the documents, two essential factors must never be overlooked: the area and equipment at the disposal of the farmer.

II

To say that the essential aim of agriculture is to provide subsistence for the population is a truism. Yet it is worth stressing that the object is above all to produce food and therefore grain. From the fertile Parisian basin to the stony soil of Provence, from the moors of Brittany to the mountain valleys of the Alps and Pyrenees, from the *terres grises* of Flanders to the hills of Forez and Vivarais, cereals—not only wheat or rye, but also barley, oats, pulses, and vetch—were basic to all forms of agriculture. The differences in patterns of cultivation between regions were determined by the necessity of growing grain, with additional crops only as circumstances permitted. We must therefore look first at grain production.[8]

Several methods of preparing the ground for sowing were current. One of three implements was used to loosen the soil, turn it over, and weed it. The first, well suited to the rich but heavy soil of northern France, was the heavy plough. This very old device, which had gradually become more sophisticated during the Middle Ages, was composed of two parts: coulter and ploughshare, generally made of iron, cut into the earth, while the mould-board turned the soil and dug the furrows. The whole was hinged on a wooden plough-beam, and a regulating mechanism controlled the depth of penetration into the soil, while a front axle ensured ease of handling despite the weight. The number of horses or oxen harnessed to the plough varied: two horses were sufficient on the light, loamy soil around Paris, though 6 or 8 were required for the heavy earth of eastern Brie; and 3 pairs of oxen were needed to till the fields of Berry. In use throughout southern France was the even more ancient swing-plough, slightly improved by the addition of a mould-board which parted the earth on either side of the ploughshare. Easy to make, this light implement was suited to light soils. In the Mediterranean region where there is only a very thin layer of arable top soil, this plough, by barely scratching the surface, avoided digging up stones and infertile clay. Only one horse, donkey, or mule was required to draw it, and even a man could manage it. But it would be wrong to imagine that all peasants used some form of plough, for a good many relied simply on hoe and spade to till the tiny plots that constituted their holdings. Such was the case on the Mediterranean terraces and on steep hillsides.

Before sowing, the fields were worked over three or four times. They were manured, though inadequately, in an attempt to maintain fertility: as well as natural manuring by animals grazing on stubble or fallow land, there might be a few cart-loads of dung from the stables; but there was never enough, even on the best-provided farms, to fertilize all cultivated areas. Sowing was done by hand and often quite densely by present-day standards: 2–3 hectolitres to the hectare to the south of Paris and in Languedoc, for example.

The peasant kept a close watch on the growing crops, dug up any weeds, and studied the skies, praying now for sun, now for rain, fearing the storms and hail which would destroy the harvest. At the appropriate time the fields were invaded by teams of harvesters, reaping with the sickle. Behind them the sheaves were gathered and tied up with long, flexible bonds of rye. Tithes and field rents in kind were levied on the spot and the crop divided between landlord and *métayer*. Only then was the harvest brought in. Threshing had to be done immediately by the small farmers who had been awaiting this time so as to feed themselves and pay the landlord, the *seigneur*, and the tax-collector; but the big farmers could afford to wait for market prices to move in their favour. Hand-threshing with the flail was to be found throughout the country; but in the south it was common for animals to tread out the corn on the beaten earth, walking round in circles in the sun and the dust.

However, grain cultivation, which was of such vital importance in feeding the population, exhausted the soil. Very early in the western world, the practice of crop rotation had been evolved, and it was certainly well established by the seventeenth century. Two broad systems are well known to have been current in France at the time. One cycle comprised an autumn crop (wheat, rye, or more often a combination of the two) and a spring crop (barley, oats, millet, or buckwheat), leaving the land fallow in the third year; such was the custom in northern and eastern France. The other was to alternate one harvest of a bread cereal with a fallow year; this biennial system was common throughout the south and nearly as far north as the Loire valley. Both practices had their merits. In the space of six years, the first rotation yielded four harvests, the other three; but all the latter and only two of the former consisted of bread grains, which were both more useful and of greater market-value. This made the two-year rotation so attractive that, even in the heart of areas that had long been devoted to a three-year cycle, there were some enclaves (near Conches in Normandy and to the north of Strasbourg in the plains of Alsace, for example) where harvests and fallow alternated.[9]

In practice, however, these two forms of crop rotation were only suited to relatively favoured areas. Over wide expanses agriculture was far less intensive. Fields were left fallow not for one year in two or three but for much longer. After two harvests in the cold areas of Berry, Maine, and Brittany, the soil was rested for two or three years. Certain poor-soil districts of Brittany were sown only every seven or eight years, some less frequently still.[10] On the margin one even found a practice (still carried out in sub-tropical regions today) of cultivating temporary fields obtained by burning off stretches of moorland about once in every twenty years; two or three crops could be grown on the ashes before the spent soil was returned to its natural state. Thus in many parts of France uncultivated areas, such as the heathlands of Brittany, Poitou, and Languedoc, supplemented the fields regularly tilled by man. These reserves of poor soil could be drawn upon in such times of food shortage and demographic pressure as occurred in most regions in the first quarter of the century.[11] But the gains from this type of cultivation were precarious and short-lived.

The returns from cereal production were extremely variable. First, the difference between good and bad years was much more marked then than today. The terrible consequences for the whole country of a bad harvest are only too well known. The transition from shortage to scarcity and thence to famine was quickly made and frequently so in the seventeenth century, bringing with it distress, epidemics, and a rapidly rising death toll.[12] In addition to meteorological conditions, disparities in soil quality, as well as differences in methods of cultivation and manuring, were clearly reflected in average yields.[13] The best harvests were to be found in the north, in the fertile Parisian basin, in Flanders, and Alsace, where for each *setier** of grain sown up to 7, 8, or even 10 times that amount might be reaped. In Beauvaisis, Brie, and on the Hurepoix plateaux, this multiple stood more commonly between 5 and 7, which represents an average yield of 1,100 to 1,500 kg per hectare in areas where today one would expect 4,000 to 5,000 kg. But even these figures were exceptional. Around Alençon and Neufbourg, both fertile regions, the proportion was more in the order of 4 or 5 to 1; in northern Burgundy, in good years, it was between 3 and 5 to 1; in the Forez plain and in Brittany farmers were happy to reap 3 times the quantity sown; and on the borders of Berry the return was as low as 2 to 1. Differences were even more marked on the varying soils of southern France: on some the ratio was 3 to 1, on others 5 or 6 to 1. Mediocre returns were thus the rule in most provinces, other than in a few favoured areas, mostly to the north of the Loire.

The varieties of cereals cultivated also left much to be desired. Wheat remained the exception, even on some of the most fertile land. Certainly it already predominated on the plains of Île de France and in parts of Vexin, Multien, and Alsace. But it was only at the very end of the seventeenth century that it gained a firm hold in Valois, Beauvaisis, and Beauce. In certain

* A measure of capacity of different value in different areas.

areas its cultivation appeared even to have declined somewhat since the Middle Ages. On rich soils there was a preponderance of maslin (a mixture of wheat and rye in varying proportions). Elsewhere rye was most prevalent, as was the case throughout western France, from the Avranchin in western Normandy to upland Poitou, and in the centre, in Quercy, Vivarais (with the exception of a small wheat-growing area), and Forez.

In addition to these cereals which were common to most areas, others were to be found only in specific regions. Millet had long been cultivated in the south-east. Barley, a Mediterranean cereal, was grown further north only in limited quantities; although a spring cereal, serving mainly as fodder, it could in case of need be used for bread, and in Flanders and Alsace it was also required by the breweries. The cultivation of oats went hand in hand with three-year crop rotations and with the use of horses as draught animals, and it was thus virtually confined to the north.

Throughout the period, two cereals which had been introduced in the sixteenth century continued to gain ground. Buckwheat, a low-quality cereal which grew easily and rapidly, was well suited to the cold regions of the west and centre, and its success was considerable. In 1667 Froidour, a forestry commissioner, reported that the valleys of Ariège on the Spanish border produced the best millet and buckwheat.[14] Thus in a wide area of France, buckwheat mash and pancakes replaced the scarce bread. The role of maize was to prove even more important. Green, it could be used as fodder, or its grain could provide food for both men and animals; it was well suited to regions where the summer was hot and humid and where wheat, therefore, would not thrive; and as it was more nourishing and productive than other secondary cereals, in certain areas it found its way into the regular cycle of crop rotations. Maize thus spread to the valleys of Aquitaine and upper Languedoc, and around 1640 to the Rhône valley, but not until the eighteenth century did it appear on the heights of Vivarais or in the plains of Alsace.[15]

III

Cereal cultivation was the main concern of agriculture in the seventeenth century. Livestock breeding, with only a few exceptions, was therefore subject to the needs and land use of such crops. It had a double function to fulfil: the provision of both draught animals (oxen, cows, or horses) for ploughs and carts and of manure for grain cultivation. In general, however, the livestock was quite inadequate, in both quantity and quality, to meet the real needs of agriculture, as the few examples already quoted have shown.[16] Animal husbandry presented a number of problems which primitive agriculture never solved. In many parts of the country there was little natural pasture and even that was subject to the necessity of tilling any land capable of producing cereals. Hardly surprisingly, those areas least suited to cultivation (mountainous regions, moors, and waste land in the west, the wet bottoms of the great river valleys) were the only ones to support relatively large herds. The average farm of upland Poitou, which covered some 50 hectares, usually had 4 pairs of oxen, 3 or 4 heifers or steers, 3 or 4 milking cows, and about 50 sheep. In Beauvaisis the numbers were much smaller, and on the tableland of Caux, which is now fairly equally divided between arable and pasture, there were rarely more than 6 or 7 head of cattle even in medium-sized undertakings.[17]

In all grain-growing areas sheep were the main form of livestock. The flocks were quite large (3 head per hectare to the south of Paris). They were led from one bit of the property to another, grazing on fallow land and thereby manuring it between crops. They were to be found as much on the vast plains of northern France as in the rocky areas and moors of the south and, in the summer, would gradually move to higher ground in search of pasture.

In addition to motive power and manure, livestock breeding provided some valuable by-products, though far different from those expected of it today. Animals were not reared for meat. In only a few areas was it possible, because of favourable natural conditions, or profitable, because of the proximity of a large consumer market, to fatten animals for slaughter. Herds of cattle and sheep from Auge, Beauce, and even Poitou were driven to the markets of Poissy and Sceaux, which supplied the Paris meat trade. But it was not until the following century that parts of Normandy were turned over to grazing. Nor were dairy products an important concern of farmers. In the whole of the south, cows were used for ploughing rather than milking. In areas which produced olive oil (Provence, Languedoc), grew walnuts (Quercy), or reared pigs (Vivarais), there were substitutes for most milk products, other than the few essentials which were provided by ewes and goats. In the north, on the other hand, milk, butter, and cheese were commonly produced and consumed. In this area, in fact, farmers' contracts often contained an obligation to supply the landlord with pots of butter and a few cheeses. Indeed, some of the varieties of cheese common today were already known in the seventeenth century. But it must not be forgotten that in Louis XIV's day hides and wool were by far the most important by-products of livestock breeding, providing both a lucrative trade and the material for a sizeable rural industry.

The nature and extent of cultivation also determined the types of livestock kept on a farm. Horses and teams of oxen were associated with tenant-farms, mules and donkeys with small-holdings, cattle with ownership of grazing land, flocks of sheep with large domains. Pigs were universal; but in general their numbers were much smaller than might have been supposed, except in those areas (such as Vivarais and the surrounds of Paris) where oak forests provided the acorns to feed them. Thus, merchants from Dourdan contracted with the villagers around Arpajon (some 10 km away) to graze their pigs in the Ouye forest from mid-October to the end of November.[18]

The movements of herds in search of pasture had important implications for the whole of rural life. In a large part of the country, custom limited individual property rights on some of the land at given times of the year, in favour of the community at large. After the first mowing, or at least between the second haymaking and mid-March, free access to the meadows had to be granted for grazing. Similarly, after the harvest, stubble and fallow land were common property until ploughing started in the following year. And these grazing rights were occasionally extended to neighbouring parishes. As a result, enclosure was prohibited or at least made virtually impossible. In other areas, however, custom had narrowly restricted such collective rights. Quickset hedges in the wooded regions of the west and low stone walls surrounding the small fields of Provence testified to and ensured a more complete appropriation of the fruits of the earth by the farmer himself. Both systems had their *raison d'être* and their relative merits.[19]

The scenic contrast provided by open and enclosed fields survived until quite recently. Around Paris and in Lorraine, for example, the horizons were wide and empty, with few trees and with villages clustered tightly around the church. In Maine, Puisaye, Brittany, and southern Berry, on the other hand, the countryside was a maze of lanes running between high banks or hedges, with individual farms nestling in the greenery. In the Mediterranean region the cultivated fields, which had been wrested by hard labour from infertile ground, were interspersed with large stretches of scrub, coarse grass, and stony outcrops. To these varied landscapes correspond different methods of cultivation. In open-field areas cereals, with their natural concomitant, sheep rearing, predominated. There was little alternative in these wide open spaces where common grazing rights and the obligations imposed by crop rotation and tradition weighed so heavily on the farmer. Secondary crops were confined to special plots separated from the rest of the fields. The hemp and flax spun by all countrywomen, for example, were grown in carefully tended enclosures, which were tilled by hand and more heavily and frequently manured than the rest of the holding. But, according to Meuvret, the garden was the main experimental ground.[20] Of variable size, but often tiny, it was surrounded by a hedge or wall. Here the farmer could grow vegetables, fibrous plants, and some fruit trees. Here lucerne, clover, and sainfoin first made their appearance in the sixteenth century. Town-dwellers instructed their gardeners to try also some rare species. Thus in 1643, a Conseiller du Roi had a plot in the garden of his house in Thiais sown with common sorrel, red sorrel, purslain, chicory, chervil, parsley, and burnet; in another patch were white cabbages, cauliflowers, leeks, and chives; and in a third, pumpkins, cucumbers, melons, asparagus, and artichokes, while gooseberries, strawberries, cherries, and jasmin were grown in the orchard.[21] In the north of France these secondary crops were cultivated mainly on medium- and small-sized farms. As already mentioned, the larger ones, which often accounted for the greater part of the total cultivated area, remained devoted primarily to grain.

In those districts where a spirit of innovation had developed earlier and more rapdily, cereals, while retaining their predominant role, were not cultivated exclusively. In their search for additional resources, these poorer regions had displayed a time-honoured ingenuity. In many parts of central France chestnuts became a staple product of a subsistence economy in which they served to feed both men and pigs: single trees and forests together covered about one-quarter of Vivarais in the seventeenth century.[22] Further south was the domain of the olive tree which grew both on the terraces and in the fields, providing shade for the cultivation of wheat and barley, the main grain crops of the south. Although a delicate tree, sensitive to winter frosts and giving poor returns, it was none the less a fundamental element in the agricultural system and daily life of Provence and Languedoc. From the end of the sixteenth century the mulberry gained in popularity.[23] The history of the Lyons silk industry is well known, and obviously the development of silk-worm breeding was closely tied to it. Without having read Olivier de Serres' treatise, farmers in Vivarais and the Cévennes acted in accordance with the advice he gave to his housekeeper at the beginning of the century and made room for this lucrative occupation. In and around their fields they planted mulberries on which the silk-worms fed during May. The eggs were kept and hatched in special cases carried around by the women. The worms were reared in a nursery until they had spun their precious cocoons, when it was time to harvest, unwind, and spin the silk. In the large uncultivated expanses of the west such secondary crops, which provided small farmers with valuable additional resources, were largely replaced by livestock breeding.

Thus agriculture not only varied widely from one area to another but was continually being adapted to soil conditions, the level of technological development, and the changing markets for its products.

IV

Little mention has been made so far of one essential element: wine-making.[24] Vineyards had been cultivated for centuries, playing a fundamental role in the life of a whole section of the French peasantry by providing it with the means of buying basic foodstuffs. At this time viticulture could still be found in many areas from which it was to disappear in the next two centuries. In the north, the vineyards of Champagne and Laonnois stretched on to the hillsides of Artois. The area around Beauvais produced small quantities of pale red wines which were either consumed locally or, until the middle of the century, sold on the Amiens market. The Paris region was one of the greatest wine-producing districts, in both extent and output; the hillsides around the city were covered by vineyards. Around Thiais, Bagneux, and

Antony, vine-growing occupied more than a quarter of the cultivated area. In the Alps, vines hung from the southerly slopes of the valleys, and they also lined the Loire valley. The true home of wine-producing, however, was in the south, where the vines formed an integral part of the landscape: growing among the olive groves, in rows in the fields, and even clinging to trees, they were as characteristic of the area as the round-tiled roofs and low stone walls.

According to Estienne and Liebault, vineyards were profitable, although much time, care, and effort had to be devoted to the frail plants.[25] Pruning, hoeing, layering, and tying up are all delicate operations; and the wine-grower was thus the skilled worker of the peasant world. The tools, however, were neither elaborate nor costly: a pruning-knife, a hoe, and a special spade. Manual dexterity was the main requirement. On the other hand, the equipment used in wine-making, including vats and barrels, represented a considerable investment; in fact, the presses were generally owned by the *seigneur*.

The history of viticulture in modern France has been well told in Roger Dion's great work. In the seventeenth century a complex evolution took place, a distinction gradually appearing between quantity- and quality-producing areas. Those regions favoured by climate, soil, or the proximity of a large market began to specialize, while less privileged areas went into decline.[26] In western France, all trace of the medieval vineyards finally disappeared: in Normandy, Picardy, and to the south-west of Paris, vines, already sparse and frail, were losing ground to apple-trees and, in the villages, cider was taking over from wine or *piquette*.* On the other hand, the large, quality vineyards were consolidated and extended. Bordeaux retained its reputation and supremacy, while claret had not yet been supplanted in England by port and sherry. The wines of Beaune, which had been exported since the Middle Ages, were now joined by the great Burgundies. Along the Côte, government officials and wealthy Dijon merchants bought up existing vineyards and established new ones. It was under their influence that, in the middle of the century, a more rational classification of wines according to area was established. At about this time, religious communities that had fallen into debt made over to such persons the vineyards of Chambertin, Fixin, and Vosne. Louis XIV's predilection for Burgundy and his court's readiness to follow his example did the rest. During the seventeenth century also, the white wines of the côte of Champagne, so far undistinguished from the wines of Île de France, were launched on their own great career. Here again the impetus was given by a powerful family, the Brularts de Sillery: tailoring their interests to contemporary tastes, they popularized the new wine. Around 1668 the vineyards and cellars of the abbey of Hautvilliers

* Weak, sour wine produced by pouring water on the residue of pressed grapes and allowing it to ferment.

were entrusted to Dom Pérignon, to whom has been attributed the invention and perfection of the process to which champagne was to owe its world-wide fame.

While the prestige vineyards grew in size and reputation, producing luxury wines for export as well as for wealthy domestic custom, the development of quantity vineyards was even more important. This was owing to the fact that, from the sixteenth century, wine was quite commonly consumed, especially in the towns. Thus, in answer to a rapidly rising demand, wine-producers extended their activities, choosing the more productive strains and generally sacrificing quality to quantity. In the vicinity of towns, and especially of Paris, a general debasement of viticulture took place. As early as 1600, Olivier de Serres had feared that the Parisian vineyards would fall into disrepute, and by 1650 the process was complete, though it was yet to spread, as shown by Dion, to the whole of the very wide area supplying the capital. Elsewhere opportunities for exporting low-quality wines led to the same results. On the Languedoc moors, limestone plateaux that had hitherto been abandoned to sheep and goats were gradually turned over to wine-producing, leaving the plains to grain cultivation. Genoese boats called for their cargo of wine at the ports of the Gulf of Lions. On the Atlantic coast, the extension and transformation of vineyards was due to the influence of the Dutch who bought not only white wines, which they sweetened for re-selling in northern Europe, but especially the spirits produced in the Charente and Adour valleys.

v

This description of agricultural production, technology, and returns, of regional variations in a barely unified country, is relevant to the whole of the seventeenth century. But it would be a mistake to think of things as set in rigid medieval ways. Like all other fields of activity, agriculture was subject to the general economic climate; the total volume of output was determined by demand, labour supply, profit expectations (of both landowners and farmers), and also by political circumstances. With the help of research work already published it is possible to detect a general trend of production. I shall merely attempt to describe it without going into the problems of its interpretation.

The starting-point at the beginning of the century was extremely low. Throughout the country the religious wars had exacted their toll, especially in their closing years: production had been disrupted, notably in Normandy and Île de France, the richest regions of the kingdom; during the course of military operations whole areas had been sacked and extortionate demands made of the people, many of whom had had to flee from their villages; houses had been burnt to the ground, buildings untended for a quarter of a century, vineyards neglected, fields left fallow for years on end, while epidemics had decimated the population.[27] Such then was the situation at the end of the wars. However, when peace returned, a rapid improvement was brought about by wise legislative measures and especially by the combination of peasant labour with urban capital. From 1600 to around 1630 or 1640, as population and demand increased, so did agricultural production. Of course it is impossible to quantify this growth, but there is ample evidence of it.[28] Obvious signs can be found in the rise in real prices and ground rents. Further indications are provided by the various attempts to increase output: vineyards encroaching on the moors of Languedoc; Dutch engineers called in by Henri IV to advise on the draining of coastal marshes: landowners in Poitou reclaiming heathland to create new holdings; the monks of St. Germain des Prés adding to their cultivated area 100 arpents of hitherto untilled hillside near Arpajon; farmers nibbling at the edges of forests to extend their fields by a few furrows.[29] And as well as the exploitation of new areas, efforts were also made to raise productivity.

Peasants and their landlords from the cities were well aware of the constraints imposed on production by nature itself. At a very early stage the most enterprising members of the rural community experimented, more or less successfully, with ways of improving traditional methods of cultivation. The pressure of consumer demand seems to have led to the multiplication and extension of these experiments, certainly in the richer and more advanced parts of the country.

The most obvious course was to use at least some of the land traditionally left fallow. Cereals were tried. Already at the end of the sixteenth century, in the fertile northern regions of France, the normal cycle of crop rotations was being violated to allow additional cultivation of wheat. But the result could only be mediocre and landlords actually forbade the practice as it exhausted the soil. Yet needs and price rises induced farmers to lay custom aside in their attempts to force nature. The environs of Paris, especially from the 1630s, witnessed the spread of cultivation on fallow land of pulses (peas or beans), for which there was an assured market in the city. Some landowners specifically authorized the growing of such leguminous crops having no doubt realized that, unlike grain, they did not impoverish the soil. But the significance of these experiments must not be exaggerated as they alone could not operate a radical change in production methods.[30] It still remained essential to leave some land uncultivated in order to feed the herds that manured the soil. Thus the real problem to be solved was that of fodder.

The quality of sainfoin grown in Burgundy had long been recognized. As early as 1564 Estienne and Liebault claimed that there was no more valuable or suitable cattle food and that the profits to be derived from its cultivation were such that any good farmer must devote his best land to it.[31] Gardens and enclosures often contained a patch of clover or lucerne to provide much-needed winter fodder. Towards 1630, however, in certain favoured areas, sainfoin began to be grown in the fields. On the large farms around Paris, and in Normandy, Amiénois, and Brie, some of the arable land was being converted to permanent artificial grassland. But this too was only a limited development; cultivated fodder did not yet enter into regular crop rotations. The idea was simply to take advantage of a privileged proximity to the Paris market by growing a speculative crop, and it therefore had nothing in common with the fundamental transformation in rotations which was to characterize the true 'agricultural revolution'.

The rising trend of production appears to have reached a peak towards the middle of the century, slightly earlier in the north (where Pierre Goubert dates it around 1630), later in the south (where René Baehrel puts it between 1680–90, though Emmanuel Le Roy Ladurie's seemingly more realistic assessment is 1670).[32] A number of factors contributed to the difficult times that followed: the ravages of the Fronde, the shortages that coincided with the accession of Louis XIV (and which hit the north severely but spared the south), and a run of poor harvests at the close of the century. The state of French agriculture was to deteriorate until after 1715. Prices (including those of land and rents) suffered an enduring decline. Many tenant-farmers were ruined because they could not honour their contracts. Western sharecroppers were in a precarious situation. In short, the whole of the peasant community was in debt. There are many contemporary accounts of the attendant misery: in La Bruyère, Vauban, Fénelon, Boisguillebert, in the correspondence of stewards and the minutes of small village notaries, everywhere the same facts, the same complaints recur. And rural poverty seems to have brought with it a considerable reduction in total output. Colbert, who saw only the beginnings of this prolonged crisis, fought against the spread of vineyards because of the grain shortages.

Here again generalizations partly obscure the facts. Some areas of production and some regions fared better than others. Despite the extensive nature of the economic crisis, urban markets continued to exert the pull so often mentioned above. Around Paris, the spread of semi-permanent artificial grassland did not slow down: on the morrow of the Fronde the abbess of La Saussaye, in Villejuif, allowed the new tenant-farmer to convert 50 of his 270 arpents to sainfoin. A similar trend was apparent in Brie. And in 1669 the steward of Alençon, in a memorandum, advocated the widespread cultivation of such crops because they nourished the soil and enabled it to produce good harvests for several consecutive years.[33]

But on the whole, these were exceptions in an otherwise sombre picture. By 1700 Burgundy was crippled by taxation, whole communities were in debt, and harvests were poor. In Beauvaisis the small farmers failed, while the larger ones barely subsisted. In Provence excessive land-clearance in the middle of the century had led to soil erosion. In Poitou the system of share-cropping survived only because landowners made advances and peasants went into debt. Regional studies show that everywhere rural activity and production were severely depressed. It was only after 1720 that a new era was to begin. But that is another story.

VI

Despite technical deficiencies, despite the scale of farming—often too small to be viable—despite the deterioration in economic conditions, France appeared to contemporaries, both French and foreign, as a rich country. The fertility of her soil and the abundance and variety of her agricultural products were widely praised. 'The true wealth of a country [wrote Vauban at the beginning of the *Dixme Royale*] lies in plentiful food supplies . . . and it can be said that France possesses this wealth to the highest degree . . .'

Certainly, despite some unfavourable aspects, France compared well with other areas of western Europe. Only in the Low Countries and United Provinces were the fields better cultivated: efforts to overcome adverse natural conditions from the Middle Ages had led to a system of intensive cultivation. No land was left fallow; there were often two harvests a year; and cattle breeding was not considered a necessary evil but an integral part of agriculture. However, these technically more advanced countries were those without vineyards, olive groves, or fruit trees.

The British system, which had been developed gradually by the large landowners, was still far from having reached the perfection that was to make it a model for eighteenth-century agriculturalists. It sacrificed small- to large-scale farming, led to the eviction of customary tenants and others without full title to their land, and generally set too much store on the extensive and all-pervasive rearing of sheep. Thus it could not lay claim to the relative stability, in both human and economic terms, achieved to some extent in France.

For the Mediterranean countries the seventeenth was a bad century. In southern Italy as in Spain the creation of large domains devoted entirely to livestock was an obstacle to land improvement. The irrigated *huertas* fell into decay through neglect. In central Italy, where the *mezzadria* predominated, the farmer was caught in a tight net of obligations which the restoration of the manorial system tended to strengthen further. Diversified farming in Tuscany and Romagna was little more than the picturesque sight much admired by travellers.

Elsewhere on the continent, the Swiss cantons were only poorly endowed by nature, and central Europe had been devastated by the Thirty Years War and its long-lasting effects. By contrast, therefore, France's position appears in a relatively advantageous light.

But does this mean that France was self-sufficient or could even, in an ordinary year, produce enough to allow for some export? Vauban in fact claimed that this was the case and that France was well able to come to the aid of her neighbours by exchanging her surplus for their gold and silver. He even listed her export products: wines, spirits, salt, grain, and cloth. As this was written in 1707, at the height of the economic crisis, it does seem that this otherwise keen observer had allowed himself to get carried away in trying to prove too much.

First, distinctions must be made between regions. In the seventeenth century France had not yet achieved economic unity. Every province, every area, practically every rural community, possessed some degree of autarchy. The balance of production and consumption varied greatly from one to another. Two forces pulled in opposite directions. On the one hand there was a tendency for permanent trade links, motivated by profit opportunities, to be established between surplus and deficit areas. The Haut Vivarais could sell rye to the more densely populated Rhône valley; the tablelands of Brie and Beauce, Vexin, and Île de France fed the huge Paris market; Normandy was so fertile as to produce surplus grain and cattle. On the other hand these natural flows were continually being impeded not only by regulations and internal customs-duties, but also by transport problems and even more so by the doubts and worries that continually assailed the population: the fear of famine was such that it acted as a brake in times of difficulty, despite the attraction of profit.

The sale of agricultural produce, nevertheless, was an important part of both internal and external commerce. Richelieu claimed in his *Testament politique* that France was so productive of grain, wines, flax, and hemp that Spain, England, and all her other neighbours relied on her to help meet their needs. Vauban has already been quoted, and many similar statements can be found, mentioning the same products and the same trading partners.

Without impinging on the subject of another lecture in this series,[34] it might be useful just to mention here the foreign outlets for French agricultural products. Despite people's anxieties and despite strict regulations, cereals were the object of a more or less legitimate trade, for commerce in grains was usually forbidden unless the harvest was good. Between 1675 and 1683, for example, the king's Council issued more than 30 edicts on the subject. But the pressure of local conditions was often stronger than the law. Thus buckwheat left the country by the Breton ports which had close links with Spain and Portugal, and Languedoc could look to the east for markets for its grain.

Some agricultural products, however, were exported regularly and with full official authorization. These were not basic necessities, and therefore mercantile logic saw only gain, in the form of gold and silver specie, to be had from their sale abroad. The list of such products is headed by wines and spirits. (I have already mentioned the part played by Dutch merchants in the development and spread of Atlantic-coast vineyards.) Next came fibres and natural dyes: flax and hemp grown in the west, in Maine and Brittany, saffron from Quercy, woad from the Garonne. The south exported its surplus oil. And tobacco, which had been introduced in the sixteenth century and had been made a state monopoly under Colbert, was sold to Holland.

However, this is but an enumeration of small details which must not detract from the over-all picture. The bulk of agricultural output was consumed at home or processed on the spot. Agriculture was the principal occupation of more than three-quarters of the French population; it was the main component of national product; but its contribution to savings and investment was minimal. Productivity was too low, and offered too little hope of improvement, to enable real economic progress. Other forms of economic activity—industrial production and colonial trade—were to be left to provide the capital accumulation necessary to operate the radical changes in economic and social structures of the following century.

NOTES

1. Within the limited framework of this survey it is impossible to give a complete list of sources or an extensive bibliography. I will therefore make only a few general remarks. The archives still contain many neglected documents. Of special interest are the notarial Minutes (Series E in the *Archives Départementales*, ZZ1 in the *Archives Nationales*, Minutier Central Parisien). In addition to the texts of leases, which often contain instructions about cultivation, they include agricultural contracts and harvest surveys. A systematic study of inventories drawn up on decease could provide information on farming equipment, livestock, extent of cultivation, crops grown, and returns. Similar information can be obtained from judicial sources (Series B in the *Archives Départementales*, ZZ2 in the *Archives Nationales*). Descriptions of individual domains, as well as more or less uninterrupted series of leases, are to be found in the following archives: ecclesiastical (Series S in the *Archives Nationales*, H in the *Archives Départementales*), lay landowners (Series R and T in the *Archives Nationales*, E in the *Archives Départementales*), and Crown lands (Series O in the *Archives Nationales*).

A general survey of the subject is provided by H. Sée, *Histoire économique de la France*, vol. i, pt. 4 (unfortunately less detailed about the 17th than the 18th century). M. Bloch, *Les Caractères originaux de l'histoire rurale française* (2nd ed., 1952), with a supplement by R. D'Auvergne, throws light on economic and social developments. And for an indication of the current trend of research, the following two works should be consulted: J. Meuvret, *L'Agriculture en Europe aux XVIIe et XVIIIe siècles* (10e Congrès des Sciences Historiques, Rome, 1950, *Relazioni*, iv. 139–68); and E. Le Roy Ladurie, 'Voies nouvelles pour l'histoire rurale (XVIIe–XVIIIe siècles)', *Études rurales*, Nos. 13–14 (1964), pp. 79–95 (which includes a bibliography).

Since G. Roupnel's thesis, *La Ville et la campagne au XVIIe siècle: Étude sur les populations du pays dijonnais* (Paris, 1922, reprinted 1955), there have been a number of regional studies relating, to some extent at least, to the 17th century: R. Baehrel, *Une Croissance, la Basse-Provence (fin du XVIe siècle–1789)* (Paris, 1961); M. Fontenay, 'Paysans et marchands ruraux de la vallée de l'Essonne dans la seconde moitié du XVIIe siècle', in *Paris et Île de France*, ix (1957–8), 157–282; P. Goubert, *Beauvais et le Beauvaisis de 1630 à 1730* (Paris, 1960); R. Latouche, *La Vie en Bas-Quercy du XVIe au XVIIIe siècle* (Toulouse, 1923); A. Lugnier, *Cinq siècles de vie paysanne à Roche-en-Forez (Loire)* (Saint-Étienne, 1962); A. Plaisse, *La Baronie du Neubourg* (Paris, 1961); L. Merle, *La Métairie et l'évolution de la Gâtine poitevine* (Paris, 1958); P. de Saint-Jacob, *Les Paysans de la Bourgogne du Nord au dernier siècle de l'ancien régime* (Paris, 1960); H. Sée, *Les Classes rurales en Bretagne du XVIe siècle à la Révolution* (Paris, 1906); E. Sol, *La Vie économique en Quercy aux XVIe et XVIIe siècles*

(Paris, 1950); M. Venard, *Bourgeois et paysans au XVIIe siècle* (Paris, 1957). In addition there have been a number of articles, some of which I will mention.

Some useful information, though not always very detailed, can be found in a wide variety of theses on regional geography, from R. Blanchard, *La Flandre* (Paris, 1906), to P. Bozon, *La Vie rurale en Vivarais: Étude géographique* (Clermont-Ferrand, 1961). P. Brunet, *Structure agraire et économie rurale des plateaux tertiaires entre la Seine et l'Oise* (Caen, 1960), deserves a special mention for its consideration of historical factors.

2. H. Sée, *Histoire économique de la France*, i. 176.

3. P. Goubert, op. cit., p. 169; M. Philipponeau, *La Vie rurale de la banlieue parisienne* (Paris, 1956), pt. 1.

4. R. Baehrel, op. cit.; L. Merle, op. cit., pp. 100–8; M. Venard, op. cit., ch. v; J. Jacquart, 'La Vie paysanne au sud de la capitale sous le règne d'Henri IV', *Bull. Soc. Hist. de Paris et de l'Île de France* (1960–1), pp. 97–107, esp. p. 101.

5. L. Merle's study documents the economic and social history of *métayage*. See also R. Baehrel, op. cit., pp. 368–72.

6. G. Fourquin, *Les Campagnes de la région parisienne à la fin du Moyen-Âge* (Paris, 1964), pp. 91–8 (with detailed bibliography).

7. *Archives Nationales*, S207; P. Brunet, op. cit., p. 365.

8. A brief general survey of agricultural techniques is given in D. Faucher, *Histoire générale des techniques*, ii. 143–68. And there is some useful information in P. Goubert, 'Les Techniques agricoles dans les pays picards aux XVIIe et XVIIIe siècles', *Revue d'histoire économique et sociale*, xxxv (1957), 24–40.

9. On these oases of biennial crop rotations, see A. Plaisse, op. cit., pp. 233–7; E. Juillard, *La Vie rurale dans la plaine de Basse-Alsace* (Strasbourg, 1953), pp. 40 *et seq.*

10. F. Gay, 'Production, prix et rentabilité de la terre en Berry au XVIIe siècle', *Revue d'histoire économique et sociale*, xxxvi (1958), 399–411 (applies also to the earlier period); R. Musset, *Le Bas-Maine* (Paris, 1917), p. 288; H. Sée, *Les Classes rurales*, p. 382.

11. E. Le Roy Ladurie quotes the case of the Languedoc moors in his article 'Histoire agricole et phytogéographie', *Annales* (1962), pp. 434–47.

12. Mention must be made here of J. Meuvret's standard work, 'Les Crises de subsistences et la démographie de la France d'ancien régime', *Population* (1946) pp. 643–50.

13. More or less detailed estimates of average returns are to be found in most of the works quoted. Many contributions on this subject were also made at the Third International Conference of Economic Historians in Munich, August 1965.

14. M. Chevalier, *La Vie humaine dans les Pyrénées ariégeoises* (Paris, 1956), p. 146.

15. The historic geography of maize cultivation is covered in several articles by D. Faucher, collected in *La Vie rurale vue par in géographe* (Toulouse, 1962).

16. There are some interesting comments in P. Goubert, *Les Techniques agricoles*, pp. 30–2.

17. L. Merle, op. cit., pp. 110 *et seq.*; P. Goubert, op. cit.; M. C. Gricourt, 'Étude . . . de cinq paroisses', in *A travers la Normandie des XVIIe et XVIIIe siècles* (Caen, 1963).

18. P. Bozon, op. cit.; *Archives Départementales de Seine-et-Oise*, E 4473 (9 Oct. 1601), E 4531 (29 Nov. 1607), 4591 (12 Oct. 1612), 4759 (9 Oct. 1630).

19. On agricultural landscapes see: M. Bloch, op. cit.; R. Dion, *Essai sur la formation du paysage rural français* (Tours, 1934); and a general survey by A. Meynier, *Les Paysages agraires* (Paris, 1958) (incl. bibliographical notes).

20. J. Meuvret, 'Agronomie et jardinage au XVIe et au XVIIe siècle', in *Mélanges, L. Fébvre*, ii. 353–62.

21. *Archives Nationales*, ZZ463, f. 204 (29 Oct. 1643).

22. P. Bozon, op. cit., pt. I.

23. D. Faucher, *Plaines et bassins du Rhône moyen* (Paris, 1927), pp. 348–60.

24. The basic work on this subject is R. Dion, *La Vigne et le vin en France* (Paris, 1959).

25. C. Estienne and J. Liebault, *La Maison rustique*, book V. This dates from 1561 and was reprinted several times in the 17th century.

26. R. Dion, ibid., pt. III.

27. P. de Saint-Jacob, 'Mutations économiques et sociales dans les campagnes bour-guignonnes à la fin du XVIe siècle', *Études rurales*, i (1961), 34–49; J. Jacquart, op. cit., note 4; and by the same author 'Propriété et exploitation rurales au sud de Paris, dans la seconde moitié du XVIe siècle', *Bulletin de la Société d'histoire moderne*, xii (1961), 15–16.

28. P. Goubert, op. cit.; R. Baehrel, op. cit.

29. E. Le Roy Ladurie, op. cit.; G. Debien, in *En Haut-Poitou, défricheurs au travail* (Paris), quotes an example in Avrainville, taken from the *Archives Nationales*, LL 1045, f. 159 (7 May 1612), whereby the tenant undertook to clear, if possible, all his land, to plough it, and grow cereals or vines on it.

30. Many instances could be found around Paris, on the Villejuif plateau.

31. C. Estienne and J. Liebault, op. cit., book V, chap. 29.

32. There are many articles on the question of this reversal in the economic trend, as well as a recent study by P. Chaunu, 'Le XVIIe siècle. Problèmes de conjoncture. Conjoncture globale et cojonctures rurales françaises', *Mélanges, Antony Babel* (Geneva, 1963), i. 336–55.

33. *Archives Départementales, Seine-et-Oise* (*État du revenu en 1600*); P. Brunet, op. cit., p. 316.

34. J. Delumeau, 'Le Commerce extérieur français au XVIIe siècle', *XVIIe siècle* (1966), pp. 81–106.

9

Italy in the Crisis of the Seventeenth Century

RUGGIERO ROMANO

*Translated by Anna Hearder**

IN order to avoid misunderstandings, it seems necessary to make one thing clear at the outset. By crisis, in this context, I mean a prolonged period, in which certain structures become eroded, break up, and collapse, while others (or at least the conditions for new ones) become established. It must be clear, however, that even what one may call the *new* structures show signs of erosion from their very inception. There has never been, I believe, a completely new structure, shining and durable as steel and impervious to all possible pressures.[1]

I have already had occasion to treat elsewhere the problem of the European seventeenth-century crisis[2] and would now like to deal with the same problem in relation to Italy above. The general background, however, obviously remains the same in outline.

What, then, is the general picture of Italy in the 1580s and 1590s? The country had shown an extraordinary capacity for adaptation; after her political 'misfortunes', a certain kind of economy and a certain social system had re-emerged. I must make it clear that nothing casual or accidental is intended by 'misfortunes': they were, I am convinced, closely linked to the failure of a given economic and social structure. Yet the indications are that, in the course of the sixteenth century, that same structure re-established itself, however precariously. The myth of Italian economic decadence in the sixteenth century has been severely shaken by the work of Fernand Braudel, and yet his researches have not been able to show a revival in Italian economic life. The façade has simply been repainted: in place of the predominant activity of Florentine bankers, we are shown greater activity by Genoese bankers ...: the examples could be multiplied. These adjustments do not, however, alter the valuation of the inner dynamics of the economy. There are admittedly a few changes, if one looks closely enough: how could it be otherwise? The fact is that any marginal changes, detachable here and there, do not modify the general picture.

What is this general picture? On the economic front, as we said, the indications are positive (at least in terms of quantity; a qualitative judgement would have to be more cautious). In the social field, the problem is more

* From 'L'Italia nella crisi del secolo XVII', *Studi Storici*, ix (1968), 723–41.

complicated. It is certainly true that some new men had actively entered the country's productive life and the ruling social class as early as the end of the fifteenth century. But the relevant point is that they were few, and, in the course of a few generations, the descendants of those new men had nothing left in common with their ancestors.[3]

It is now possible, I think, to enter into the main analysis of my present theme.

The important publications which have appeared in the last few years about different aspects of seventeenth-century Italian economic life allow some general conclusions to be reached: let us try to sum them up.

(a) With regard to demography, two assertions can legitimately be made: (1) urban population in Italy contracted in the course of the seventeenth century; (2) the total population of the country increased in the same period. The rate of growth was certainly not as high as that typical of sixteenth-century Italy, and even less than that of the eighteenth century, but growth there was nevertheless.[4]

(b) Production in the great classic centres (in Florence as in Milan, in Venice as in Naples) shows a considerable contraction in the textile sector. The contraction in these centres was an absolute one: in other words, no other branch of activity flourished to balance, for instance, the decline of wool. The process of substitution of economic activities, often witnessed in the history of various Italian cities, does not appear in the course of the seventeenth century. It must be added that, in the collapse of traditional textile manufacture, the heaviest blows were suffered in the production of the poorer textiles; richer fabrics (velvets, gold-threaded silks) fared rather better. As far as is known, there are no positive signs of devolopment in sectors other than textile manufacture: rather the reverse. One must also bear in mind that those other sectors of the economy, even if they had been quite flourishing, never had sufficient importance to reverse the economic conditions of a city, let alone of a region. There is, admittedly, the building sector, at least as important as textile manufacture, though it has not so far received its due attention. Looking at the seventeenth century, one has the impression that urban construction was subject to a considerable contraction—though it is really impossible to go beyond impressions in this case, owing to the almost total lack of research on the subject. Churches and palaces were indeed being built, but the genuine revolution in urban building that had taken place in the sixteenth century and had given their character, lasting almost to the present day, to the towns of Italy, came to a halt. On the contrary, the impression is that, in comparison with the sixteenth century, seventeenth-century growth took place rather in the number of towns-people's country residences.

(c) In the field of the distributive trades the picture is certainly no livelier than in that of urban production. Harbour and alpine tolls, when they can be studied, certainly show as a whole (with the exception of Leghorn) a remarkable picture of stagnation. It is useful to turn, even more than to the scant figures available at present, to the descriptions of travellers and foreign diplomatic agents. A picture of extraordinary squalor then emerges everywhere; already very clear in the first half of the century (with 1620 as the turning-point), it becomes gradually worse in the course of the second half. Nor, understandably, is there any compensating factor in the volume of internal trade, since a diminished urban population would only need for its provisions a more circumscribed hinterland than had been necessary in a phase of growth. An indirect pointer to the breakdown occurring in the seventeenth century can be found, as Emilio Sereni has observed in his masterly essay, *Mercato nazionale e accumulazione capitalistica*, in the fact that co-variant indexes of wheat prices on different Italian markets show a definite tendency to slacken between the end of the sixteenth and the beginning of the seventeenth centuries. After a tendency, however relative, 'in Italy, to the formation of a *national market* for wheat, in the sense of a more intimate link, which seems to become established at least between some of our local and regional economies',[5] a break in this development becomes apparent from the very beginning of the seventeenth century.

(*d*) Several other phenomena, linked to those so far examined, show a very similar orientation: a contraction of the monetary issue and, in general, a contraction in the circulation of money; a downward trend in the prices of manufactured goods; fairly static wages. There is perhaps no clearer piece of evidence highlighting the dismantling of the Italian urban economy than the number of paupers and vagrants, which appears to have been extremely high during the century. In Florence at the end of the seventeenth century unemployment was rampant; in Milan already in 1620 'about half of the 500 carders, 10,000 women spinners, and 10,000 stocking-makers were unemployed; out of 20,000 workers at the silk mill, 33 per cent were out of work'.[6] The evidence on this point could be multiplied; it could also be invalidated to a certain extent by the consideration that idlers, vagrants, and beggars are not typical of the Italian scene in the seventeenth century only, but were present before and after. There is, however, a considerable difference between sixteenth- and seventeenth-century vagrants: the former, in a sense, can be considered a 'reserve army' of workers and therefore always hopeful of finding employment; the latter, on the other hand, have no other prospect but the status of a vagabond, without any hope. It is certainly no coincidence that what can be called the greatest manual of vagabondage saw the light in 1627 by the hand of the Dominican, Giacinto Nobili.[7]

All these factors taken together show quite clearly, in their interaction, that Italian urban economy was having a rough passage during the seventeenth century. It is worth making a short pause here for a few clarifications.

First of all, it is obvious that we have so far dealt with the economy without taking agriculture into account; and for the moment I will continue to
leave this sector aside, although it is undoubtedly the most important in the
Italian economy. It can therefore be said that Italian economy, to the exclusion of agriculture, was in an extremely depressed state throughout the
seventeenth century. But where are the significant end-dates of the century
for this economy (always excluding agriculture)? A sufficiently firm answer
seems to be, between 1620 and 1740.

It remains to be added that the European economy as a whole (with the
exceptions, limited to some essentially qualitative features, of England and
the Low Countries), shows the same depressed characteristics. This is an
important consideration, since the seriousness of the internal Italian crisis
was sharpened by the fact that other European countries were also going
through difficult times.

So far this has been a rapid survey; but agriculture still has to be considered. Italian agriculture also suffered a crisis, but of what kind, and from
what point in time? It seems important, for the purpose of this essay, to
begin by establishing this second point. Both in Italy and in other European
countries, the agricultural crisis and that of the urban economy do not seem
to have coincided in time. The first largely preceded the second by about
thirty years. It is important to establish this, since it points quite clearly to
the separation, almost amounting to a complete divorce, between the two
economies, but it also points to the fact that urban economy cannot subsist
indefinitely when its foundation—agriculture—is failing.

After this preamble, one can perhaps trace the symptoms of the agricultural
crisis. A very recent trend in historiography—no doubt fully justified—sets
out to detect, in the seventeenth century, any positive aspects that may be
found in agricultural history (in particular, for instance, any trace of capitalist development). There is nothing arbitrary in this procedure and I myself
will later call attention to these aspects: but for the moment I would like to
keep to more general trends. And these are, without a doubt, negative. In
Milan in 1688 the Senate, in one of its councils, presents this bleak picture
for the whole of the state: 'jamdiu intermissus agri cultus multis in locis
nondum repetitur; incolae, profugi, abiecta omni spe melioris fortunae, in
alienas regiones transmigrant'.[8] Still in the State of Milan: in the district of
Casalmaggiore alone, the river Po had covered 90,000 perches of vineyards:
'the "ragone", or flooded lowlands, from Cremona to Casalmaggiore,
covered 300,000 perches, and probably more for the rivers Serio, Adda, and
Oglio'.[9] In the Monferrato, the consistently low price of land—as Giuseppe
Prato has skilfully shown—is a certain index of stagnation in agricultural
life; Prato himself suggests that 'it is unlikely that the price would have been
noticeably higher in other parts of Piedmont, which are described by contemporary historians, in the middle of the century, as terribly depopulated'.[10]

For the district of Imola, as Claudio Rotelli demonstrated in his excellent essay, 'the fall in productivity, foreshadowed in the crisis of 1562–4 and again in 1569–72, takes on, after the black quinquennium 1588–92, the features of a depression'.[11] For the whole Sienese district, a substantial 'stagnation of the over-all average production'[12] is reported for the years between 1630 and 1692. In the Roman countryside at the end of the seventeenth century only approximately one-tenth of the arable land was cultivated: the rest was by then given over to rough pasture.[13] In Apulia—even if the available figures are not strictly reliable[14]—it is certain that the proportion of land given to pasture increased considerably.

All these are isolated examples which, from different aspects, express fairly clearly the general involution of Italian agrarian economy. A black outline, undoubtedly. But it would not be impossible to paint a brighter picture, either by considering large economic units as a whole, or by looking at smaller details.

The only example of the first type seems to be provided by Venetia. The impression has indeed gained ground that 'from the second half of the sixteenth to the end of the seventeenth century, the Venetian provinces show: (1) an absolute increase in the total population, with a higher increment in the rural population; (2) the introduction and widespread diffusion of maize culture; (3) the execution of large-scale works of land reclamation and the transformation of estates; (4) the freeing of the land (especially towards the end of the period under examination) from many traditional bonds, in particular the sale to private individuals of common and ecclesiastical property'.[15]

Apart from point (4), which in any case does not apply to the period here under discussion,[16] I would not feel inclined to share such optimism; or rather, would apply it to different periods. Beltrami himself, in a publication subsequent to the one quoted above, has considerably toned down his enthusiasm. What must be noted in particular is that the conquest of the land (in the sense of 'execution of large-scale works of land reclamation' and 'transformation of estates') on the Venetian mainland was accomplished in two phases: first in the sixteenth century (and not only in its latter half); then in the eighteenth. In between, there is a vacuum.[17] But more about this later. As for the more detailed 'optimistic' pictures, reference should be made to the excellent synthesis traced by Villani.[18] But it should be mentioned here that it is not impossible to find clear negative indications even in some of the areas which are quoted as centres of positive development during the seventeenth century.[19] The point, though, is not so much to draw a kind of balance sheet between 'positive' and 'negative' signs. Numerically, there is no doubt that the latter are far more frequent than the former. The real problem is that of judging whether the positive traits can really be interpreted in the light of productive investment of personal capital; investment, that is, that would justify the description of rural capitalism. The problem is an extremely important one in the history of Italy. It must not be forgotten that a long and slavish adherence to the myth of medieval capitalism has wasted the time of a whole generation of scholars. It would indeed be a pity if, at a time when a rich vein of Italian studies in agrarian history is being opened up, the concept of rural capitalism in the seventeenth century came to trouble us.

The case of Venetia, as the most obvious and loudly-quoted example, provides a good starting-point. There is no doubt that many thousands of 'fields' were put to cultivation in the sixteenth and eighteenth centuries, and it may seem that a phenomenon like land reclamation could not be accomplished without cash investments. But the reality of sixteenth-century Venice is quite different. The problem has already been studied some time ago by Cessi,[20] though with a rather simplistic approach: he is concerned to find out whether Cornaro or Sabadino was the better technical expert—almost, which of the two was the 'nicer' man. It is of course important to establish the merits of a technical solution, since the choice of one method in preference to another nearly always implies an economic and political choice; but it is not enough. What then is the next step? These are the terms of the problem:

And therefore Your Lordship (the Doge) must with good grace and rightly accept my record, which is, that I find in Your Lordship's lands, that is in the countryside of Friuli, Treviso, Padua, Verona, and Polesine, a third of that countryside useless and uncultivated, and this third amounts to fields 800,000, and in these I include all the arid lands in the above-mentioned districts, and these are arid, because they have no water, and the marshes are marshy, because they have too much.

Of these 800,000 'fields', 200,000 cannot be reclaimed, and the remaining 600,000 can, 'but only by your Lordship alone, and not by their owners, since all those fields, which up to now could be put to cultivation by their owners, have been so put, and those that have not been are useless, because they have not been able to do it, and never will'.[21] Can one then talk of investments? The doubts raised by Alvise Cornaro's letter are, I think, fully confirmed by Elsa Campos in her good book,[22] which has not met with much favour among our historians. Essential works of land reclamation can be accomplished directly by the state (i.e. with public money) in the public interest (drainage, embankments, 'cutting' of rivers, etc.) or by the state on behalf of private owners. The first case obviously presents no problem: private citizens gain advantage from public expenditure. The second case requires closer examination:

The experts estimated the sum which would have to be allocated for the completion of the works. The interested owners were informed of the amount and given the option to deposit it within a given time. If they made the deposit, the work would be carried out by the Provveditori, to ensure certain and proper execution, but the reclaimed land would remain private property. If they did not, the work would still be carried out by the Provveditori, but the Republic would retain, as compensation for the expense undertaken, one half of the reclaimed land, while the other half would be returned to the owners at no expense to themselves. The property acquired by the Republic in this way was divided in 24 lots, called carats, and sold by public auction on the Rialto.[23]

There is also, obviously, the case of reclamation carried out directly by the owners, but such cases are in a minority and destined to 'disappear completely',[24] with the increase in the number of 'Consortia' between state and private landlords. Nor did things go otherwise for the subsequent maintenance of the completed works: though by law the onus of conservation should have fallen on the landlords, it was very often carried by the state.

But who was, in Venice, the state? Families such as the Gritti, Morosini, Trevisani, Contarini, Pesaro, da Mula, Pisani, da Canal, Giustiniani. These are the very same names we find among the improving landlords.[25] Given the close symbiosis between state and patrician families, it is not arbitrary to think that this grandiose work of land reclamation was essentially charged to public funds, and it would be hard to attribute any 'capitalist' features to an operation, undoubtedly on a grand scale, but 'political' in the worst sense of the term. If this is obdurate pessimism, it is hard to avoid it.

The situation I have just outlined belongs, it is true, to the sixteenth century. If I have proposed it in what I consider to be its real terms, it is because these facts, arbitrarily extrapolated to the seventeenth century, have been taken as proof of productive investment of liquid capital into real estate. This is not admissible. It remains to find out whether the conservation and exploitation of this new land in the course of the seventeenth century were achieved by recourse to management capital, to complementary investments, to a new entrepreneurial spirit. This seems rather difficult to prove: even though improvements did take place in some areas, the manner in which they were carried out was rather old-fashioned. It is significant that, while Venetian landed property on the mainland, in the mid-seventeenth century, bore 'by this time, the true characteristics of latifundia', tenancy contracts remained tied to the old criteria of production and to the old relationships, the norm being 'small and very small tenancies with payment in kind or partly in cash'.[26] To this must be added the surviving bonds, weighing heavily on every aspect of Venetian agrarian life: quarterage, feudal taxes, annuities, grazing dues. Peasants were very heavily in debt. Even if we do not want to call this feudalism, it cannot be denied that, on the whole, Venetian agriculture was geared to a system of abuses. It is not a paradox to say that some of the 'investments' consisted not so much of gold coins as of abusive practices.

The Venetian mainland, however, cannot be the main observation point for researching the penetration of money in the Italian countryside: the focal point is Lombardy. Is it not there that 'the equivalent of a thousand million was buried'?[27] There is no need to contradict Cattaneo: it cannot be doubted that such an amount was sunk into the Lombard plain: but how much of it was actually invested in cash, and how much during the seventeenth century, and in what way?

In the heart of Lombardy, the region of Lodi remained strongly feudal up to the beginning of the eighteenth century.[28] Zaninelli tentatively suggests that the fiscal exemption enjoyed by feudal estates (as well as by ecclesiastical land) constituted an advantage and certainly contributed to the almost total elimination of uncultivated land; but it remains hard to believe that the irrigation works were carried out during the seventeenth century. The region of Lodi is certainly the 'jewel' of the state of Milan, but—as Sergio Pugliese judiciously and precisely observed[29]—it must have been so already in the sixteenth century. It could not be otherwise: the whole Lombard countryside remained unchanged between the sixteenth and the eighteenth centuries. Comparing the

land capable of providing income, either by human effort or by spontaneous production, there is no variation, after two centuries, in the proportion between arable on the one hand and pasture, sedge, and woodland on the other (27% and 27·6%); nor is there any change in the relative percentages of land put to mixed culture of fields and grass with vines, and dry pasture. It would seem rather that, in the interval, there was an increase in irrigation (unless the difference can be explained by the greater diligence of the Austrian surveys), since the proportion of non-irrigated arable fields falls from 33·8% to 24·9% while fields and meadows in rotation and irrigated meadows go up from 12·3% to 15·8%. The culture showing the greatest percentage increase is that of rice, which appears for only 85,512 perches in the Spanish survey (0·5%) but for 591,316 in the Austrian (3·9%).[30]

We are thus left with a single real, solid change which can be credited to the seventeenth century: the rice-field. This calls for the use of not very fertile land, of few farm buildings, few animals, and not much labour (except, of course, temporary labour at certain times). This rather pessimistic interpretation could be reversed if, turning to look at contracts, we were to find any noticeable development: but, on the whole, we do not seem to find any substantial change in the type of contracts used during the seventeenth century.[31] This also applies to Lombardy: real tenancies will only begin 'to come into practice at the beginning of the eighteenth century in a few of the best estates'.[32] It may be as well to remember here that one cannot confuse, under the generic name of tenancies, situations which have often nothing in common; how, for instance, can one put together the tenants of the Roman countryside,[33] who already appear in the sixteenth century, with Lombard tenants of the eighteenth century?[34] Their contracts may be similar in form, but only the latter, well into the eighteenth century, will constitute that important development, the tenancy of the self-contained individual farm operating on rented land.[35]

At this stage a point should be made. The relevant historiography has been too eager, I believe, to establish a link between the end of mercantile activity and the beginning of investment in land. Was there really no alternative, for the men of the seventeenth century, between commerce and agriculture? There was one, of primary importance: excise-contracting and loans to the state. Moreover, the disappearance of some more obvious kinds of commercial investment does not exclude the persistence of other forms of investment in this sector. A few years ago, when I was analysing with José Gentil da Silva the fluctuations in the exchanges of the 'Bisenzone' fairs, we came to the conclusion that, after the troubled decade of the 1620s, the character of the fairs changed: we went so far as to talk of 'embourgeoisement';[36] profits became more limited, but also less hazardous, and capital could safely be invested at the exchanges.

In conclusion, between commercial and 'industrial' profit on one hand, and agricultural rents on the other, there was another very attractive source of revenue (excises, exchanges, loans to the exchequer) which for convenience may be called urban. And here is the heart of the problem. There is no doubt that a few oases existed in Italy (particularly, if not exclusively, in Lombardy) where it is perhaps possible to see a deliberate movement towards profit-seeking. But it is also true that, on the whole, it was the preference for 'rents' which more frequently provided a closer and, one could say, more stifling link between capital and agriculture in the history of Italy as a whole. This inclination towards 'rents' developed through what may be termed the 're-infeudation' of Italy.[37] Commerce and 'industry' could have provided the only check to this trend; but neither was to recover after the joint crisis of 1619–22. Thereafter, the process of re-infeudation went on unchecked: the signs of this are present in every Italian region. Lombardy was not to escape the trend (even leaving aside the fact that, with the exception of border territories which were immune from it, the process of infeudation was carried out with great intensity throughout the seventeenth century).[38] What is more significant, and cannot be overstressed, is that all kinds of abuses regained life, strength, substance: the sale of the feud and of its fiscal dues was accompanied by the sale of the very powers of jurisdiction: 'such as civil and criminal notary prerogatives; the appointment of the mayor and of the actuary'.[39] Hence the way open to pressures, violence, impositions, which in the last resort led to direct and, above all, indirect economic advantages. In this sense it is difficult to study many of the agricultural account-books—in Lombardy and elsewhere—in the light of modern economics: there is an 'extra' which it is impossible to quantify. It was against this 'extra' that the population tried to protect itself. Why would the people make incredible efforts to obtain redemption from the feud or to avoid being infeud-

ated, if not because the Lombard feud—or any feud—was extremely oppres-
sive? The fear of infeudation centred on the inhabitants' apprehension that
the new lord would burden them with 'sentences, fines, and annual confis-
cations' in order to 'recover his expense' incurred in obtaining the feud itself.
A fear all the more justified since on the whole these were new nobles,
who had previously belonged 'almost exclusively to the bourgeoisie which
had become rich in public offices or by the collection of duties and excise'.

The Italian economy—all of it, in every sector—went through some hard
times. But the beginning and the end of the crisis do not coincide for each
sector. I mentioned above that the first difficulties were already being felt
in agriculture at the end of the sixteenth century, while commerce, 'industry',
banking, the exchanges, etc., were not affected until the joint crisis of 1619–22.
For the end of the difficulties, too, it seems that a different time-scale applies.
In Italy the sector of commerce, 'industry', etc., does not seem to show a
genuine trend towards recovery before 1740. It is possible to find some advance pointers here and there, but examination will reveal that, when they
are present, they develop against a substantially negative background. On
the other hand, there are advance signs of recovery in agriculture at the turn
of the century. The foundation for the subsequent recovery of those that can
be described as 'urban' activities must be seen precisely in this earlier recovery of agriculture, however partial and relative.

For about 150 years, then, Italian economy had to struggle against grave
difficulties. The rest of Europe however was no better off;[40] and this is why
the true problem of the Italian 'crisis' cannot be solved by itself, but only in
comparison with parallel conditions in Europe. The Continent was going
through the same 'crisis'; but this does not imply that the crisis had everywhere the same intensity, the same development, and above all the same
conclusion.

These differences, it must be added, are to be found as much in the effects
as in the causes of the crisis. Moreover, just as there are variations within
Europe, so one can talk of a differential geography of the Italian 'crisis'.
This multiplicity of variables can however be reduced to the same principle,
by referring to the fundamental definition of crisis given at the beginning of
this essay.

As regards Europe, one can summarize as follows: in England and the
Low Countries the crisis had essentially liberating effects; in France, it did
not release energies but it certainly sowed the seeds which were to bear
fruit later; in the rest of Europe, it meant nothing but involution. Italy is
undoubtedly to be included in this last part of Europe, under the label of
involution.

This large problem, I am sure, must be looked at in perspective within a
very long historical period, going from the thirteenth to the eighteenth centuries (if not to the present). Italy (together with Europe, one should add)

had two great historical opportunities for renewal: the 'crisis' of the fourteenth century and that of the seventeenth. Both opportunities were missed.

The first was missed because of the great 'bourgeois' flowering ('capitalist',
it has even been argued with great eloquence) of the twelfth to thirteenth
centuries. In reality, that boom had very deep 'non-bourgeois' roots, tied as
it was to a feudal world which, in spite of having shed at an early stage many
of its external forms, maintained its fundamental characteristics as an economic force, a force all the more active in Italy for being armed here with
more advanced techniques and a more sophisticated philosophy than in
the rest of Europe. It was because of this 'feudal-bourgeois' blend that the
'crisis' of the fourteenth century had only a few slight positive consequences
in Italy, and many extremely damaging ones. The façade was saved, but
Charles VIII's adventurous expedition was enough to show that Italy was,
indeed, only a façade. Those who should have buttressed it and made it
into a solid construction (if they had been performing their function) were a
ruling class who did not rule, but usurped offices and corrupted, at every
level, minds and consciences. In spite of all this (perhaps even because of it)
there followed in the history of Italy about a hundred years (say, between
1480 and 1580) of splendour and full maturity. But within that renaissance
(which, as far as the economy was concerned, was directly linked with the
contemporary European boom) negative forces regained strength and the
ground on which they were rooted became ever more favourable to bearing and nourishing them. The crisis of the seventeenth century therefore
found a whole ruling class ready to withstand it: economically ready, since it
had been acquiring strength throughout the sixteenth century; ideologically
ready, since it had already absorbed the country's intellectuals;[11] socially
ready, since it had shrewdly incorporated new men, who were quickly absorbed and conditioned by the old system, so that their 'newness' only served
to strengthen the 'old' with new blood; politically ready, since it had made
its definitive choice by becoming anchored to foreign power and played, at
most, a political game between the Empire or Spain, Spain or France. This
ruling class was to suffer blows from the crisis, but it would come through
the long night: weakened, no doubt, but still strong enough to be able to
take advantage—once again—of the favourable international circumstances
of the eighteenth century. It is arguable that the scheme proposed here does
not take into account the factual differences manifest in Italy at the regional
level. On this subject we are perhaps too inclined to notice differences which
on the whole appeared only after the seventeenth century. In any case the
problem of regional and local diversity, which undoubtedly exists in the
earlier period as well, does not eliminate the fundamental problem. This
great diversity, in essence, is that between the centre and the north (with the
exception of the Papal States) on the one hand, and the kingdom of Naples
on the other. But we cannot ignore the fact that the Neapolitan ruling class,

even if it did not display so strongly the phenomenon of interpenetration with the 'bourgeois' world which is apparent in Florence, Venice, or Genoa, was indirectly tied, ever since Angevin times, to that same northern ruling class. One of the more significant books on economic history is still, in my opinion, that by the late Georges Yver;[42] but his lesson seems to have been forgotten and should, I think, be taken up again. In it the links, the ties, the community of interests between the ruling classes of the two parts of Italy are made evident: Florentine patricians and Neapolitan barons are old accomplices. Later there will follow the new marriage with Genoa. There are differences, to be sure: but beyond them the common standpoint cannot be mistaken.

Any study which raises problems concerned with capitalism cannot, I am convinced, leave aside the fundamental consideration that *capital* is older than *capitalism*. I am aware that this is an accepted truth; but it is worth recalling from time to time, and this is what I have attempted to do here, perhaps in too hurried and categorical a fashion. I never claim a monopoly of truth and certainty: there are, rather, problems and doubts which one must try to resolve without worrying about incurring contradictions (only the intellectually sterile fear contradiction). What matters is that, without academic or conceptual compromise, problems should be put clearly and in such terms that further debate—on the intellectual level and no other— becomes possible.

NOTES

1. With this I hope to go some of the way towards agreement with R. Zangheri's explanatory notes, 'Ricerca storica e ricerca economica. Agricoltura e sviluppo del capitalismo', *Studi Storici*, vii (1966), 453, note 6.

2. R. Romano, 'Tra XVI e XVII secolo. Una crisi economica: 1619–22', *Rivista Storica Italiana*, lxxiv (1962). Unfortunately, though I tried to make my views clearer in a subsequent article: 'Encore la crise de 1619–22', *Annales* (1964), that essay has sometimes been misinterpreted. To recapitulate: the first, most important, determining breakdown—in agriculture—comes at the end of the 16th century; the commercial and 'industrial' breakdown comes later: it is set in 1619–22 in the sense that *after* the short crisis of those years, commercial and 'industrial' activity enters into a longer crisis.

3. Reference can be made to my essay, 'Rolnictwo i chlopi w Wloszech w XV i XVI wieku', *Przeglad Historyczny*, liii. 2.

4. See C. M. Cipolla, 'Four Centuries of Italian demographic Development', from *Population in History*, edited by D. V. Glass and D. E. C. Eversley (1965), p. 573.

5. E. Sereni, *Capitalismo e mercato nazionale in Italia* (Rome, 1966), p. 61.

6. For Florence: L. Cantini, *Legislazione toscana raccolta e illustrata* (Florence, 1803), xix. 267; for Milan, E. Verga, *Il Comune di Milano e l'arte della seta*, p. xx.

7. R. Frianoro (pseudonym for G. Nobili), *Il Vagabondo, overo sferza de bianti e vagabondi* (Venice, 1627, and numerous Italian editions and French translations).

8. 'The cultivation of the land, interrupted for a long time in many places, has not been resumed; the country people, uprooted, abandoning all hope of better times, are migrating to foreign regions.' Quoted by B. Caizzi, *Storia di Milano* (Milan, 1957), x. 366.

9. Ibid.

10. G. Prato, *La Vita economica in Piemonte a mezzo il secolo XVIII* (Turin, 1908), p. 195.

11. C. Rotelli, 'Rendimenti e produzione agricola nell'Imolese dal XVI al XIX secolo', *Rivista Storica Italiana*, lxxix (1967), 1.

12. G. Parenti, *Prezzi e mercato del grano a Siena* (1546–1765) (Florence, 1942), p. 99.

13. Ibid., p. 102.

14. See P. Villani's correct observations in *Feudalità, riforme, capitalismo agrario* (Bari, 1968), p. 119, note 11; see also G. M. Galanti, *Nuova descrizione storica e geografica delle Sicilie*, ii (Naples, 1788), 298–9.

15. D. Beltrami, *Saggio di storia dell'agricoltura nella Repubblica di Venezia durante l'età moderna* (Venice–Rome, 1955), p. 11.

16. Point (2) also lacks conviction: maize may have been known in Venetia already in the sixteenth century but it should be remembered that it did not carry real economic weight before the first decades of the seventeenth.

17. D. Beltrami, *Forze di lavoro e proprietà fondiaria nelle campagne venete dei secoli XVII e XVIII* (Venice–Rome, 1961).

18. P. Villani, op. cit., pp. 117–25.

19. See for instance, for Mantua, C. Vivanti, *Le Campagne del Mantovano nell'età delle riforme* (Milano, 1959), pp. 24–5.

20. R. Cessi, 'Alvise Cornaro e la bonifica veneziano nel secolo XVI', *Rendiconti della Reale Accademia Nazionale dei Lincei (Classe di Scienze, Morali, Storiche e Filologiche)*, s. VI, vol. xii, Nos. 3–4 (1936), and id., *Premessa a Antichi Scrittori d'Idraulica Veneta*, ii. 11 (Venice, 1941).

21. Alvise Cornaro, 'Aricordo de —, molto bello et utile alla conservation perpetua di questa alma città', *Antichi Scrittori*, op. cit., p. 38.

22. E. Campos, *I Consorzi di bonifica nella Repubblica Veneta* (Padua, 1937).

23. Ibid., p. 35, note 1.

24. Ibid., p. 38.

25. Alvise Cornaro, 'Replica di —, alle opposizioni sopra gli arzeri di Fogolana', *Antichi Scrittori*, op. cit., pp. 17–18.

26. D. Beltrami, *Forze di lavoro*, pp. 96 and 99.

27. C. Cattaneo, 'Industria e Morale', in *Scritti Economici*, edited by A. Bertolino, iii (Florence, 1956), 4.

28. S. Zaninelli, *Una grande azienda agricola della pianura irrigua lombarda nei secoli XVIII e XIX* (Milan, 1964), p. 30.

29. S. Pugliese, *Condizioni economiche e finanziarie della Lombardia nella prima metà del secolo XVIII* (Turin, 1924), p. 31.

30. Ibid., p. 34.

31. See P. S. Leicht's introduction to *Testi e documenti per la storia del diritto agrario in Italia, secoli VIII–XVIII* (Milan, 1954).

32. S. Pugliese, op. cit., p. 47.

33. See W. Sombart, *La Campagna romana* (Turin, 1891), pp. 82 *et seq.*

34. See L. Cafagna, 'La "Rivoluzione agraria" in Lombardia', *Annali dell'Istituto Giangiacomo Feltrinelli*, ii (1959), 398–9. Indirectly, additional information can be drawn from C. Saibene, *La Casa rurale nella pianura e nella collina lombarda* (Florence, 1955), pp. 200–1.

35. See L. Dal Pane, *Storia del lavoro in Italia dagli inizi del secolo XVIII al 1815* (Milano, 1958), p. 45.

36. J. Gentil da Silva, R. Romano, 'L'Histoire des changes: les foires de "Bisenzone" de 1600 à 1650,' *Annales* (1962), p. 720.

37. In addition to my article quoted in note 3, see R. Villari's perceptive observations, *La Rivolta Antispagnola a Napoli. Le origini (1585–1640)* (Bari, 1967), pp. 216 *et seq.*, and the general picture drawn by A. De Maddalena, 'Il Mondo rurale italiano nel Cinque e nel Seicento', *Rivista Storica Italiana*, lxxvi (1964), 362–3.

38. B. Caizzi, op. cit., p. 341.

39. Ibid., p. 340.

40. See *Crisis in Europe: 1560–1660. Essays from Past and Present,* edited by Trevor Aston (1965), and my two articles quoted in note 2.

41. See A. Tenenti and R. Romano, 'L' Intellectuel italien dans la société italienne des XVe et XVIe siècles', in *Niveau de culture et groupes sociaux. Actes du colloque réuni du 7 au 9 mai 1966 à l'École Normale Supérieure de Paris* (Paris–The Hague, 1967), pp. 51–65.

42. G. Yver, *Le Commerce et les marchands dans l'Italie méridionale au XIIIe et au XIVe siècle* (Paris, 1903).

10

Economic Fluctuations and Trade in the Netherlands, 1650–1750

J. G. VAN DILLEN

*Translated by Alice Claire Carter and Sytha Hart**

SEVERAL historians have argued erroneously that fluctuations in trade in the seventeenth and eighteenth centuries were of the same character and were due to the same causes as the modern trade cycle. Posthumus, for instance, thought that the crises in various branches of the Leiden textile industry in the seventeenth century 'showed no essential differences from those of this age'.[1] Groeneveld used statistical material to make the same point with reference to a large part of the early capitalist economy.[2] Such a thesis is untenable before the Industrial Revolution, since the amount of fixed capital employed was so very small. It is true that there were many wind- and water-mills and that machine tools were sometimes used; indeed some of the tools made by the specialized millwrights and artisans were quite sophisticated. But in relation to the whole economy the capital-goods sector was very small. Both the large-scale manufacturers and the numerous artisans were mainly engaged in the production of consumer goods. The almost total absence of a real capital-goods industry meant that the tendency towards regularly recurring over-production that was characteristic of later periods was not yet present in the seventeenth and eighteenth centuries. There were periods of prosperity and adversity, but such fluctuations were not caused by the structure of industry. They were due to exogenous factors.

For Europe as a whole one can discern periods of economic growth alternating with periods of slow development, but one has to beware of unreal, schematic generalization. The sixteenth century, for instance, has acquired the reputation of being a period of almost revolutionary change and modernization of the economic system, accompanied by high prices and a tremendous growth of trade and industry. This 'modern' character, thought to be peculiar to that period, calls however for serious criticism. The seventeenth

* From Chapter 23 of *Van Rijkdom en Regenten: Handboek tot de economische en sociale geschiedenis van Nederland tijdens de Republiek* (The Hague: Martinus Nijhoff, 1970). Some alternations and rearrangements of material have been made in order to enable this chapter to stand up as an article in its own right. These alterations have been approved by Dr. W. M. Zappey who prepared the late Professor van Dillen's book for the press.

century, on the other hand, is sometimes depicted as having been as con-servative as the sixteenth was revolutionary. According to Mousnier there was a permanent crisis in the latter century,[3] not only in the economic field but also in those of politics, science, religion, and the arts. Others do not speak of a crisis but of a prolonged economic depression, in sharp contrast to the prosperity of the sixteenth century. This opinion is to be found in the works of French historians such as Braudel, Labrousse, and Goubert, and in those of the English writer F. C. Spooner; among Dutch writers Slicher van Bath subscribes to this theory. These authors point in the first place to the fact that the supply of bullion from Spanish America attained its peak in the years around 1600, but then began to decrease, slowly at first but later more and more rapidly. By 1651–60 the supply was only one-sixth of what had arrived in the last decade of the sixteenth century. This phenomenon, coupled with the increasing outflow of silver and gold from Europe to the East Indies, decreased the circulation of money with a resultant fall in almost all prices.

From data published by Posthumus and from research into price move-ments in other countries it appears that there was also a general fall in prices in the Netherlands. It also seems that the prices of agricultural products, and in particular those of grain, show a greater fall than those of other products. This can be explained by the fact that, at least from the middle of the seventeenth century, Spain and Italy no longer needed rye and wheat from the Baltic countries. The reduced buying-capacity of the farmers influenced the prices of industrial products, thus intensifying the tendency towards a general fall in prices caused by the decreasing circulation of money. The falling population in Spain and Italy, the fact that Germany was ravaged by the Thirty Years War, and the slower increase of population in some other countries are also said to be characteristic of this period, called 'la grande depression' by some French authors.

Some historians date the beginning of this great depression from as early as around 1620. The copper inflation which plagued Germany from the begin-ning of the Thirty Years War also caused much harm to the exporters of English cloth to Germany. Since cloth occupied such a dominant position in English exports, one can assume that for England economic conditions began to deteriorate around 1620. And by the time the German copper in-flation had come to an end, the English Civil War had begun, with its ex-tremely harmful influence on trade and industry. For Germany and England, therefore, the beginning of the depression can be dated from the year 1620. The date was probably even earlier for Spain and Italy. But, in contrast, the Dutch Republic saw its greatest prosperity around 1650, and any argument for an early dating of the beginning of the depression in the Netherlands is contradicted by the fact that the general fall in prices, and in particular those of grain, begins only between 1650 and 1660.

This is why Slicher van Bath and other authors date the beginning of the great depression as late as around 1650,[4] even though by that date the greatest misery was over in Germany and England. It is assumed that the depression lasted to about 1750 when there began a long period of rising prices and in other respects the economic climate was altogether more favourable. One must remember, however, that between 1685 and 1720 prices, and again grain prices in particular, were considerably higher, leading to a prolonged interruption of the depression. In addition to his use of price data Slicher van Bath reinforces his argument for the dating of the beginning and the end of the great depression by pointing out that, for the Netherlands at least, the interest in land reclamation and poldering dwindled considerably from around 1665 but recovered a century later in 1764. It is more than probable that this decline in interest was related to the fall in agricultural prices and to the lower purchase- and rental-value of land, but it should be remembered that, with the exception of the Haarlemmermeer, the lakes presenting the greatest hazards had already been reclaimed, and that poldering had often been financially disappointing for the shareholders. And the renewed interest after 1764 was very slight compared with the preceding century.

These reservations aside, it is clear that there was a fall in prices, particularly agricultural prices, in the century between 1650 and 1750 interrupted only during the long period of general warfare between 1680 and 1720. What caused this depression of prices and what effect did it have on the Netherlands economy? Though it is not subject to absolute proof, it seems probable that the general fall in prices from 1660 onwards was at least partly due to the reduction in the supply of silver from South America and the increasing export of silver to the East Indies by the Dutch, English, and French companies. Monetary reasons can be discovered for the upturn of prices in the eighteenth century too. From the beginning of the century the supply of gold from Brazil increased and around 1750 the production of silver in Peru and Mexico also began to increase, at first slowly but later more rapidly, as can be seen from the data obtained by Soetbeer from the archives of Seville.[5] But there were real as well as monetary factors at work. Why, for instance, should grain prices have fallen so much further than other agricultural prices? Certainly not because of a deluge of foreign grain. The main reason seems to be that there was a considerable change in the relationship of grain production to population in many parts of Europe. There was an increase in the production of corn in Spain, Portugal, and Italy and also of rice in the plain of the river Po in Italy. In western Europe and also here in the Netherlands the production of buckwheat was considerably increased. At the same time the population of southern Europe which had grown rapidly in the sixteenth century was now decreasing in this time of depression, while in western Europe, although the population increase continued, it was at a much slower pace than in the sixteenth and in the first half of the seventeenth centuries. In France there was probably little or no population growth because of the less favourable economic climate during the wars of Louis XIV and the emigration of many Protestants. It is plausible that population was stable in Germany, too, where certain areas had been devastated during the Thirty Years War. The grain market in Italy and Spain may have been further disturbed by the cessation of the Turkish government's prohibition on the export of grain from the Morea and the islands of the Greek Archipelago. In any case, by the eighteenth century, southern Europe was no longer an important market for the Amsterdam grain trade. The densely populated southern Netherlands, however, still bought a great deal of grain from Amsterdam while France was also a good customer in years of bad harvests.

What effect did the agricultural depression in the periods 1650–80 and 1720–50 have on the Netherlands economy? It should be noted that the depression mainly concerned grain; the prices of commercial crops and pastoral products also fell, but much less than those of grain. During the depression the wheat farmers of Zeeland and of the islands of Zuidholland and the rye farmers of the eastern provinces and Brabant decreased their production of grain and increased their production of commercial crops such as flax, madder, and colza. Stock-farming also increased, at least until the rinder-pest became epidemic from 1714 to 1720. In so far as the change-over to commercial crops or stock-farming was successful there can have been no important decline in the prosperity of the farmers concerned.

The grain trade was also affected, but not necessarily disastrously. The import of grain from the Baltic was a good deal smaller than in the preceding period, but as soon as poor harvests caused a rise in prices the grain trade once more became active and import from the Baltic increased. This happened around 1680 and the following years and even more in 1693–4, while in 1697–8 all of western and southern Europe was stricken by famine. Notwithstanding the war, France had to call upon the Amsterdam grain market in 1707 and again in 1709. After 1720, however, there ensued a long period of low prices and little activity in the grain trade. Only in the fifties was there a change when conditions became once more favourable. For the Amsterdam grain trade in general the reduced supply of grain from the Baltic was of course an unfavourable development. On the other hand there was a growing trade in timber and colonial goods. J. A. Faber's argument[6] that this in no way compensated for the decline of the grain trade is rather one-sided. According to Faber the major role played by the grain trade was 'not primarily the result of the total monetary value of the imported grain but rather of the physical size of that quantity of grain', because this determined the amount of tonnage, hold capacity, warehouse space, and labour required. It is true that in the course of the eighteenth century the number of grain-porters and grain-lighters in Amsterdam decreased, but there is little or no evidence of unemployment among the Amsterdam dockworkers or of warehouses standing empty. New Baltic trades grew to replace the old ones. The decline of the grain trade was matched by a decline in the shipment of the traditional outward cargoes, herrings and salt. But compensation for this was provided by an enormous expansion of imports of timber from the Baltic area and of exports of textiles and colonial wares to it. The imports of timber from the Baltic, mainly oak, but also pine, from the forests of Livonia and Estonia, grew at a truly astonishing rate. From the decade 1661–70, when imports amounted to no more than about one million 'pieces', the supply of timber grew to almost five million in 1721–30 and reached an ample ten million 'pieces' in the next decade, a high level which was more or less retained until 1780. But for Dutch trade to the Baltic as a whole it was an ominous sign that during the first half of the eighteenth century the supply of grain from and the export of salt and herrings to that area was at a much lower level than it had been in the last decades of the preceding century. The greater supply of timber and the export of textiles and especially of colonial products did not sufficiently compensate for this loss. And in so far as the volume of Dutch shipping through the Sound remained at its former level, its share in the total of Sound shipping was reduced as a result of the increases in English and Scandinavian shipping and in that from the German cities.

During this period Amsterdam remained by far the most important world-market for colonial products. As Henri Sée wrote of the first half of the eighteenth century: 'Amsterdam est toujours le grand marché des denrées coloniales: les prix de cette place, en ce qui concerne le sucre, le café, l'indigo, le poivre, s'imposent aux autres places de commerce.'[7] The city held this position owing to the successful development of the East India Company as a commercial enterprise. The market value of goods shipped from the East Indies which had amounted to 8·7 million guilders in the period 1648–50 rose to more than 23 million in 1738–40[8] and the number of large ships engaged in this trade had risen from fifteen to thirty or more. Besides the traditional spices and pepper, such goods as tea, coffee, and textiles—raw silk and cotton, and silk and cotton fabrics—had grown to be of major importance. These goods were re-exported not only to the Baltic but also to Russia, Germany, France, and the southern European countries. In South America the loss of Brazil had been made good since the last decades of the seventeenth century by the flourishing colony of Surinam with its 400 or 500 plantations. In addition there were Berbice, Essequibo, and Demerara from whence every year several million guilders' worth of sugar, coffee, tobacco, cocoa, and cotton were shipped to the Dutch staple-market. Though the earlier trade to the English and French Caribbean islands had become almost impossible because of protectionist measures, there was also an active and profitable contraband trade from Curaçao and St. Eustatius to the Spanish colonies in South America and to the English colonies in North America.

One feature of colonial trade that was of major significance to the Dutch was the fact that English merchants had driven them from first place in the slave trade. Since the beginning of the eighteenth century the slave trade had become an essential part of economic life in England, not only because slave labour was indispensable to the West Indian colonies, but also because the British possessed, through the Assiento agency in Jamaica, the monopoly of slave deliveries to the Spanish colonies.

The prosperity of the colonial trade of the Republic was threatened in 1723 by the foundation of the Company of Ostend, whose ships made successful journeys in the early years to the East Indies and to China. This new competitor caused anxiety not only to the Republic but also to England, though not for long. For the Company was obliged to cease its operations in 1728 on the orders of the Emperor Charles VI, and it was dissolved in 1731. The emperor took this measure after both sea-powers had agreed to the Pragmatic Sanction guaranteeing the succession of Charles's daughter, Maria Theresa, to her father's hereditary lands.

The progress of other trades was less satisfactory than those in timber and colonial products, mainly because of the increasing pressure of French and English competition. Sometimes this was not too serious, as in Russia where Dutch trade remained important throughout the eighteenth century, despite the conclusion by the English of a most advantageous commercial treaty with Russia in 1734. All classes of trade with Germany and the southern Netherlands remained intensive in the first half of the eighteenth century, partly as a result of the prohibition on transit trade through the latter. But elsewhere the strength of the two competitors began to tell. In the eighteenth century English and French competition in the trade from Cadiz to the Spanish colonies, which had been mainly in Dutch hands in the seventeenth century, grew stronger. The carrying trade to Portugal still had some importance in the eighteenth century, but after the Methuen Treaty of 1703 England outstripped the Republic in this trade so that Brazilian gold reached the Amsterdam specie market partly by way of England, but also from France, especially in the years between 1715 and 1725. Shipping through the Straits also decreased since Italy no longer needed Baltic grain and the export of Leiden textiles to the Levant diminished after 1672 in the face of French and English competition. Yet trade to the Levant remained important.

Until about 1730 the Netherlands remained the centre of distribution for English cloth and colonial products, but after that date the English merchants began to make their own contacts with other countries to the detriment of the Republic. Rotterdam, however, profited from an increased supply of goods destined for transit to the Rhineland area.

French protectionist measures had an unfavourable influence on Dutch trade and industry, but because of increasing rivalry between France and England, the French government was more lenient towards Dutch interests in the first half of the eighteenth century than it had been in the time of Colbert, and the commercial treaty concluded in 1739 was very favourable to the Republic. But the time had long since passed in which Dutch merchants settled in Bordeaux, Nantes, and La Rochelle had given the lead; Netherlands trade in French wines was decreasing in the last decades of the seventeenth century and the increasing quantity of French colonial wares could dispense with the Dutch staple-market.

Dutch industry, like trade, was affected in diverse ways during this century of predominantly falling prices and increasing foreign competition. Some industries, like the Amsterdam soapworks, started to decline as early as 1660. Many other industries met the challenge of new conditions quite successfully for a long time but showed a tendency to decline from about 1730. But decline in some industries was compensated to a certain extent by the continued prosperity or recovery of many old industries and the introduction of completely new industries.

The textile industry was one that had mixed fortunes during this period. The decline of the Leiden wool industry after 1672 and that of the Haarlem linen industry which was also beginning to be noticeable was only partly compensated for by the growth in the weaving industry in the agricultural areas. The scale of the cloth industry declined rapidly around the turn of the century because of the imports of English cloth, now being finished and dyed in England. But one bright feature in textiles was the prosperity of the silk industry which, however, diminished in turn after 1720 as a result of French competition and the rise of this industry in England, Prussia, and elsewhere. Compensation for the decline of other sectors was found in the rise of the important new industry of cotton-printing, connected with the onset of new fashions and with the over-supply of cotton from the colonies in the East and West Indies. Over-all, with the exception of the Leiden cloth and Haarlem linen-weaving, the textile industry was still prosperous in the first half of the eighteenth century.

Saw-milling and ship-building too continued to be of great importance. These related industries increased slightly in size in the second half of the seventeenth and at the beginning of the eighteenth centuries. The saw-mills continued to work for export as well as for the home market and around 1730 there were still more than 250 saw-mills in the Zaan area, though this number was to decrease later. Although the ship-building industry felt the effect of a slackening in shipping through the Sound between 1652 and 1678 there was compensation in other trades. Expansion of the whale fishery and of the Iceland cod fishery from the middle of the seventeenth century led to an increase in the number of ships employed, and the ship-building industry was also busy replacing vessels destroyed in the not infrequent shipwrecks in these trades. There was also an increase in the number of ships sailing to the East and West Indies. Foreign customers remained important too. The English merchant navy still required the help of Dutch ships in the second half of the seventeenth century, notwithstanding the prohibiting measures of the Navigation Acts. Danish ship-owners used fly-boats built in the Netherlands, and in years of peace the French government on several occasions had ships built in Amsterdam. In 1707 more than 300 ships were under construction in the sixty ship-yards of the Zaan area. But, as a result of heavier foreign competition, a decline in ship-building and saw-milling set in between 1730 and 1740, at first slowly but later more rapidly.

Other industries also began to decline. As we have seen, the Amsterdam soapworks began to decline as early as 1660. Salt-making was still relatively prosperous, but received a heavy blow when the import of raw salt began to decline, and the glass-blowing industry was handicapped not only by the import of cheap glass from Germany and Bohemia but above all by imports from England. But such decline was matched by the progress or continued prosperity of other industries. The oil-crushing industry of the Zaan area was still prosperous, as was the paper-making industry which was improved technically by the invention of the 'hollander'. The same is true for the printing, publishing, and book-selling industries, all of which were greatly indebted to the arrival of French refugees. The important industry of sugar-refining, at a low ebb after 1660, went through a new long period of great prosperity after the beginning of the eighteenth century, and one also sees a prosperous state of affairs in other finishing industries such as diamond-cutting, tobacco, distilling, and white lead. Finally, the prosperity of Delft ware lasted until the end of the period under discussion.

The financial sector of the economy remained prosperous. From the enlargement of the stock-exchange building in 1660 it appears that the Amsterdam Bourse drew an increasing number of visitors, a great number of whom were foreign businessmen. Amsterdam had also become an important financial centre as the international staple-market of goods and bullion. After 1683 it had become possible to deposit specie with the Exchange Bank which resulted in a considerable increase in the trade in specie. From the fact that in 1737 Spanish silver to the total value of 15·5 million guilders was deposited with the Exchange Bank,[9] it appears that heavily loaded silver fleets must still have been arriving in Cadiz in the first half of the eighteenth century. Silver and gold were also obtained from England. And because exchange rates were more stable in Amsterdam than elsewhere merchants in foreign countries preferred to pay their debts with bills drawn on Amsterdam. This money and exchange business and the issue of numerous foreign loans meant very profitable business for the bankers of this period.

It is clear that, just as in the preceding period, much new capital was also created in the period 1650–1740. Historians have not always been fully enough aware of the great importance of this creation of capital to the political and economic position of the Republic. One need only think of the acquisition of allies by means of subsidies. And in so far as the newly created capital had been invested in foreign loans, the inhabitants of the Republic could claim important annual sums in payment of interest from abroad, favourably influencing the Republic's balance of payments.

Until now no mention has been made of the yields of the import and export duties (Convoy and Licence duties). Naturally it is mainly the proceeds from the offices in Amsterdam and Rotterdam which should be considered. But since complete tables of the quantity of imports and exports have been preserved for only a few years, the total figures of the annual proceeds are an imperfect source for discerning changes in the Dutch staple-market. There are other problems in using these statistics. Variations in the exports of untaxed or lightly taxed goods cannot be discerned. The import and export of money and bullion, for instance, went untaxed, so that the prosperity of the trade in specie does not appear in the statistics. Nor was the export of spices—a product of great value—taxed. The analysis of colonial trade is made even more difficult by the fact that from 1683 the East India Company paid a fixed sum annually that is not included in such tables as survive, so that the steady increase in the import of colonial products from the East Indies is not reflected in the statistics, and their re-export is observable only to a very small degree. Another drawback attaching to these tables is that many merchants practised fraud, and it is impossible to tell whether smuggled goods invariably represented the same percentage of total tonnage. In the grain trade, at least, there was much more smuggling in a period of low prices and small profits than at other times.

Notwithstanding all these drawbacks the statistics of the yields of the import and export duties are of some interest. It appears that during the period 1652–80 the proceeds of the Amsterdam office exceeded one million guilders only twice, in 1660 and again in 1668, whereas this figure was exceeded no less than eight times in the shorter period 1681–1702, confirming the theory that the latter period was economically a favourable one.[10]

But the statistics of the proceeds of the import and export duties at Amsterdam and Rotterdam give a rather one-sided picture of the economic cycle because they only concern overseas trade. In an attempt to broaden this picture Oldewelt published tables and graphs of the proceeds of three imposts, those of the *Waag*, the *Ronde Maat*, and the *Grove Waren* in Amsterdam and Rotterdam.[11] One or other of these imposts had to be paid every time a sale of merchandise took place in these cities, except in the case of re-exports —a considerable exception. So, since it was expressly stipulated that export duties but not imposts should be paid on exported goods, Oldewelt's theory that the proceeds of these three imposts reflect the size of almost all trade is therefore not completely tenable.

In many respects the tables of the import and export duties give a different picture from what emerges from the imposts. Where the former suggest stagnation for the period 1652–78 and strong growth for the following period, and another decline during the War of the Spanish Succession, the picture is almost reversed in the tables of the imposts. This may be explained as follows. Although the levying of impost affected goods supplied from overseas, this was only when these were sold on import. The proceeds of the three imposts, therefore, probably reflects mainly the sale of domestic products and products obtained by land from neighbouring countries. This branch of trade flourished in times when overseas trade was severely hampered by privateers and war fleets, as happened in the years 1672–8 and 1702–13. During the Nine Years War, however, England and the Republic were more successful in controlling the activities of the French navy, though they suffered serious setbacks in the southern Netherlands which explains, according to Oldewelt, why trade by land went through a period of depression while overseas trade flourished. It is however a fact that in this war the Dunkirk privateers inflicted much damage on the Dutch merchant navy and on the herring fishery. The high proceeds of the import and export duties were really the result of the flourishing Baltic trade which had expanded once more, because of the great demand for grain.

Thus statistics that are based only on data from the import and export duties collected at Amsterdam and Rotterdam give a distorted picture of the course of the economic cycle. On the other hand one must remember that domestic trade and trade by land with the Rhine area and with the southern Netherlands were far less vital to the prosperity of the Republic than the extremely profitable overseas trade. The amount of trade by land with Germany and areas further afield was somewhat limited even in war years by heavy transport costs due to the many high river-tolls along the Rhine, while transport along the usually bad roads using horse-drawn carts was slow and expensive. Merchant wealth was for the most part the result of extensive overseas trade, the woe and weal of which is well reflected by the data of the import and export duties. There is no doubt that the statistics of the three imposts are important for our knowledge of the prosperity of the population but, besides the shortcomings mentioned above, they have the objection that they do not reflect the actual proceeds but give merely the amounts of rentals and it is a well-known fact that there were often illegal agreements between tax-farmers and municipal authorities in fixing these rentals.

Summarizing the qualitative and quantitative evidence for the economic life of the Republic we find a decline in some areas and progress in others. The powerful economic growth before 1650 seems to be followed by a long period of stability, though on a lower level than had been reached in the very steep upward swing of the 1640s. It is not easy to determine the terminal point of this period of stability but there are strong arguments for placing it around 1735 or 1740. The data of the first four decades of the eighteenth century, with the exception of those for the textile industry, point to a relative rather than to an absolute decline.

How should we explain this change in the Republic's relative position? Because of the country's geographical position economic progress was dependent upon its part as an intermediary in trade relations between different parts of Europe and was therefore greatly influenced by natural and economic factors such as the succession of runs of good or bad harvests, changes in the population size of different countries, the increase and decrease in the production of bullion, and in the import of colonial wares. One should not, however, forget to take into account the influence of political circumstances—alliances, wars, and peace treaties between the states—or the steady increase in protectionist measures in many countries. Because of its financial capacity and its large merchant fleet the Republic was considered to be a valuable ally; it could also profit from mutual competition between the great powers. On the other hand its prosperity gave rise to jealousy. Because of the prevailing static conception of the size of commercial traffic, merchants and statesmen of other countries were convinced that they would be able to increase their own prosperity by military violence at the cost of the Republic. Charles Wilson demonstrated that this conception was an important factor in the outbreak of the Second Dutch War as well as of the First. An English merchant expressed this idea in 1664 with the words: 'that the trade of the world is too little for us two, therefore one must down'.[12] It may be true that Louis XIV's inclination towards imperialism should be seen more from a psychological than from an economic viewpoint, but this king, like his minister Colbert, was aware of the fact that his desire for power could not be gratified without the necessary means. He was equally aware that the political power of the Republic that opposed him had an economic basis. The coveted southern Netherlands had not only strategic but also considerable economic importance; one has only to think of Antwerp and Ostend. That Louis XIV was realistic enough appears also from a letter written by him in 1709, that is during the War of the Spanish Succession, in which he says: 'le principal objet de la guerre présente est celui du commerce des Indes et des richesses qu'elles produisent'.[13] In this connection India means Peru and Mexico.

Both the great coalition wars against France in which the Republic became involved were economically very detrimental. This was especially true of the War of the Spanish Succession. Trade to Cadiz was hampered and Dunkirk, now in French hands, was a base for privateers, as it had been in the earlier war with Spain. French privateers inflicted great losses on the

Dutch fishery and merchant navy and the economic curve that had been rising fast at the end of the seventeenth century flattened out considerably during this period. Moreover, the Northern War, even though the Republic was not involved, proved harmful to Dutch Baltic trade. After the end of this war in 1721, and especially after the resulting tariff revision, the economic climate once more became favourable.

War was not the Republic's only problem. As we have seen, the protectionism of France, England, and other countries diminished the outlets for various branches of Dutch industry. English ship-building began to supersede that of the Republic. In the preceding century English cloth was dyed and finished in Dutch towns but now the English had learned this craft themselves. French and English textiles drove Leiden cloth from the Levant. Notwithstanding these developments the economic position of the Republic remained relatively strong until about 1740 thanks to the staple-market, the flourishing banking business, the prosperity of some industries, and most of all to the possession of important colonies. The tremendous increase in the supply of colonial products, not only from the Dutch colonies but also from France and other countries, reinforced the position of the Amsterdam staple-market where the competition of Hamburg which was to prove so formidable later in the century caused no anxieties before 1740.

NOTES

1. N. W. Posthumus, *De geschiedenis van de Leidsche lakenindustrie* (The Hague, 1939), iii. 1141.

2. F. Ph. Groeneveld, *De economische crisis van het jaar 1720* (Groningen, 1940).

3. R. Mousnier, *Les XVIe et XVIIe siècles* (Paris, 1954); I. Schöffer, 'Viel onze Gouden Eeuw in een tijdvak van crisis?', *Bijdrugen en Nededelingen van het Historisch Genootschap te Utrecht*, lxxviii (1964), 45–72. [See *Acta Historiae Neerlandica*, i (1966), 82–105 for English translation.]

4. B. H. Slicher van Bath, *De agrarische geschiedenis van West-Europa, 500–1850* (Utrecht, 1960), pp. 227 ff. [English translation, *Agrarian History of Western Europe* (1963), pp. 206 ff.]

5. J. G. van Dillen, 'Amsterdam om wereldmarkt der edele metalen in de 17de en 18de Eeuw', in *Economisch-Historische Herdrukken* (The Hague, 1964), p. 236, note 1.

6. According to the calculations of Faber the average numbers of lasts of grain imported yearly from the Baltic, in three periods, the first and second halves of the seventeenth century and the first half of the eighteenth century, were respectively: 68,500, 55,800, and 31,800. The Dutch share in the total transport of grain through the Sound remains more or less the same, viz. about 80 per cent. See J. A. Faber, 'Het probleem van de dalende graanaanvoer uit de Oostzeelanden in de tweede helft van de 17e eeuw', *Afdeling Agrarische Geschiedenis*, ix (1963), 3–28. [English translation in *Acta Historiae Neerlandica*, i. 108–31.]

7. H. Sée, 'Le Commerce de Saint-Malo dans la première moitié du XVIIIe siècle', *Revue internationale du commerce*, xxv (1924).

8. K. Glamann, *Dutch Asiatic Trade, 1620–1740* (The Hague, 1958), p. 14. In 1778–80 the figure was even higher, 28·1 million.

9. J. G. van Dillen, *Bronnen tot de geschiedenis der Wisselbanken* (1925), ii. 898.

10. J. C. Westermann, 'Statistische gegevens over den handel van Amsterdam in de 17de eeuw', *Tijdschrift voor Geschiedenis*, vol. lxi (1948).

11. W. F. H. Oldewelt, 'De Hollandse imposten en ons beeld van de conjunctuur tijdens de Republiek', *Jaarboek Amstelodamum*, xlvii (1955), 58–64. Approximate translations of these three imposts are (*a*) impost of the weighhouse, (*b*) of round measures, and (*c*) of bulky wares. The *Ronde Maat* was a complement to the weighhouse impost levied since 1600 on all goods sold by measure such as grain, beans, coal, etc. The *Grote Waren* was an impost on building materials such as wood, bricks, etc.

12. C. H. Wilson, *Profit and Power* (1957), p. 123.

13. E. W. Dahlgren, *Les Relations commerciales et maritimes entre la France et les côtes de l'Océan Pacifique* (Paris, 1909), i. 561.

11

Government Control and Free Enterprise in Western Germany and the Low Countries in the Eighteenth Century

MAX BARKHAUSEN

*Translated by Elisabeth Johnson and Martin N. Topping**

'THE development of Rhenish industry in the eighteenth century and the birth of an industrial upper class' have been described by me in the *Rheinische Vierteljahrsblätter* (1954). Without mercantile aid from the rulers, local industry, based on the availability of local raw materials, mineral resources, and water power, had developed out of centuries-old crafts. However, already at an early stage, the import of foreign raw materials was necessary, and industry developed beyond the demands of the area into an export business; parallel to this development there arose an industrial bourgeoisie which took on the management of production and foreign trade independent of any state control. Industry did not develop throughout the Rhenish-Westphalian area, but predominated in the hills, in small towns which had no guilds, and in the country, while the old centres of the economy remained untouched. There were three particular industrial areas which stood out clearly among the old towns and the fertile plain. In the first instance there was Berg with the neighbouring Sauerland; then the area round Aachen; and thirdly the flax-growing land on the Niers to the left of the lower Rhine. It is especially noticeable in the two lower Rhine areas on the left bank that industrialization moved beyond the narrow territorial frontiers; it was not determined by the sovereignty of the land.

This sudden industrial growth started about the beginning of the eighteenth century, a long time before the general flowering of the European economy in the second half of the century. The Peace of Utrecht (1713) brought an end to the long period of war which had suppressed economic life in the ancient and culturally well-developed areas of the Southern Low Countries and the lower Rhine since the rising in the Low Countries (1568) and the Cologne

* From 'Staatliche Wirtschaftslenkung und freies Unternehmertum im westdeutschen und im nord- und sudniederländischen Raum bei der Entstehung der neuzeitlichen Industrie im 18. Jahrhundert', *Vierteljahrschrift fur Sozial- und Wirtschaftsgeschichte*, vol. xlv (1958). This translation has been approved by Dr. Christel Barkhausen, daughter of the late Professor Max Barkhausen.

War (1583). Contemporaries were hardly aware of the significance of this economic development; it happened away from the main movements of the armies, and even at present its importance is overlooked by economic historians, probably because it is thought that tight mercantilist control and promotion of industry were the necessary preliminaries for its development in the eighteenth century, and because research was striving to establish from the records what the governments contributed towards the furthering of industry. Although imposing buildings in the west German industrial areas testify to the flowering of the economy, little of this is to be found in the archives, as the governments of the small territories allowed the economy to take its course, and indeed had to act in this way. The researcher has to restrict himself to the history of individual firms and families, for which sources are fragmentary and subject to the accident of survival.

PREREQUISITES TO MERCANTILIST PROMOTION OF INDUSTRY

With his specialized knowledge of the Prussian development, Gustav Schmoller defined the nature of mercantilism as 'in its essence nothing else than a product of state-building, but not just straightforward state-building, but state and economy action at the same time, state-building in the modern sense, of making the state community simultaneously into an economic one and thereby giving it greater importance'. According to Schmoller, the aim and achievement of mercantilist policy consisted 'in the total reorganization of society as well as of the state and its institutions, in [the substitution] of the local and agricultural economic policy by a state and national one'.[1]

It is obvious that the success of a mercantilist policy, which at the same time is a policy of state formation, is dependent on three prerequisites. The state has to be so large and unified that the creation of a unified economic area could at least be envisaged as an aim. The power of the state has to be strong enough to be capable of asserting itself in the face of a medieval economy and the encapsulation of various parts of the country, and it also has to have the authority to assert itself against foreign competition and to expand its own field of influence.

Absolutism, mercantilism, and increase of military and maritime power tend to go hand in hand. In western Europe these conditions were fulfilled in Elizabethan England, and the England of the first Stuart rulers and of Cromwell. They were, to an even greater extent, fulfilled in France under Louis XIV and Colbert, even though under the Ancien Régime economic unification was not complete. In the eighteenth century, the rising central and east European powers, Austria, Russia, and Prussia, were anxious that their industry, too, should catch up with western Europe and become independent. But what about the old heart-land of Germany?

Schmoller, in his *Basic Principles of Economics*, after describing western European development in the seventeenth century, described the decay of

Germany in the Thirty Years War, and continued: 'it was made worse by the fact that Germany was fragmented into several hundred, now completely independent, small states; the smallest were villages and manors, small towns and abbeys; even the counties and principalities were often only 500 to 5,000 square kilometres; there were only ten to fifteen larger territories' (which he did not name) 'which became the perpetuators of economic progress in Germany; but some of these were not even entities and were scattered among other territories'.[2]

AN INTEGRATED TERRITORY OF CONSIDERABLE SIZE DID NOT EXIST IN THE RHENISH-WESTPHALIAN AREA

In the eleventh to thirteenth centuries neither the Rhenish counts nor the archbishops were able to become leading powers; there arose territories of middling size which kept a balance among themselves.[3] At the beginning of the fifteenth century, Cleves, Mark, and Jülich were united dynastically with Berg and Ravensburg, and in 1511–21 the two groups were joined under the dukes of Cleves. In this way there arose a territory of considerable size, but it was not integrated; the territories of the Church, above all the archbishopric of Cologne, remained separate until the end of the old empire, and the most important towns, Cologne, Aachen, and the previously important Dortmund, remained excluded as imperial towns. With the extinction of the ducal family in 1609, the lower Rhine area was torn apart into two areas, just as the Low Countries were distributed between Spain and the States General; one part fell to Brandenburg, and the other to Pfalz-Neuenburg.

The border between the northern and southern Low Countries was an ossified military front line that separated people of the same extraction. It had been drawn eastward across the Rhine and divided territories that formed an organic whole. From that time, apart from some very small groupings, the territorial division resulted in three pairs of medium-sized territories, each of which was physically separated from its partner.

The Brandenburg possessions consisted of the duchy of Cleves (1,852 square kilometres), which spanned both banks of the lower Rhine, and the Westphalian earldom of Mark (3,142 square kilometres); they were connected by the rivers Ruhr and Lippe, but they were divided by Recklinghausen, which belonged to Cologne, the religious foundations of Essen and Werden, and the Bergian dependency of Broich (Mühlheim an der Ruhr). The Neuberg-Palatinate lands consisted of the duchy of Jülich on the left bank of the Rhine (3,557 square kilometres) and the duchy of Berg on the right bank of the Rhine (3,192 square kilometres); but these were separated on the left bank by the long-stretched territory of the Archbishops of Cologne's foundation (2,660 square kilometres). The latter also owned the duchy of Westphalia and the Sauerland of Cologne (3,774 square kilometres), but they were separated by the duchy of Berg.

Each of these closely interlaced Rhenish-Westphalian territories belong to the medium-sized type which, according to Schmoller, had no economic future; even if one totalled up their areas, the share of Brandenburg-Prussia would still fall below the lower limit of 5,000 square kilometres, and the areas by which Cologne and the Palatinate exceed this are too insignificant to produce a qualitative difference. But, most important of all, in no case do we find a continuous territory.

Although the distribution of territory may look very similar, a great deal of difference emerges as soon as one takes a good look at the territorial rulers. The princely Houses to whom the inheritance of Cleves had fallen owed their success to the fact that they were powerless and had to place themselves under the protection of one of the two enemies who faced each other on the lower Rhine. But then began the climb to power of the House of Brandenburg-Prussia. Its homeland in the March of Brandenburg measured 36,000 square kilometres. The duchy of Prussia, far away in the east, that came into its possession in 1618, was of equal size. Dating from the territorial acquisitions of the Peace Treaty of Westphalia the continuous heart-land of the state measured already 70,800 square kilometres, ten times the size of the scattered West German possessions. The first king of Prussia succeeded against the wish of the Estates General in rounding off his possessions on the lower Rhine by acquiring the Orange earldom of Mörs with Krefeld (216 square kilometres) and of Spanish Obergeldern (1,163 square kilometres). But when the line of Pfalz-Neuenburg became extinct in 1738 the Great Powers prevented him from acquiring the much-coveted duchy of Berg. They would not permit a further strengthening of Prussian military power on the lower Rhine. Because of this the young King Frederick concentrated on the extension of his power through enlarging the heart-land and waived his claims in the west.

When King Frederick William constructed a state based on army and bureaucracy, the eastern regions presented the pre-conditions for mercantilist policies: the vast expanse of territory, the powers of the ruler by virtue of his position internally and his military machine externally. The far-flung heterogeneous possessions in the west that constituted only a small part of the state could not be brought into one unit with the main territory; it was logical, when constructing a mercantilist economy, to treat them as foreign countries. No policy of integration of state and economy could bring far-away minor territories within its system. On their own, the Prussian possessions in the west could not form an economic whole. The instruments of mercantilist economic organization such as protective tariffs, import embargoes, monopolies, and control of commerce could not be applied to such a mosaic of medium-sized and small territories: the counter-measures of neighbouring states would have severely disrupted their economies. Their internal market was too small: craft-production could only be turned into viable industries with the aid of export opportunities, and in this respect the native state could offer no assistance.

The duchies of Jülich and Berg, although rich in possibilities for the future, had also become subsidiary territories ever since their ruler had been made Count Palatine. The famous Jan Wellen still held brilliant court in his beloved Düsseldorf; in 1720 his successor made Mannheim the capital of the Palatinate and never set foot in his possessions on the lower Rhine. The distance from the centre of government increased even more when Karl Theodor became Elector of Bavaria in 1777 and was obliged to live in Munich. The abnormality of these west German territories consisted of the absence of that characteristic feature of the Ancien Régime: the hereditary line of rulers, the 'Residenz', the court. Although the Prussian possessions were ruled very strictly from Berlin, they had only an administration but no government. The Wittelsbach rulers left their Rhenish possessions to their own devices: for this reason Düsseldorf adapted itself to the economic and social developments that were arising in the duchies.

IS THE FLOURISHING OF KREFELD INDUSTRY A SPECIAL CASE?

The essence of this case of industrial prosperity becomes clear by comparing the founding of the silk-weaving industry in Berlin and Krefeld under the same Prussian régime. Hintze, discussing the Prussian silk industry in his third descriptive volume of Acta Borussica, says that a silk industry had existed in seventeenth-century Frankfurt, Augsburg, Cologne, and Hamburg, which had faded away during the eighteenth century, and he continues in the spirit of Schmoller: 'These minor municipal economies had long ceased to be centres of German economic activity, and large-scale production in particular could only be energetically and successfully tackled by the large consolidated territories . . .'[4] Now the four imperial cities mentioned by Hintze had been for centuries important centres of commerce and trade, whose economic spheres of influence exceeded by far their actual tiny territories and therefore should not be referred to as 'minor economies'. But the decline or stagnation of industry in the ancient cities is also typical of the large territories; it did not prevent the brilliant rise of the commercial cities of Frankfurt, Hamburg, and Leipzig in the eighteenth century.

Hintze, with the support of documentary evidence, demonstrates how Frederick the Great, by bringing to bear all the powers of the absolute state, through subsidies and import embargoes, the recruiting of entrepreneurs and workers, had called into being and nurtured the Berlin silk industry; but he also mentions how, from 1731 onward, the silk-weaving concern of the brothers von Leyen in the Prussian-Mörsian possession of Krefeld grew into a firm of world-wide importance. This came about without the aid of the ruler and despite the fact that the import of its products into Prussian territory east of the Weser was prohibited. Hintze writes: '. . . It was an industry that had developed completely independent of the State, far away from the great stream of mercantilist practices ... Berlin represents the bureaucratic principle and Krefeld the limitless autonomy of the entrepreneur ... It did not need the support of the State, which was therefore not forthcoming ...'[5]

From the point of view of the state-sponsored creation of the Berlin industry, the success of Krefeld appears to be a special case, which Hintze explains by the exceptional ability of the entrepreneur and the fact that he was following the Dutch example; but the thing he particularly emphasizes, the independent spirit of the entrepreneurs, is the hallmark of west German industry in general, which only flourished where the former was in evidence. Economic, social, and cultural forces and circumstances that required no government directions and managed to evade those that existed must have been the decisive factors, and neither the Prussian government nor that of the Palatinate attempted such direction on any significant scale. In the case of Krefeld it would have been impossible on the one hand and unnecessary on the other. If this is so, then we have here an early example of a free-enterprise industrial economy of the kind that was already revealing itself on a spectacular scale in England, and which would establish itself throughout Europe from the turn of the century on.

THE RISE OF WEST GERMAN INDUSTRY MUST BE RELATED TO DEVELOPMENTS IN THE NORTHERN AND SOUTHERN LOW COUNTRIES

The area where the formation of the three west German industrial centres took place in the eighteenth century is not large: it comprises today's administrative districts of Düsseldorf, Cologne, and Aachen—no more than 12,600 square kilometres, and if one includes all of Westphalia south of the Lippe still only 20,000 square kilometres. This adds up to very little when compared with the vast spaces of Prussia, the classical example of German mercantilism; and what a territorial patchwork it looks on the historical map! And yet, this is where the export industries came into being, whose markets lay far beyond their narrow immediate frontiers. In other words, they were not contained within a wall of mercantilist restrictions. In this connection Hintze's mentioning Holland is perfectly justified. West Germany had always formed a living entity with the territories along the estuary of its great river, and the same applies to the highly developed regions in the west, Brabant and Flanders. This had shown itself in the development of the north European towns during the Middle Ages and had never ceased to continue. In the seventeenth century the northern Low Countries constituted the most flourishing country in Europe; in the eighteenth century the industrial centres on the left bank of the Rhine had the closest possible contacts with the northern and southern Low Countries, and in the first half of the nineteenth century Belgium was the leading industrial power on the Continent. In my opinion it is essential to the understanding of the situation to look at the industrial progress of west Germany in the eighteenth century in relation to the developments in the northern and southern Low Countries. This has now become possible owing to the recently published *Algemeene Geschiedenis der Nederlanden.*[6]

With the publication of the twelfth volume this splendid work has now been completed. Political, economic, social, and cultural developments are delineated in every volume by experts in the field, and the introduction by the editor summarizes the character of each period. Ample bibliographies enable the reader to study the material in depth. All contributions are published in Dutch; the work impressively bears witness to the fact that both countries belong together.

Our own investigation confines itself to volumes 5 to 8, 1568–1795; they deal with the period from the Revolt of the Netherlands to the invasion by the French revolutionary armies. I shall now not simply recapitulate what I have said in my previous work on the subject of the rise of industry in the eighteenth-century Rhineland, but underline what seems to me to be its theoretical implications; then we shall turn our attention to the development of industry in the northern and southern Low Countries, finally glancing at the Prussian possessions in Rhenish Westphalia.

THE HEY-DAY OF INDUSTRY IN EIGHTEENTH-CENTURY BERG

The extent of industrial advance can be easily assessed by looking at population increase.[7] Round about 1600, the fertile duchy of Jülich with its 50 inhabitants to the square kilometre constituted one of the most thickly-populated areas in central Europe. Not until 1720 did it regain the pre-war population figure of 180,000; by 1767 the figure had risen to 217,000. The duchy of Berg, in 1600, was still a remote forest-land with little more than half the population of the duchy on the left bank of the Rhine, but it had already made good its wartime population losses by 1680. By 1722, during the period of economic advance due to craft-production, the population had increased to 263,000. These are figures that are unique in the Germany of the period; they can only be compared with the contemporaneous increases in the industrial areas of England, and the storm-fraught developments of nineteenth-century Germany. As the population figures demonstrate, economic expansion had already begun in the seventeenth century. We can trace the beginnings by means of the geographical description presented to the Elector Johann Wilhelm in 1715 by E. Ph. Ploennies.[8] He says of the town of Lennep: '... In addition to agriculture, the inhabitants are also engaged in the cloth trade and many of them are also weaving cloth; they rarely stay at home during the summertime but usually go abroad and gain their bread by trading at the fairs of the district; some sell cloth by the ell at the said fairs, others take a cart-load of cloth to a staple-town and from here they send it by the piece into the country ...' Lennep is also said to have been working up Spanish wool since 1695; this represents the beginning of the manufacture of high-quality cloth, in which Lennep followed the development in the area of Aachen and Verviers.

A different picture is drawn in the memorandum handed in 1729 to the Elector Karl Philipp by Hofkammerrat Johann Wülfling. There it is said of Lennep:

> For some years now this town has been flourishing on account of its extremely high-quality cloth in all imaginable colours, and also its medium-quality cloth. This fast-growing craft, which admits weavers, shearers, and workers of many different nations without regard to the three Roman-Catholic and Protestant religions, provides a livelihood for the inhabitants of many of the surrounding market-towns, cities, and administrative centres.... In short, this town may be considered a noble commercial city in the land of Berg ...
>
> The far-famed city of Elberfeld is a commercial city of great wealth, situated on the river Wupper, and by virtue of its world-wide trading connections can be justly called Little Amsterdam. Here merchants can be found engaging in trade, who are comparable to the Dutch in world-wide commercial experience and wealth.

Buildings of note are, in addition to the Reformed Church and the Town Hall, the almshouses where '... the poor are fed, clothed, entertained, and prevented from begging from house to house ...', as well as the shops and bleaching-grounds.

> ... Adjoining this famous town of Elberfeld lies the equally pleasant village and administrative centre of Upper and Lower Barmen, mostly consisting of bleacheries for linen-yarn, as well as merchants and traders. In the summertime, it does one's heart good to see all these bleaching-grounds ...
>
> The town of Solingen is a world-famous centre of commerce; here they not only manufacture all manner of high-class blades and knives, but all things imaginable that can be worked or manufactured in steel and iron, and every year they invent and bring to light something new ... [underlining the necessary personal initiative]; ... its merchants and their commerce extend far into the world, and these merchants stand in the highest esteem with kings, princes, and lords on account of their trade in fair blades.
>
> Remscheid, a market-town on a mountain: here as well as in the parish of Remscheid there are many steel-smiths and all manner of their manufactures are produced here: great plenty of skates, locks, and all manner of iron goods are wrought here, neatly finished and dispatched as exports into foreign lands. In this market and parish there are many noble merchants ... This place is famous for its commerce.
>
> Kronenberg, a market-town in the district of Elberfeld.... In this place and parish there are being manufactured spades, axes, pick-axes, locks, and other smiths' work. Here also can be found many different steel-smiths, iron-hammers, and grinding-sheds, and merchants as well as common artisans are engaged in a flourishing trade.
>
> Langenberg is a large market-town, beautifully situated on the Ruhr; here can

be found a preponderance of noble merchants and traders who deal in a variety of goods in many parts of the country.

The widespread trading by pedlars based on Langenberg as described by Edmund Strutz is said to have been made obsolete by economic developments; Langenberg now houses a considerable silk industry.

> The said land of Berg consists mainly of skilled craftsmen as previously described, far-famed and noble merchants who import gold and silver coins from foreign parts and provide plentiful work and sustenance to citizens and traders, craftsmen and carriers, so that neighbouring countries cannot get at them. In this land no denizen needs to beg from door to door; children of five and six years old can get their bread in the Bergian capital of Lennep by sorting, combing, and spinning wool, and in the town of Elberfeld by spooling, bleaching, combing, and spinning yarn; the old and disabled are supported by the parishes out of alms collected in Church; but as in the neighbouring countries begging from door to door as well as the giving of alms are prohibited, so that no beggars are tolerated. The land of Berg is crowded, not with native but foreign and alien idlers and beggars. As far as is known unto me, this land, praise be unto God, is in a flourishing state ... the level of taxation is tolerable ... the subjects of this land can sleep and wake in peace.

This is clearly pointed against Prussia and possibly Hesse.

This description from the first third of the eighteenth century is most revealing. We can recognize how far industrialization had already progressed. The author distinguishes between the noble merchants, who specialize in trade—the Estate from which he himself has sprung—and the artisans, that is, the skilled craftsmen and other workers. Child labour is praised as an opportunity to work; behind all this lies the worry and fear caused by the proletariat of beggars. This I shall discuss elsewhere. Spinning and weaving are largely carried on in the countryside, centred on Lennep and Elberfeld, the nascent capital. The working of iron is carried on with the aid of iron-hammers and grinding-sheds in the many valleys, where water power is preserved with the aid of weirs. The entrepreneur is still referred to as a merchant and not a manufacturer. The terms 'manufacture' and 'factory' are not yet used; they are yet to be formulated in the course of the century. We do not hear anything about trade control and support of the industry by a government.

THE TEXTILE INDUSTRY IN THE DUCHY OF BERG[9]

The great textile industry of the duchy of Berg did not develop out of an urban craft. Elberfeld is not an old town and was, in the Middle Ages, smaller than Lennep and Wupperfürth, the 'capitals' of the duchy. Its basic industry was yarn-bleaching for which the water of the Wupper was eminently suited. Flax had always been grown here, the fibre spun and the yarn woven. Therefore the weaving of linen was not a guild and an urban craft, and was not considered very important. But the bleaching of the yarn demanded specialist knowledge and suitable water. In 1527 the duke gave the central area of Wuppertal the privilege of yarn-bleaching. Already at that time the craft had grown beyond local demand. The owners of the bleaching grounds on the river were the most privileged; they gradually became tradesmen and not only processed local produce, but bought yarn in the Weser area, in Hanover, and Hesse, and sold it again after bleaching. Trade of this kind demanded considerable capital. The trade in yarn was not controlled by a guild, but the amount of yarn which a member could process was limited. In 1610 Elberfeld was made a town; at that time it counted 1,000 inhabitants. By 1700 it had grown to 3,000 inhabitants and had its own independent law court like the 'capital towns'.[10] But Elberfeld was not a town in the old style, with guilds and boundary. The narrow town walls had to go. The town expanded up-river and eventually joined up with the village which stretched along the river banks in that area. The latter became known as Barmen and had no freedom of the city.

The cause of the expansion was that people had gone over to processing their own bleached yarn. They wove linen cloth (lint) and material for clothing and underwear. The dyeing business was devoted to this, and the recently introduced 'Turkey red' dyeing was particularly successful. In 1762 the production restriction in bleaching ended, and it became a profitable trade. Most of the 'yarn merchants' turned to processing yarn. Cotton began to supersede linen, although people still wove *Siamosen*, a material made from linen warp and cotton woof, because as yet it was still not known how to spin strong warp thread from cotton. For a long time people in rural areas continued to spin yarn on spinning wheels. In 1738 the weavers had obtained a privilege for their guild from the Elector: at that time there were 1,000 weavers and as many journeymen. The contractors now agreed, however, to deal with the preparatory work, that is to say the spooling and warping, in their own workshops. Thus the factory was born. But the new system met with trouble in 1783, when a yarn merchant objected to the goods delivered: it was, in fact, the guild's job to examine these goods. The militia had to intervene. Elector Karl Theodor decided the case in favour of the manufacturers, while his diet supported the weavers. The privilege granted to the guild was retracted. Likewise in Lennep, in 1790, the shearers' privilege was suspended. The odious 'Zunftzwang'* was broken. In the textile industry of the Berg region freedom of trade had been asserted by the end of the century.

Even silk became a domestic industry of the Berg region. In 1714, after Bergian liberty had been granted, ten wealthy Lutheran merchants from Cologne settled in Mühlheim, which lay slightly lower down the Rhine, over on the right bank. The imperial city had several times (most recently in 1615) checked the establishment of businesses in the region of Berg, because they

* 'Zunftzwang' was the system whereby an obligation was placed on all artisans, tradespeople, etc., to join a guild.

contravened the legal boundary limits. But now this establishment could no longer be prevented. The settlers found here unrestricted economic movement and religious tolerance. The strength of their capital resources ensured the continued vitality of the little town. The Andreä family, untroubled by the *Zunftzwang*, founded here the velvet factory which still exists today, and the Elector granted them the monopoly. Silk-weaving grew up in the Wuppertal. The silk industry of Cologne, on the other hand, languished under the *Zunftzwang* system.

THE HARDWARE INDUSTRY IN THE DUCHY OF BERG[11]

The diversity which distinguishes the Bergian textile industry is also the distinguishing feature of the hardware industry. Its origins went back far into the Middle Ages, and it started operating on its own local production of iron. But it very soon went over to processing better iron from the Sauerland, and above all from the Siegerland. This iron was made into steel in valley forges, which were driven by the powerful waterfalls of the local streams. The grinding-mills were also situated here. The construction of these forges required considerable capital, and it can be said that their owners were the original 'Captains of Industry'. The open industrial site was first developed as a result of this new dependence on water power, and businesses became far more widely dispersed.

Solingen swords and Kronenberger scythes were already known in 1200. At that time there was an iron market in Cologne, and the fact that it was constructed on a guild system shows the great age of the industry. There were the three parallel fraternities of swordsmiths: the Temperers, the Grinders, and the Sword-Cutlers (i.e. those who finished off the work). Only they were allowed to go abroad as merchants, and there was good reason for this supervision on the part of the guilds: inadequate goods could bring the trade into disrepute. The sword-blades had to bear the hereditary mark of their makers. The manufacture of knives and shears in Solingen was later added to the production of purely military weapons. It was not, however, until the eighteenth century that tools began to be manufactured in the remote town of Remscheid: by Wülfing's time this is still not mentioned. The trade soon took on world-wide dimensions. Only a merchant who knew the trade inside out was able, by travelling abroad, to get to know the wishes of clients, who were used to particular models and types. On his return home he could then direct production according to his findings. He could not rely on the big export firms of the great commercial cities. Thus there arose in Remscheid large houses of commerce with connections overseas, but there also arose innumerable medium- and smaller-sized firms, which manufactured, with excellent quality, a restricted number of models and types. In 1800 there were calculated to be as many as 4,000 different models.

In 1809 Nemnisch[12] described Remscheid as a village with 100 houses, although the parish itself had a population of 6,000. He also counted 18 streams in the area, which were used by nearly 200 forges and grinding-mills. There was no space left for new constructions.

The emergence of the tool industry led to conflict, however. The new profession of tool-making had never been organized on a guild basis. The many forms the industry took did not allow of strict regulation: nevertheless, it was obvious what this development was leading to. The grinders insisted on their guild privilege, but, as it was granted in a time when only scythes were produced, the tool-makers did not regard it as valid for their new profession. They allowed 'blacklegs' to grind in Solingen, where work was short due to the decline in demand for weapons after the Seven Years War. Every night there were clashes in the woods when the illicit workers made their way back from Solingen. As always the law decided in favour of the old traditional Right: (one can compare this with Turgot's attempt in France in this period to quash the guilds; an attempt which floundered on the opposition of the Parlements). Although the government wanted to promote the blossoming new trade, it was unable to assert itself. In the long run, however, freedom of trade was won under the threat of workers migrating to the neighbouring region of Mark, as had already happened in the scythe industry. The proclamation of the basic principle of freedom of trade, announced by the French government of Berg in 1809, was thus only the end of a gradual development.

THE MAIN CHARACTERISTICS OF INDUSTRIAL DEVELOPMENT IN THE DUCHY OF BERG

The industry of Berg was originally based on natural local resources. Yarn-bleaching depended upon the excellent quality of the water in the Wuppertal, and the hardware industry drew its power for processing imported iron from the numerous local streams. These were the main pre-conditions of the industrial development. This can be concluded from the fact that the fertile plain at the foot of the Bergland was unaffected by the development. To a great extent the Bergian area was new ground for settlers, and this also was an advantage. These industrial centres had nothing in common with the privileged towns of the Middle Ages, for which industry was a reserved right. Economically and legally there was no difference between town and country, and, as far as industrial development was concerned, it was of no importance whether a place had 'town rights' or not. There was no serfdom, nor obligation to work among the rural population. Industrial centres involved in the same line of business were at that time as near together as Solingen, Remscheid, and Kronenberg—the same with Elberfeld and Barmen. But this did not give rise to competition and struggle for the local market, because they all specialized in particular articles and were geared towards exports. The demand for labour resulted in a large population influx; this can be seen from the fact that in Calvinist Elberfeld no more than half the population belonged to the official religion. As everywhere, however, the crafts-people who had been longest established formed the basic core of the population. The leaders of economic life were strict Calvinists, the merchants and manufacturers, descendants of the founding fathers. But one must guard against the crude theory of Max Weber's, which stresses the economic pre-eminence of the Calvinists. The most important industrial centres, Lennep and Remscheid, were Lutheran. There was nowhere a patriciate to stand over the merchants and manufacturers, as there had been in the old towns.

In the case of the hardware industry, the widely spread settlement was necessitated by the natural circumstances. The textile industry of Elberfeld and Barmen, on the other hand, had to stick close to the river Wupper, as it was so dependent on flowing water. It was because of this that long, narrow twin towns formed, which are such a unique feature of the area. But whereas Barmen remained substantially an industrial town, Elberfeld was always a commercial town as well: a point which Wülfing stressed. All the raw materials which the textile industry of Berg processed were imported from abroad. It not only needed linen yarn, but also Spanish wool, cotton from overseas, Italian raw silk, and foreign dyes. Important houses of commerce dealt with the purchasing, and gave the manufacturers credit against what they would in time produce. From them banks evolved. Independent of Cologne, Elberfeld thus became the financial centre of Berg. Thus we can see that the old towns were not the main force behind the industrial advance.

THE BASIC STANDPOINT OF THE GOVERNMENT

Soon after the Seven Years War a general boom began in Europe, which was to last almost until the French Revolution. These were the great years of prosperity for the industries of Berg. We can get a picture of what it was like from the memoirs of Friedrich Heinrich Jacobi, a friend of Goethe's, written in 1773–4.[13] This young merchant from Düsseldorf was appointed by the Stadholder, Count Goltstein, to the posts of councillor in industrial affairs and chamberlain in the government of Jülich-Berg. He calculated the profits of industry in the duchy by itemizing the costs of running the various branches of industry, and balancing the revenue against them. From his book we can see that there was a significant export industry. A general introduction prefaces the book and outlines a physiocratic line of thought. Jacobi suggested that, in view of the danger of industries moving out, the guild privilege granted to the bleachers in the Wuppertal be suspended, and advised that modern roads (highways) be built to connect the Bergland to the Rhine. The Stadholder,[14] an excellent man who did much to improve his own neglected palace, but who also lent great support to road construction, was in complete agreement with the measures proposed by his councillor,

After Karl Theodor came to govern Bavaria in 1777, his minister, the Rhenish Count Hompesch, suggested that Jacobi should be appointed a Privy Councillor and recorder of taxes and commerce in Munich. In his new post, however, Jacobi was not able to put his ideas into practice. He published *Zwei politische Rhapsodien*, a small volume 'directed against the idiocy of conducting trade through the imposition of taxes and prohibitions'; in this he represented the views of Adam Smith, still little-known at the time.[15] Because of his views he quickly fell from grace, and was regarded as 'a presumptuous and contrary-minded man'. By June 1777 he was back in Düsseldorf. He was a wealthy man, largely through his wife's inheritance—she was the daughter of von Clermont, a cloth manufacturer from Vaals near Aachen—and he lived out his years happily on his estates at Pempelfort, which became a meeting-place for German intellectuals. (Visitors included Hamann, Stolberg, Herder, Forster in 1790, and Goethe in 1774 and 1792.)

Jacobi's demands in Munich, which struck people there as so outlandish, were, however, not in any way merely based on ideology, but had been well proven by practice and experience in his own country. Highly developed industry needed neither guidance nor support, but exports were essential, as were imports from abroad. Industry depended upon free trade. In Düsseldorf affairs were conducted much more on a basis of free trade and commerce. It is calculated that in the prosperous years which followed Jacobi's statistical survey, industrial profits rose by one-third. In 1793 E. F. Wiebeking published in Heidelberg and Mannheim his *Essays on the History of the States of the Palatinate, with particular reference to the Duchy of Jülich and Berg, 1742–92*.[16] These essays can be regarded as semi-official sources. Among other things he asserts:

> Of all the states of the Palatinate, it seems to me that the Duchy of Berg-Jülich has reached the highest stage of prosperity. The general well-being of this land has resulted from the freedom of commercial action, and from the factories and businesses which have developed in this freedom. Trade and factory business have risen to a peak since 1742, and particularly in the last ten years, because of an undisturbed freedom of trade. It is a peak which the other German states will strive in vain to reach, so long as they continue to allow monopolies, controlled markets, and the like. Commercial freedom, which many a foreign country would make such a show of, is enjoyed here by every manufacturer and merchant without fuss and without public advertisement. Here there is no inspection by excise-officers and such like.

In his excellent book about the grand duchy of Berg, Charles Schmidt says that after the economic crisis during the French supremacy, and the consequent flooding of the market with English goods, Berg became once more through the foundation of the Zollverein what it had been in the eighteenth century: 'une des régions les plus industrielles du globe'.[17]

THE ADVANCE OF THE FINE-CLOTH INDUSTRY IN THE
AACHEN AREA

While the industry of Berg blossomed forth in new territory, free from the traditional economic and social restrictions, Aachen remained an industrial town in the old manner; the fine-cloth industry, the major trade, had originated in Aachen in the Middle Ages, but its recent development had taken place in the area around the imperial city. The area which the city controlled, the Aachen Reich, measured 87 square kilometres, and bordered directly on to the lands of the 'reichsfrei'* Cistercian monastery at Burtscheid, some 8·5 square kilometres, the lands of the imperial abbey of Cornelimünster, 100 square kilometres, and the little village of Vaals, which had belonged to the States-General of the Netherlands as an exclave since 1648. The duchy of Jülich lay to the east of this region, and to the west lay the Austrian (formerly Spanish) duchy of Limburg, and the 'reichsfrei' bishopric of Lüttich. A unified economic control of this politically divided region was impossible, but nevertheless a development took place here which is comparable to that of the industries of Berg.

Aachen was always the second most important town in the lower Rhineland (after Cologne), and was the natural market town to serve the agricultural plain of Jülich, the pasture land of Limburg in the west, and the wooded Eifel hills in the south. It was an often-visited place of pilgrimage, and with its hot springs it numbered among the fashionable bathing resorts of the eighteenth century. At that time it had a population of 25,000. Its grandiose late-gothic town hall bears witness to its former economic prosperity. In the second half of the sixteenth century, however, it had begun to decline as a result of the wars in the neighbouring Netherlands, and the religious strife within the town. Twice the Spaniards had made sweeping changes and reimposed the absolute authority of the Catholic religion. The Protestant coppersmiths moved out to Stolberg, where they processed and manufactured brass from the fine-quality local zinc-ore (galmey) and imported copper. Innumerable cloth merchants also moved out and re-established their businesses in places where their faith was tolerated. And here, in small towns and in the countryside, arose the businesses of the future.

Since time immemorial people had used the wool of the region between the Rhine and the Meuse for spinning and weaving, and, as Plönnies recounted, coarse cloth was sold in the markets. But the good-quality, finely coloured cloth which was in demand among the upper classes could only be manufactured from fine foreign wool by trained, specialist craftsmen. The fine-cloth trade was reserved for craftsmen of the towns. The various stages through which the work had to go—the sorting, combing, washing, and spinning of the wool; then the fulling, dyeing, shearing, and pressing of the

---

* 'Reichsfrei': a term meaning subject to the emperor alone.

material took place under strict supervision and regulation. The finished goods were tested in the workshops of the master-craftsmen, and then authorized with the trademark of the town: only then were they permitted to go on to the market. Only trademarked goods could be exported, nor indeed did they pass straight to the consumer, but went to the *Verleger*,* who dispatched them or sold them direct from the warehouse to a bulk purchaser. Fine-cloth goods constituted the staple export of the Middle Ages.

THE DECLINE IN THE IMPERIAL CITY

The cloth trade of Flanders and Brabant had also operated on this regulated guild basis. The *Verleger* held the key position. He bought the expensive raw materials and channelled them into the different work sectors. He also undertook to distribute and market the goods. He needed considerable capital for purchasing the raw materials, paying his workers, and managing foreign trade. He was not a manufacturer, however. The master-weaver may have seemed an independent agent, but this was illusory: he was in fact a salaried employee. He was not allowed to operate more than four weaving-looms, though this was in fact the most that a craftsman, who worked himself, could have managed. He needed a small financial outlay for the workshop and its equipment, but he was not allowed to expand his business, and he had very little chance of promotion to the level of a *Verleger*. On the other hand the work was evenly distributed; the *Verleger* was not allowed to select his own master-craftsmen, and it was the job of an official board, not of the employer, to test the finished products. In Aachen, then, the *Verleger*, or merchants as they were known, formed the town's upper middle class; the broader-based lower middle class was formed by the master-weavers, and after them came the many levels of journeymen, who had absolutely no chance of improving their social lot. With the decline of the trade in about 1700 master-weavers were only allowed to employ two journeymen each: this was later cut to one. We can see from the account given by Georg Forster (*Ansichte vom Nieder-rhein*)[18] that there was a large beggar population in Aachen. That the cloth trade did not completely succumb is due to the fact that the Council had, by force of necessity, to allow craftsmen to work for the big contractors in the surrounding region. But the Council did not dare to disregard the position of the guilds, because this would have been received by them as an economic and social degradation, and would have caused a guild revolt. The imperial city thus took no part in the advance of the fine-cloth industry in the Aachen region.

* *Verleger*. The merchant who organized the production and sale of cloth under the putting-out or domestic system. There is not really a single-word English equivalent.

THE MIGRATION OF THE 'VERLEGERS' FROM AACHEN TO
NEIGHBOURING NON-GUILD TOWNS, AND THE BEGINNINGS OF
FACTORY BUSINESS

Early in 1700 the cloth merchant von Lövenich, a Mennonite, moved house
from Aachen to the tiny near-by domain of the abbess of Burtscheid, which
was free from guilds. He erected there the magnificent factory-building which
Forster went especially to see. In it the most important stages of cloth-work
were brought together—the fulling, dyeing, shearing, and pressing. His
example was followed by the long-established Lutheran merchant family of
Pastor.[19] An example will show what motivated these entrepreneurs. The
family firm of von Lövenich, whose colour-dyeing was unsurpassed, produced
Cardinals' red robes for the Vatican. As he did not want to let the Dyers'
Guild into his secret, von Lövenich could only have this work done in his
own dye-house and under his supervision.[20] There was, however, no religious
freedom even in the diminutive realm of the abbess; the church which the
Calvinists built in 1635 had to be pulled down on orders from the emperor
in 1714. After that the Protestants attended their services in the Dutch
village of Vaals, where all creeds enjoyed religious tolerance. Here the most
important of the Aachen cloth merchants, the Lutheran Esajas von Clermont,
constructed the extensive factory lay-out which Forster described with such
admiration. The head of the firm was F. H. Jacobi's brother-in-law, and his
father was visited by Tsar Peter the Great, and raised to the aristocracy by
Karl VI. His widow left capital assets worth 500,000 Rtl.*

   The migration from Aachen was caused by these well-respected and solid
firms, whose owners wanted to use a great deal of capital and labour to
expand their businesses. They had realized that it was better to have production in the unrestricted control of the employers than in the control of the
guilds. Being near to the big city they would also have all the advantages
which a trading centre could offer—a large pool of skilled craftsmen, an
ample supply of the required raw materials, and the rest of the labour-force
without which no great undertaking can succeed. Things were admittedly
more difficult in the more remote villages, where the cloth trade took a long
time to develop from a local craft into a business of international significance.
In these up and coming industrial localities we can best see the conditions
under which modern industry has grown up.

THE RISE AND PROSPERITY OF THE MONSCHAU FINE-CLOTH
TRADE[21]

The 'Monschauer Land' was the southern part of the so-called 'Waldgraf-
schaft' (forest dukedom) in the Bergland, south of Aachen and Düren. The
counts and dukes of Jülich had always possessed the northern part, which

* Reichsthaler.

extended to Heimbach and Nideggen, but it was only in the fifteenth century that they gained the southern part as well. The insignificant little town of Monschau lay on the Roer, at the foot of the powerful Monschau fortress, which was once the seat of a minor branch of the ducal house of Limburg. In 1543, during the Guelders war, the town was burnt by imperial troops and 'all the inhabitants slaughtered'. Then came the rise of the cloth trade, under the same natural conditions as were found in Verviers and Eupen. The sheep of the high Venn country yielded coarse wool, and on the moors there was peat, which could be used for fuel. For the washing, fulling, and dyeing processes, however, the most important thing was the clear, lime-free water of the Roer, which with its powerful waterfalls also drove the fulling-mills.

As with linen-weaving, the production of coarse cloth was not one of the guild trades of the towns. The Monschau weavers were linked with the Company of Coarse Clothiers and occupied the same fulling-mill, but they were not organized as a guild. The finished goods were sold from house to house or in the markets, as happened in Lennep and throughout Berg. This is how affairs were originally conducted in Verviers and Eupen as well. The fine-cloth industry was first introduced from Aachen.

Towards the end of the sixteenth century Arnold Schmitz, a Lutheran cloth merchant, had to 'withdraw from my homeland (Aachen) because of insufferable religious persecution', and moved to Monschau, where he established 'The House of Schmitz', a cloth business of the type found in Aachen. A dam diverted the water of the Roer for his use, and he did all his own fulling and dyeing. Schmitz had nothing to do with the Company of Coarse Clothiers. With all the work processes united in it, his workshop was really a small factory, and this had to be so, because Aachen, with its countless auxiliary trades, was a long way away. In Monschau the manufacturer had to stand on his own two feet. The extent of the manufacturing works he set up was a sign of prosperity, and his family connections with the Stolberg master coppersmiths (originally from Aachen) also bore witness to this prosperity. The sons and sons-in-law of the original founder themselves established businesses which manufactured high-quality cloth. Each owned his own dye-house and fulling-mill, and this cleared the way for private production and started a development which only reached fulfilment in the eighteenth century.

In the village of Imgenbroich, the last village on the high plain before the descent into the Roer valley, a Lutheran family of big farmers, the Offermann family, went over to manufacturing cloth. They were closely related to the Monschau manufacturers. Imgenbroich became a village of cloth-makers. During the religious dispute between Kurbrandenburg and Pfalz-Neuenburg, the Lutherans of Monschau and Imgenbroich declared that in 1624, they had held a service in a barn in Menzerath, a little hamlet between Monschau and Imgenbroich, and they maintained a free religious practice there, though not in the two home towns. The care of the Lutheran diaspora in Jülich was directed from Lennep, the centre of Bergian Lutheranism, and was mainly in the hands of a family of pastors, the Scheiblers—there had been 24 ministers in the Scheibler family, and 12 daughters had married ministers. Johann Heinrich Scheibler, son of a Bergian minister, came to work in Imgenbroich as a 14-year-old apprentice in the Offermann firm. Four years later, when Scheibler had finished his apprenticeship, his master's son-in-law died: he had been a cloth manufacturer in Monschau. Scheibler then married this man's 22-year-old widow and carried on the firm's business in his own name. He must have been a very gifted manufacturer and merchant. He started processing fine Spanish wool, which had already been going on in Verviers and Eupen, and within a few years he had attained such a high standard that his cloth compared with the best that England and France could offer, and his dyeing was even better. A speciality of his firm was dyed-in-the-wool and patterned cloth goods, as distinct from the piece-dyed goods which Aachen, Eupen, and, in the main, also Verviers produced. Selling this costly cloth on the home market was out of the question. It was sold at big display fairs, especially the Frankfurt fair, and went from there to north, west, and south Europe. The markets of France and England were barred. One can tell the extent of Scheibler's business from the report which he wrote to the local governors towards the end of his life. It stated that he himself employed 4,000 men, but that this figure reached 6,000 if the businesses of his two elder sons were included. In this number one must of course allow for the numerous spinners spread around the countryside. The immense 'Red House' with its magnificent carved staircases is a monument which marks the rise of this great trade. The same industry developed even more extensively in Verviers and Eupen. I would therefore like to go into this development in more detail by dealing with the bishopric of Lüttich and the duchy of Limburg, and emphasizing the features which emerged, particularly those which distinguished Monschau.

The great period of prosperity in the Monschau industry, as indeed in the whole of this industry, was the three decades between the end of the Seven Years War and the outbreak of the French Revolution. While old Scheibler was still alive, his two elder sons had founded independent firms with their own manufacturing works. The separating and regrouping of firms was not difficult at that time, because the amount invested in buildings and machines did not come to much (5 per cent of the total is the figure suggested by the financial accounts of Monschau and Krefeld, which I have detailed in another work). The crucial considerations were stock-in-trade, outstanding debts, and liabilities. At this time there were eight fine-cloth firms in Monschau: they were headed by sons and in-laws of the Schmitz, Offermann, and Scheibler families. They joined together to form the Company of Fine Clothiers (as distinct from the Company of Coarse Clothiers). In the 1780s this had 46 members, made up of active but mainly quite small businesses. We know the production figures too. The total production of all the eight fine-cloth firms was eight times as much as that of all the coarse-cloth firms put together. To graduate from making coarse cloth to manufacturing fine cloth was difficult in view of the amount of capital required, and in the eighteenth century this transference did not occur on a large scale.

The difference in social standing between these two types of manufacturer can be seen in their family connections. Obviously religion had an important influence here, but apart from that it would have been out of the question for a fine clothier to marry into a local, Lutheran, coarse-cloth family. On the other hand the family connections of the 'merchant aristocracy', as people called the fine-cloth families, were very widespread. They not only reached Aachen and Burtscheid, but also as far afield as Krefeld and Elberfeld in Berg, Mülheim on the Rhine (the Andreä family), Hagen and Iserlohn in the region of Mark. Indeed these families even spread as far as the Mosel (the Böcking family in Trarbach), the Saar (the Stumm and Röchling families), Frankfurt, and Amsterdam. This new industrial upper middle class can be compared with the merchant aristocrats of the old commercial cities.[22]

Bernhard Scheibler, the eldest and most talented of J. H. Scheibler's sons, chose himself a wife from a Hagen family of cloth manufacturers (originally from Lennep). He founded a cloth factory near Hagen, in Herdecke, which he later moved to Iserlohn. With the outbreak of the Seven Years War he moved back to Monschau, and his business there became the largest in the area. He also established a branch firm in Eupen, but the unified control of factories in Prussian, Palatine, and Austrian areas did not fit in well with the concept, held in a mercantile age, of administratively divided territories. In 1781 Bernhard Scheibler was knighted by the Elector, Karl Theodor. His brother, Wilhelm Scheibler, also built factories in the Limburg area, in Eupen and Dison. The brothers not only achieved an increase in production, but also a wider range of manufacture in that piece-dyed goods were also produced in their factories. The pattern book of Wilhelm Scheibler, which still belongs to the family, gives us an impression of the extent of this range in production. It contains 2,500 patterns, and has a clasp arrangement designed on the Leporello system, so that when it is shut it can be fitted into a saddle-bag, but when unclasped it measures 13 metres in length.

THE STRUGGLE FOR TRADING FREEDOM AND THE BEGINNINGS OF FACTORY BUSINESS

The industrial boom met with opposition in the little town. The influx of foreign workers led to price increases and a shortage of houses. The farming townsmen and the coarse-cloth manufacturers felt their position threatened, and the town council, which represented their interests, resented the Lutheran fine-cloth manufacturers, who were not eligible for the council. When a dispute broke out, the council thus supported the workers, and their religious differences added fuel to the fire. The trouble began with the shearers. Cloth-shearing was difficult and responsible work, which could only be done by trained craftsmen. Few shearers were needed in the production of coarse cloth, but rather more were needed for fine cloth. They had to be brought in from other areas. If they came from places where guilds operated, they insisted on working with fellow guild-members, and regarded all others as 'idle' and disreputable. But there were no guilds in Monschau: the shearers were employed direct by the manufacturers.

The dispute which broke out was not just a local one, for disturbances occurred at this time among the shearers of Aachen, Burtscheid, Eupen, and Düren. Old Scheibler had tried as far as possible to recruit Protestant shearers from non-guild places, and it was these people who suffered the brunt of the attack. In 1762 these 'High Germans' were hounded out and beaten up. They found refuge in the palace. The mayor, a coarse-cloth manu-facturer, did nothing to expel them, and the fine-cloth manufacturing works thus lay dormant for a month. The militia was summoned from Jülich, but they needed five days to cover the distance to Monschau. The dispute was finally settled by granting the shearers a 10 per cent wage increase, in return for which the shearers renounced their guild demands. The freedom from guilds in Monschau after that served as a precedent to which the Lennep government appealed when they disbanded the Lennep shearers' guild in 1790.

In 1769 the weavers caused trouble because of the 'foreign middle-men'. Because there were not sufficient craftsmen in Monschau, the fine-cloth manu-facturers had for a long time had some of their spinning and weaving done in the Limburg area. Middle-men (*Baasens*) collected the dyed wool in Mon-schau and distributed it to spinners and weavers. Then they brought the unfinished cloth back to Monschau for its final processing. In 1773 Jacobi reported that two-thirds of Monschau fine cloth was produced in this way, and the traffic was unrestricted. The manufacturers claimed that work was more efficient in the Limburg area, and the government rejected the weavers' pro-tests. But in 1774 increasing unemployment led to open rebellion. The weavers unloaded the wool trucks of the 'foreign middle-men', and shut off the road to Eupen. At this the shearers intervened, as they were now threatened with unemployment, and took the wool trucks over the border under escort. The government imposed harsh penalties, for to ban the middle-men was imprac-ticable. An industrial court had been set up in 1769 to settle disputes of this kind, and peace once more prevailed. When business took a turn for the better, jobs became available for everyone, and no further difficulties arose with the town's administration either, since the mayor was paid a compen-satory allowance from the funds of the fine-cloth manufacturers.

So it went too with the building of the Lutheran church. Since Joseph II's edict of toleration this project could not easily be refused. This magnificent building coast 27,000 Rtl. to construct, but 3,269 Rtl. had also to be put aside for donations and gifts to the other religious bodies. The French government of Berg was not mistaken when it later stated that, in contrast to the Prussian and Nassau authorities, the Düsseldorf authorities were corrupt.[23] But quite apart from that, the industrial development in Berg and in Monschau had assumed such dimensions that it proved impossible for the government to maintain its outmoded economic system: it carried out independent and localized measures, and, like the Ancien Régime, cautiously and hesitantly followed the trend of a development, which finally led to a factory system controlled by independent contractors. It was left to the French Revolutionary government to carry through the final and complete establishment of trading freedom.

In the 1780s completely self-contained factory sites were built in Monschau. The greatest of these was the building which Bernhard Paul von Scheibler built to finish off his father's project. It had nineteen windows along the front, four down the side, and was four stories high. With water power provided, this construction housed all the activities needed for the trade, even the weaving, for which a separate building with especially good lighting was put aside. The factory, whose beauty of form made a pleasant contrast to later buildings, served as a spinning- and weaving-mill for many years. Unfortunately it has now been dismantled, because its rooms were not large enough to take big modern machines. But in the year of its completion, the French Revolutionary armies invaded, and brought an end to the industrial prosperity of the Rhineland and of Monschau.

THE LINEN AND COTTON INDUSTRIES OF THE NIERS[24]

If a merchant from the Wuppertal visited the lowlands of the Niers in the eighteenth century, it seemed as if he had travelled back a century in time, so humble were the conditions there. An excellent type of flax grew there, however: the farmers prepared it, spun it, and took it to the *Verleger* who had the yarn woven for linen by rural weavers. Only the woven fabric, not the original yarn (as in the Wuppertal), was bleached and dyed in the Niers region, and used for bed-linen or clothing. More refined goods were also produced, such as top linen and diaper; they were sent to the famous bleaching yards of Hagen, and appeared on the world market as fine Dutch linen.

Cotton first became popular in the eighteenth century because of its pliancy as a material. It was used at first, as we have already seen, in the production of *Siamosen* (from linen warp and cotton woof). The masters in this field became contractors in the Wuppertal, who, because of the lower pay there, then moved across to the Gladbach-Rheydt region. In the nineteenth century this became the most important area for the cotton industry in Germany.

Here the fragmentation of territories was particularly bad. At the head of the river Niers lay the imperial free dominion of the Calvinist counts of Quadt (now princes of Quadt in Bavaria); following the course of the river, there was Odenkirchen, an exclave of the Electorate of Cologne; the Dependency of Rheydt and the town of Gladbach, which belonged to Jülich; the Prussian-Geldrisch exclave of Viersen, and Süchteln and Dülken to the west, which both belonged to Jülich. Only Gladbach, Süchteln, and Dülken had town rights, but they were unimportant. The straggling village of Viersen was, through its trade, the most populous of these places: none of them had guilds, nor had they any connection with the trade of the old towns. Most of the *Verlegers* lived in the countryside. The Pfalz-Neuenburg, as governors of Jülich, had seriously checked the development of the linen trade by driving out the Mennonites, and thereby indirectly brought about the development of the Krefeld silk industry. The governors of the large territory of Rhine-Westphalia had failed to secure the right to determine the religion of their vassals, and when the area was divided up in 1609, the Calvinist Brandenburgs and Catholic Pfalz-Neuenburgs had to decide which creed should be officially adopted. The matter was finally settled by letting each town and village decide for itself. But the Mennonites, or 'anabaptists' as their opponents called them, had no rights; their expulsion began under the first Palatine Count, and the Calvinists had no objection to continuing it: religious and economic jealousy went hand in hand. The linen trade was in the hands of the Baptists: most of them were weavers, although there were also one or two financially powerful *Verlegers* among them. In 1622, 151 Mennonite families and individuals were registered in the town of Gladbach. This constituted one-fifth of the population, and it is thus no wonder that after their expulsion, the bailiff stated that he could not raise more revenue from taxes. In fact the town remained at a population of 1,000 until 1800. The expulsion of the Mennonites from Rheydt in 1694 was violent and rapacious: they had enjoyed protection there only as long as the Calvinist branch of the counts of Byland were in power. William III, king of England, Stadholder of Holland, and count of Mörs, forced the Elector Johann Wilhelm to compensate the people he had expelled.

The Mennonites found refuge in the tiny town of Krefeld, a southerly exclave of the county of Mörs, which had belonged to the House of Orange since 1600. The Mennonites in the Netherlands had enjoyed tolerance and civil rights since 1622, but this did not mean that the same applied in the county of Mörs, which was not Dutch, as people are often told, but rather the private property of the House of Orange. There was, however, a Dutch garrison in Mörs, the fortress serving as a strong-point for the States General in the lower Rhineland. The county itself was solidly Calvinist, as was the parish church in Krefeld, but a large proportion of the town's population was Catholic. Brushing aside the objections of the Calvinist ministers, the rulers of Orange allowed these Catholics to attend services in the small monastery there. In the Thirty Years War both the county of Mörs and the town of Krefeld were neutral, and it is a strange fact that a possession of the leader of the opposing army should have been spared by the enemy. But so it was, and it resulted in the rise of Krefeld which, with the arrival of the Mennonites, became the business centre of the linen trade. But even before this influx from Rheydt the town needed to spread outside its walls. The new extension to the town in 1692 was named 'Konigstrasse' in honour of its governor, now the king of England. The town needed to be expanded again in 1711, this time to twice its former size; a new market was also built there. This took place when the Prussians controlled it, because in 1702–12 Frederick I, as heir to the last of the Orange line, took possession of Krefeld and the county of Mörs. At that time Krefeld was the prosperous centre of the linen trade, but this was soon outstripped by the silk industry.

THE ORIGINS AND ADVANCE OF THE KREFELD SILK INDUSTRY[25]

In the previously mentioned towns and country areas, the origins of the industry were favoured by natural conditions: this was not the case in Krefeld. As a town of exile it had grown quite large, but whereas the emigrants from the Lower Rhineland had made Krefeld the centre of the linen trade, its silk industry was established by a single family, that of von der Leyen. The same rulers drove the von der Leyens from their home in Berg as had driven out the other exiles. It has been thought that the family originated in the Netherlands. Schmoller and Hintze, for example, stated (and apologized for the fact) that the silk industry of Krefeld, unlike that of Berlin, had arisen without state aid, because it was not, like Berlin's, a new creation, but rather an extension of the highly developed Dutch industry.

Researchers are no longer of the opinion that this family came from the Netherlands. The proof for this rested on the evidence that in 1555 a certain Anneke von der Leyen, and in 1559 one Lorenz von der Leyen, died as martyrs in Antwerp. But their connection with the Berg family cannot be proved; indeed, von der Leyen was a local name, and was recorded as early as the fifteenth century. Ribbon-weaving was also a local trade arising from the yarn-bleaching business of the Wuppertal, and it still prospers in Barmen today.

The ribbon trade, or haberdashery trade, as it was known at the time, was much more important in the seventeenth and eighteenth centuries than it is today. Men's coats were made from plain-coloured, piece-dyed cloth, but were embroidered with ribbons, lace, and braiding. Towards the end of the sixteenth century the ribbon-mill was invented, which made it possible to produce a greater number of ribbons at a time. This time-saving machine was not allowed by the guilds and was officially banned by the Reich, albeit unsuccessfully. In towns like Cologne, however, where there was a guild organization, such technical progress was impossible.

In 1638, in the remote Bergian village of Radevormwald, which was not granted town rights until 1746, fourteen Baptist families were registered by the authorities and forced to leave the Land. Ten of them were lace-workers, including the widowed Entgan von der Leyen. Although she owned two houses the authorities regarded her as a debtor. Her husband, Adolf, however, had been no mere humble weaver. In 1623 and 1624 he had been a dealer in linen, silk ribbons and cloth at the Frankfurt trade fair. He had not only been a craftsman but a businessman as well. His son, also called Adolf, belonged, as we can see from his family connections and endowments, to the class of highly esteemed merchants in Krefeld, where he finally settled in the 1650s. Once in Krefeld, he naturally entered the linen business which was dominant at the time, but he brought to it his experience from ribbon-making and silk-weaving, indeed from the silk business in general. It can be assumed from this that, quite early on, linen-weavers were trained in the more refined art of silk-weaving. But in the main Adolf and his sons were export merchants, as the firm's accounts show, not only of their own products, but also of goods which they were able to procure from their business friends and fellow Baptists, and in addition of domestic goods. Their business affairs and contacts extended on the one side from the Lower Rhineland to the Netherlands, and on the other southwards to the great Frankfurt Fair, and even further to Zürich, where Italian raw silk could be purchased.

THE VON DER LEYENS BECOME MANUFACTURERS. THE RISE OF WORLD-WIDE FIRMS

The grandchildren of the von der Leyen family were the first to make the transition from being *Verlegers* and merchants to being manufacturers. In 1724 the three family firms joined together in establishing a mutual dye-house. We have already seen how the methods of business in the fine-cloth industry of the Aachen area were improved in this period, in that the contractor himself began to supervise all the most important stages of production, as well as dealing with the sales and distribution of the finished goods, thereby being able to adapt his manufacture to the needs of the market. Silk-dyeing was, and still is today, difficult and financially risky, in view of the high cost of materials. Up to that time the dyeing of raw silk had mainly been done in Cologne, but also to some extent in Frankfurt and the Netherlands. The von der Leyen family sent a representative, a man called Gerpott who came from the Netherlands, to train in Rotterdam: he became the manager of their dye-house. Obviously there were hitches to start with, and it took a few years to get everything to work satisfactorily. In 1731 the two brothers, Friedrich and Heinrich von der Leyen, established their business, which was to become a firm of international importance. They each invested the considerable sum of 18,900 Rtl. in this new business, and the accounts of June 1756 show that the capital resources of the concern already amounted to 317,000 Rtl. In 1763, after the end of the Seven Years War, the firm apparently employed 2,800 men, which was almost half the town's population. In 100 years the firm had increased tenfold, but after the 1750s the number of employees increased only a little more to just over 3,000. This might seem to suggest that stagnation had set in, but in fact the capital resources of the owners reached the proud figure of 1,279,000 Rtl. in 1794, shortly before the French invasion. The population of this sovereign territory, including the area immediately outside the town walls, had risen to 7,896 by 1787. This figure suggests that other firms had taken root there, and that the great firm of von der Leyen had reached the limits of its growth.

Through this one family, then, the silk industry of Krefeld came into existence. Aided by the technical and merchant experience of generations of von der Leyens, they trained a labour-force, which was practised in the art of linen-weaving, to weave silk. That this labour-force existed in the first place shows the great advantage of a town which had become a refuge for exiles. Water power, which was otherwise so important, was not needed in the silk industry, and the water in Krefeld was not particularly suited to dyeing as it was in Monschau. It was to the advantage of the silk industry that there was a decline in linen exports, and that silk paid higher wages, as it was a very fine craft which needed great care and skill. It must have been the great firm's object to pay their weavers handsomely, in order to counter the enticement to skilled workers to go and work in the region of Berg. The firm had to make silk-weaving looms available to the linen-weavers it wanted to win over, but these looms remained the firm's property. One could say that the weavers were in bondage, but it meant that they were kept on even in times when jobs were scarce, and in the eighteenth century there were no wage disputes.

THE RISE OF NEW FIRMS

The situation was different with the linen *Verlegers*, however. They started turning to the silk industry from the 1750s onwards, but disputes with them did not cease until the break-up of Old Prussia (in 1815). During the Seven Years War the family received from the Austrian authorities (and after the peace, from the Prussian authorities) exclusive rights in some important branches of production. Such privileges or monopolies (similar to modern patents) were quite common at the time in order to encourage the advance of new industries: the velvet monopoly which the Palatine government granted to the Andreä family after they moved from Cologne to Mülheim on Rhine is a comparable example. When competition increased the von der Leyen family tried to assert their privilege, but was it advisable for the government to hold back rising businesses and cause the emigration of valuable industries? Much was written on this question between Krefeld, Cleves, and Berlin, which shows how opinion was divided on the subject. The king always decided in favour of the great firm; for him one big business was always preferable to ten little ones. The firm of Preyers did, in fact, move to Kaiserswerth, but did not achieve much by this move. The great firm's biggest competition, as regards capital assets, was the firm of Flöh,[26] which concentrated on velvet and velvet-ribbon production, a sphere that was not monopolized. By doing this it acquired great wealth. The velvet industry later became as important as the silk industry. Indeed the 'outsiders' were by no means small fry in the eighteenth century.

In the second volume of documents in the 'Acta Borussica', Hintze mentions some Prussian statistics for 1788,[27] in which the number of silk factories, looms, and workers are listed for Krefeld, as well as the value of manufacture and foreign sales: a column for Mörs and Xanten is added in smaller figures. He concludes from these statistics: 'only 30% of the total production came from the five firms which operated besides the great von der Leyen firm; in 1790 this was reduced to four firms, a conclusive proof of the complete dominance of the one concern'. Hintze further concludes that, because Krefeld industry was almost entirely controlled by one firm, no strict controls were placed on it from Berlin: he also assumes that Berlin industry was three times as big as that of Krefeld. But one cannot judge the extent of the latter merely by counting the number of weaving looms and workers it employed on Prussian soil. After all, the linen industry had extended itself into the villages around Cologne and they were outside the Prussian exclave: they became industrial villages. If the linen *Verlegers* had their local weavers trained in silk-weaving, they cannot be reproached with stealing labour from the linen trade. The older Hermann Keussen estimated the number of these weavers at between 2,000 and 3,000.[28] These firms had their own dye-houses in the town, and that in itself suggests they were quite large. In the district created by the last extension to the town these contractors also built magnificent houses which speak of good standing and wealth.[29] This is suggested too by the tax assessment figures, which Hintze did not mention.

The excise duties, raised at the gates of towns, were an important part of Prussian finances. This system made necessary the strict division of the countryside—which paid land tax—from the town, which had trade rights. But the spread of industry into the countryside meant that this system could not be operated strictly in western Germany, and the cumbersome excise levy with its 35 items led in small territories to the diversion of trade traffic (to avoid payment): little exclaves could easily be circumvented. The government of western Germany thus gradually restricted the excise levy to one or two lucrative items, such as food and drink, and to replace the old levy it introduced a fixed tax, which was paid directly by the inhabitants of the town. This was really a kind of income tax, which was graded by a special commission made up of representatives of different professions. In Krefeld there were 27 tax gradations.[30] The poor did not have to pay anything, and the contribution of the middle classes was not very high. In the highest grade, with a contribution of 82·5 Rtl., came the three von der Leyen partners and their great competitor, Kornelius Flöh; in the second grade came two Beckerath silk manufacturers and in the third three others. Two of them were Councillors of Commerce. The von der Leyen brothers were Knights and Privy Councillors of Commerce. By today's standards these tax payments were not high, but they were higher than in other places at that time. In Elberfeld, as Wiebeking proudly emphasizes, a man worth 1,000,000 Thalers only paid 24 Rtl. in tax. In 1790, then, besides the great von der Leyen firm there were four other sizeable firms in the silk industry.

We read of the long business trips made by the heads of all these firms,[31] and the impression we gain is similar to that of the fine-cloth industry in the Aachen area. The high price of raw materials and the long-term credit, which it had to have, made great demands on the industry's capital strength. This was no place for small businesses, for the industry was capable of competition on a European scale. But how did this silk industry of western Germany stand in relation to the industry which the King himself had nurtured in the eastern part of his monarchy?

THE DIFFERENCE BETWEEN THE INDUSTRIAL DEVELOPMENTS IN BERLIN AND IN KREFELD

When King Frederick began to build up the silk industry in 1746, specialist workmen, master-craftsmen, and contractors were brought in from outside, mainly from Lyons. A group of 100 families formed the basic core of skill and experience from which domestic labour received its training. Houses, workshops, and weaving looms had to be provided for the immigrants; they were also paid pensions (i.e. supplements to their work wage), and given pew-rent. The wages and benefits must have been very high, for why else would these people leave their homes and venture into the distant unknown? Among the new immigrants there were some rather dubious adventurers. In 1752, in his political testament, the king wrote that 100,000 Rtl. a year had to be put aside for the silk industry, and during his reign he spent 2,000,000 Rtl. on it. To begin with, wages were higher than in Lyons, but the quality of the goods was worse, and the work less efficient. Lyons could offer its goods in the Leipzig market at a cheaper price than Berlin could. It was also known that a third of all silk goods consumed were smuggled in. The contractors and local merchants who had been urged into the silk manufacturing business were short of capital, and for this reason a state warehouse was set up, where manufacturers could purchase raw materials on credit, which, in the event of a sales shortage, could be repaid in finished goods. This served as a 'substitute' for the contractors' capital resources. In Krefeld and western

Germany people got by without state aid. Even today, governments who want their countries developed industrially have to face the question whether to leave the development to foreign capital, or whether they themselves should aid and direct it with their own capital. Only the latter course was possible for the Prussian state. For as long as it was not fully competitive, the success of the new industry depended upon securing the home market. The import of foreign silk goods was thus restricted by ever increasing duties, until finally it was banned altogether. This ban even applied to products from Krefeld. The Prussian territory west of the river Weser was foreign as far as customs policy was concerned. As business in the eastern part of Prussia was not as active as that in the west, the government aimed to secure the Polish market for its eastern industry. Therefore the transport of Berlin goods to Poland was rewarded with a bonus, whereas a duty had to be paid on the transport of Krefeld goods.

Berlin industry was hard-hit by the European crisis which followed the Seven Years War, and had to resort to heavy state subsidies for support. In 1766 regulations were enacted which gave the state strict powers of supervision over the industry. Two supervisors had to visit each firm, without warning, twice a week; on Saturdays an inspector did the round of firms, and on Mondays they all went to the palace, to Department No. 5 of the Board of General Directors, to report their observations, and to tell them if the regulations (the conditions of which occupied several pages) were being complied with. This was the height of state supervision. But the crisis passed, and the general advance, of which we have already spoken, began. The silk industry of Berlin also began to prosper, and the supervision became less stringent.

These regulations had not been devised for the industry of Krefeld, but the von der Leyen brothers received questions from Berlin, asking them if they wanted such regulations introduced in their town. They declined the offer, and wrote among other things that

the factories in this town came into being solely through our own efforts, expense, equipment, and technical discoveries: in this manner they reached their present perfected and prosperous state. This position would be threatened and damaged by all these changes and innovations. With all humility and obedience we therefore ask that you most graciously exempt us from these regulations, and allow us to keep the freedom we have so far enjoyed while this continues to serve the best interests of the factories, manufacturers, and indeed the whole town of Krefeld.

There the matter rested, and it would have been a mistake to interfere with the business methods of such an important and successful concern. None of the firms in Krefeld ever had state supervisors or factory inspectors.[32]

King Frederick turned down the repeated requests of the great firm (von der Leyen) to allow their goods to be sold in the eastern part of the kingdom, but he invited them to open a branch-firm in the east in order to exploit that market. Excusing themselves by reference to their advanced years, the von der Leyen brothers declined this invitation, and elaborately explained how, after decades of effort, they had raised their firm to its present proud peak, and emphasized again that any interference in their business methods would be harmful. The implication of these explanations was that the type of business they had created could not be transferred elsewhere.[33] None of the other firms were prepared to transfer their businesses either.

In its dealings with Krefeld and western Germany in general, the Prussian government had had to adapt itself to circumstances and did not exert any pressure, but these concessions did not affect the basic standpoint of the monarchy. The silk industry which Frederick the Great had built up was almost exclusively situated in Berlin. Because of the high wages here the government suggested to employers that they move their businesses out of the capital city and into smaller towns in the area; they refused, because these towns would not be able to provide the necessary skilled workers: on the other hand, Krefeld was a small town, and yet its industry and business had become world-wide, and had spread itself across the country, regardless of territorial boundaries. This would not have been possible in eastern Germany, even staying within the Land's boundaries, because of the bondage and labour-obligations of the rural population. As a rule, the industrialization of the country areas led to open developments, as we have seen in the area of Berg. The industrial town of Elberfeld had long since sprawled outside its old town walls, and the Prussian exclave of Viersen with its long straggling rows of courtyards became an industrial village. But Krefeld remained a closed town, within town walls. These walls and gates were no longer needed for defence purposes, but they were indispensable for collecting excise duties. I have already spoken of the first two extensions to the town in 1692 and 1711; there were three more after that, in 1738, 1752, and 1756. With each extension the walls and gates of the town had to be pushed back or rebuilt. Compared with the elaborate expansion of the big residential towns this procedure might seem somewhat niggardly, but it was not prompted by a desire for display, rather from a need to accommodate the stream of newcomers within a restricted area. The Councillor for War, Müntz, told King Frederick William I that he reckoned on a contribution of 2·5 Rtl. from each new citizen for the outlay on the third extension to the town. Thus arose, with the keen co-operation of the royal house, the industrial town of the eighteenth century, built without pretensions to splendour, with straight, right-angled, grid-like streets, whose beauty of form delighted contemporaries.[34] After the walls and gate-towers had fallen into decay during the French rule, the architect Vagedes, who still held the views of the eighteenth century on civic design, began in 1819 to construct a rampart around the old rectangular foundations. This shows posterity more clearly

than any building could have done what the industrial town of the eighteenth century looked like.

THE COMPOSITION OF THE POPULATION

Where did these immigrants come from, whose arrival over the decades increased the population of the little town tenfold? The migration of the Mennonites from the area of Berg to the lower Rhine was prompted by religious reasons: they made up one-tenth of the population. Hintze suggests that many of the immigrant workers came from the Dutch silk industry, but there is no record of this in the town registry. Most of the new citizens came from the surrounding regions and were Catholics. After the fourth extension to the town in 1752 they got their own parish church. By the end of the century they accounted for two-thirds of the population. There were, however, no Catholic employers in the silk industry, nor were there any from among the local Calvinists. The Mennonites were superior here because of their merchant training and business skill, acquired over many generations, and also their capital wealth, which was necessary for running a silk business. Here I am not going to attempt an evaluation of the religious factor in their success. The successful transference of the Dutch silk industry to the lower Rhine could only have been achieved by contractors, and not by workers: that such a transference took place cannot be established, since the von der Leyen family cannot be counted as Dutch. The foreign merchants who married into the families of silk industrialists came from merchant and business families in the Palatinate. In the course of the century a social gap emerged between the 'merchant aristocrats' and the local middle classes; but, on the other hand, people of the same class formed much closer links with each other at this time throughout the whole of western Germany, and the differences between the various Protestant beliefs gradually lessened.

In observance of the 'old rule', only Calvinists were eligible for election to the Council. The public authorities refused on principle to recognize the Mennonites. The von der Leyen family, however, stood outside the town's authority and were directly subject to the government in Mörs. But the social and economic development proceeded regardless of political boundaries or religious differences. Two new social classes, the upper-middle-class employers and the workers, determined in essence the character of the town, and the constitution of its population. In the working class the domestic weavers were predominant, and they, although economically dependent, really had a lower-middle-class mentality and outlook on life.

THE FLOURISHING OF DUTCH INDUSTRY IN THE SEVENTEENTH CENTURY AND ITS DECLINE IN THE EIGHTEENTH[35]

The seventeenth century was the great period of prosperity for the independent Netherlands. Ever since Antwerp had lain idle, after the closing of the

Scheldt, Amsterdam had become the trade centre and emporium of Europe. One would have thought that the individual contribution of this small country would be trifling when compared with the huge turnover in goods from the rest of the world which it handled. (Leaving out of account the yield from the fisheries, that is.) But in fact Holland was at that time the leading industrial nation in Europe. I use the name of the leading province, because the industrial development of the Netherlands took place almost entirely within Holland. It is worth noting the nature of this industry, because the character of the modern industry of the eighteenth century clearly owed much to it.

The word 'industry' evokes today pictures of the great works of the iron, steel, or chemical industries, but up to the middle of the nineteenth century the textile industry was much more important, and it was in the field of textiles that Dutch industry dealt. In the later Middle Ages the English began to process their own excellent wool, but the famous English cloths, which the Merchant Adventurers brought across to continental markets, were neither dyed nor finished. It has been thought that this was because the English were not very skilled in the art of dyeing. It is more probable, however, that, in view of the distances involved, it was more expedient and business-like if the cloths were finished in the area where they were sold, according to the customer's wishes[36]—assuming, that is, that there were suitable processing means in that area. But Holland had a fine-cloth industry of her own—the leading one in Europe, in fact. Leiden, which we remember today as Rembrandt's birthplace and home of the most important university in the seventeenth century, was at that time no mere scholastic retreat, but the centre of the cloth industry, and second in size of population only to Amsterdam. Leiden owed this prominence to immigrants from the south Netherlands, mainly Walloons, who had introduced new types of material, and new manufacturing methods. In his account of this prosperous period, J. G. van Dillen writes:

Except for Lyons, the main city of the silk trade, Leiden was perhaps the largest industrial town in Europe. Travellers to the town could see, while still some distance away, its 25 fulling-mills (which were driven by the wind, as there was no water power), and its 30 fields of tenter-frames ['Rahmen', which were used for stretching the cloth; you will recall the 'Rahmenberg' in Monschau]. Once in the town, the traveller stopped to admire the huge houses of the cloth wholesalers, which contained living-space and work-shops; in the suburbs lived the spinners, weavers, fullers, and dyers. In population the town was the second largest in the Republic.[37]

The wholesalers ('Reder') had, through middle-men, a great many cloth-makers dependent upon them. They also had to have large and mobile capital resources. A cloth-maker could seldom work his way up to the position of a *Verleger*, in whose service the middle classes (i.e. the 'drapers' or cloth-makers, fullers, and dyers) worked. Each of these employed one or two

journeymen. Below them came the proletariat, the wool-combers and spinners. 'But one should not overestimate the power of the "Reder"; it paled by
comparison with that of the Amsterdam merchants.' Wages were low by
general Dutch standards. There was no limit set to the amount a master-
craftsman was allowed to produce or to the number of workers he could
employ, as there had been in the Middle Ages, and still was in Aachen. But in
no way can it be said that there was freedom of trade. Once finished, the
woven fabrics were taken to the 'Sales Hall', and there subjected to the inspection of the *Staalmeesters*. There were regulations for every stage of production. The raw materials, the measurements, and the quality of the fabrics were
all tested. The *Gouverneures* and the 'Staalmeesters' were appointed by the
municipal council from among the small group of big contractors. The
master-craftsmen had no say in this, and merely enjoyed the honour of belonging to the Corporation. The 'Reder' supplied the great Amsterdam cloth-
traders with export goods.

There was also an important cloth trade in Amsterdam; its dye-houses
were particularly famous. In 1661–2 Rembrandt painted for the *Staalhof*
that splendid picture of the *Staalmeesters* working out their accounts. This
masterpiece which catches our eye in the Rijksmuseum can also serve as a
memorial to the contemporary economy.

In the seventeenth century the silk industry was brought to Amsterdam
through the influence of the *marranos* (Spanish moors who were forcibly
Christianized). There were 25 to 30 silk dye-houses, for which strict rules were
drawn up. It is a fact typical of Amsterdam, at that time, that guild regulations were made to apply to the new trade as well. There was more freedom
with silk-weaving, however: this sphere was also divided up into silk-
merchants, *Verleger*, and *Fabriqueurs*, who owned the workshops. After
1685 the industry made new progress, this time under the influence of the
Huguenots.

The centre of linen-weaving was Haarlem. Here the impetus was given by
Flemish immigrants in exile. The area around the town was famous for its
bleaching. Flemish, French, and Schleswig linen was given its final preparation here. As we have already seen, raw fabrics were sent from the Lower
Rhine to Haarlem right up to the end of the eighteenth century, and then went
on to the world market as fine Dutch linen ('Gebild').

All in all we get the impression that an astonishing industrial growth took
place. It was largely caused by the influx of immigrants, who were readily
welcomed. It was an export industry whose sales were supported by the great
Amsterdam market and the power of her capital. The conditions of trade
were, on the whole, those of the Middle Ages and guilds, except for one or
two capitalistic relaxations. All products were strictly examined and tested.
And above all, it was an urban industry. Leiden, Haarlem, and Amsterdam
were all old towns with fully developed guilds, to which even the new-

comers had to adjust themselves. As in the Middle Ages, trade was reserved for the towns, in contrast to the wider-ranging expansion of the new industry of the eighteenth century. This concentration in towns explains the astonishing size of Leiden's population.

THE ECONOMIC DECLINE OF THE REPUBLIC (ACHTERUITGANG)

This is the title of the ninth chapter of vol. viii of the *Allgemeine Geschichte der Niederlande*, dealing with the second half of the eighteenth century. At that time England's economic predominance was becoming evident. The proportion of Dutch sea-going ships to English ones was 6 to 7; London had taken the place of Amsterdam as the staple-market of Europe. However, the volume of trade and above all the financial power of Amsterdam remained considerable. Thus, it was a case of a relative lag in the face of English competition. But industry was falling into real decay at a time when elsewhere, especially in England, a brilliant upswing was taking place. At Leiden, the decline began with the French invasion of 1672. Production had reached its peak in 1671 with 139,000 pieces of cloth. The town then had 72,000 inhabitants. Production sank to 72,000 pieces of cloth in 1725, to 54,000 in 1750, to 41,000 in 1775, and 28,000 in 1795. At the end of the century, the town had a population of only 30,000. Chronic unemployment and pauperism led to idleness and decreased efficiency, when there was work. Firm measures had to be taken against the rapid increase in begging. In the first decades of the century, a large amount of cloth from England was still being imported and finished, but then England set about exporting only finished cloth, and so the trades of dyeing and finishing went into decline as well.

Already in the seventeenth century, competition had made itself felt. At the small town of Tilburg in the General Territories to the south of the Meuse, wages were lower, and the big Amsterdam cloth merchants succeeded in getting the import of Tilburg cloth permitted, at first for a short period and then permanently. Today, Tilburg is the centre of the Dutch wool industry. Like the rest of the formerly Spanish General Territories, the town is completely Catholic, the businessmen as well. Imports from the up-and-coming industrial town of Ypres in the formerly Spanish and later Austrian duchy of Limburg were becoming an even greater threat. At the customs post at Hertogenbosch, at first coarse woollen cloth and then soon fine cloth was imported from Ypres in great quantities. Fine cloth was also supplied by Verviers in the bishopric of Liège. It is the same development as at Monschau. Wages at Verviers were said to be only a third of those at Leiden.

The industrial decline was not restricted to the cloth industry. The Haarlem linen industry had to struggle against competition from Ireland, Flanders, and Silesia, and the Amsterdam silk industry was in decline. In 1767, the firm of von der Leyen wrote to King Frederick that they had eliminated the

Dutch competition.[38] The cotton industry of Amersfort (in the province of Utrecht) moved away to Enschede in the marshes of eastern Overyssel, where there were no guilds. On the other side of the border is the German town of Gronau. Both towns are now centres of a large cotton industry. This example, like that of Tilburg, shows that modern industry, which is not tied to local natural resources, frequently began to flourish in poor districts with low wages.

THE CAUSES OF THE DECLINE

How is this decline in a period of general expansion to be explained? As it was of a lasting nature, was not restricted to the textile industry, and was not interrupted by a period of recovery, it was not a case of a temporary depression but rather of a structural crisis. Blok and de Vries[39] explain it by the high level of wages, enforced guild-membership, and the prohibition of rural industry. They refer to the measures taken by England, France, and Prussia to exclude imports; however, these measures did not prevent the expansion in Belgium and the Rhineland. Wages were the decisive factor; for, in the age of handicraft, industry was much more labour-intensive than it is today. Restriction to the towns was part of the medieval economic structure, with which the 'regents' did not dare to interfere. In the Dutch towns the cost of living had been driven up by the excises, which threw the burden on to the masses. In over-populated Amsterdam one-eighth of the rent had to be paid in tax. One should not imagine, on account of the high level of wages, that the republic was a country of widespread affluence like the United States, Switzerland, or Sweden today. 'In contrast to the closed circle of the patricians and the wider groupings of the wealthy and of the small bourgeoisie, there was the much more numerous class of the poor, who lived permanently on the verge of starvation. That is how it was in the golden age.' In the eighteenth century things got worse. 'Het gemeine arbeidsvolk vergaat van kommer en gebrek.'*[40] There is no mention at this time of intervention by the state to protect industry, and this was a time when, elsewhere, new industries were nurtured with protective tariffs, prohibitions on imports, and monopolies. The northern Low Countries were a trading nation, and the interests of trade took precedence; cheap goods had to be imported which could be sold on the world market. Due to the high level of wages, a change in the economic system would hardly have held any promise of success. The state constitution, the social and economic structure, had taken shape in the golden age, and adaptation to the new age would have amounted to a revolution. Possibly it is more difficult to adjust than to start again from scratch. This brings to mind the biological law of evolution which states that specializations cannot be reversed. In the northern Low Countries there was 'no climate for an industrial revolution' (de Vries).[41]

* Trans. note: 'The common working people are perishing from misery and disease.'

The fate of Dutch industry is not an isolated one. In the imperial city of Aachen the fine-cloth industry withered away under the guild obligations, while it flourished in the neighbouring towns that had no guilds. In Cologne, the silk industry went into decline because the guild held back technological progress. At Basle, where the council permitted the use of the ribbon-loom, the silk industry exists to this day. In the commercial town of Frankfurt, which was developing into the economic centre of southern and western Germany, no industry was allowed to be established after the (Fettmilch) uprising of 1612–14, whereas Offenbach, Hanau, and Höchst became industrial towns. Where the old type of bourgeoisie had a say in affairs, they ruled in an oligarchic manner and did not interfere with the old social order; they were a part of the Ancien Régime just as were the king and the nobility of France. This was the case in the Low Countries, in Switzerland, and in the imperial cities. It gave rise to dangerous tensions; in the Low Countries these tensions had already erupted before the French Revolution in the insurrection of the 'Patriots'. The same thing happened at Liège in 1789, while the Brabançonne Revolution was directed against the precipitate reforms of Joseph II. Thus, the title of the eighth volume of the 'General History of the Low Countries' is as follows: 'De Revolutie tegemoet!' ['Forward to the Revolution!']

THE ECONOMIC RISE OF THE SOUTHERN LOW COUNTRIES IN THE EIGHTEENTH CENTURY[42]

As a result of the War of Spanish Succession the southern Low Countries had come under Austrian rule. It was a fertile country with an old culture, but it had been badly mutilated. The industrially most advanced areas around Lille and Valenciennes, and the port of Dunkirk, had been lost to France in the reign of Louis XIV; this is the Département du Nord, the most important industrial region of France. To this day, one can tell from the density of population which areas were once part of the Low Countries. But still, the southern Low Countries were ten times the size of any single one of the western German territories. However, one of the three pre-conditions for a mercantilist policy, namely independence, did not exist. The emperor was not the sole ruler in the country. In accordance with the Barrier Treaty the fortresses were garrisoned with Dutch troops, four-fifths of whose pay had to be raised by the southern Low Countries. At the same time, the tariffs, which had been reduced by the maritime powers during the war in order to improve imports of their goods, were not allowed to be raised. Antwerp remained cut off from the sea. Be that as it may, after 145 years of insurrection and war there came an age of peace, which, until the French Revolution, was interrupted only by the hardly noticeable Austrian War of Succession. While at that time English agriculture, with its system of extensive tenant-farming on large estates, was making great advances, agriculture in the southern Low Countries was developing in the shape of small-scale, extremely intensive cultivation. Already in the late Middle Ages, free contracts of tenancy had taken the place of the earlier ties. It was now that there came into being the form of landscape that has been called an extended garden and which presents such a surprising sight when coming from southern England and its pasture land. The chief benefits were enjoyed by the landowners, who had done a great deal for cultivation and for the reclamation of land from the sea (the dukes of Arenberg), but the tenants were well off too.[43]

THE ECONOMIC STAGNATION IN THE TOWNS

The situation was quite different in the towns. The population had declined, and it was estimated that a quarter of what remained received public assistance. The industrial advance which, in the first half of the nineteenth century, made Belgium into the leading industrial country on the continent, did not originate in the large and small towns with which Flanders and Brabant had for centuries been so densely studded. They were old towns with a medieval organization of trades. At Bruges there were 74 guilds, at Antwerp 60. And because of this very decline, they stubbornly defended their privileges. This was, of course, also the case at Cologne and Aachen. In the early years of Austrian rule, on account of a number of encroachments on the old privileges, the governor got into a dispute with the citizenry of Brussels which degenerated into mob rioting. It was only when the army had been brought in from afar that the riots could be put down. Annessens, the mayor, a brave and honest man, who had stood up for the old privileges, was executed in the market-place, as were Egmont and Horn in their day. After this experience, the government was more cautious.

In 1748, the Peace of Aachen freed the southern Low Countries from customs obligations. But for measures aimed at industrial self-sufficiency this country, too, was too small. The export trade across the near-by French border and to England was blocked by tariffs and import embargoes. Other ways had to be looked for. Pauperism in the towns and the prevention of trade by sea pressed for the stimulation of industry. The Austrian Low Countries were now ruled in accordance with the precepts of the Enlightenment. It was not the governor Karl von Lothringen (the brother of the emperor and a brother-in-law of Maria Theresa) whose authority was decisive, but rather the Chancery at Vienna, together with the Chancellor of State, Count—and later Prince—Kaunitz, the antagonist of the king of Prussia. From 1744 to 1746 he had been minister at Brussels.

THE RISE OF RURAL INDUSTRY

As the government had to take guild obligations into consideration in the old towns, it promoted new branches of industry with monopolies and privileges, but without much success. Of greater importance was the rise of the old rural industries. In Flanders, the linen industry flourished on the basis of flax-growing. In the countryside, the peasants spun and wove their own flax. At Ghent, the dealers bought the linen in the market, had it finished, and saw to selling it. Most of the export trade went via Ostend to Spain. It was estimated that half the population of Flanders, 200,000 in all, were employed in the linen industry. The old system was able to endure, since linen was a staple commodity that was not subject to fashion. It was only in the 1840s that machine-spinning in factories began, together with terrible misery in the countryside. In Flanders, too, there was a period of great misery for the weavers. In the meantime, as in the Niers region, the cotton industry had developed with its centre at Ghent.

Already in those days, in the region between the Sambre and the Meuse, the Borinage district (which, nowadays, besides Liège, is the other region of Belgian heavy industry), iron extraction and processing were flourishing, based on the coal and iron-ore deposits of Mons and Charleroi.[44] But in those days, coal was used only for forges; the blast-furnaces had to be fired with charcoal. The main product was nails (*clouterie*); they were manufactured by 10,000–15,000 rural forges and distributed by retail dealers. It is surprising how little iron was manufactured and consumed in those days. The success of mercantile promotion of industry was not very great. The state did much more indirectly for the economy by the extension and improvement of the trade-routes, and in this the provincial diet co-operated willingly. Unlike in western Germany, the territories had been joined together for centuries. Modern paved highways were built, and good quarries were available. 'From 1715, when what is now Belgium had 61 km, the number increased by 1795 to 925 km. Under French rule only 40 km were added.' Already in 1750, Voltaire wrote: 'De toutes les nations modernes, la France et le petit pays des Belges sont les seules qui aient des chemins dignes de l'antiquité.'[45] In addition there came the construction of a canal network, whose centre came to be Louvain. Whereas the navigable rivers like the Meuse and the Scheldt flowed to the north and had their outlets in a foreign country, the canals provided the east–west communications. They also served the passenger traffic with comfortable mail boats. Georg Forster wrote on this subject.

In the southern Low Countries, farming still predominated; it was an area of surplus like the lower Rhine. Together with the splendid court that the governor was allowed to conduct, the nobility was held in high esteem, and the rich bourgeoisie endeavoured to increase its importance by acquiring titles of nobility. This was quite different from the situation in the Dutch Republic with enmity between the Stadholder and the Regents, and also from the lower Rhine, where apart from Bonn there was no longer any court and where confessional differences made the bridging of the social divisions more difficult. But one must also be aware of the reverse side of the splendid life of the upper strata of society.

PAUPERISM IN EIGHTEENTH-CENTURY BELGIUM[46]

We have seen that, due to the economic decline in the northern Low Countries in the eighteenth century, the situation of the masses was very unfavourable. But in the south things were no better in spite of the economic expansion. A few important conclusions from Paul Bonenfant's book should be mentioned.[46] We have already seen the misery in the towns. For the countryside, where conditions were more favourable, there is no documentation, but due to the very low level of wages there was a lot of female and child labour. In the towns, the masters of trades prevented the advancement of their badly-paid journeymen. On top of the material poverty of the masses came cultural and moral degradation. Three-quarters of the population were illiterate. Alcoholism was very widespread. Beggars and vagabonds led the badly-paid workers astray; yet there was a shortage of skilled workers. At Brussels, the number of foundlings rose from 671 in 1771 to the enormous figure of 2,570 in 1785. At that time the city had a population of 70,000. The number of beggars was huge. In the towns they importuned the citizens, in the countryside there was highway robbery; tramps made themselves a nuisance at farms.

The author's acknowledgement that wars and famines were not the cause of these conditions is important. Wars and famine were temporary phenomena. It is a case of endemic, chronic conditions, which can be identified at least from the end of the Middle Ages. They prevailed in the golden age of the fifteenth and sixteenth centuries in the reign of Philip the Good and Charles V, and in the eighteenth century. Bonenfant believes that in the periods of expansion the increase in population kept ahead of the expansion of the food supply. Just as pauperism had already existed for such a long period in history, equally it was not geographically limited to the Low Countries; it existed throughout the whole of western Europe. This leads the author to the conclusion that it was not caused by modern industry. On the contrary, he is of the opinion that nineteenth-century industry absorbed most of the old proletariat and 'after a terrible crisis adjustment' brought about an astonishing material, cultural, and moral improvement for the broad masses of the people.

Industrial work in the eighteenth century was handicraft work. Because of the imperfection of tools and machines it placed high demands on craft skills. These skills were difficult to pass on, and that was the strength of the industrial regions of that day. These workers were not proletarians, either with respect to their skill or their mental attitudes. The fact that there was a particularly numerous working class in the old towns pressed the governments to promote industries, and the entrepreneur who created work was regarded as a benefactor, not as an exploiter. The existence of mercenary armies must also be seen in this light.

Although the Austrian government was, in principle, in favour of mercantile promotion of industry, the really big industrial expansion in its duchy of Limburg and in the episcopal principality of Liège was accomplished without state assistance.

ALREADY IN THE EIGHTEENTH CENTURY THE OLD MEDIEVAL CITY OF LIÈGE BECOMES A MODERN INDUSTRIAL CITY

Liège is one of the old cities of the Middle Ages, and had always been a meeting-point of many routes of commerce, and a political, economic, and cultural centre. It is situated on the navigable parts of the Meuse, which comes from far in the south in France but turns eastward at Namur; at Liège it bends to the north again, soon enters the low plain, and joins further north the area of the Rhine and Scheldt estuaries. At Liège a number of Ardennes valleys debouch together from the south and east into the Meuse valley. Here, the coal deposits were easily accessible on account of a deeply cut valley, and had been worked for centuries. The name Wahl, which occurs quite commonly in the Sauerland, indicates that in the Middle Ages Walloons were the instructors in mining and iron-smelting. Already in early times, Liège had surpassed Maastricht, which was situated further north and where the road from Cologne to the Low Countries had crossed the Meuse since Roman times, and had taken its place as a bishop's see. Liège was one of those cities that had always rebelled against their rulers and become almost independent. Subjugated by Charles the Short, it regained its freedom after his death, and, unlike Utrecht, the bishopric remained immediately subject to the imperial government. After the Thirty Years War the military power of the cities was finished. In 1684, after a revolt by the guilds, the bishop and lord of the country, Maximilian Heinrich of Bavaria, archbishop of Cologne, marched unopposed into Liège with Bavarian infantry and French cavalry. Both the mayors were executed. The régime of 1684 put an end to the independence of the city, and thereafter the senators were appointed by the bishop. They were landowners, judges, and eminent merchants, the upper strata that existed in every old city. The guilds were no longer of any economic or political significance. The cloth manufacturers, who previously had always had the biggest say, are described by Pirenne as 'boutiquiers ruinés par la concurrence verviétoise'. The same reorganization of the senates and councils took place in the country towns of the bishopric. However, it was just as little a case of the establishment of absolutism as in the other ecclesiastic territories of the empire. The bishop continued to rule with the Estates: the cathedral chapter, the nobility, and the bourgeois upper strata of the towns. This subjection signified for Liège the beginning of a new development.

Whereas the cloth industry was dying away, the iron industry was making an amazing advance. The industry was not limited to iron production; it led above all in the manufacture of small arms and does so to this day. After all, at that time wars were in full boom. As the demand for iron could not be fully met by local production, 'Arenberg' iron had to be imported from the Schleide valley in the Eifel. The industry was managed by entrepreneurs and, as at Solingen and Remscheid, the various stages of manufacture were managed in the form of cottage industries. The industry had no guilds.

The medieval town, the 'cité', was no longer enough for this new influx. Here we have the unusual case of a medieval town that had already become a modern industrial city in the eighteenth century. The city precincts became workers' suburbs and lost their rural character. Towns were no longer places exempt from outside judicial and economic obligations, closed off by a ring of walls and surrounded by an empty space (as was Cologne); they became *foci* of activities that radiated far abroad and encroached ever more on the countryside. The differences between town and country no longer divided the population as in the Middle Ages; the privileges of the townspeople disappeared under the common law. There were no longer any distinctions between country folk and town people besides those arising from their occupations. Wherever industry penetrated, it broke down the divisions that the past had created between people. But if industry no longer took into account the former differences before the law and reduced the differences between townfolk and peasants, it did, on the other hand, intensify the contrast between rich and poor, capitalists and proletarians, a contrast that stood out all the more clearly in view of their equality before the law.[47]

In 1790 the Liège district had a population of 83,224; of these, only 32,964 lived in the medieval town, the *cité*, and 50,260 in the suburbs and city precinct. Thus, Liège was more populous than the big cities of the Austrian Low Countries and surpassed even the capital, Brussels, with its population of 70,000. Birmingham, which now has a population of one million, had only 66,000 at that time. Thus, Liège was already in the eighteenth century what is called an 'agglomération' in Belgium and France, where amalgamation of towns is not readily done. The dense concentration in the Meuse valley, in contrast to the usual sprawling of industry in the eighteenth century, is to be explained by the fact that the workshops sprang up close to the coal mines, which were situated immediately around and under the city. In 1790, Georg Forster took delight in the heavy traffic in the streets and the not exactly courteous miners, mirror-workers, and fitters, and from the escarpment above the Meuse valley he looked down upon a view similar to that to be seen today. Only the gigantic blast-furnaces were still lacking; it was not until the nineteenth century that they were built, when it had been learnt how to charge them with coke.

VERVIERS, THE NEW TOWN OF THE FINE-CLOTH INDUSTRY[48]

The greater part of the bishopric of Liège was situated in the Ardennes; this was a poor country of woods, bogs, and infertile farmland. The poverty of the soil stimulated industrial pursuits, as it did at Tilburg and Enschede, at the edge of the Eifel and in Berg. Sheep-breeding on the pastures supplied the raw material for the coarse cloth worn by the rural population. It is a matter of controversy as to where the stimulus to manufacture fine cloth came from; the *Algemeene Geschiedenis* points to Leiden; Pirenne and Dechesne point to the more near-by Aachen. Verviers's decisive advantage lay in the pure and soft water available for fulling and dyeing. Flowing westwards from the Hautes Fagnes is the rivulet called the Weser in the German-speaking area around Eupen and Vesdre by the Walloons. It was on the excellent qualities of this water, which also supplied power for fulling, that the fine-cloth manufacture of Verviers was founded. I base my account on Pirenne's portrayal in his *Histoire de Belgique*; he was born at Verviers in 1861. One can sense his intimate knowledge of the situation, the direct observations, and the living traditions.[49] His father and both his grandfathers were cloth manufacturers.

In contrast to Liège, Verviers has the appearance of a modern industrial town. Cloth manufacturing began in the fifteenth century; in the seventeenth century they changed to the manufacture of fine cloth from Spanish wool. The rise came so suddenly that all connections with tradition were broken. Only the somewhat rural church at the cemetery serves as a reminder of the past. In 1657, Verviers was elevated to the status of a town; it had never had walls or known guilds and privileges. 'Industry had always developed under conditions of free work and competition.' Unconfined, the town grew along the Vesdre and the factory canal. Along its irregular streets the brand-new 'hotels' of the manufacturers stood beside the workshops with their small windows; behind them in high buildings without light or air, that stood over narrow alleys, were the homes of the weavers, fullers, dyers, and shearers. The town was a confusion of warehouses and fulling, dyeing, and shearing workshops. The spinning was done in the countryside. The raw material, Spanish wool, was made even more expensive on account of the long distance it had to be transported by sea and roads that at first were still quite bad. To compensate for this, Verviers had excellent water, cheap fuel from the near-by coal mines, and cheap labour. And as for the population: 'The young middle class is composed only of manufacturers, all of whose resources are tied up in their businesses and who possess neither government securities nor real estate.[50] Under them there toils from early in the morning an industrial proletariat specialized in the many different operations required for the preparation of the wool and the dressing of cloth. There is nothing here which reminds one of the guilds which still survive in the old urban centres.

... The originality of the industry of Verviers consists precisely in its independence from the supervision of the guilds. It was born in complete freedom.'
Even though, as elsewhere, wages were low and working hours long, the workers were, in contrast to the mendicant proletariat of the old towns, highly qualified skilled workers whose traditional skills are admired to this day.

At the end of the Ancien Régime, Verviers had a population of 15,000, about as large as that of the Wupper valley, where industry also crowded along the river that gave it life. As England and France were closed to its exports, the market outlet for Verviers, as for the fine-cloth industry of the Aachen area, was, besides the Low Countries, the interior of Germany with its fairs that mediated in the trade with northern, eastern, and southern Europe. This is a manifestation of the economic and cultural advance of central and eastern Europe, which also makes itself felt in the rising power of the three eastern powers. The Mediterranean area and the Orient also became market outlets, which until then had been supplied by the industry of southeastern France via Marseilles. At Marseilles, the French products were once again rigorously inspected by the French trade inspection. Even without inspection at home, and in spite of the great distance, the competition from Verviers was successful, even against English fabrics. One might think that close proximity of fine-cloth manufacturing towns in such a small area would have resulted in sharp competition. But we hear nothing about that. However, the various industrial towns certainly applied themselves to particular branches of manufacture in which they distinguished themselves. Aachen and Eupen produced piece-dyed cloth, Monschau produced patterned cloth, and Verviers piece-dyed and medley cloth. This kind of specialization tends to develop even today in the larger industrial regions.

In the eighteenth century, the bishopric of Liège, which had an area of 2,100 square kilometres, became together with the district around Limburg the industrial region of modern Belgium. The industry was Walloon, but the commonplace notion about the desire of every Frenchman to be of private means cannot be applied to the Walloons with their enterprising spirit. What did the rulers contribute to this development? In a word: nothing. Or, in other words: the best thing they could have done: they left well alone. Pirenne says: 'It was not on principle, but from impotence that the ruler left the fervid enterprising activities to themselves and refrained from subjecting them to any restraint. The ruler "is a physiocrat without knowing it and writers such as Quesnay and Gourney could have quoted him as an example in support of their theories".'[51]

EUPEN, A LITTLE VERVIERS[52]

The bishopric of Liège was bordered on the north by the small duchy of Limburg, the Overmaas district, which belonged to the Spanish and later to the

Austrian Low Countries. The hilly pasture land that extends as far as Aachen is distinguished by highly developed cattle-breeding. When I was a boy, I asked at Eupen: 'why aren't there any fields here?', and received the reply: 'that would be a waste of good land'. The population had long since specialized in the production of butter and cheese; their hands are not as rough as those of the peasants who cultivate the soil, and they were skilled at spinning the fine Spanish wool. The wool was distributed by middle-men, the *baases*, who also arranged to have the yarn woven. They worked for Eupen and Verviers, but also for Burtscheid, Waals, and Monschau. Independent cloth manufacturers were to be found above all at Eupen, situated on the Vesdre, 15 km up-river from Verviers. Here the river water was even more suited for fulling and dyeing than at Verviers. Like Barmen, this sprawling town enjoyed no municipal privileges and, of course, it had no guilds. One can tell how insignificant Eupen had formerly been from the fact that it was only in 1695 that it became a separate parish. There was also a small reformed parish, one of the six parishes in the Spanish Low Countries which after the death of Phillip II had been tolerated *de facto*, even if not before the law. One of these existed also at Hodimont in the Limburg district, which was situated opposite Verviers on the other bank of the Vesdre and also had a considerable cloth industry. Exports from Eupen to the northern Low Countries in competition with Leiden were already taking place; their volume in 1764 was 21,780 pieces of fine cloth. In 1803 the population is given as 10,000, in 1815 as 8,600. At all events, Eupen was at that time approaching the important industrial towns in the lower Rhine region and the region of Berg. The entrepreneurs in the fine-cloth industry were not exclusively Protestant as at Monschau. There was a good deal of friction between the Limburg and Liège territories until the Liège transit duties had been abolished; between Monschau and Limburg, traffic had long since been free from duties. Due to the requirements of co-existence, free trade had succeeded against mercantile isolation.

In a description of industry at Eupen written in the last decade of the eighteenth century, the anonymous author says, quite in keeping with the spirit of his time: 'the merchant or manufacturer is the prime driving force and soul of everything; he keeps very many people occupied, who all work for him and receive their livelihood from him, which is certainly worth more than receiving the best administration of justice under conditions of starvation and misery, and it is this which determines the merit of the merchant in the state and makes his existence palpable.' There then follows a description of how the merchant obtains the raw materials and conducts them through the various stages of production. 'The *baases* see to the weaving and spinning. The fulling is undertaken by the fuller. Only the finishing of the cloth takes place on the manufacturer's premises under his supervision: the raising of the nap, shearing, and pressing. Only a few (big) manufacturers have their own dye-houses, the other (small) ones have their cloth dyed either by dyers or in the dye-houses of the big manufacturers. The shearers are not organized into guilds either, and some manufacturers employ 50–100 of them.' One can tell that freedom from guilds is evidently more important than the concentration of all the productive processes in one hand in a factory.

At Eupen alone there are 60 manufacturers and 1,500 shearers. This industry brought very considerable sums of money into the district, and this wealth is visible everywhere. Some people own palaces and make a display of lavish expenditure that many a count is unable to equal. They have coaches and splendid horses and servants in livery, and their household is magnificent. A manufacturer worth 10,000–20,000 talers is considered to be neither rich nor poor. In Germany where not many have that kind of money this would be considered a very big amount. Many fortunes are estimated in hundreds of thousands, and there are even some amounting to millions.

The last two sentences agree almost word-for-word with Wiebeking's reports from the Wupper valley in the same year. The number of shearers is surprisingly large; together with their families they must have made up half the population of Eupen. In the decades that followed, most of them were put out of work by the introduction of the cross-shearing machine.

Pirenne estimates the number of those employed in the Vesdre region towards the end of the century at 25,000; in 1810 the same number is reported with surprise by the prefect of the department of Ourthe. Eupen was a small-scale Verviers; it had risen as an industrial town even later than its big industrial neighbour. The fact that it had no municipal privileges was of no consequence. The industrial towns were fundamentally different from the old type of town. Their loosely built-up areas are reminiscent of the many industrial towns of the lower Rhine region and of the region of Berg. The fact that the population was Walloon at Verviers and German at Eupen did not interfere with their common pursuits. It was not until the frontiers of 1815 and 1919 that the population was divided.

I would like to draw special attention to two points made in Laurent Duchesne's book *L'Industrie drapière de la Vesdre avant 1800* (Paris and Liège, 1926). The author stresses the high transport costs of Spanish wool with which the region was burdened, as compared with the competition in southern France. The lower margin of profit could be partly made up for by lower wages, but also by the human factor—first-rate craftsmanship— and that was in fact the case. One chapter bears the proud heading: 'Population d'élite dans un milieu ingrat'. This is of course applicable to the entire region of this industry, and might equally well be said of the population of Berg. The other point is the relation to the European market. The bishopric of Liège was a small country with a big industry. It could only exist through its exports, with which the essential raw materials and food were paid for. Protective measures that injured a country to which one exported were out of the question due to the political and economic situation, just as they were in Berg. Free trade, under which goods succeed according to their quality, had to be striven for without constraint by economic theories.

In taking the example of Berg by way of comparison, one has to compare it to the whole area between Liège and Aachen. The brass industry of Stolberg, the incipient coal-mining near Aachen, and the needle industry of Aachen are also to be included in this area. Thus, the two industrial regions are more or less on an equal footing. The western region is more divided-up politically. But it had two old towns of inherited culture; this is evident in the grand houses of the burghers and the magnificent furniture. In this respect Berg was left behind; its rise was more recent. The area of Aachen and Verviers was dominated by the fine-cloth industry; Berg was character-ized by versatility, and the two areas are very different in their later develop-ment. The fine-cloth area did not escape the dangers of a single-industry economy. Today, Verviers is a middle-sized town with a population of 40,000, and Eupen is not much bigger than 150 years ago. In contrast, the Wupper valley which is now incorporated in the one large town of Wuppertal has a population of 400,000. New industries, such as the Bayer Dyes and Glanzstoff [viscose rayon], have grown so big that they had to be moved from the con-fined valley.

INDUSTRIAL DEVELOPMENT IN CLEVES AND MARK[53]

After the Peace of Utrecht (1713) industry in the western German and Belgian area began to develop on the basis of free enterprise. With the accession to the throne of Brandenburg-Prussia by Frederick William I in the same year, there began the establishment of a military–bureaucratic state which directed and promoted industry with every mercantilist means. How did this administration come to terms with the different conditions in western Germany?

Frederick I had financed his extravagant court by hiring out Prussian troops; his son put an end to that, but he doubled the size of the army from 38,000 men to 76,000; he did it without subsidies, but with harsh conscrip-tion. In small districts it was easy to escape conscription by moving away. Thus, the population of the duchy of Cleves declined by 10,000[54] between 1722 and 1734, and between 1714 and 1740 the town of Duisburg lost 8 per cent of its population.[55] It was only when Frederick the Great abolished conscription in Cleves, Mörs, and the industrial part of the county of Mark in 1748 in return for compensation payments, that the economy was released from this burden. In 1789, conscription was finally abolished by the Director of the Chambers [of Cleves and Hamm], Baron von Stein, in an agreement with the estates.

The limiting of consumption by the court was a catastrophe for the capital, whose livelihood it had been. In accordance with the king's desire, Berlin was to become—and did become—an industrial city, at first through the promotion of the wool industry. Carl Hinrichs[56] has given us a detailed account of these efforts by Frederick William I: the interconnecting system of prohibitions on the export of local wool, of the supply of the wool on state credit to the guild weavers in the towns, who were placed under inspecting masters of the guild, factory inspectors, and commissioners, whose job it was to improve quality and to supervise; of warehouses as finishing places for coarse cloth, and as fine-cloth factories; of the army as a bulk purchaser; and of an embargo on foreign woollen goods as a protective barrier.

State direction of industry, begun under Frederick William I with the wool industry and extended to the silk industry by his famous son, was successful and lasted until 1808. But in the Prussian possessions in western Germany it was as impracticable as conscription. The industry in Cleves, which manufactured fine cloth, was obliged to exchange the coarse local wool for better foreign wool in the Low Countries. No attempt was ever made to put into effect the prohibition on exports of wool. The embargo on woollen goods was met with countermeasures by the neighbouring areas and soon dropped. Cloth from Cleves had a considerable market not only in western Germany and the Low Countries, but also in the central Prussian provinces and above all in Berlin. It provided sharp competition for the new fine-cloth manufacture of the *Lagerhaus*. The king imposed a tariff on this cloth, which amounted to an embargo. Hinrichs says the following about it:[57] 'The exclusion of goods from Cleves from the market of the central provinces took place in the same year as industry in Cleves suddenly began to expand beyond all previous limits.' (The expansion in question is that of the fine-cloth industry, an expansion we had already encountered at Lennep and in the Aachen area.)

Here, in the western part of the state that was so different in character there arose on a completely individualistic basis a splendid bustle of industrial activity, the effects of which were immediately felt in the more passive east that had to be roused from above and had been driven to industrial activity only with the greatest of efforts. The King devoted all his affection to this enterprise of his in the east, to this land that had been roused by force and compulsion from its lethargy and misery: he could not but regard with jealousy anything that threatened, or merely made difficulties for his enterprise. For the King there was no question as to what choice he was faced with, the less so as the choice between the east and the west was also a choice between an industry governed and directed by the state on the one hand, and individual enterprise on the other, which the King regarded with the greatest mistrust.

The ministers were of the opinion that a big industry could be created more easily in Cleves-Mark, and were in favour of removing the tariff on cloth from Cleves; but in their report to the king they only dared to present the figures on the expansion of the industry in Cleves. 'The King wrote in the margin that it would be a million times more profitable to him if the good news were to come from Magdeburg, Halberstadt, the Kurmark, Pomerania, and Prussia, and thereby he expressed clearly and unmistakably his decision in favour of the east.' The king did not even stop at the exclusion of western goods, but also lay claim to the west as a market for the goods produced by the eastern provinces. He decreed in 1726 that the towns of Cleves-Mark had to buy 30,000 Rtl. worth of goods from the Kurmark, and the towns of Minden-Ravensburg 12,000 Rtl. worth. After some delay, the order was in fact put into effect by the General Directory. Thus the western German provinces were not only treated as foreign countries with respect to tariff policies, but on top of that also burdened with compulsory purchases. Their industry was expected to turn to export. Hinrichs writes:[58] 'In character, Cleves-Mark was part of the Dutch–Belgian industrial region, with which it was most intimately involved with regard to the supply of raw materials and to markets, and with whose organization of enterprise and system of work it was completely in accord.' (It would have been even more to the point to mention Berg and the Aachen area.) 'The problems of the wool industry in the eastern part of the monarchy did not apply here.'

'This is one of the first conflicts between true Prussianism and the liberal-minded west, a conflict in which the latter, which was only in the first stages of its individualistic economic development, could still be repulsed.' Attempts to persuade western entrepreneurs to move met with complete failure (as was later the case at Krefeld).

Just as protective measures in the west were impracticable, state direction of production was equally impossible. In 1753, the General Directory inquired whether the Berlin regulations and inspection system could be adopted. The officials responsible for Duisberg and Orsoy both replied that this would be impossible: the manufacturers had to be able to comply with the demands of their foreign customers.[59] Things remained that way, as was later the case at Krefeld. No compulsion was used, and apart from places where old guild privileges existed, there were no inspecting masters and no factory inspectors or commissioners in the textile industry. The advances in cloth manufacturing were not brought about by regimentation, but were transmitted by manufacturers who had moved from Lennep to Hagen (Moll) and to Duisburg[60] and from Monschau to Herdecke near Hagen and to Iserlohn (Schreibler). They were assisted in their move by family connections. Two entrepreneurs from Berg made Duisburg into the Rhine port serving their industrial region; they organized regular river-transports[61] to the Dutch ports, and up the Rhine there came the overseas goods that the area required. This is how the Duisburg tobacco industry came into being. The over-land route from Düsseldorf would have been shorter, but ships from Cleves paid only a quarter as much duty at the six Prussian customs posts on the lower Rhine.

It was the hilly part of the country of Mark, the Märkisches Sauerland,[62] which became the actual industrial region. Here there was iron ore, coal was mined in the Ruhr valley, and there was a plentiful supply of water power; these were lacking in the lowlands of Cleves and in the fertile northern part of the country of Mark, the country around Hellweg, which is today known as the Ruhr. This district remained untouched by the industrial expansion. Since times of old, the industrial town had been Iserlohn; here, calamine deposits were worked and brass goods were manufactured as at Stollberg, and needles as at Aachen. But iron production and processing became ever more important, the hardware industry of Berg expanded into Mark, the rivers and streams became crowded with forges, while the textile industry declined in significance. Wire-drawing in the area of Altena experienced a particularly great development.

As everywhere else, mining in the country of Mark was under state control; this control did not have its origin in the age of mercantilism, but was founded on the mining royalty. The mining enterprises had to pay considerable taxes. That is why they had factory inspectors and factory commissioners, who were not necessary in the case of the textile industry. The technology and organization of mining and smelting were backward in comparison with the regions in the Harz and in Saxony known to the Minister of State von Heinitz and the young Baron vom Stein, whose appointment to the mining board at Wetter on the Ruhr Heinitz had arranged. To further the promotion of the hardware industry, the Royal Industrial Commission organized industrial conferences on an open space near Sprockhövel, at which the gathering of managers, delegates, and doyens of the trade discussed technical matters and advances. It was hoped that the factory inspectors would have a stimulating function.

The long-planned canalization of the Ruhr had been held up by the jealousies of the small dominions situated between Cleves and Mark (Essen, Werden, Broich); after laborious negotiations Prussia succeeded in carrying out the scheme. Eleven locks had to be built past weirs, and in 1780 the first barge-load of coal from Mark sailed down the river to the Rhine. From now on, Ruhr coal was able to enter into competition with the English coal which reached the Low Countries by sea. It was then that the rise of the coal-shipping and coal-trading firms began which, later, when deeper mining became possible, were big enough to undertake the opening-up of the Ruhr district: the firm of Stinnes at Mülheim on the Ruhr and the firm of Haniel at Ruhrort.[63]

The condition of the roads was of greater importance to the mining and iron industry than to the textile industry. A good road from the south was needed for the transport of the superior iron from the Siegerland, and from the north Ruhr coal was brought to the forges. Equally, a modern road from the east was lacking, from Soest towards the lower Rhine on the route of the Hellweg. It is known that Frederick the Great was not interested in roads, but later vom Stein managed to put through the construction of roads on these two routes, even though at that time it was not easy to make Berlin come up with funds.

From the 1780s onwards, the Prussian government began to adopt a more positive attitude towards the western provinces, which G. Ritter has called the step-children of the Frederician state. This new attitude was represented by Heinitz and Stein. In the west the sharp contrast between town and country was unknown. For, unlike the situation in the eastern part of the monarchy, industries had settled in the countryside on a considerable scale, and by their very nature could not be confined by the barriers of the excise authorities in the towns. As the frontiers were so near, the country folk were accustomed to evade the burdensome duties (to be paid at the city gates on leaving) by buying what they needed in towns outside the Prussian domain. This situation led to the following compromise: 'The payment of fixed lump sums (fixa) by the rural manufacturers to the excise office in the nearest town; complete exemption of rural enterprises, at least of those already in existence, from guild and excise obligations; restriction of excises in the towns to a small number of profitable items, mainly food; the removal of the obligation on the rural population to buy what they needed at the local towns, in other words, a sort of freedom of trade for the countryside; and finally, offsetting the loss of revenue by direct taxes on trades in the towns and in the countryside.'[64] It is the same arrangement we have already encountered at Krefeld. Stein brought it about in the county of Mark through laborious negotiations between town and country. It would now have to be proved whether it was a case of necessary adaptation to western German conditions, or a case of a general European development, whose effects even the eastern part of the monarchy would not be able to avoid in the long run.

We obtain a vivid impression of the conditions under which the industrial advance took place from the recent history of the Harkort family, which is also a history of their firm.[65] And to this day the buildings of the Harkort manor are immediately evocative of their history. For centuries, this family of free peasants had resided on the high ground above the Ennepe valley just up-river from Hagen, and in the seventeenth century, after the Thirty Years War, they took up the manufacture of iron products at the forge in the valley; yet they held tenaciously on to their land, which was inherited undivided. At the magnificent mansion built in 1756, 150 account-books, and 40,000–50,000 letters and documents have been preserved—a unique source of historical information. In their hey-day, around 1780, when Luise Katharina Harkort, née Märcker, was running the farming and manufacturing enterprises, the family owned and had in operation two bar-iron forges, two crude-iron forges, and five scythe forges. The dispersion of the workshops was made necessary by the limited efficiency of water power. All sorts of iron goods were produced. The market was northern Germany and the Baltic region. The customers were old-established reputable trading firms, with whom connections had existed for generations, and every year these were visited on long business trips. At one time Dortmund and Soest had prospered through trade with the Baltic region, but now the manufacturers took over the marketing. They were better equipped to satisfy the customers' manifold requirements, so mediation by export dealers became unnecessary. A new type of manufacturer came into being. Mercantilist control and promotion of commerce was impossible.

Wide travelling broadened their outlook and raised their level of culture. Family connections expanded from the vicinity of Mark to the Wupper valley and to the Aachen area. Peculiar to the Harkorts is their clinging to their landed property, and also their Prussian sentiments bound up with the desire to maintain and advance the liberal Westphalian ways. These sentiments were the basis of the political activities of Fritz Harkort, who was born in 1793 at the Harkort family seat.

The natural advantages to which the Märkische Sauerland owed its rise lost their importance in the nineteenth century. Coal production in the Ruhr valley became insignificant in comparison with the vast quantities mined at the deep workings further to the north, which was also where the huge coke-fired blast-furnaces were built. Water power, which was already becoming short of supply in the eighteenth century, was insufficient for modern industry and could only be used as an auxiliary source of power. But in contrast to the Eifel, situated off the main trade-routes and where the iron industry died out, manufacturing carried on busily with iron and coal available in the immediate vicinity. This is evident when one travels down the Ennepe valley from Schwelm below Wuppertal towards Hagen, or from this new capital of the Sauerland southward towards Siegen. All through the wooded Lenne valley one factory closely follows upon another along the river. They are not huge factories, employing thousands of workers, but for the most part middle-sized factories. The rust-stained concrete weirs show that iron is processed here. After all, it is not only the large producers of iron and steel goods that are responsible for the huge consumption of iron and steel, but also a multitude of plants which specialize in the manufacture of a few separate products with all the experience of generations. Such a development can only take place where worker and entrepreneurs are firmly rooted in the district, and firm-rootedness is the distinguishing mark of this industry just as it was in the eighteenth century.

SUMMING UP

We have seen that state direction of industry in western Germany and in the Low Countries, regarded as a pre-condition of expansion in the eighteenth century, never existed, and we have seen why it could not exist. The big eastern German states of Austria and Prussia directed industry in their heartlands in a mercantilist manner. But in the area of western Germany and the Low Countries they adapted to the different development which was already in full swing. However, industry was not expanding everywhere. We have heard about the catastrophic decay of industry in the towns of Holland, and decline or stagnation of industry were also to be found in the southern Low Countries and in the old towns of the Empire. Other regions, which had been backward in the past and were for the most part situated in hilly areas, became industrial regions. And it was in such regions that modern industry and 'industrial society' had their origin, just as had happened in England. This development took a long time and in some places it had already begun in the Middle Ages, at first with the exploitation and use of local mineral resources; but most important of all was the abundant supply of flowing water that was eminently suited for bleaching, dyeing, and fulling, and also supplied the power for the fulling-mills, for the blast-furnace bellows, the tilt-hammers, and the grinding wheels. The forests supplied charcoal for smelting iron ore, and where coal was available it was used in the forges. This is the natural material basis of the industrial expansion. The unfavourable location with regard to communications was compensated by the low wages in the poor hill-country. It was the organization of trades which was decisive. The remote regions were little-accessible to town-settlements and were, therefore, predominantly free from guilds. There was no difference between town and country as far as the trades were concerned; those workshops that relied on water power could not be forced into the towns. Here we have a rural industry of the kind that had already developed in England in the late Middle Ages.

In the old-style industrial town the quality of the goods was assured by inspection by the guilds; in these new industrial regions, the manufacture was controlled by the entrepreneur, who had the important stages of production carried out in his own workshops and who also saw to the selling of the finished product, so that he was in a position to adjust to market requirements. Considerable capital expenditure was required for the supply of raw materials, wages for the domestic industry, credit to customers, and for the entrepreneurs' own workshops and equipment. An industrial bourgeoisie arose that had not existed previously. One manufacturer or another may have risen from the artisan class, but in the main the bourgeoisie was formed out of the rural and small-town upper strata; in the Wupper valley it was formed out of the owners of the bleaching grounds, in the hardware industry out of the forge owners, and elsewhere out of those who financed domestic industries and out of merchants in the export trade, but also out of landowners who had turned to industry. The numerous working class was employed predominantly in domestic industries. Weaving was such a domestic industry; it demanded much more skill than tending a machine does today. These skills had been acquired through a succession of generations and could not be transmitted. By contrast, spinning was a wide-spread rural part-time trade.

Under such conditions, these industrial regions of the eighteenth century went through a splendid expansion and were fully capable of competing on the European market without government assistance or protective tariffs. The superiority of this form of organization of industry is evident in the fact that important entrepreneurs in the domestic industries moved from the two imperial cities to towns which were free from guilds, and in the fact that manufacturers from the Prussian possessions in western Germany refused to move to the eastern part of the monarchy with its regimentation of industry. In the regions we have scrutinized, we have already seen the birth of modern industrial society. And the industrial towns, whose population increased many times over within a few decades, have more in common with the towns we live in today with respect to their function and the social composition of the population, than with a medieval town. In the hey-day of industrial advance, the second half of the eighteenth century, the inventions that gave rise to the 'industrial revolution' were made in quick succession and in another part of the world—England. We shall consider this in conclusion; the question is how industry in western Germany and the Low Countries came to grips with this development.

A COMPARISON WITH THE DEVELOPMENT OF ENGLISH INDUSTRY[66]

Medieval England was an agrarian country; the fertile south predominated. With the exception of the capital, the towns were insignificant and quite incapable of furthering the interests of their industries in the way that the towns of Flanders had been able to. The unequalled wool was exported to the continent and was burdened with an export duty of one-third of its value which had to be paid by the purchaser, for English wool was indispensable to the Flemish fine-cloth industry. Towards the end of the Middle Ages England began to process its own wool. There was a financial advantage over the continental competition in that the export duty for cloth was quite low, and England was technically superior on account of its machine-fulling which was very labour-saving, whereas in the Flemish plains water power for the fulling-mills was lacking. The cloth industry moved north to take advantage of the water power which was abundantly available on both sides of the Pennines; on the eastern side in the West Riding of the large county of Yorkshire, and in the west in Lancashire. Parallel to this regional move was the migration of industry to the countryside and the market-towns. This was mainly determined by the dependence on water power, but it also offered freedom from the guild obligations of the towns ('freedom to experiment had always characterized the rural industry').[67] It was from market-towns, not old cities that the big English industrial towns originated: Sheffield (iron industry), Leeds and Bradford (wool industry) in Yorkshire; Manchester (cotton industry) in Lancashire; and Birmingham (iron industry) in the Midlands.

Thus, the regional move of industry and its expansion in the countryside occurred earlier in England than in the industrial areas we have looked at so far, and became the basis of modern development.

In the sixteenth and seventeenth centuries, governments, above all those of the big western European states, sought to promote industry by laying down trade regulations that were binding on the guilds; in this way, output was raised and the uniformity of the goods that was so important for export was guaranteed. This is what happened in Elizabethan and early Stuart England; and in France under Colbert, industry was controlled by state-employed factory inspectors subordinate to the intendants. Beneficial as state supervision may have been, there was nevertheless the danger that it would hold methods of production down to a certain level. Since the revolution there had no longer been a bureaucratic apparatus in England. Local administration was carried out by the justices of the peace, who were members of the gentry and not professional administrators. State inspection fell in to disuse, and the higher courts tended to declare regulations which stood in the way of progress to be outdated and ineffective. Heckscher writes in terms of legal relics; the regulations were not repealed, but they were no longer observed. This is how the great expansion of the English cotton industry was possible, while in France the industry was unable to develop on account of the trade regulations and the objections of the dyers' guild to textile printing. In Prussia, the cotton industry was even prohibited in favour of the local wool industry. In England, by contrast, there existed—*de facto* though not under the law—the same freedom of industry, that was the prerequisite of the economic expansion in the industrial regions of western Germany and the Low Countries. This expansion was, therefore, caused less by new techniques in manufacturing than by the new form of organization of the economy; free enterprise was superior to an economy tied to guilds. There arose the 'modern industrial society' which was based on this new form of economy. It is a case of the same development as in the industrial regions we have examined so far, but on a more grandiose and comprehensive scale. England was, after all, in a more favourable position in having at its disposal its own excellent raw material, wool; in addition to the availability of water power there were abundant and easily worked deposits of coal and iron in immediate proximity; the centuries-long experience of the workers and entrepreneurs, backed by the technical experience of Flemish and Huguenot immigrants; and also its uninterrupted peaceful development and the advantages of naval supremacy. Under these conditions, English industry developed on a scale far exceeding continental circumstances; this is to be seen in the much higher population figures of the industrial towns. Then, in a time of general economic expansion, in the 1770s and 1780s, the technical advances which brought about the 'industrial revolution' were achieved in England. Why did it happen at that particular time and why in England?

Otto Brunner[68] points to the importance of new horizons in mathematics and the natural sciences. I would like to draw attention to a different point of view. When examining the industrial development in the region of western Germany and the Low Countries one has the impression that the limits of technical efficiency had been reached in the course of the economic expansion. How primitive spinning by hand appears, and how difficult it was to achieve uniform quality when it was spread all over the country! Was it possible to increase its output many times over when the demand so required? Water power (apart from weirs and reservoirs) was limited in output and could not be increased at will. Industry overcame this problem to a certain extent by spreading over a larger area, as we have seen in the region of the fine-cloth industry. The situation was no different for the iron industry. The Harkort family had nine separate forges; at Remscheid all available water power was already being used to the fullest extent. The bigger the industry became, the more urgent was the desire, the compulsion even, to raise human performance by mechanical means. How much more did this apply to England!

The decisive inventions were made by practical, self-educated, and self-made men.[69] Arkwright, who constructed the first efficient spinning machine, was a barber by trade; at the age of 50 he was still making efforts to spell correctly. With a rare combination of spirit of enterprise and inventiveness, he achieved his goal by ruthlessly appropriating the technical pioneering work of others. With mechanization he succeeded (1769–75) in increasing output, improving quality, and reducing prices. When he died in 1792 at the age of 60, he left, beside his factories, a fortune of £500,000. It was he who made possible the manufacture of calico, and the English cotton industry soon dominated the world market. Imports of raw cotton, which had cost £3·2 million in 1782, rose to £31·5 million by 1790, and £132·5 million by 1810. Between 1780 and 1800, the value of exports rose from £12·6 million to £43·2 million, and £58·8 million by 1810.

Arkwright's spinning mills were still water-powered. In order to raise output, Arkwright had to establish several mills. In the long run, only the steam engine would provide a solution to the problem.

James Watt, who constructed this steam engine, was a mechanic by trade; in 1776 he entered into partnership with the factory-owner Boulton, who assisted him unreservedly. In 1790 Georg Forster visited their factory near Birmingham, which already employed a thousand workers who manufactured mainly metal buttons. It was here that the machine to which the future belonged was developed. Its first task was to pump water from coal mines. This led to an increase in coal production and provided fuel for the steam engines. For millennia, iron ore had been smelted with charcoal; what would happen when the forests could no longer meet the demands of the blast-furnaces? It turned out to be possible to fire the blast-furnaces with coke. This gave rise to transport problems, which were not solved until the arrival of Stephenson and his locomotive. Stephenson had no school education and at the age of 18 was still unable to read or write. He started as a stoker and then became attendant of a steam engine at a coal mine. All these developments represent an amazing interlocking of technical advances. England was in the process of becoming the workshop of the world.

The industrial regions of western Germany and the Low Countries endeavoured to follow this example. However, the export of machines from England was prohibited and the emigration of engineers was severely punished. But, of course, it could not be prevented,[70] and there was no lack of capital for new factories. However, there soon came the revolutionary wars and the two decades of French rule. The pillage in the first years, the interruption of the supply of raw materials, and the cutting-off from the markets all led to terrible losses of capital, and the recuperation under Napoleon cannot be compared with the hey-day in the eighteenth century. Markets were flooded with English goods—the prices for cotton goods sank to a fifth of their previous level. France protected itself in the customary manner with high protective tariffs; but the tariffs of the United Netherlands (8 per cent) and of Prussia (10 per cent) were no protection against superior competition. Impoverished and technically backward, these industrial regions did not, however, suffer the fate of industry in the Low Countries in the seventeenth century; they were able to survive the terrible test and to adopt England's technical achievements. This was only possible because already in the eighteenth century there had come into being an industrial society which had arisen out of the activity of generations of entrepreneurs and workers. In England this industrial society was the prerequisite, not the consequence, of the great inventions; it was also the pre-condition of the industrial resurgence in Belgium and western Germany. It was a matter of acquired characteristics that had to be constantly reassimilated, and the intellectual climate, the industrial environment were also part of it. The importance of this human factor can be seen in the fact that there are industrial towns still flourishing today, whose natural advantages of former days have no longer any significance—take, for example, the Wupper valley and the hardware industry of Berg.

The examination of eighteenth-century industry in the area of western Germany and the Low Countries shows that it was the necessary preliminary stage of the expansion in the nineteenth century.

NOTES

1. *Schmollers Jahrbuch*, viii (1884); 'Studien über die wirtschaftliche Politik Friedrich des Grossen und Preussens überhaupt 1680–1786', p. 43.

2. *Grundriss der Allgemeinen Volkswirtschaftslehre* (1904), 2nd pt., p. 594.

3. Franz Steinbach wrote about this development in 'Geschichtliche Räume und Raumbeziehungen der deutschen Nieder- und Mittelrheinlande im Mittelalter', *Annalen des Hist. Vereins für den Niederrhein*, vols. 155–6 (1954).

4. Acta Borussica, *Seidenindustrie*, vol. iii, Description, p. 27.

5. Op. cit., pp. 102 and 273.

6. *Algemeene Geschiedenis der Nederlanden*, in 12 vols., published by J. A. van Houtte, Leuven *et al.*

7. According to Helmuth Dahm, 'Die Verluste der jülich-bergischen Landmiliz im 30jährigen Krieg', *Düsseldorfer Jahrbuch*, xlv (1951), 280–8.

8. *Zeitschrift des Bergischen Geschichtsvereins*, xix (1883), 81–170.

9. Bernhard Schonneshöfer, *Geschichte des Bergischen Landes* (2nd ed., 1908). Wolfgang Köllmann, *Die Garnnahrung in Wuppertal. In Unsere Heimat*, supplement to the *Generalanzeiger der Stadt Wuppertal*, No. 12 (Dec. 1953). Edmund Strutz, 'Die Ahnentafeln der Elberfelder Bürgermeister und Stadtrichter 1708–1806', *Berg. Forsch.*, vol. 3 (1936).

10. Henceforth the judiciary had no authority in Elberfeld. The town paid 5,000 Reichstaler for this privilege. Why then did it not also insist on representation in the Berg diet? It had long overtaken the old 'capitals' Wipperfürth, Ratingen, and Lennep, which together with the seat of the government, Düsseldorf, did have this privilege. I believe Elberfeld did not consider this important. The guilds would have felt envy and ill will towards the parvenu town. The high amount of the payment proves that it was nevertheless possible to assert oneself in Düsseldorf.

11. Max Schmidt, *Geschichtliche Wanderungen durch Solingen* (1922); *Chronik der Stadt Solingen* (Berlin, 1937); Hendrichs, *Solingen und seine Stahlwarenindustrie* (1952); Julius Bernhard, *Zur Geschichte der Solinger Industrie* (1952). Other literature on this subject includes Wilhelm Engels and Paul Legers, *Aus der Geschichte der Remscheider Werkzeug- und Eisenindustrie* (2 vols., Remscheid, 1928).

12. Philipp Andreas Nemnisch; *Tagebuch einer der Kultur und Industrie gewidmeten Reise* (Tübingen, 1809), p. 440.

13. *Ztschr. d. Berg. Geschichtsvereins*, xviii (1882), 1–148. Josef Wilden, *Das Haus Jacobi* (1943); 'F. H. Jacobi' in *Allgemeine Deutsche Biographie*, by Prantl.

14. *Allgemeine Deutsche Biographie*, 'Grat Goltstein', by Harless.

15. In *Bayerische Beiträge zur schönen und nüklichen Literatur* (Munich, 1779).

16. For greater detail of the contents of Wiebeking's *Essays*, see my work in the *Rheinisch Vierteljahrsbl.* (1954), pp. 141–3. I refer once more to Fritz Schulte's work, 'Die wirtschaftlichen Ideen F. H. Jacobis', *Düsseldorfer Jb.*, vol. xlviii, pp. 292 ff. The author regrets the exclusion of Jacobi from the government: except for the suspension of a few privileges and monopolies, none of his intentions or suggestions was realized. But a fundamentally new order did not come about anywhere in the age of absolutism, until Joseph II, whose measures were caused by the Brabantine revolution. The influence of Count Goltstein is not mentioned, and the author does not seem to be familiar with the 'Essays' of Wiebeking, which give a rather different picture.

17. Charles Schmidt: *Le Grand-Duché de Berg, 1806–13* (1905), p. 420.

18. J. G. A. Forster, *Ansichten von Niederrhein* etc. (Berlin, 1791).

19. The famous historian of the Papacy also belonged to this family: his father was a convert.

20. Whenever Herr v. Lövenich went to the Frankfurt Fair he gave Goethe's father some of this cloth for the family. The young Goethe was made great fun of as a student at Leipzig when he wore clothes—especially a laced coat—made from this material by the family tailor: *Dichtung u Wahrheit*, pt. 2, 6th Book, *Gottasche Jubiläumsausgabe*, xxiii. 42.

21. The history of the cloth industry of Monschau was depicted by my late brother, Ernst Barkhausen, in Viersen, *Die Tuchindustrie in Monschau, ihr Aufstieg und Niederļang* (Aachen, 1925). For a shorter account on the basis of this work see *Westdeutschen Ahnentafeln*, vol. i, 'Scheibler' by Hans Carl Scheibler and Karl Wulfrath, a publication of the Gesellschaft f. Rhein (Geschichtskde., xliv, 1939). The documents of the fine clothiers were stored in my parents' house. They were burnt in the winter of 1944–5 by occupying troops. They contained exact production figures because the figures of each individual firm were collected when the cloth was fulled. The financial accounts of the family firm were also at our disposal. As an experienced cloth manu-

facturer and a man with a merchant's understanding, my brother was particularly suited to his work, being aided also by the family tradition. Walter Scheibler has written a history of the family firm: *Geschichte und Schicksalsweg einer Firmer in 6 Generationen, 1724–1937*. Also more recently, though undated: Peter Scheibler, *Imgenbroich, ein ehemaliges Tuchmacherdorf*, publ. by the Geschichtsverein des Kreises Monschau.

22. For more precise details I refer you to my essay in the *Rheinisch Vierteljahrsbl.*, xix (1954), 170–6.

23. Charles Schmidt, loc. cit., p. 244.

24. Ernst Brasse, *Geschichte der Stadt und Abtei Gladbach* (2 vols., 1914–22). Ludwig Schmitz, *Rheydter Chronik, Geschichte der Stadt und Herrschaft Rheydt* (2 vols., 1897). F. W. Lohmann, *Geschichte der Stadt Viersen* (1913). There is a good account of the linen trade in the sixteenth, seventeenth, and eighteenth centuries in Friedrich Otto Dilthey, *Geschichte der niederrheinischen Baumwollindustrie* (1908).

25. Hermann Keussen, *Geschichte der Stadt und Herrlichkeit Crefeld mit steter Bezugnahme auf die Geschichte der Grafschaft Mörs* (1865). Acta Borussica, 'Die Preussische Seidenindustrie im 18 Jh. und ihre Begründung durch Friedrich den Grossen', vols. i and ii by G. Schmoller and O. Hintze, vol. iii by O. Hintze. Wilhelm Niepoth, 'Zur Frühgeschichte der Familie von der Leyen', *Die Heimat*, vol. xxi, pts. 3/4 (Krefeld, 1950); id., 'Das Bürgerbuch der Stadt Krefeld (1644–1794)', *Die Heimat*, vols. xxi and xxii. Gerhard von Beckerath, *Die Wirtschaftliche Bedentung der Krefelder Mennoniten und ihrer Vorfahren im 17. und 18 Jh.*, Bonner Phil Diss. (1951). Hermann Keussen, 'Crefeld vor 100 Jahren', *Krefelder Zeitung* (1894) which can be found in *Beiträge zur Geschichte Krefelds und des Niederrheins* (Cologne, 1898). Comprehensive accounts are to be found in Buschbell-Heinzelmann, *Geschichte der Stadt Krefeld*, vol. i (1953); 'Scheibler' in *Westdeutsche Ahnentafeln*, vol. i by Karl Wülfrath. Also on Krefeld, Walter Föhl, 'Krefeld und das Fürstentum Mörs, Verwaltung u. Wirtschaft, 1787/1788', *Die Heimat* (1955), and 'Die Träger der Krefelder Wirtschaft im 18. Jh.', *Die Heimat* (1957).

26. In a letter of 13 Oct. 1810 to the Minister of the Interior, the prefect, Ladoulette, names among the seven most powerful manufacturers of the Department of the Roer Heinrich van der Leyen in the first place with 3,000 employees, production valuing 3,000,000 francs, and capital assets also worth 3,000,000 francs. In second place is Gottschalk Flöh with 1,500 employees, production valuing 1,500,000 francs, and capital assets worth 3,000,000 francs. That this new wealth was not due to the French occupation can be proved by the tax assessments of the Prussian authorities. The two manufacturers were the richest in the Department of the Roer. From Richard Zeyss, *Die Entstehung der Handelskammern und die Industrie des Niederrheins während der Französischen Herrschaft* (Leipzig, 1907).

27. Acta Borussica, ii. 1194. Interpretation by O. Hintze, iii. 269.

28. *Beiträge zur Geschichte Krefelds*, p. 238. On the question of the other firms, see also Gerhard von Beckerath, op. cit., p. 73. Nothing can be found in the Düsseldorf State Archives dealing with the Cologne villages around Krefeld. We are often told, however, that several thousand workers and loaders drew their daily wage and keep from the factories in Krefeld. It was paid in Prussian money. See further Walter Föhl, 'Die Träger der Krefelder Wirtschaft im 18 Jh.', in *Die Heimat* (Krefeld, 1957).

29. On the corner of Friedrichstrasse and Friedrichplatz the house of Heydtweiller, later of Scheibler, was built, with ten windows facing on to Friedrichstrasse and five facing out on to Friedrichplatz. On the ground floor, with its high ceilings, there were offices and store-houses, and the living quarters were in the two upper stories. Since hand-weaving had been superseded by more mechanized methods, the weaving-mill had been in the suburb of the town. The old building was used as a velvet store-house. This stood as a monument to eighteenth-century industry, until it was destroyed in the blitz of 1943.

30. Düsseldorf Staatsarchiv, Mörs, *Kammer*, c. 49 and 50. Also Ludwig Friese, *Die verwaltung der Stadt Krefeld in 18 Jh.* (Krefeld, 1936), pp. 93 f.

31. Acta Borussica, ii. 1,196, Düsseldorf, Staatsarchiv. Also see *Handelsstatistik, no. 7*, for Cleves-Mörs.

32. The Regulations of 15 Mar. 1766 are set out in Acta Borussica, vol. i, No. 501; von der Leyen's letter of refusal is in Acta Borussica, vol. ii, No. 1,170. See also O. Hintze in Acta Borussica, vol. iii, No. 596. At the twenty-third Assembly of German Historians in Ulm on 14 Sept. 1956 W. Treue delivered a lecture on 'The Relation between Prince, State, and Contractor in the Mercantile Age'. G. Schilfert, from the University of Humboldt, criticized the opinion expressed by this speaker, namely that Prussian economic policy in its Rhineland possessions managed without the regulations, and claimed that documents in Acta Borussica, vol. i, show that the reverse was the case. The critic did not however realize that the first volume of Acta Borussica only contains documents from the silk industries of Berlin and the Märkisch region; the Krefeld documents are to be found in the last part of vol. ii, and also the above-mentioned letter of refusal from the von der Leyen brothers. It was as O. Hintze described it in the third volume of Acta Borussica: official guidance was not necessary and it was therefore withheld, and he could have added here that it was not a possibility either. The states of the eighteenth century did not form a unity, and nor could Prussia claim to be a harmonious unity. This is demonstrated not only in this particular case, but in the disputes with the western provinces in general.

That there were never any state regulations in Krefeld while it was a part of Old Prussia is shown in the following documents: on 22 July 1810 the French minister of the interior inquired whether the regulations guiding the Krefeld silk industry, which he assumed existed as they did in French industry, had had a beneficial effect, or whether it was advisable eventually to reframe them. The prefect for Krefeld answered on 24 Aug. 1810 (Acta Borussica, vol. ii, No. 1,200) to this effect: 'Le petit nombre de manufacturiers en ce genre réglaient entr'eux tout ce qui était convenable à leurs intérêts. Ainsi il n'y avait point de règlements publics: tout ce réglait d'après les évènements et les circonstances.' The regulations of 1786 for the von der Leyen factory and the joint regulations of 1788 for the other four firms were drafted without official scrutiny, and they only deal with the question of workers, particularly with job-stealing, but not with the manufacturing itself. It seems that the French authorities were inclined to return to the regulations which had been temporarily suspended by the revolution.

33. Acta Borussica, vol. i, No. 596: the protocol declaration of the von der Leyen brothers (7 Mar. 1768) along with their rejection of the suggestion to move part of their manufacturing to the east. (It is the only document concerning Krefeld in vol. i.) It also contains the impressive explanation as to how their factory was built after long years of toil.

34. The young Wilhelm von Humboldt wrote of Krefeld in his diary: 'This town looks quite different from any other in Westphalia and indeed in the whole of Germany. Walking through it one can see that it is very prosperous, and one immediately sees that the sources of this prosperity is hard work and skill. During my stay of 24 hours I do not recall seeing any genuine poverty—the whole town puts on a pleasant smiling face.' From Wilhelm von Humboldt's diaries in his *Gesammelte Schriften*, vol. xiv, publ. by Albert Leitzmann (1916), pt. 1, p. 80. A detailed and enthusiastic description of Krefeld can be found in the account by Humboldt's companion on these travels, J. H. Campe, in *Reise von Braunschweig nach Paris in Heumonat 1789* (Braunschweig, 1790).

35. In *Algemeene Geschiedenis der Nederlanden*, vol. v, pt. 7: 'De economische opbloei van het Noorden', by T. S. Jansma, pp. 210–45. vol. vi, pt. 3: 'De economische en sociale ontwikkeling van het Noorden', by T. S. Jansma, pp. 86–147. vol. vii, pt. 10: 'Honderd Jaar economische ontwikkeling van het Noorden', by J. G. van Dillen, pp. 277–321. vol. viii, pt. 9: 'De economische achteruitgang van de Republick', by Joh. de Vries, pp. 222–61; 'Licht en schaduw en de nyverheid', pp. 246–53.

36. An example of this: Around 1585 Pierre Aubin, an ancestor of Professor Aubin of Freiburg, left his home-town of Valenciennes on account of his religious beliefs, and established a 'Grobgrün' dye-house in Frankfurt, which had three boilers. Emigration was allowed under the treaty between the Estates of the southern Netherlands and the Stadholder, Farnese. The word 'Grobgrün' (coarse green) does not refer to colour, but to the weaving method used. The word is the germanicized form of the French 'gros grain' (coarse grain), and means rep. At that time this thick woollen

material was exported from the southern Netherlands to Frankfurt in large quantities. Pierre Aubin and other emigrants brought the difficult art of dyeing this material to the great trade market from its place of production. (*Frankfurter Handelsgeschichte*, by Alexander Dietz, ii. 388.) In England in the seventeenth century the dyers and cloth-preparers wanted to have it that only completely finished cloth be exported, but the export traders declared that only unfinished cloth was in demand on the Continent, and the weavers, who depended on the export trade, argued that there were ten times as many weavers in England as dyers and preparers. It was not until the first half of the eighteenth century that England went over to exporting finished cloth.

37. *Algemeene Geschiedenis*, vol. vii, pp. 295 ff. and pp. 390–6.

38. Acta Borussica, ii. 1,173.

39. P. J. Blok, *Geschichte der Niederlande* (Gotha, 1918), vi. 158. J. de Vries, in *Alg. Gesch.*, viii. 251. Also C. H. de Pater, *Geschiedenis van Nederland*, iv (1936), 124.

40. *Alg. Gesch.*, vi. 119, and viii. 255.

41. *Alg. Gesch.*, viii. 252.

42. *Alg. Gesch.*, vol. v, ch. 6: 'Het economische Verval van het Zuiden', J. A. van Houtte, pp. 174–210; vol. vii, ch. 10: 'Economische en sociale entwikkeling van het Zuiden, 1609–1748', J. A. van Houtte, pp. 390–1,748; vol. viii, ch. 10: 'De economische opbloei in de zuidlyke Nederlanden', H. Coppejans-Demandt, pp. 261–89; vol. viii, ch. 12: 'De Generaliteitslanden van 1648–1795', L. P. Pirenne, pp. 315–52; vol. 8, ch. 8: 'Het Prinsbisdom Luik van 1477–1795', P. Harsin, pp. 195–222. Henri Pirenne, *Histoire de Belgique*, vols. iii–v, in particular v, from 1648 to 1795 (2nd ed., 1926).

43. In the northern Low Countries the big Amsterdam merchants had a part of their capital securely invested in reclamation of land from the sea. It is remarkable how internal colonization, which was undertaken by the kings in Prussia, was carried out in the Low Countries by the big landowners and big financiers. However, these strata with a lot of capital at their disposal were not involved in the building up of industry.

44. Here in the Borinage in the second half of the nineteenth century, Meunier found the subject-matter for his paintings and sculptures; and it was here that Van Gogh painted the pictures of his first period.

45. H. Pirenne, *Histoire de Belgique*, v. 276.

46. Paul Bonenfant, *Le Problème du paupérisme en Belgique à la fin de l'ancien régime*. Acad. roy. de Belgique, classe des lettres et sciences morales et politiques. Mémoires. Deuxième série, vol. xxxv (1934). See, in particular, the summing up on pp. 558 ff.

47. By way of comparison, I will quote Pirenne's definition (in *Les Villes et les institutions urbaines* (1939), ii. 118) of the medieval town: 'La ville du Moyen-Âge est une communauté vivant à l'abri d'une enceinte fortifiée du commerce et de l'industrie et jouissant d'un droit, d'une administration et d'une jurisdiction d'exception qui font d'elle un corps privilégié.' For a description of eighteenth-century Liège see Pirenne, *Histoire de Belgique*, v. 354 ff.

48. For Verviers see: Pirenne, op. cit., v. 363 ff., also *Les Villes et les institutions urbaines*, ii. 151 ff.: 'Coup d'oeil sur l'histoire de Verviers'.

49. Biography of Pirenne: Charles Verlinden, 'Henri Pirenne', in *Architects and Craftsmen in History*. Commemorative volume in honour of Albert Payson-Usher. Publications of the List-Society, vol. ii (1956).

50. A pertinent observation. The up-and-coming entrepreneur needs all his money for his business; the old upper strata in the towns were considerable landowners. Reinhold Koser quotes from a French memorandum in 1764 the following definition of the bourgeoisie: 'The bourgeois are those people who by birth and wealth are enabled to live decently without having to work for gain. Among those who pretend to the title of bourgeois, one frequently encounters persons who have a right to it only with respect to their idleness, while in other respects they lead obscure and unrefined lives. The bourgeois should, on the contrary, always distinguish themselves by their wealth, birth, talents, manners, and style of life.' The merchants who worked for gain were not considered part of the bourgeoisie. See p. 243 of the volume entitled 'Staat und Gesellschaft der neueren Zeit, Abschnitt: auf der Höhe des Absolutismus', in the

anthology, *Die Kultur der Gegenwart* (1908). This old type of bourgeoisie also existed in the old German towns; it is understandable that the entrepreneurs wanted to give expression to the importance of their class by building fine houses.

51. *Histoire de Belgique*, v. 354.

52. *Die feine Tuchmanufaktur zu Eupen, ihre sämtlichen Geheimnisse, Vorteile und Preise, nebst Tabellen* (Gotha, 1796). The aim of this book is to transplant the manufacture of fine cloth to the interior of Germany—a vain endeavour. It was impossible to transplant the experience of centuries and the symbiosis of cattle-breeding, spinning, and weaving. The book must have been written before the French invasion of 1794 which abruptly interrupted the flourishing industry. The author estimates the volume of production on the basis of the consumption of Spanish wool; accordingly, Aachen and the surrounding area consume approx. the same amount as Verviers, each being responsible for a third of the total consumption; of the last third, Eupen consumes twice as much as Monschau. The branches at Eupen of the big Monschau firms are probably included in the calculation. The most recent account is in the 1955 yearbook of the Eupen Chamber of Commerce.

53. Wilhelm Steffens, 'Die linksrheinische Provinze Preußens unter französischer Herrschaft, 1794–1802', in *Rheinische Vierteljahrsblätter*, xix (1954), 402 ff., gives information on conditions in the possessions on the left bank of the Rhine before the French occupation.

54. Max Lehmann, *Freiherr von Stein*, i. 106.

55. Averdunk-Ring, 'Geschichte der Stadt Duisburg', revised by Walter Ring (Ratingen, 1949), p. 117.

56. Acta Borussica, 'Die Wollindustrie in Preußen unter Fr. Wilhelm I', an account with an appendix of documents, by Carl Hinrichs, 1933. In the introduction, Otto Hintze, with the silk industry in mind as well, expresses the opinion that 'In both cases it is a matter of the introduction of a capitalist mode of production, which in Prussia at that time was promoted and directed from above for reasons of state. At the same time, it was only with difficulty that private enterprise, which was regarded as the truly desirable goal, was forced to make do without state assistance. As a result, a system of state capitalism which intruded to a greater or lesser degree never quite disappeared against the background of mercantilist industrial policy.' Thus it is stressed that state capitalism was only a means of bringing industry into existence. Where industry was already thriving, state assistance was not necessary.

57. 'Wollindustrie', p. 19. In this article, the term 'Cleves' is applied to the district administered by the Chamber (Kammer), that is to say it applies also to Mark.

58. 'Wollindustrie', p. 286.

59. Secret State Archives, Berlin, General Directory Cleves, XLVII, section I Town of Duisburg No. 8. From Ilse Barleben, 'Die Wesel-Orsoyer Tuchmacherfamilie Lüps. Ein Beitrag zur Geschichte des preußischen Merkantilismus am Niederrhein', *Rheinische Vierteljahrsblätter*, vi (1936), 46.

60. Ring, *Geschichte von Duisburg*, pp. 140 ff.

61. Gisela Vollmer, 'Eine Fabrikenstatistik des Herzogtums Kleve aus dem Ende des 18. Jahrhunderts', *Düsseldorfer Jahrbuch*, xlvi (1954). The figures for the cloth industries of Duisburg and Orsoy, which are most prominent, do, however, lag behind the expansion in Berg and the Aachen area.

62. *Die Grafschaft Mark* (Dortmund, 1909), published on the occasion of the 30th anniversary of the union with Brandenburg-Prussia, section entitled 'Handel, Gewerbe, Industrie, Bergbau', by A. Meister. See also the introductory description by Ludwig Beutin in his *Geschichte der südwestfälischen Industrie- und Handelskammer zu Hagen und ihrer Wirtschaftslandschaft* (1956). For the activities of Baron von Stein in the county of Mark and western Germany see *Freiherr von Stein. Persönlichkeit und Werk in Briefen und politischen Dokumenten*, compiled by Erich Botzenhart, vol. i (1958), and the selection published in 1955 in one volume.

63. Max Lehmann, *Stein*, i. 39 ff.

64. Gerhard Ritter, *Stein*, i. 60.

65. Ellen Söding, *Die Harkorts* (2 vols., Münster, 1957).

66. For the Middle Ages see: *The Cambridge Economic History of Europe*, vol. ii: *Trade and Industry in the Middle Ages* (1952). Vol. iii has not yet been published [in fact it now has. Trans. note]. Of importance is chapter vi by Eleonora Carus-Wilson, 'The Woollen Industry', especially section 5: 'The Triumph of the English Industry', pp. 413–28. In particular, the author shows clearly the origin of industry in the country-side and the market-towns, and also the importance of water power. For later centuries see: Cunningham, *Growth of English Industry and Commerce in Modern Times*, and Eli F. Heckscher, *Mercantilism* (2 vols., authorized translation Jena, 1932), section on England, pp. 201–304. [Trans. note: English edition: authorized translation by Mendel Shapiro (2 vols., 1934); see vol. i.]

67. *Camb. Econ. Hist.*, ii. 423. Also p. 422: 'The ancient proverb: "City air maketh free" could have had little meaning for an Englishman of the later fifteenth century, least of all for an aspiring captain of industry.' Heckscher, p. 224 [Trans. note: p. 244 in the English edition]: In a report of 1588 to Elizabeth's minister Cecil, it is said of the inhabitants of the market town of Halifax: 'They excell the rest in policy and industry, for the use of their trade and grounds, and after the rude and arrogant manner of their wild country they surpass the rest in wisdom and wealth. They despise their old fashions if they can hear of a new, more commodious, rather affecting novelties than allied to old ceremonies … It should seem that desire of praise and sweetness of their due commendation hath begun and maintained among the people a natural ardency of new inventions annexed to an unyielding industry.' One can sense the writer's combination of admiration and disquiet.

68. *Neue Wege der Sozialgeschichte* (Göttingen, 1956), in essay iv, 'Stadt und Bürgertum in der europäischen Geschichte', p. 95. Adolf Weber, 'Drei Phasen der industriellen Revolution', *Bayerische Akademie der Wissenschaften*, Report of the proceedings of the philosophical–historical section (1957), book 10. In Brunner's and Weber's work, the significance of the economic expansion that provided the stimulus for technical advance is not brought out.

69. Bernhard Guttmann describes the personality of the inventors in *England im Zeitalter der bürgerlichen Reform* (1923).

70. Already in 1784, Brögelmann from Elberfeld established the first spinning-mill near Ratingen with the assistance of English workmen; he called the place Cromford after Arkwright's first spinning-mill (Otto Redlich, *Geschichte von Ratingen*, 1926). The most important transmitters of technical progress were Cockerill and his sons, from Lancashire. The big smelting works near Liège still bears their name.